LEARNING Microsoft Office 2010

Other Titles by the Same Authors

- Learning PageMaker 7
- Learning 3D Max
- Learning Computer Fundamentals
- Learning Java 7
- Learning Internet & E-mail
- Learning HTML 5
- Learning JavaScript with HTML 5
- Learning Visual Basic 6
- Learning SQL
- Learning Web Designing
- Learning Multimedia
- Learning Networking
- Learning PC Hardware
- Learning Desk Top Publishing
- Learning C
- Learning C++
- Learning Windows XP
- Learning Windows Vista
- Learning Windows 7
- Learning Windows XP, Vista, Office 2007 & Internet & E-mail
- Learning MS Office XP
- Learning MS Access 2003
- Learning MS Excel 2003
- Learning MS Word 2003
- Learning MS Office 2003
- Learning MS Access 2007
- Learning MS Excel 2007
- Learning MS Word 2007
- Learning MS Office 2007
- Learning Tally 9.0
- Learning Dreamweaver CS4
- Learning CorelDRAW X4
- Learning Photoshop CS4
- Learning Flash CS4
- Learning Illustrator CS4
- Learning Microsoft Access 2010
- Learning Microsoft Excel 2010
- Learning Microsoft Word 2010
- Learning Microsoft Office 2010
- Learning AutoCAD 2010
- Learning Dreamweaver CS5
- Learning CorelDraw X5
- Learning Flash CS5
- Learning Illustrator CS5
- Learning Photoshop CS5
- Learning ASP.Net 4.0
- Learning C# 4.0
- Learning ASP.Net and C#.Net
- Learning Tally 9.0 (Hindi)
- Learning Internet & E-mail (Hindi)
- Learning Desk Top Publishing (Hindi)

LEARNING Microsoft Office 2010

Ramesh Bangia
B.Sc., Dip. Comp. Sc.
Formerly Managing Editor, Software Today
Formerly Incharge Computer Centre, Hindustan Copper Ltd., New Delhi

KHANNA BOOK PUBLISHING CO. (P) LTD.
::: Publisher of Engineering and Computer Books :::

Head Office : 4C/4344, Ansari Road, Darya Ganj, New Delhi-110002
Phone: 011-23244447/48 Fax: 011-23244447
Regd. Office : 1694-95, Nai Sarak, Delhi-110006
Phone: 011-23283211 Fax: 011-23256658
E-Mail : contact@khannabooks.com
Website : www.khannabooks.com

Learning Microsoft Office 2010 — Ramesh Bangia

ISBN: 978-93-81068-04-5

Published by:
Khanna Book Publishing Co. (P) Ltd.
4C/4344, Ansari Road, Darya Ganj, New Delhi-110 002
Phone: 011-23244448 Telefax: 011-23244447
E-mail: contact@khannabooks.com
Website: www.khannabooks.com

Regd. Off: 1694-95, 1st Floor, Nai Sarak, Delhi-110006 (India)
Phone: 011-23283211 Telefax: 011-23256658

Cover Design & Layout by
Chauhan Offset, Delhi

Printed in India by ZN Printers

PREFACE

Learning of a software is both easy and difficult. It depends upto what level you are planning to learn. If you are learning only for the working use, then it is very easy. But, when you try to go deep into it, then you realise how difficult it is to master it.

Microsoft Office 2010 is such a vast subject that it will take a lot of time to understand it fully. This book has been written in mind to make you aware of the options available in the software and how they can be used. It is like telling the child about the steps and stairs. You are the one who is to climb the stair. This book will just guide you how to use the stairs.

I am indeed debited to my publishers Khanna Book Publishing Co. Pvt. Ltd. for their suggestions and encouragement given in producing this book.

I would like to thank my family specially my wife Sadhna, kids Mayank and Samarth, for without their criticism this book would not have seen the day.

Suggestions for improvement of the book are indeed welcome.

Ramesh Bangia

CONTENTS

Contents

CHAPTER 1

Introduction to Microsoft Windows 7

Introduction

Windows 7 is here. It is the newer version of ever popular operating system called Microsoft Windows. Keeping in the tradition of the various versions given earlier by Microsoft, this one too has some advancements specially in the field of mobile computing, networking and other related topics. Since it forms the base of the base of Microsoft Office 2010, it is imperative to understand Microsoft Window 7, first.

What's New in Windows 7?

Faster, more responsive performance

Nobody likes to wait. So we've focused on the basics that can impact the speed of your PC. Windows 7 starts up, shuts down, resumes from sleep, and responds faster.

Improved taskbar and full-screen previews

You can use the taskbar at the bottom of your screen to switch between open programs. In Windows 7 you can set the order of the taskbar icons and they'll stay in that order. The icons are larger, too. If you point to an icon, you'll see a small, preview version of the page or program. If you point to this preview, you'll see a full-screen preview. To open a program or file, click an icon or one of the previews.

Better on laptops

Windows 7 helps extend the battery life of your laptop with power-saving features, including dimming the display if you don't use your computer for a while. Another new laptop-friendly feature, location-aware printing, can automatically switch your default printer when you go

Jump Lists

With Jump Lists, you can quickly find files that you've worked with recently. Right-click a program icon on the taskbar to see a list of recently-opened files. You can also pin files that you use regularly to a Jump List. Some Jump Lists show commands for common tasks, like playing music or videos.

A leap in efficiency: Jump Lists provide quick access to common files and tasks.

Find more things faster with improved search

Thanks to an improved search, you can find more things in more places—and do it faster—than in

Get the picture: See what's open with full-screen previews

previous versions of Windows. Just type a few letters into the search box to see a list of relevant items, such as documents, pictures, music, and e mail. Search results are grouped by category and contain highlighted keywords to make them easy to scan.

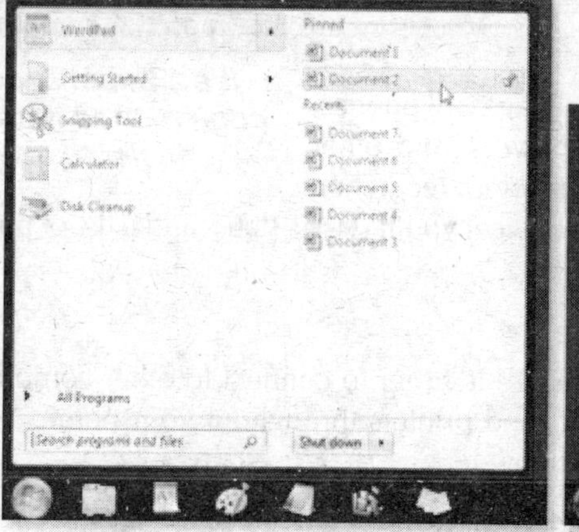

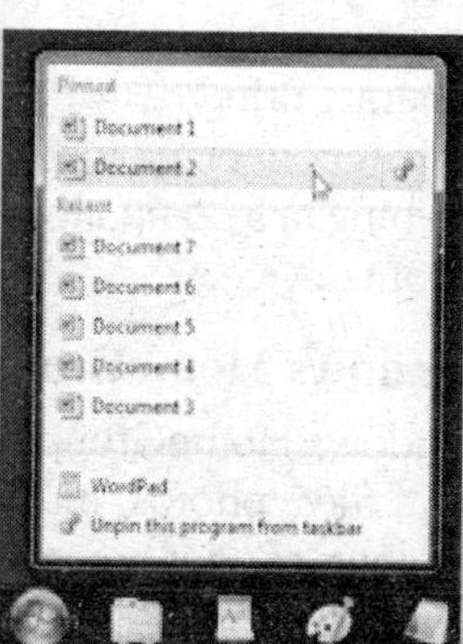

A leap in efficiency: Jump Lists provide quick access to common files and tasks

Few people store all their files in one place anymore. Windows 7 is designed to search external hard drives, PCs on a network, and other locations. It also speeds up your search by displaying recommendations based on previous queries. Overwhelmed by the results? New dynamic filters can instantly narrow results by categories such as date or file type.

Easier ways to work with windows

Windows 7 simplifies how you work with the windows on your desktop. You have more intuitive ways to open, close, resize, and arrange them.

Maximize a window by dragging its border to the top of the screen, and return the window to its original size by dragging it away from the top of the screen. Drag the bottom border of a window to expand it vertically. To compare the contents of two windows, drag the windows to opposite sides of the screen. Each window will resize to fill half of the screen.

To see all of your desktop gadgets, drag your mouse to the lower-right corner of your desktop. The open windows will turn transparent, making your desktop, and the gadgets on it, immediately visible. Want to minimize all open windows? One click and it's done. If you've moved your taskbar, you can drag your mouse to a different corner of the desktop to make open windows transparent. It's a Snap: Dragging a window to the desktop edge resizes it to fill half of the screen—making it easier to quickly compare two windows.

It's a Snap: Dragging a window to the desktop edge resizes it to fill half of the screen—making it easier to quickly compare two windows.

Better device management

Devices and Printers

In the past, you had to go to different places in Windows to manage different types of devices. In Windows 7, there's a single Devices and Printers location for connecting, managing, and using your printers, phones, and other devices. From here, you can interact with your devices, browse files, and manage settings. When you connect devices to your PC, you'll be up and running in just a few clicks.

Device Stage

Device Stage helps you manage cell phones, cameras, printers, MP3 players, and other devices connected to your computer. When you plug in a compatible device, you'll see its status and a list of popular tasks. You'll even see a picture of your device.

Windows HomeGroup

Windows HomeGroup makes it easier to connect to other computers running Windows 7 so you can share files, photos, music, and printers throughout your home. You choose what to share with other members of your homegroup.

Theme packages reflect your style

With Windows 7, you start with a clean desktop and get to decide how it looks. We provide the templates, or themes, and you can choose the color or format.

New theme packages include rich backgrounds, 16 window colors, sound schemes, and screen savers. You can download new themes and create your own to share with friends and family. There are plenty of ways to make it yours.

Take control of problems

In Windows 7 you get to choose the messages you want to see. Action Center consolidates notifications from multiple Windows features, including Windows Defender. When Windows 7 needs your attention,

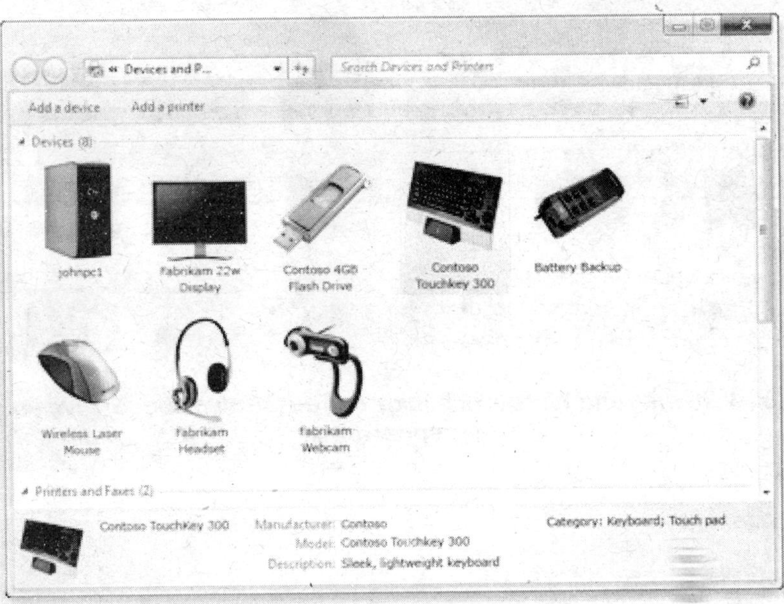

All together now: See all your devices in one place in Devices and Printers.

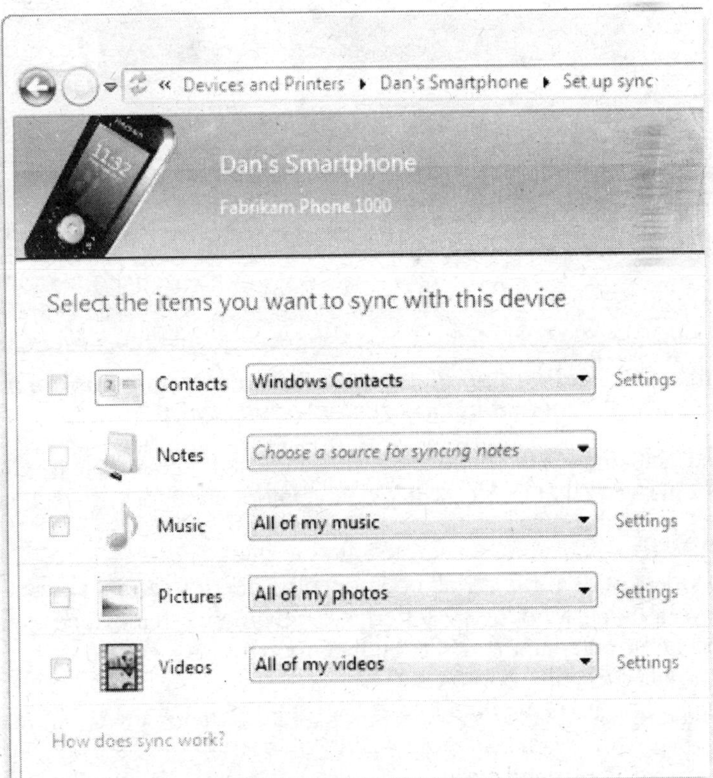

Center stage: The new Device Stage feature puts your favorite devices in the spotlight, making it easier to see status and perform common tasks.

By design: New themes and Windows backgrounds (shown above) give your desktop a personal touch.

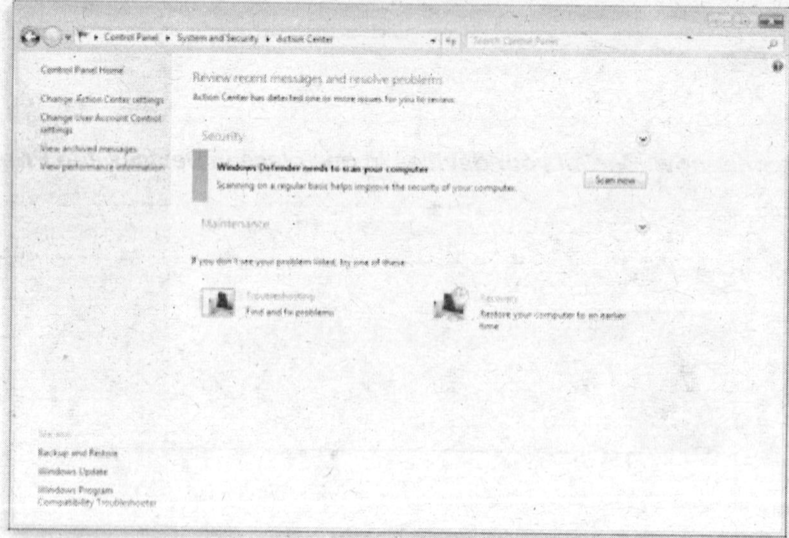

Bringing it together: Action Center cuts down on distracting pop-up messages by consolidating system notifications.

you'll see an Action Center icon in the notification area and can find out more by clicking it. No time to look at the alert right away? Action Center will keep the information for you to check later.

Share music and videos

After your pictures, videos, and music are all on your computer, it's natural to want to share them with other computers in your home. Windows 7 introduces new media sharing and streaming features that make your PC a great home entertainment hub. HomeGroup makes it easy to share music, pictures, and video with other computers running Windows 7.

With another new feature called "Play to," you can play your digital media on other devices in your home.

Introducing Windows Touch

Using a keyboard and mouse are great for many tasks, but they aren't always the easiest way to do things. If you've got a touchscreen, you can just touch your computer screen for a more direct and natural way to work. Use your fingers to scroll and zoom. Large touch-sensitive areas on the Start menu and the taskbar make Windows Touch easier to use.

Better Tablet PC support

Handwriting recognition takes a big step in Windows 7. Beginning with greater accuracy and speed, Windows 7 improves pen input in several ways. You can create personalized custom dictionaries for handwriting recognition and use the new languages supported in Windows 7. You can also use the new Math Input Panel to write math expressions. Or, just make a quick list on a Sticky Note using the tablet pen.

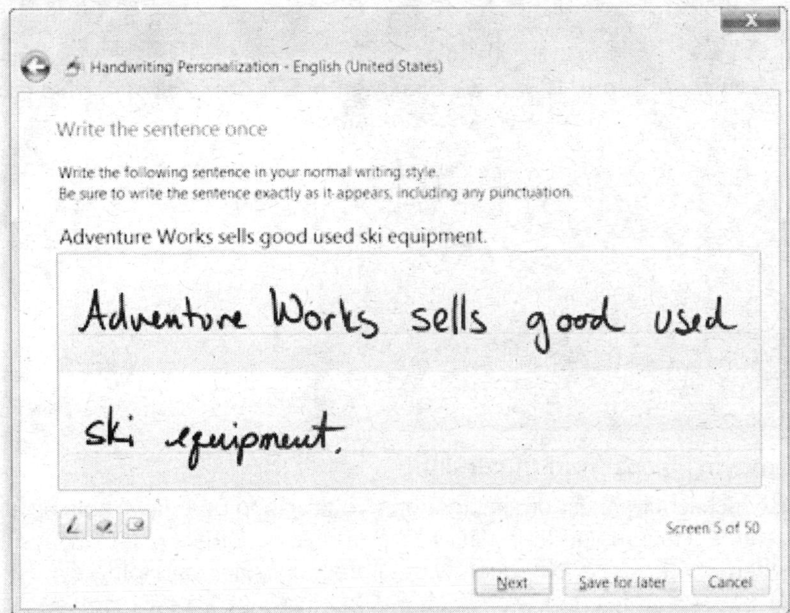

Just write it down: Handwriting recognition in Windows 7 is more accurate.

Desktop of Windows 7

The desktop is the main screen area that you see after you turn on your computer and log on to Windows. Like the top of an actual desk, it serves as a surface for your work. When you open programs or folders, they appear on the desktop. You can also put things on the desktop, such as files and folders, and arrange them however you want.

The desktop is sometimes defined more broadly to include the taskbar. The taskbar sits at the bottom of your screen. It shows you which programs are running and allows you to switch between them. It also contains the Start button , which you can use to access programs, folders, and computer settings.

Working with desktop icons

Icons are small pictures that represent files, folders, programs, and other items. When you first start Windows, you'll see at least one icon on your desktop: The Recycle Bin (more on that later). Your computer manufacturer might have added other icons to the desktop.

Taskbar

Adding and removing icons from the desktop

You can choose which icons appear on the desktop—you can add or remove an icon at any time. Some people like a clean, uncluttered desktop with few or no icons. Others place dozens of icons on their desktop to give them quick access to frequently used programs, files, and folders.

If you want easy access from the desktop to your favorite files or programs, you can create shortcuts to them. A shortcut is an icon that represents a link to an item, rather than the item itself. When you double-click a shortcut, the item opens. If you delete a shortcut, only the shortcut is removed, not the original item. You can identify shortcuts by the arrow on their icon.

To add a shortcut to the desktop

Supposing you have a program loaded into the computer and you are quite often using it. So you would like to have a shortcut for it. For example, I use **PageMaker**, quite often, so I have created a shortcut for this and it is available on the desktop.

Supposing you are using a program called **Paint** quite often during your use of the computer. You would like to create a shortcut for it. Lets see how it is created. For this you follow the steps here.

1. Minimize all your opened programs.
2. Click at the right button of the mouse on the desktop to get a menu, as shown here.
3. Click at **New** to get the new menu, as shown. Click at **Shortcut** to create one.
4. This will give rise to a dialog box, as shown. Side by side, you will notice that it has created a new folder with **New Shortcut** as the name.
5. Click at the browse button to locate the file associated with the new shortcut. In our case it will be **Paint** or **Paintbrush**. In this case, as the picture shows that the file is available in the Windows folder under the name **mspaint.exe**.

CHAPTER 1

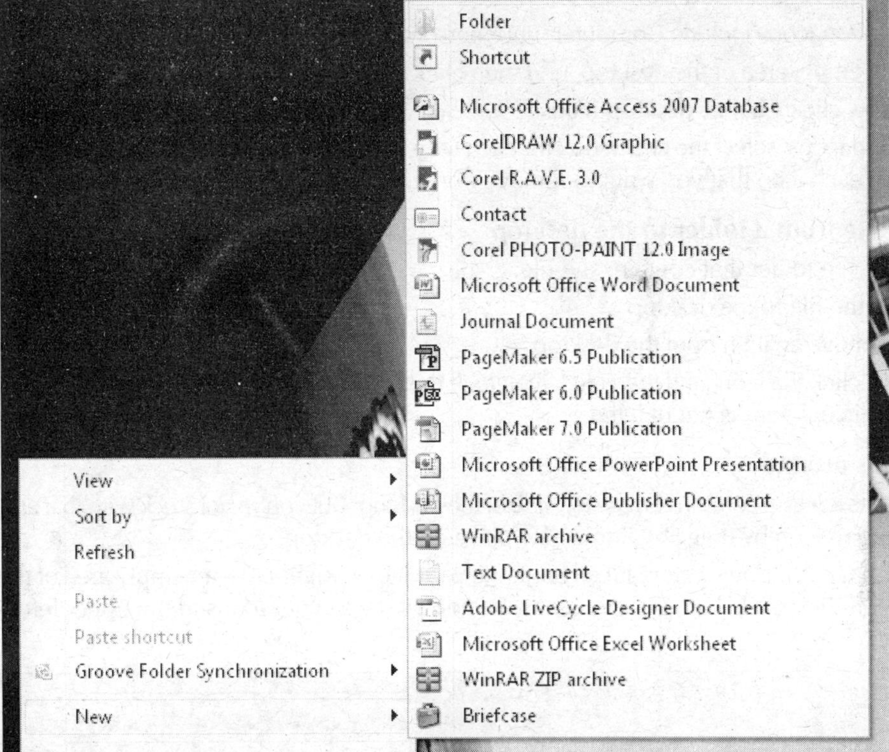

Once selected it will be filled up in the File name column. Click it to open it. This will lead us back to the main dialog box of **Create Shortcut**.

6. You will now see that the command line has been filled up with the exact location of the file which is to be Run for launching of this shortcut from the desktop.
7. Click at **Next** to get the next dialog box. This will ask you fill up the name you want to give to the shortcut. Here we have given it as **PAINT**.
8. Clicking at **Finish** will end the procedure to create the shortcut. Once done, it will create a new shortcut named **PAINT**on the desktop. You can now use it to launch Paint.
9. This can be seen on the next page.

To add or remove common desktop icons

Common desktop icons include Computer, your personal folder, the Recycle Bin, and Control Panel.

Right-click an empty area of the desktop, and then click **Personalize**.

In the left pane, click **Change desktop icons**.

Under Desktop icons, select the check box for each icon that you want to add to the desktop, or clear the check box for each icon that you want to remove from the desktop, and then click OK.

To move a file from a folder to the desktop

1. Open the folder that contains the file.
2. Drag the file to the desktop.
3. To remove an icon from the desktop

- Right-click the icon, and then click Delete. If the icon is a shortcut, only the shortcut is removed; the original item is not deleted.

Moving icons around

Windows stacks icons in columns on the left side of the desktop. But you're not stuck with that arrangement. You can move an icon by dragging it to a new place on the desktop.

You can also have Windows automatically arrange your icons. Right-click an empty area of the desktop, click View, and then click Auto arrange icons. Windows stacks your icons in the upper-left corner and

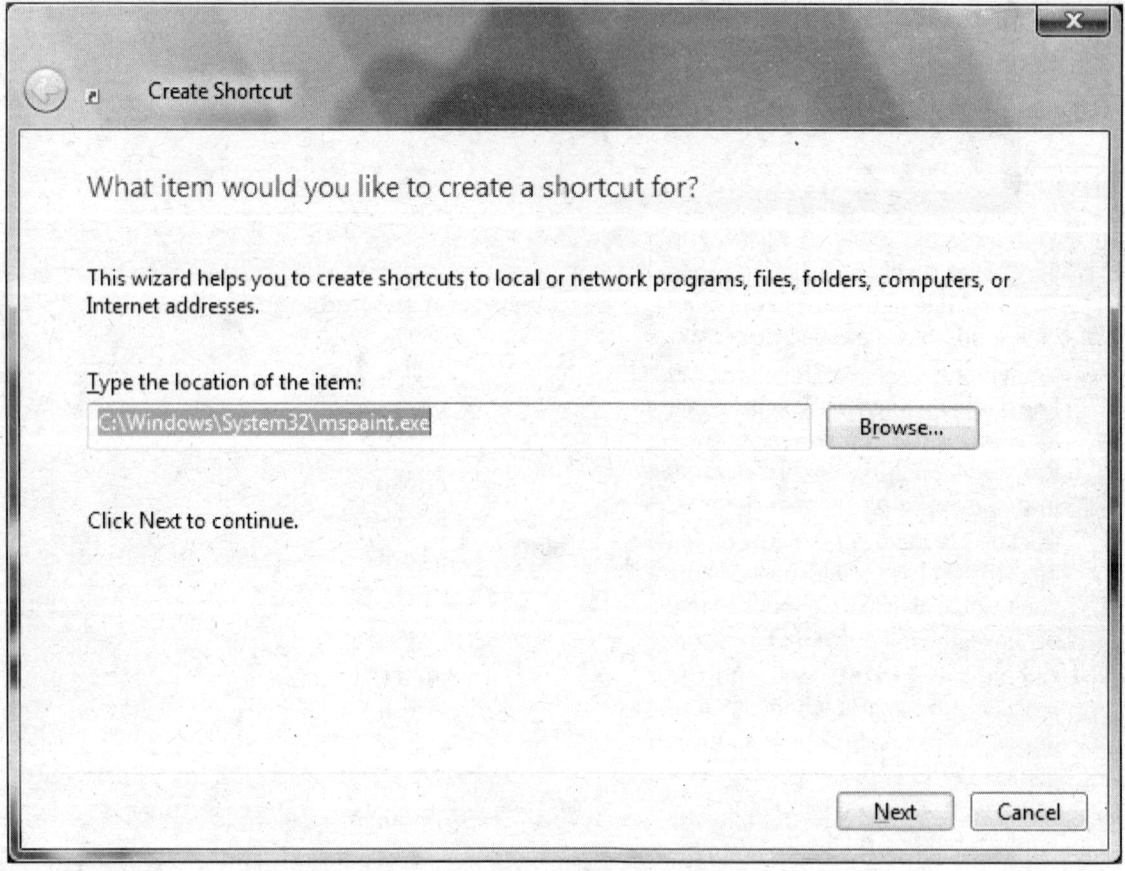

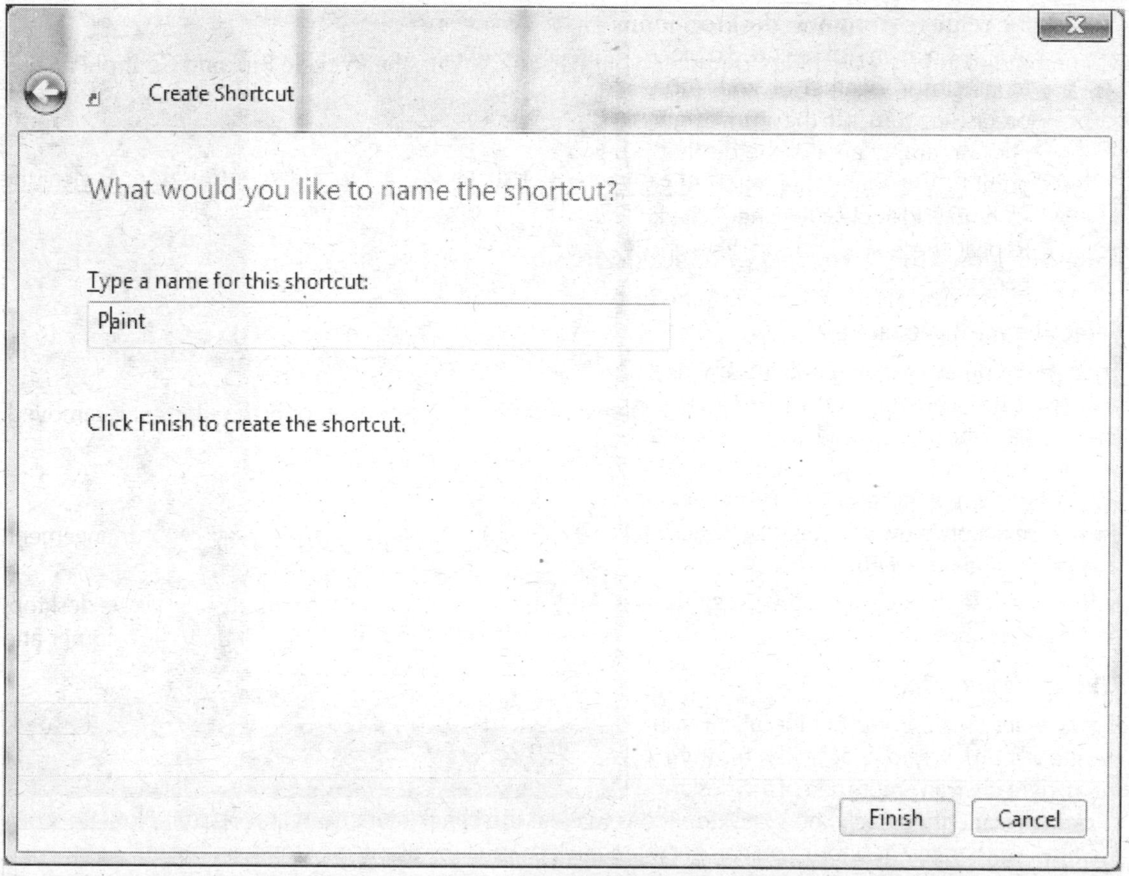

Create Shortcut
What would you like to name the shortcut?
Type a name for this shortcut:
Paint
Click Finish to create the shortcut.
Finish
Cancel

Adobe Reader 7.0
tallyrer
How to Share Feedback
Winamp
PowerDVD
Paint
Tally 9
WinZip

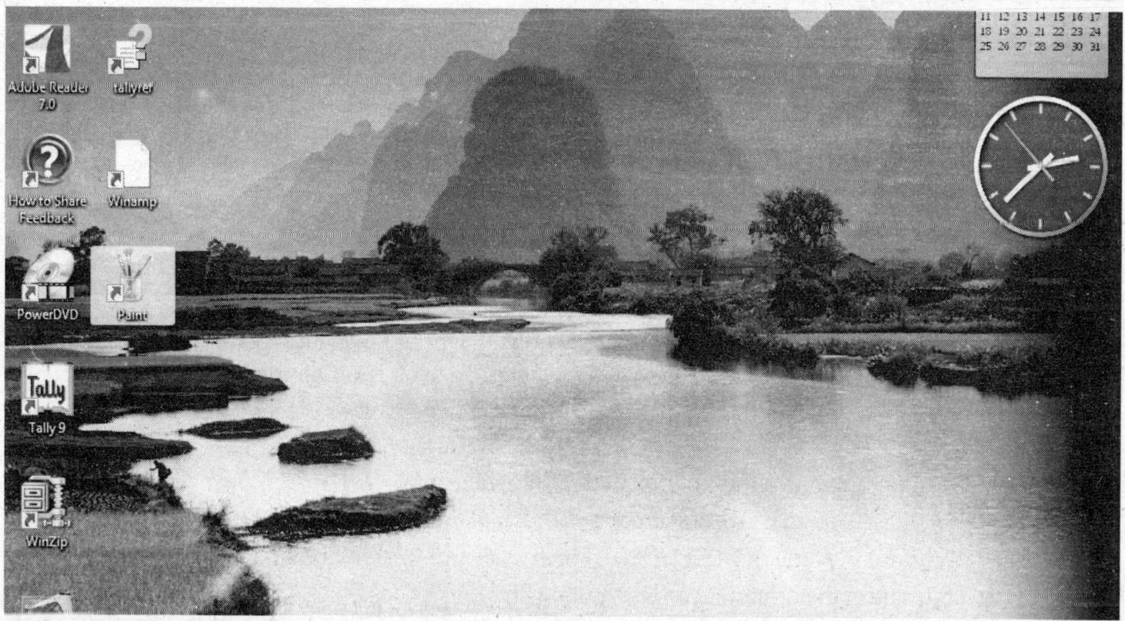

locks them in place. To unlock the icons so that you can move them again, click Auto arrange icons again, clearing the check mark next to it.

- By default, Windows spaces icons evenly on an invisible grid. To place icons closer together or with more precision, turn off the grid. Right-click an empty area of the desktop, point to View, and then click Align icons to grid to clear the check mark. Repeat these steps to turn the grid back on.

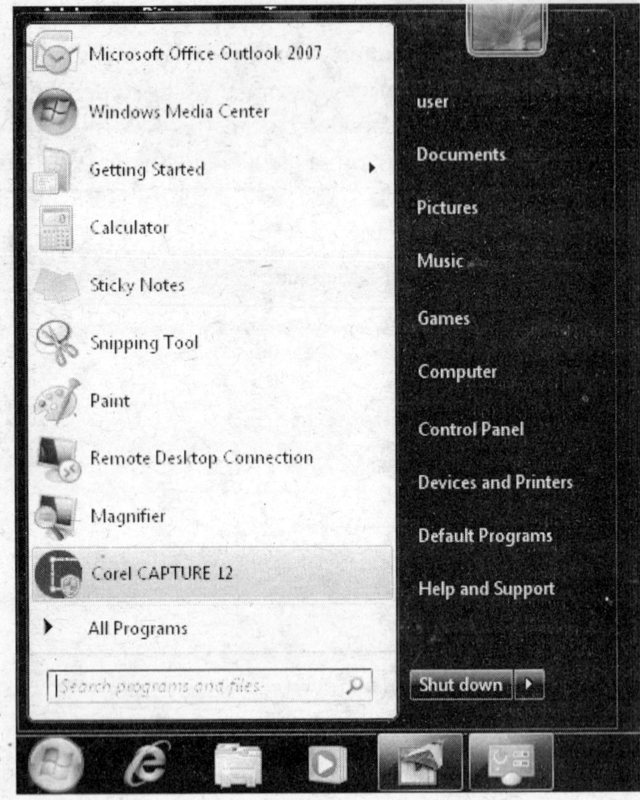

Selecting multiple icons

To move or delete a bunch of icons at once, you must first select all of them. Click an empty area of the desktop and drag the mouse. Surround the icons that you want to select with the rectangle that appears. Then release the mouse button. Now you can drag the icons as a group or delete them.

Select multiple desktop icons by dragging a rectangle around them

Hiding desktop icons

If you want to temporarily hide all of your desktop icons without actually removing them, right-click an empty part of the desktop, click View, and then click Show desktop icons to clear the check mark from that option. Now no icons are displayed on the desktop. You can get them back by clicking Show desktop icons again.

Icons on the Desktop

On pressing the Start button, as usual you would see the various programs which can be used by just clicking at them. It gives the recently used programs. On the right hand side are the programs which are always there and can be used anytime. These are: User, Documents, Pictures, Music, Games, Computer, Control Panel, Devices and Printers, Default Programs, and Help and Support.

Let us explore computer among them.

Computer

It helps you browse the contents of your computer, open folders, open documents and run your favourite applications. As shown here, it is divided into 2 sections, Favorite Links and Details. You click at any icon on the right hand side of the dialog box and then choose the option on the left hand side.

Details will give you the detail of the item selected. You can access other places by clicking at any one of them.

On the right hand side, you have the options of the followings:

Name: It gives you the option of sorting the icons by Name or by from A to H and I to Z.

Type: You can choose the type from CD Drive, Local Disk and System Folder and then Stack by Type.

Total Size: You can set the drives according to their size.

Free Space: You can set the drive to show how much space is available in them and list them according to the size, as shown below.

On the top there are buttons like this:

Organize: This allows you to organize the folders and files according to your liking. Like creating a New Folder, Cutting, copying, pasting of folders/files. Other options are shown here.

Views: It gives the option of viewing the folders/files in different views.

System properties: Shows information about your computer, such as the processor speed and the amount of installed memory.

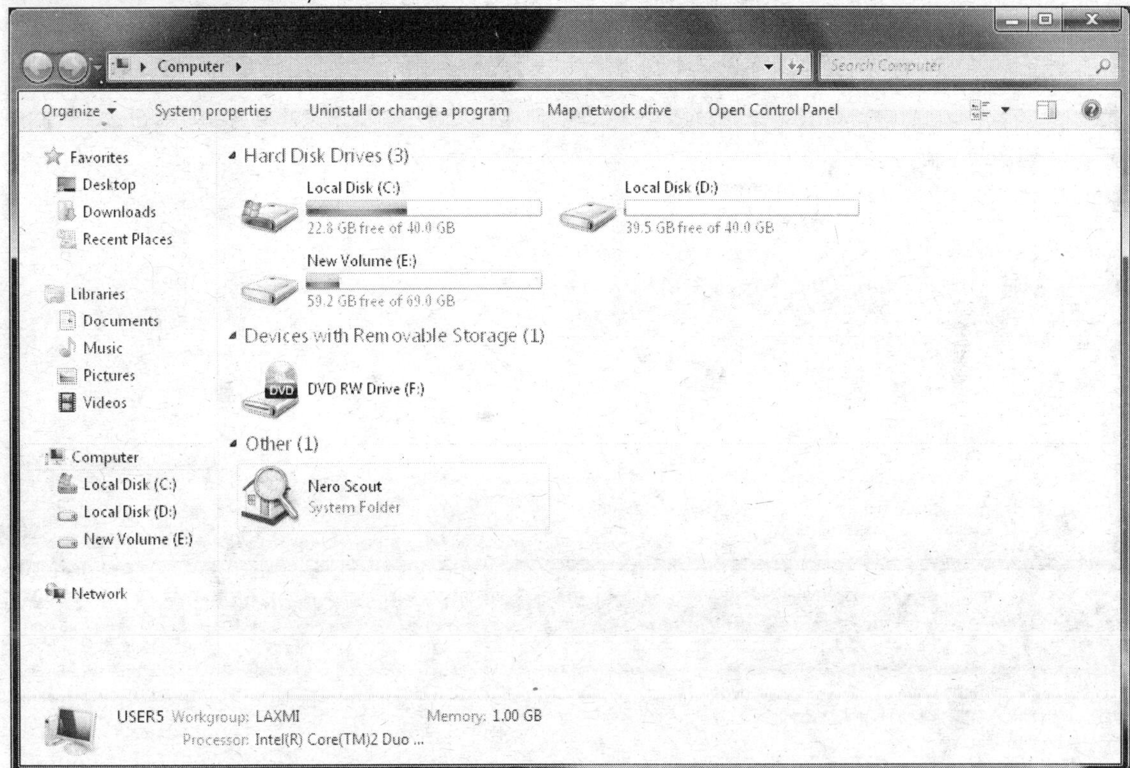

Uninstall or change a program: Allows you to uninstall or change any program in the fixed drive.

Map network drive: It allows you to map a network drive.

Details of the folders available in the hard disk drive C: are shown here.

Now let us see how **Computer** is used for working with files.

Copying of Files

Supposing you have to copy a file from one drive to another. Open the folder of hard disk and the particular file where it exists. Click the file to make it selected. Now click at Copy in the Organize menu.

Now click the other folder/hard disk where you want to copy the file. Let us say disk drive F:. Now again go to the Organize menu and click at Paste, this time. The file will be pasted in the disk drive F:, as shown next. Similary you can copy and paste folders from one place to another.

However, if you want to copy without leaving the copy of the file in the source, press **Control Key** and then click the mouse to drag the file. This will copy the file and not leave the copy behind.

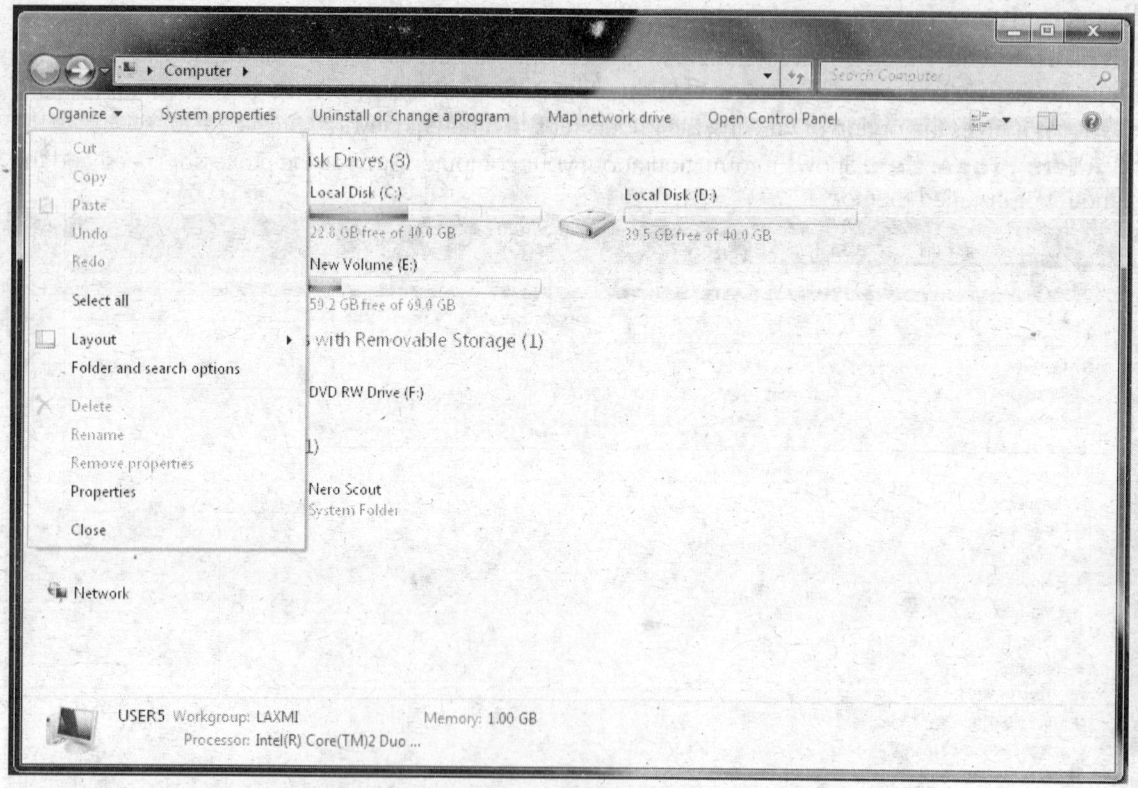

Computer ▸
Search Computer
Organize ▾ System properties Uninstall or change a program Map network drive Open Control Panel
Cut
Copy
Paste
Undo
Redo
Select all
Layout
Folder and search options
Delete
Rename
Remove properties
Properties
Close
Network
...isk Drives (3)
Local Disk (C:)
22.8 GB free of 40.0 GB
Local Disk (D:)
39.5 GB free of 40.0 GB
New Volume (E:)
59.2 GB free of 69.0 GB
...s with Removable Storage (1)
DVD RW Drive (F:)
...1)
Nero Scout
System Folder
USER5 Workgroup: LAXMI Memory: 1.00 GB
Processor: Intel(R) Core(TM)2 Duo ...

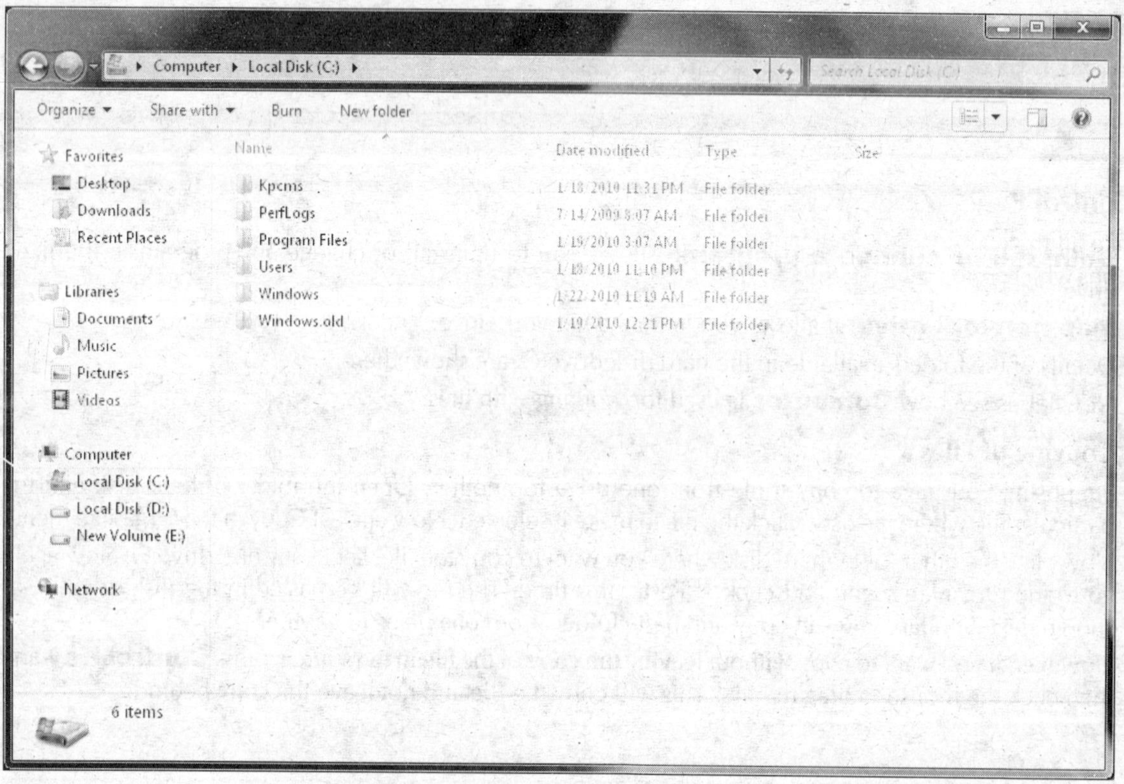

Computer ▸ Local Disk (C:) ▸
Search Local Disk (C:)
Organize ▾ Share with ▾ Burn New folder

Name	Date modified	Type	Size
Kpcms	1/18/2010 11:31 PM	File folder	
PerfLogs	7/14/2009 8:07 AM	File folder	
Program Files	1/19/2010 3:07 AM	File folder	
Users	1/18/2010 11:10 PM	File folder	
Windows	1/22/2010 11:19 AM	File folder	
Windows.old	1/19/2010 12:21 PM	File folder	

Favorites
Desktop
Downloads
Recent Places
Libraries
Documents
Music
Pictures
Videos
Computer
Local Disk (C:)
Local Disk (D:)
New Volume (E:)
Network
6 items

Recycle Bin

It is like a dust bin of the computer. All the deleted files are transferred here. You can in fact open this folder to see the files present in it. If you want at any stage to retrace any file, you can do it, if it is present in the **Recycle Bin**. However, if you choose to empty the recycle bin and delete the files altogether, then you cannot restore any of the file.

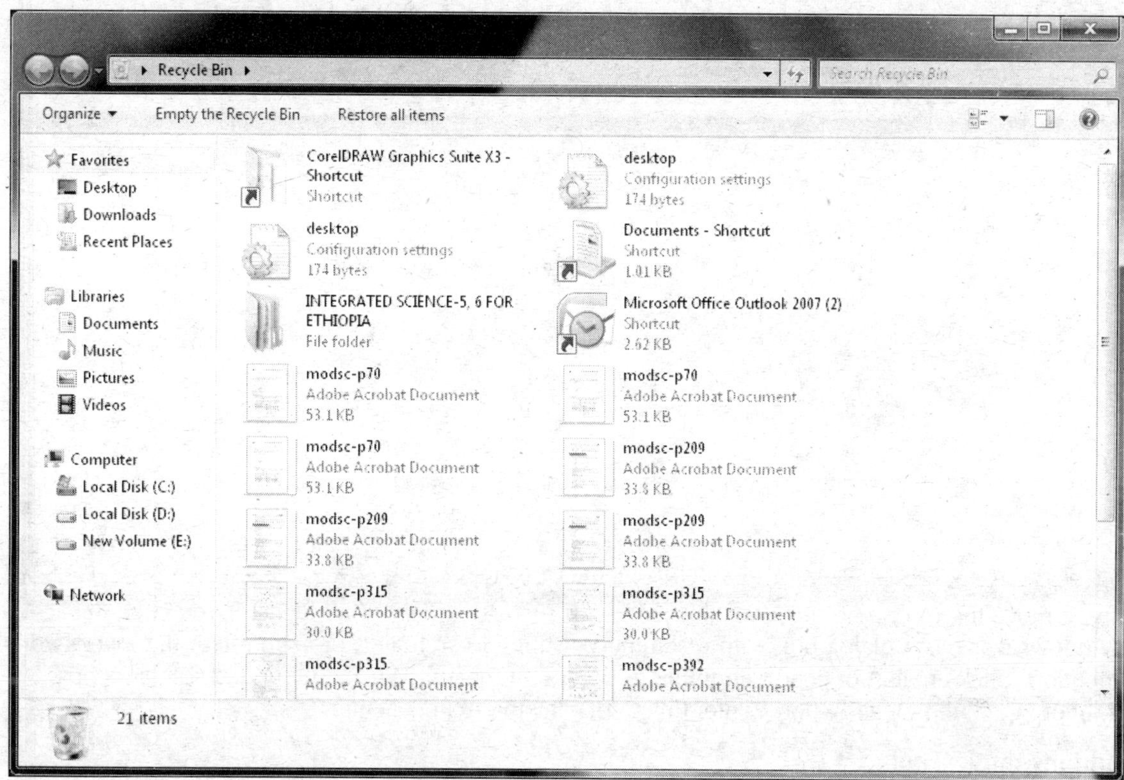

Control Panel of Windows 7

Like all the earlier versions of Windows, this Windows version too has a control panel. It is a group of icons which when selected invoke applications which allow you to change the settings of the Windows. In this chapter we will study about the various options available in the control panel.

Accessing Control Panel

Control panel can be accessed from two places: **Control Panel** in **My Computer** icon and from **Start** button on the on the desktop. When you click **Start** button, you see the different options. **Control Panel** is one of them. Control Panel can be seen in Alphabetic order of the programs or Control Panel Home view which shows the programs subjec wise. Both views are shown here.

Let us see what function each of them performs. For this I am going through it alphabetically.

Action Center

Windows 7 has a redesigned desktop with many additional customization options. By default, when you log on, the operating sysem displays an Action Center summary Icon in the notification area. This icon has a flag with a red circle with an X in it. Action Center is a program that monitors the status of important security and maintenance areas. If the status of a monitored item changes, Action Center updates the notification icon as appropriate for the severity of the alert.

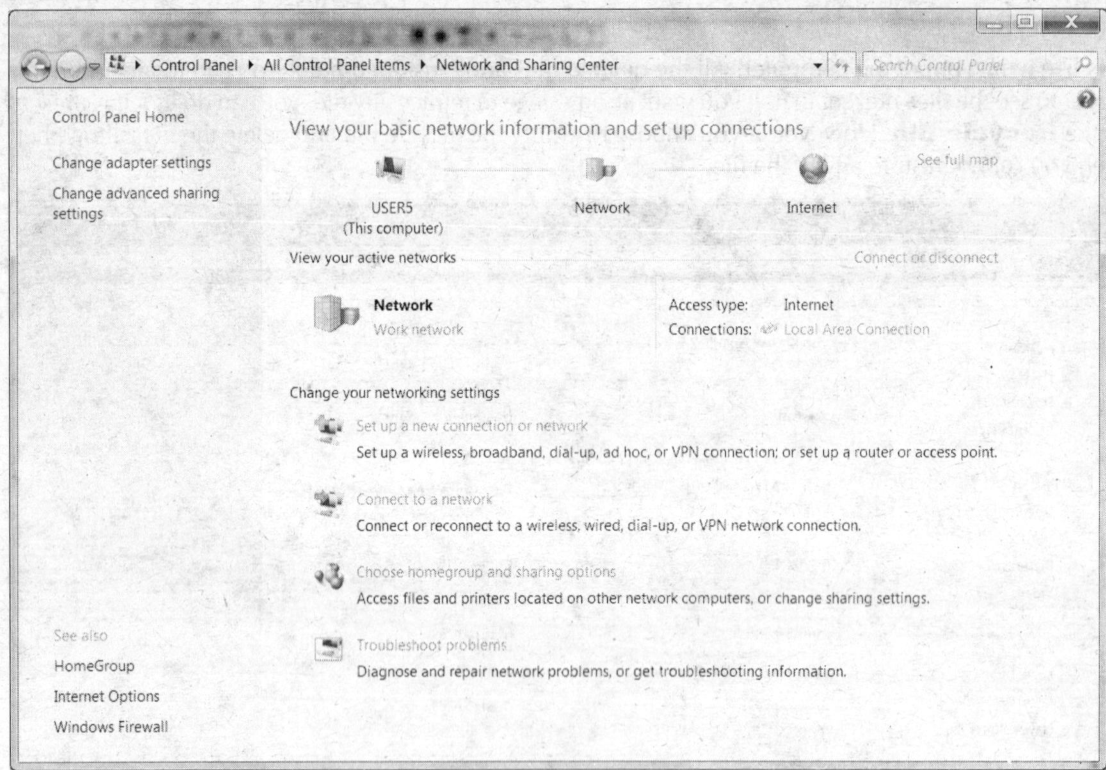

If you move the mouse pointer over this icon, you see a summary of all alerts. If you click this icon, Windows displays a dialog box with a summary listing of earch alert or action item that needs your attention. Click an alert or action item link to open your default Web browser and display a possible solution. Click the Open Action Center link to display the Action Center..

Adminstrative Tools

It has the different tools under it, they are: Computer Management, Data Sources (ODBC), Event Viewer, iSCSI Initiator, Local Security Policy, Memory Diagnostics Tool, Print Management, Reliability and Performance, Services, System Configuration, Task Scheduler and Windows Firewall with Advanced Security. Microsoft Management Console (MMC) hosts and displays administrative tools created by Microsoft and other software vendors. These tools are called snap-ins, and they are used for managing the hardware, software, and network components of Windows. Several of the tools in the Administrative Tools folder, such as Computer Management, are MMC snap-ins.

AutoPlay

AutoPlay, gives you a single place to configure how you would like your CDs and DVDs (and memory cards, flash drives, and cameras) to be run. And you can specify how audio CDs are handled, versus enhanced audio CDs.

Backup and Restore Centre

Windows 7 provides Backup and Restore Center as a central console for backing up and reovering a computer. You can acces this console by clicking Start, clicking Control Panel and then clicking the Back Up Your Computer link under the System And Security heading. Other tools for backing up and recovering a computer's data include Previous Versions, the Startup Repair tool, Windows Resume Loader, System Restore, and Backup..

Choose what happens when you insert each type of media or device

☑ Use AutoPlay for all media and devices

Media

Audio CD	Play audio CD using Windows Media Player
Enhanced audio CD	*Choose a default*
DVD movie	Play DVD movie using Windows Media Player
Enhanced DVD movie	Play DVD movie using Windows Media Player
Software and games	Ask me every time
Pictures	Ask me every time
Video files	*Choose a default*
Audio files	Play using Windows Media Player
Blank CD	Ask me every time
Blank DVD	*Choose a default*
Mixed content	Ask me every time

BitLocker Drive Encryption

Turning on BitLocker Drive Encryption (BitLocker) protects all files stored on the drive Windows is installed on. Unlike Encrypting File System (EFS), which enables you to encrypt individual files, BitLocker encrypts the entire system drive, including the Windows system files necessary for startup and logon. You can log on and work with your files normally, but BitLocker can help block hackers from accessing the system files they rely on to discover your password, or access your hard disk by removing it from your computer and installing it in a different computer. BitLocker can only help protect files that are stored on the drive that Windows is installed on. If you store files on other drives, you can help protect those files with EFS.

When you add new files to the drive with BitLocker, BitLocker encrypts them automatically. Files remain encrypted only while they are stored in the encrypted drive. Files copied to another drive or computer are decrypted. If you share files with other users, such as through a network, these files are encrypted while stored on the encrypted drive, but they can be accessed normally by authorized users.

During computer startup, if BitLocker detects a system condition that could represent a security risk (for example, disk errors, a change to the BIOS , or changes to any startup files), it will lock the drive and require a special BitLocker recovery password to unlock it. Make sure that you create this recovery password when you turn on BitLocker for the first time; otherwise, you could permanently lose access to your files.

CHAPTER 1

Protect your files and computer by backing them up

Back up files or your entire computer

Create backup copies of your files and folders. [Back up files]

Create a Windows Complete PC Backup and Restore image of your entire computer, which can be used to recover from a hardware failure. [Back up computer]

A Windows Complete PC Backup and Restore image has not been created.

Which type of backup should I make?

Restore files or your entire computer

Restore files and folders from a backup. [Restore files]

Advanced restore

You can use shadow copies to restore previous versions of files that have been accidentally modified or deleted. What are shadow copies?

Restore your entire computer from a Windows Complete PC Backup and Restore image. [Restore computer]

Use System Restore to fix problems and undo changes to Windows.

BitLocker Drive Encryption encrypts and protects your data.

BitLocker Drive Encryption helps prevent unauthorized access to any files stored on the volume shown below. You are able to use the computer normally, but unauthorized users cannot read or use your files.

What should I know about BitLocker Drive Encryption before I turn it on?

The drive configuration is unsuitable for BitLocker Drive Encryption. To use BitLocker, please re-partition your hard drive according to the BitLocker requirements.

Set up your hard disk for BitLocker Drive Encryption

A TPM was not found. A TPM is required to turn on BitLocker. If your computer has a TPM, then contact the computer manufacturer for BitLocker-compatible BIOS.

Volumes

You can turn off BitLocker at any time, either temporarily by disabling it, or permanently by decrypting the drive.

Color Management

Color management is a system used to ensure that color content is rendered to your satisfaction everywhere—including devices such as your display and your printer.

Date and Time

You can change the format Windows uses to display dates, times, currency, and measurements. You can also change the sorting order of text to match sorting rules used in a specific country or region.

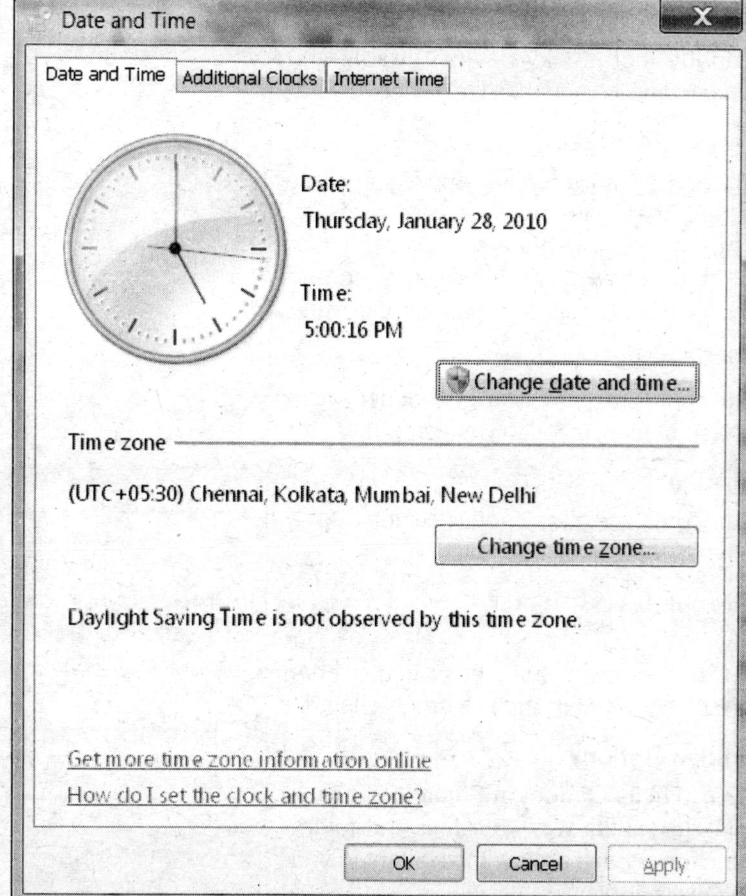

1. Click to open Regional and Language Options.
2. Click the Formats tab, and then, in the Current format list, select the locale to use for the display of the date, time, currency, and measurements.
3. You can see how these items will appear in the area below the list.
4. To customize how the date, time, currency, and measurements are displayed, click Customize this format, and then do one of the following:

- To change the way your computer displays numbers, click the Numbers tab. Items you might want to change based on the format language you chose are the decimal symbol and list separator, the format used for negative numbers and leading zeros, and the measurement system used (U.S. or metric).
- To change the way your computer displays currency values, click the Currency tab. Items you might want to change based on the format language you chose are the currency symbol, the formats used for positive or negative amounts, and the punctuation used to separate numbers.
- To change the way your computer displays the time, click the Time tab.
- To change the way your computer displays the date, click the Date tab.

Default Programs

Set Program Access and Computer Defaults makes it easy for you to change the default program used for certain activities, such as web browsing, sending e mail, playing audio and video files, and using instant messaging.

You can also specify which of these default programs are displayed on the Start menu, on the desktop, and in other locations.

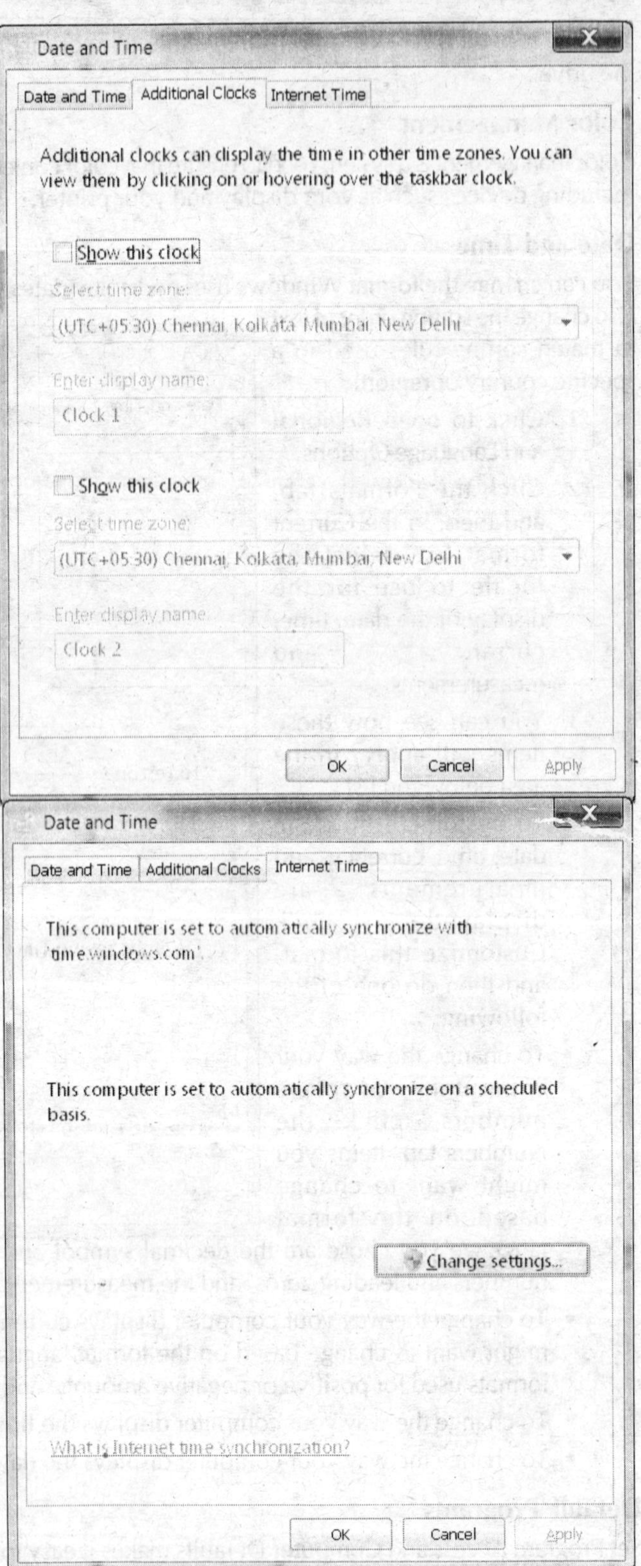

Desktop Gadgets

The device manager console shows you where all your hardware money was spent. Here, you or your tech-support person can troubleshoot a flaky device, disable and enable devices, and manage device drivers.

Device Manager

The device manager console shows you where all your hardware money was spent. Here, you or your tech-support person can troubleshoot a flaky device, disable and enable devices, and manage device drivers.

Devices and Printers

This command shows you the various devices and printers attached to your computer.

Display

This command allows you to set the display of your computer.

Ease of Access Center

This command allows you to set the various options of the dialog box. It has been discussed in details in Accessories chapter.

Folder Options

Using Folder Options in Control Panel, you can change the way your files and folders function, as well as how the content in your folders is displayed.

Click to open Folder Options.

Change the way folders are displayed

You can change the way your folders look and work to suit your needs. For example, you can open all files and folders with one click (like links in a webpage) instead of the usual double-click. Here is an overview of the settings you can change:

Choose the programs that Windows uses by default

Set your default programs

Make a program the default for all file types and protocols it can open.

Associate a file type or protocol with a program

Make a file type or protocol (such as .mp3 or http://) always open in a specific program.

Change AutoPlay settings

Play CDs or other media automatically

Set program access and computer defaults

Control access to certain programs and set defaults for this computer.

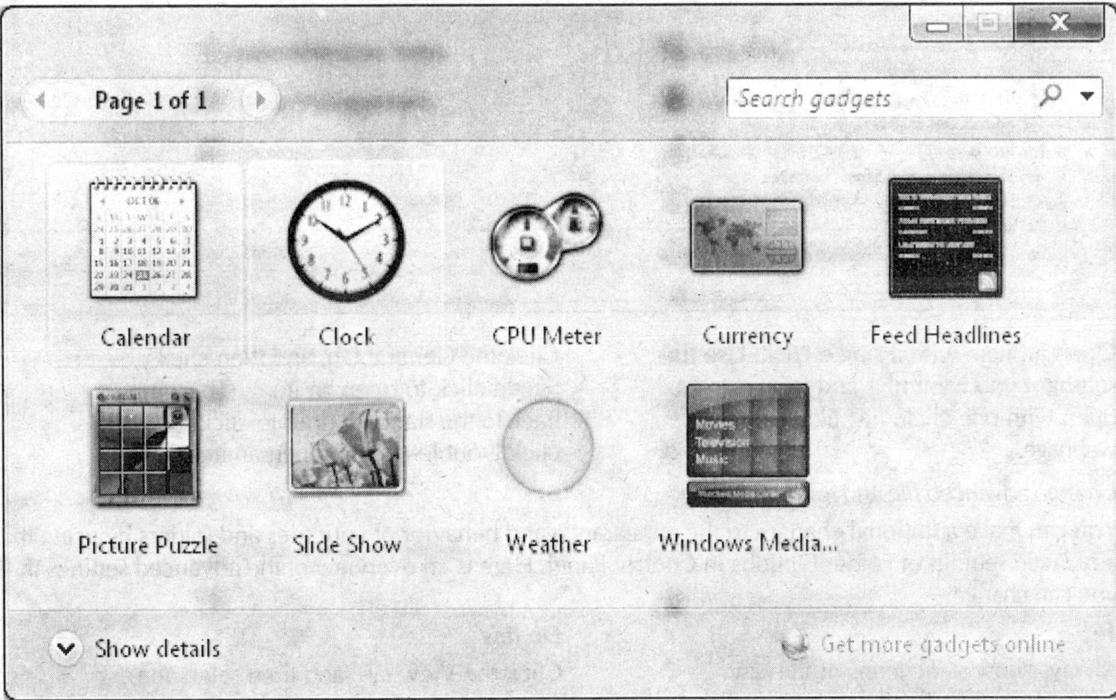

To	*Do this*
Turn off the Details pane and the Preview pane in all folders. This setting gives you more room to display files by hiding panes you might not need.	Click the General tab, and then click Use Windows classic folders. (To turn the panes back on, click Show preview and filters.)
Open every new folder in its own folder window. This can be convenient if you want to keep all the folders you are working with on the screen at the same time.	Click the General tab, and then click Open each folder in its own window. (To make each new folder replace the previous folder window, click Open each folder in the same window.)

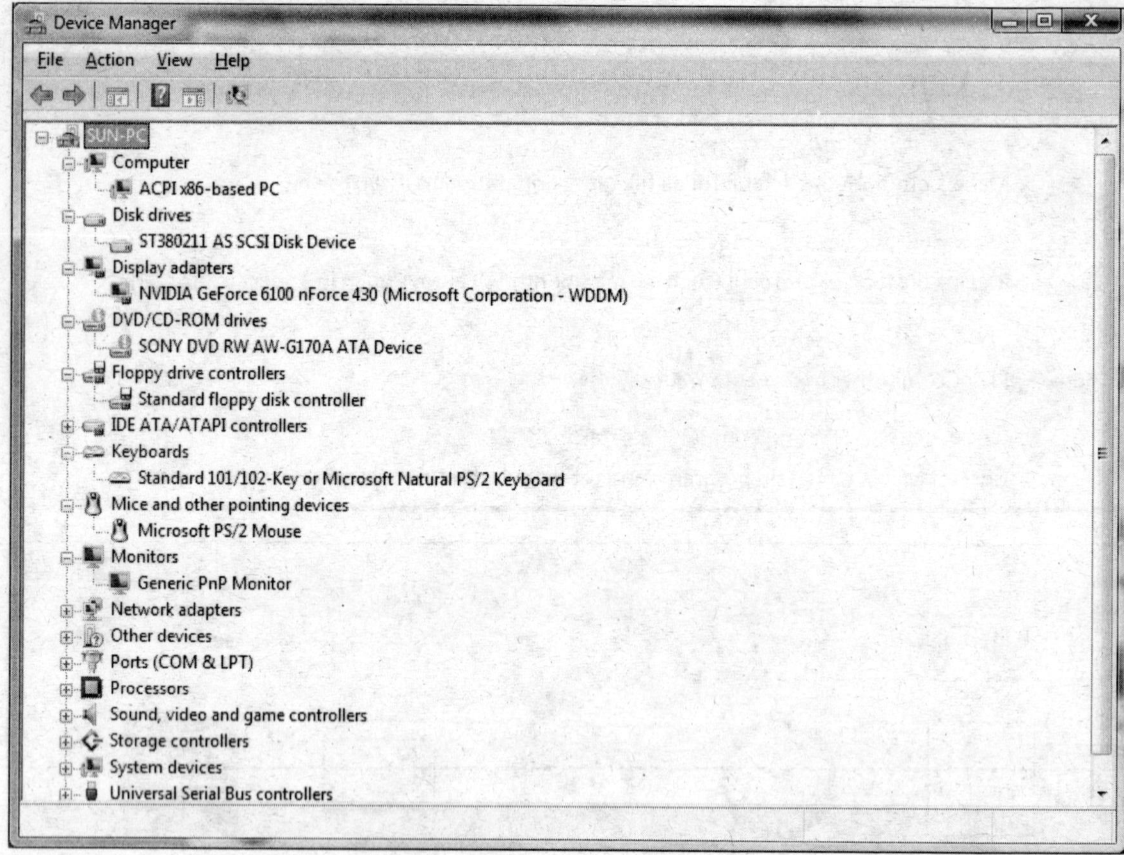

Open an item with a single click. Use this setting if you want files and folders to open with one click, just like links in a webpage.	Click the General tab, and then click Single-click to open an item. (To switch back to the standard double-click, click Double-click to open an item.)

Change advanced file and folder settings

You can make additional changes to the appearance and behavior of your files and folders by using the advanced settings of Folder Options in Control Panel. Here is an overview of the advanced settings that you can change:

To	***Do this***
Always show static icons of files and never show thumbnail previews of files. Use this setting if the thumbnail previews are slowing down your computer. You'll get better performance by using static icons.	Click the View tab, and then select the Always show icons, never thumbnails check box.
Always show the menus above the toolbar. Use this setting if you prefer to have access to the Classic menus, which are hidden by default.	Click the View tab, and then select the Always show menus check box.
See the size of a folder in a tooltip when you rest your mouse pointer over the folder.	Click the View tab, and then select the Display file size information in folder

CHAPTER 1

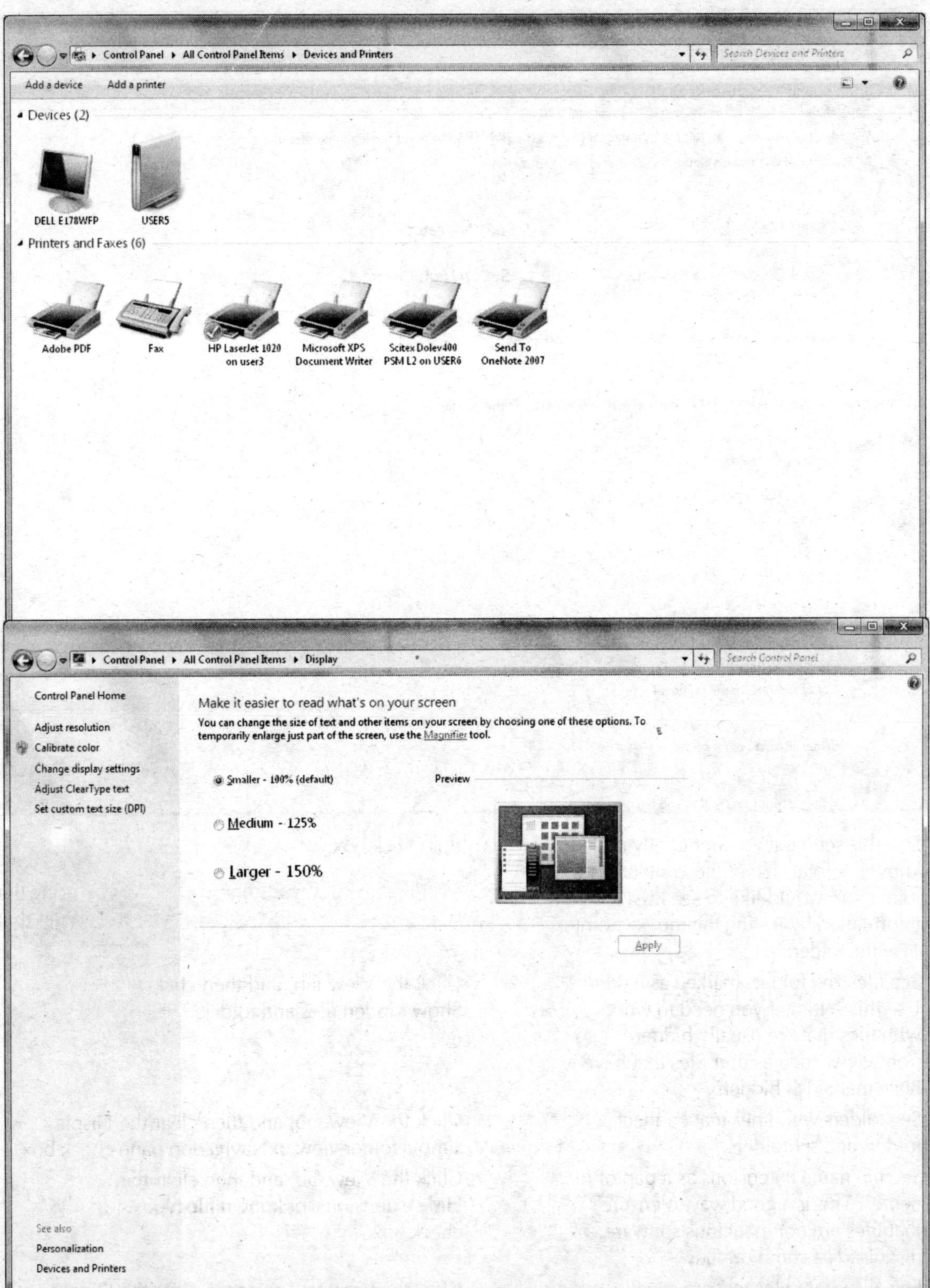
Control Panel ▸ All Control Panel Items ▸ Devices and Printers
Search Devices and Printers
Add a device
Add a printer
Devices (2)
DELL E178WFP
USER5
Printers and Faxes (6)
Adobe PDF
Fax
HP LaserJet 1020 on user3
Microsoft XPS Document Writer
Scitex Dolev400 PSM L2 on USER6
Send To OneNote 2007
Control Panel ▸ All Control Panel Items ▸ Display
Search Control Panel
Control Panel Home
Adjust resolution
Calibrate color
Change display settings
Adjust ClearType text
Set custom text size (DPI)
Make it easier to read what's on your screen
You can change the size of text and other items on your screen by choosing one of these options. To temporarily enlarge just part of the screen, use the Magnifier tool.
Smaller - 100% (default)
Preview
Medium - 125%
Larger - 150%
Apply
See also
Personalization
Devices and Printers

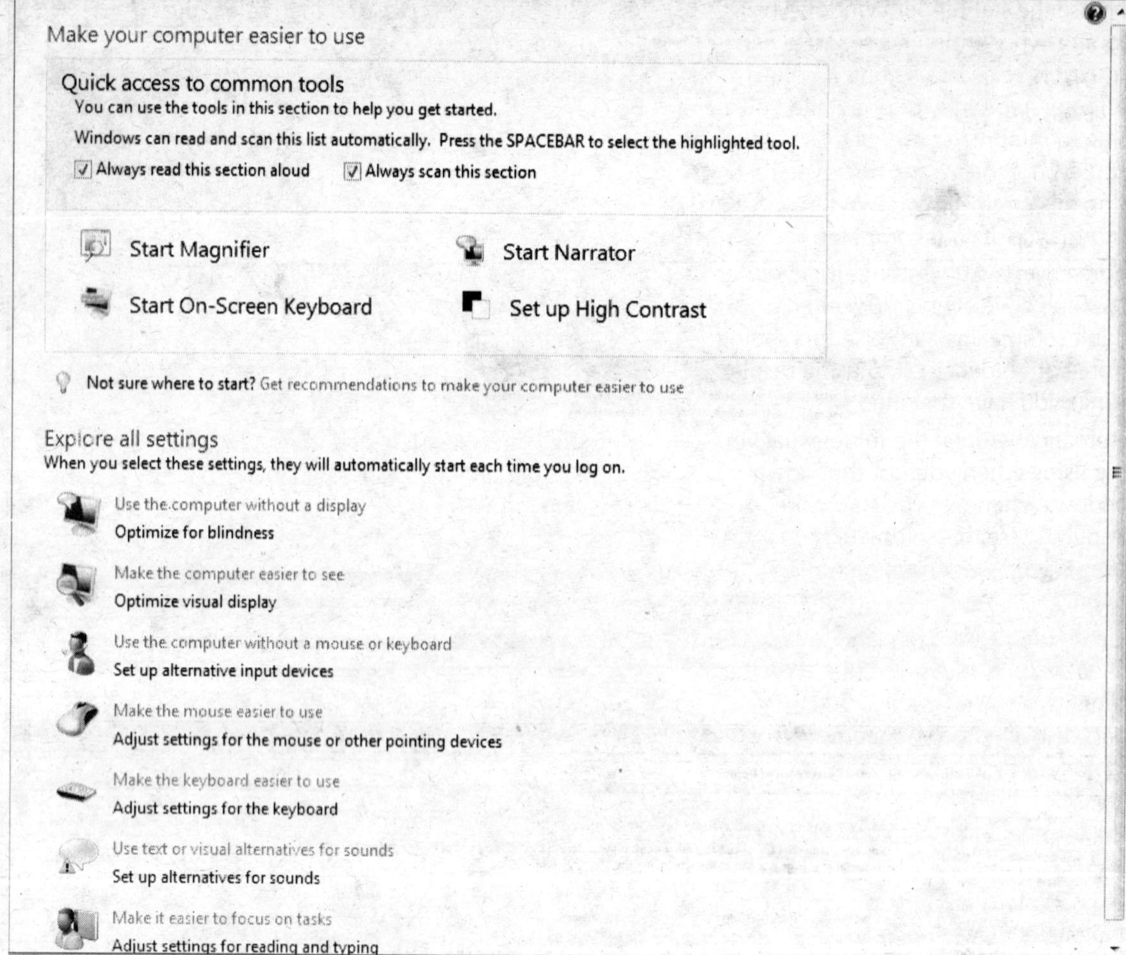

Use this setting if you frequently need to know the total size of the contents of a folder and would like to see this information by resting the mouse pointer over the folder.	tips check box.
See files and folders marked as hidden. Use this setting if you need to work with files that are usually hidden from view, such as user files that have been marked as hidden.	Click the View tab, and then click Show hidden files and folders.
See folders with lines that connect folders and subfolders.	Click the View tab, and then clear the Display simple folder view in Navigation pane check box.
See file name extensions as a part of file names. This is a good way to ensure that files are not malicious software disguised as common files.	Click the View tab, and then clear the Hide extensions for known file types check box.
See all system files that are usually hidden from view.	Click the View tab, and then clear the Hide protected operating system files check box.

Increase the stability of Windows by opening every folder in a separate part of memory. Use this setting if your computer frequently crashes, and you are trying to minimize problems or troubleshoot. Be aware, however, that doing this could slow down the performance of your computer.	Click the View tab, and then select the Launch folder windows in a separate process check box.
Ignore custom view settings for every folder and have every folder open using default settings instead. Use this setting to force all folders to stop using display settings you have specified.	Click the View tab, and then clear the Remember each folder's view settings check box.
Automatically open the folders that you were using when you last shut down Windows whenever you start your computer. Use this setting to help you preserve your work from session to session.	Click the View tab, and then select the Restore previous folder windows at logon check box.
Hide the drive letter of each drive or device in the Computer folder. Use this setting if you don't want to see drive letters displayed on your computer and prefer to see only the friendly name of each drive.	Click the View tab, and then clear the Show drive letters check box.
Display encrypted or compressed NTFS files as ordinary files, without any unique color coding to identify them. Use this setting if you have encrypted or compressed NTFS files and do not want to see them represented differently than other files on your computer.	Click the View tab, and then clear the Show encrypted or compressed NTFS files in color check box.
Turn off the tooltips that appear when you rest your mouse pointer over files. Use this setting if you don't want to see the file information that appears in tooltips when you rest the pointer over files and folders.	Click the View tab, and then clear the Show pop-up descriptions for folder and desktop items check box.
Never show the contents of files in the Preview pane. Use this setting to improve the performance of your computer, or if you don't want to use the Preview pane.	Click the View tab, and then clear the Show preview handlers in preview pane check box.
Add check boxes to file views to make it easier to select several files at once, which can be useful if it is difficult for you to hold the CTRL key while clicking to select multiple files.	Click the View tab, and then select the Use check boxes to select items check box.

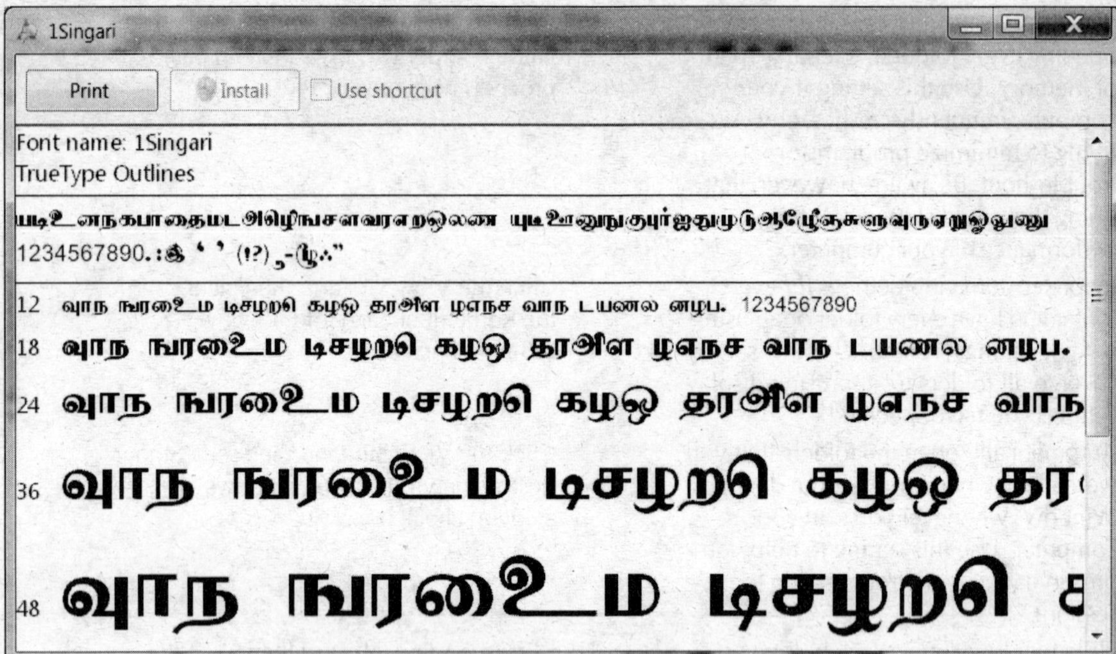

Fonts

It shows all the fonts available in the hard disk.

Getting Started

If you are new to Windows, then this is for you. From here you can work your way out to the various features of the software.

HomeGroup

Using this command you can share with other home computers running Windows 7. With homegroup, you can share files and printers with other computers running Windows 7. You can also stream media to devices. The homegroup is protected with a password, and you will always be able to choose what you share with the group.

Indexing Options

Similar to the way the index in a book helps you to keep track of its contents, the index in Windows keeps track of the files on your computer. The index stores information about files, including the file name, date modified, and properties like author, tags, and rating. You will never see the index, but it is used by Windows to perform very fast searches of the most common files on your computer.

The index is used to make searching for files much faster. Instead of looking through your entire hard disk for a file name or file property, Windows scans the index, which allows most results to appear in a small fraction of the time that a search without the index would take.

By default, all of the most common files on your computer are indexed. Indexed locations include all of the files in your personal folder (such as Documents, Pictures, Music, and Videos), as well as e mail and offline files. Files that are not indexed include program files and system files. The locations that contain those files are not indexed because you rarely need to search those files, and so not including them in the index makes your searches perform faster.

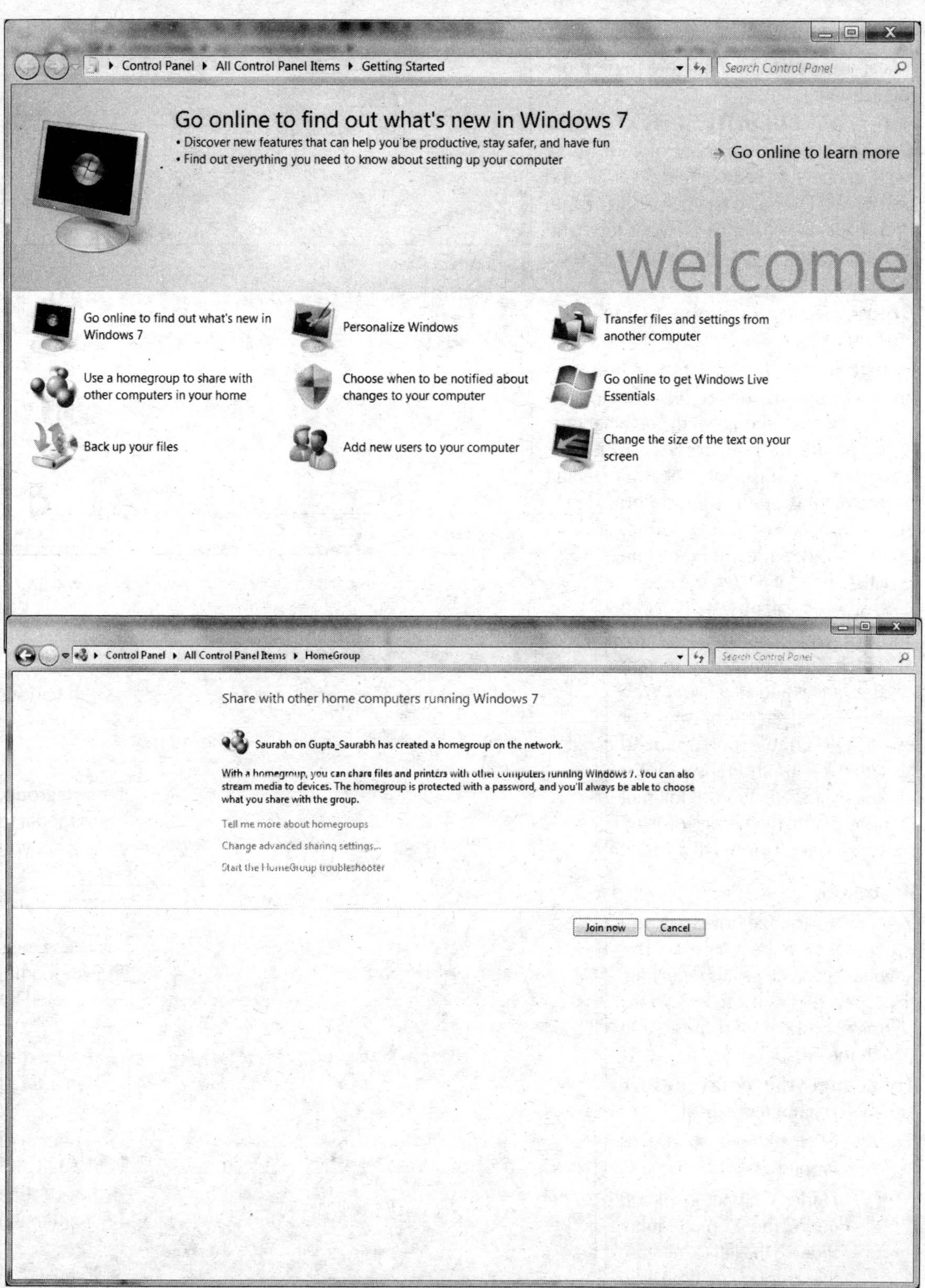
Control Panel ▸ All Control Panel Items ▸ Getting Started
Search Control Panel
Go online to find out what's new in Windows 7
• Discover new features that can help you be productive, stay safer, and have fun
• Find out everything you need to know about setting up your computer
Go online to learn more
welcome
Go online to find out what's new in Windows 7
Personalize Windows
Transfer files and settings from another computer
Use a homegroup to share with other computers in your home
Choose when to be notified about changes to your computer
Go online to get Windows Live Essentials
Back up your files
Add new users to your computer
Change the size of the text on your screen
Control Panel ▸ All Control Panel Items ▸ HomeGroup
Search Control Panel
Share with other home computers running Windows 7
Saurabh on Gupta_Saurabh has created a homegroup on the network.
With a homegroup, you can share files and printers with other computers running Windows 7. You can also stream media to devices. The homegroup is protected with a password, and you'll always be able to choose what you share with the group.
Tell me more about homegroups
Change advanced sharing settings...
Start the HomeGroup troubleshooter
Join now
Cancel

CHAPTER 1

Internet Options

As can be seen from the figure here, it has the following tabs:

General, Security, Private and Content: These tabs control your home page, cache files, search field defaults, and history list. They also let you define certain Web pages as off-limits for your kids and manage RSS feeds, as well as block pop-up windows.

Connections: Controls when your PC modem dials.

Programs: Use this tab to manage browser add-ons, decide whether or not Internet Explorer should warn you whenever it is not the default browser (for your protection, of course), or choose the default programs that open, should you click a link to email someone, open a media file, or view the HTML source of a Web page.

Advanced: On this tab, you will find dozens of checkboxes, most of which are useful only in rare circumstances and affect your Web experience only in mirror ways. For example, "Enable personalized favorites menu" shortens your list of bookmarks over time, as Internet Explorer hides the names of Web sites you haven't visited in a while.

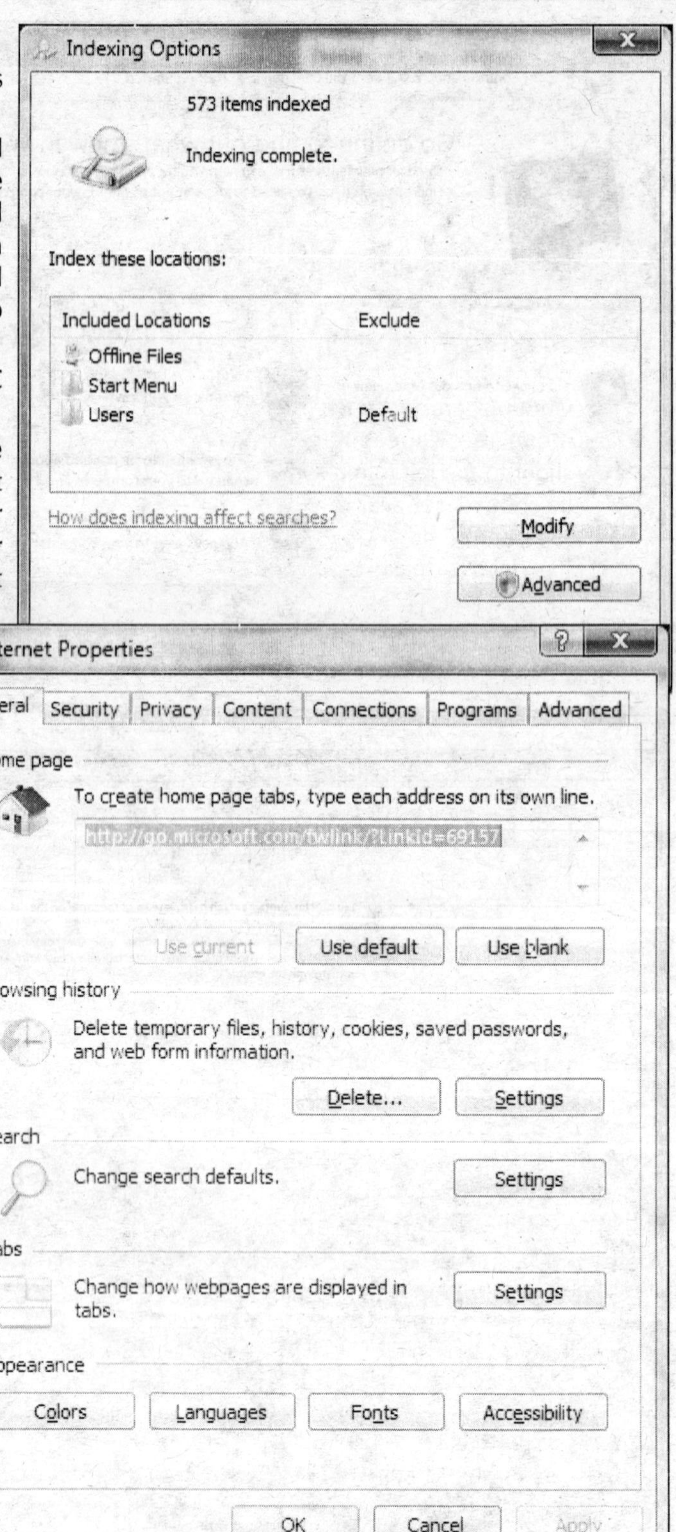

Keyboard

You can customize how long you must press a key before the keyboard character starts repeating, the speed at which keyboard characters repeat, and the rate at which the cursor blinks.

To change the delay before keyboard characters repeat

1. Click to open Keyboard Properties.
2. Under Character repeat, move the Repeat delay slider to the left to increase the amount of time you

must hold down a key before the keyboard character repeats. Move the slider to the right to decrease the amount of time before characters repeat.

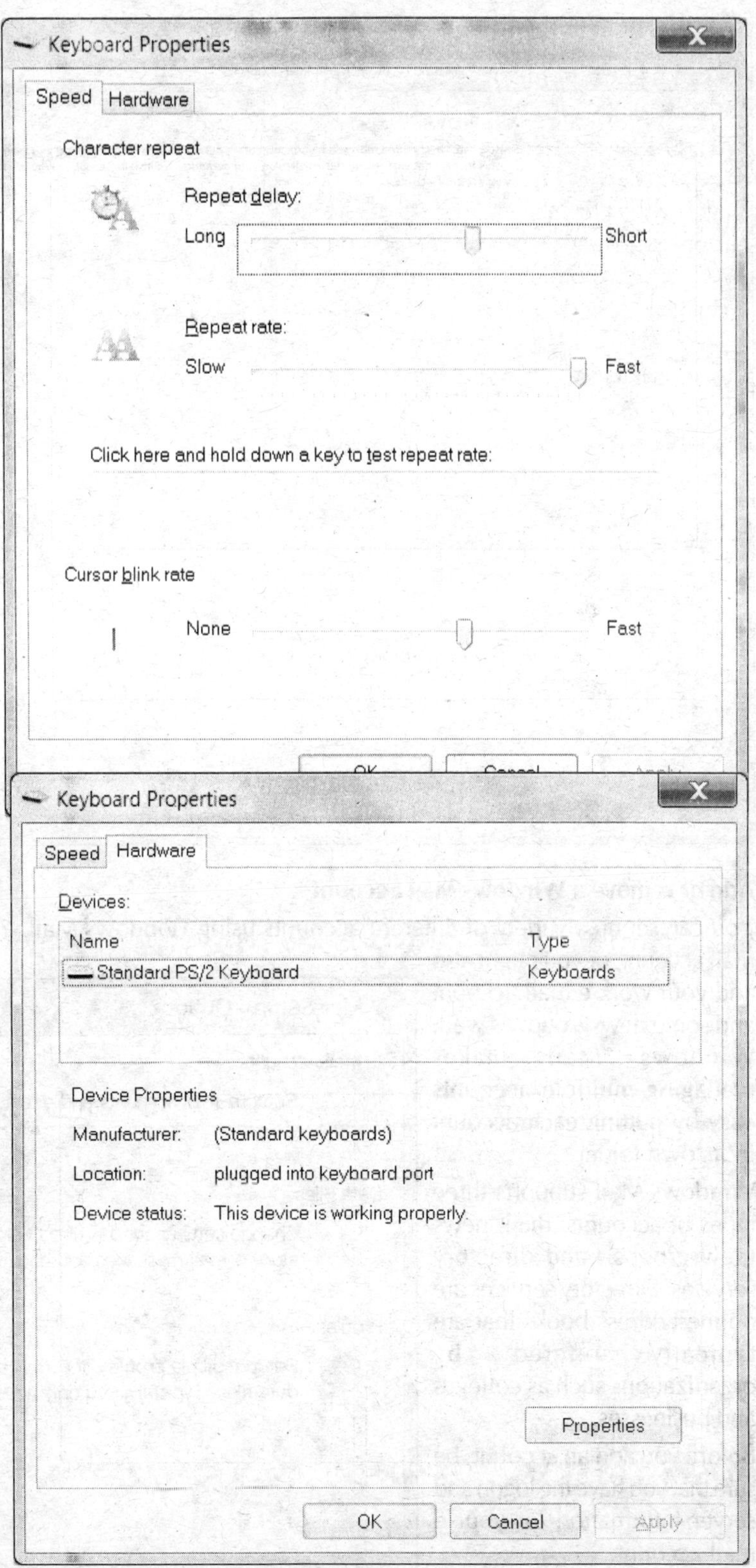

To change the speed at which keyboard characters repeat

1. Click to open Keyboard Properties.
2. Under Character repeat, move the Repeat rate slider to the left to make keyboard characters repeat more slowly, or to the right to make them repeat faster.

To change the cursor blink rate

1. Click to open Keyboard Properties.
2. Move the Cursor blink rate slider to the right to increase the cursor blink speed. If you move the slider all the way to the left, the cursor will stop blinking.

Location and Other Sensors

Sensors can detect information about your computer's current location, surroundings, and more. Once a sensor is enabled, all programs and users can access it. Sensors that are not enabled are still installed on your computer To install a sensor, see the information that came with your device or go to the device manufacturer's website.

Mail

Windows Mail has the tools you need to exchange e mail with colleagues and friends, or join newsgroups to trade ideas and information.

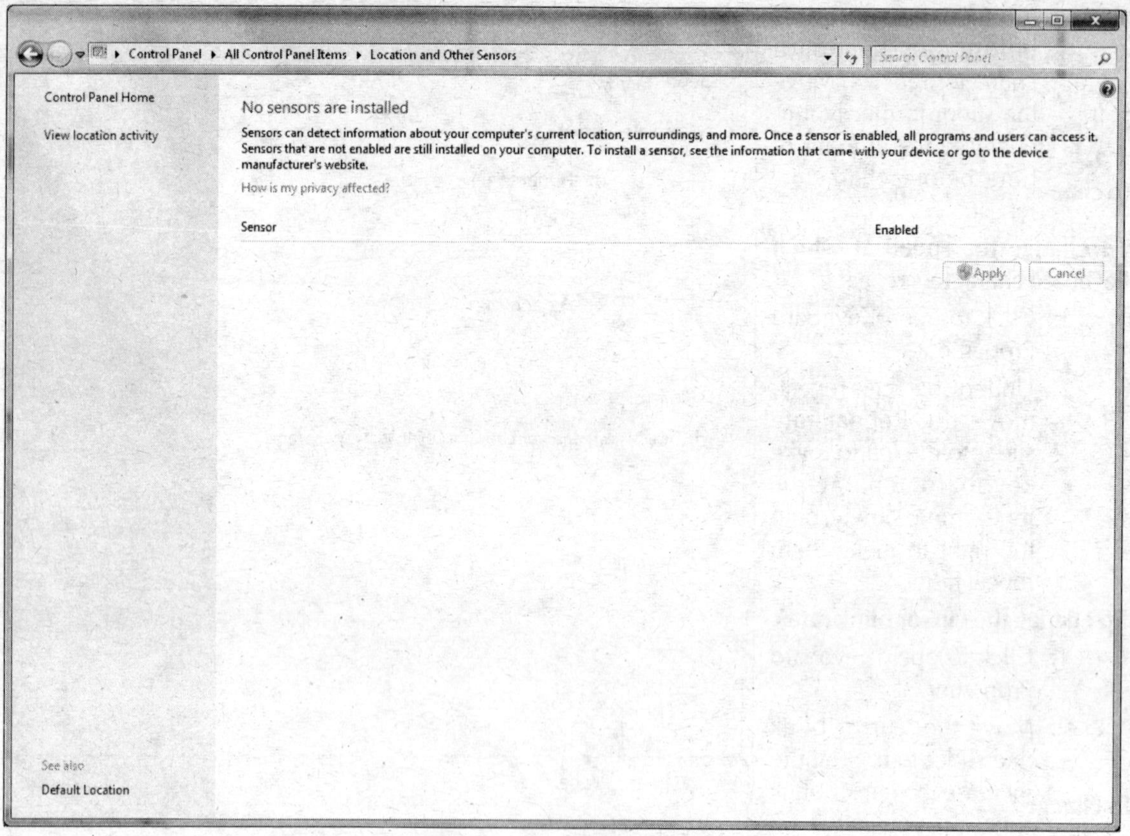

Control Panel ▸ All Control Panel Items ▸ Location and Other Sensors
Search Control Panel
Control Panel Home
View location activity
No sensors are installed
Sensors can detect information about your computer's current location, surroundings, and more. Once a sensor is enabled, all programs and users can access it. Sensors that are not enabled are still installed on your computer. To install a sensor, see the information that came with your device or go to the device manufacturer's website.
How is my privacy affected?
Sensor
Enabled
Apply
Cancel
See also
Default Location

Add or remove a Windows Mail account

You can set up a variety of different accounts using Windows Mail. You can set up a single personal e mail account, or you might also add your work e mail account and some newsgroups as well. Windows Mail makes managing multiple accounts easy by putting each account in its own folder.

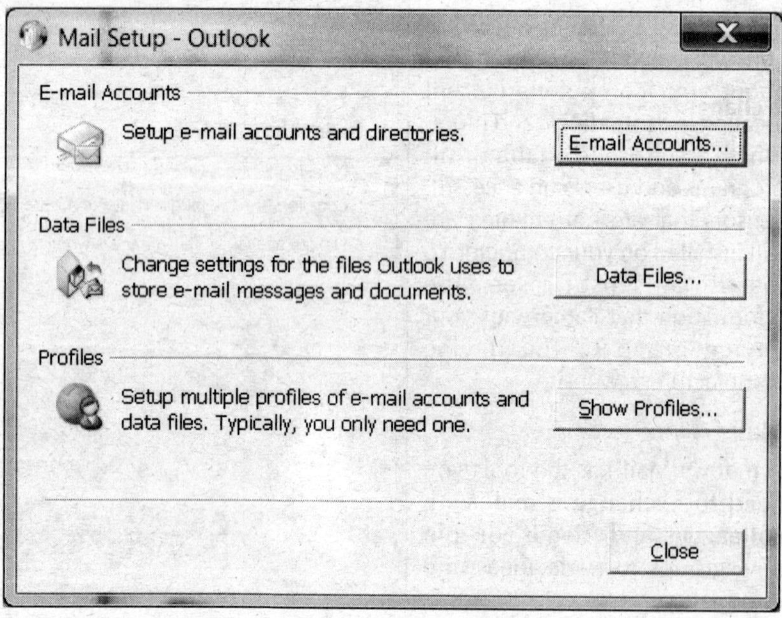

Windows Mail supports three types of accounts: mail, news (newsgroups), and directory services. Directory services are online address books that are typically offered by organizations such as colleges and businesses.

Before you add an account, be sure that you have the logon and server information for your e mail account.

Mail Setup - Outlook
E-mail Accounts
Setup e-mail accounts and directories.
E-mail Accounts...
Data Files
Change settings for the files Outlook uses to store e-mail messages and documents.
Data Files...
Profiles
Setup multiple profiles of e-mail accounts and data files. Typically, you only need one.
Show Profiles...
Close

Mouse

You can customize your mouse in a variety of ways, such as swapping the functions of your mouse buttons, making the mouse pointer more visible, and altering the scroll wheel speed.

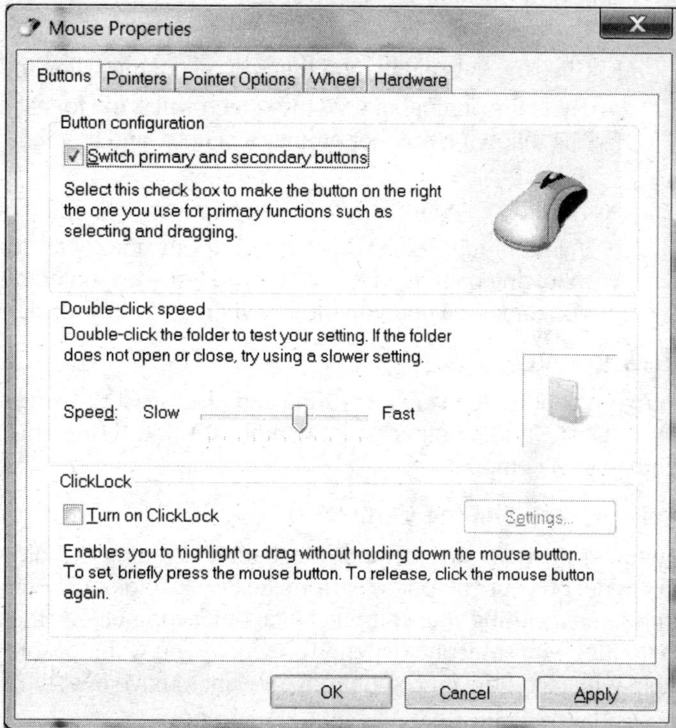

To change how the mouse buttons work

1. Click to open Mouse Properties.
2. Click the Buttons tab, and then do any of the following:
   - To swap the functions of the right and left mouse buttons, select the Switch primary and secondary buttons check box.
   - To change how quickly you must click the buttons to perform a double-click, move the Double-click speed slider towards Slow or Fast.
   - To turn on ClickLock, which enables you to highlight or drag without holding down the mouse button, select the Turn on ClickLock check box.

To change how the mouse pointer looks

1. Click to open Mouse Properties.
2. Click the Pointers tab, and then do one of the following:
   - To give all of your pointers a new look, click the Scheme list, and then click a new mouse pointer scheme.
   - To change an individual pointer, click the pointer you want to change in the Customize list, click Browse, click the pointer you want to use, and then click Open.

To change how the mouse pointer works

1. Click to open Mouse Properties.
2. Click the Pointer Options tab, and then do any of the following:
   - To change the speed at which the mouse pointer moves, move the Select a pointer speed slider towards Slow or Fast.
   - To make the pointer work more accurately when you're moving the mouse slowly, select the Enhance pointer precision check box.
   - To speed the process of selecting a choice when a dialog box appears, select the Automatically move pointer to the default button in a dialog box check box .
   - To make the pointer easier to find when you move it, select the Display pointer trails check box, and then move the slider towards Short or Long to decrease or increase the length of the pointer trail.
   - To ensure that the pointer doesn't block your view of the text you're typing, select the Hide pointer while typing check box.

- To find a misplaced pointer by pressing the CTRL key, select the Show location of pointer when I press the CTRL key check box.

To change how the mouse wheel works

1. Click to open Mouse Properties.
2. Click the Wheel tab, and then do one of the following:

- To set the number of lines the screen will scroll for each notch of mouse wheel movement, click The following number of lines at a time, and then enter the number of lines you want to scroll in the box.
- To scroll an entire screen of text for each click of the mouse wheel, click One screen at a time.
- If your mouse has a wheel that supports horizontal scrolling, in the Tilt the wheel to scroll the following number of characters at a time box, enter the number of characters you want to scroll horizontally when you tilt the wheel to the left or right.

Nero BurnRights

Nero is a popular software for writing and reading CDs. Using it you can Burn CDs with data and create DVDs/Data CDs and other type of audio CDs too. Using this option you can set the options of using Nero in your computer.

Network and Sharing Centre

Windows provides two methods for sharing files directly from your computer. You can share files from any folder on your computer, or from the Public folder. Either method allows you to share files or folders with someone using your computer or another computer on the same network. Which method you use to share files with someone depends on where you want to store the shared files, who you want to share them with, and how much control you want to have over the files.

Share files from any folder on your computer

Follow these steps to share files from their current location without copying them to another location. Using this method, you can choose with whom you want to share files, regardless of whether they use this computer or another computer on the network.

1. Locate the folder with the files you want to share.
2. Click one or more files or folders that you want to share, and then, on the toolbar, click Share.
3. In the File Sharing dialog box, do one of the following:

- Type the name of the person you want to share files with, and then click Add.
- Click the arrow to the right of the text box, click the person's name in the list, and then click Add.
- If you don't see the name of the person you want to share files with in the list, click the arrow to the right of the text box, and then click Create a new user to create a new user account so that you can share files with the person using this account.

4. The name of the person or group that you selected appears in the list of people you want to share files with.
5. Under Permission Level, click the arrow next to the permission level for that person or group, and then do one of the following to set sharing permissions:

- Click Reader to restrict the person or group to viewing files in the shared folder.
- Click Contributor to allow the person or group to view all files, add files, and change or delete the files that they add.
- Click Co-owner to allow the person or group to view, change, add, and delete files in the shared folder.

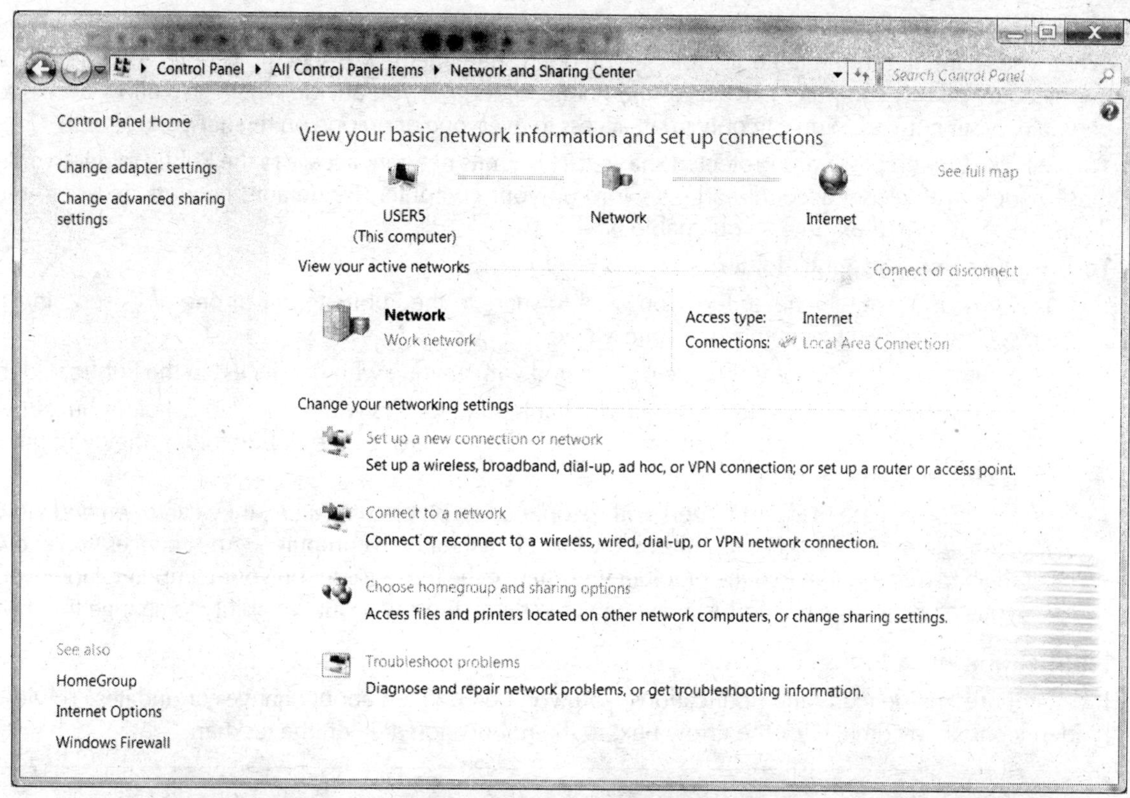

- If you are sharing a file instead of a folder, there is no option to set the permission level to Contributor.

6. When you are finished choosing the people or groups you want to share files with, click Share. If you are prompted for an administrator password or confirmation, type the password or provide confirmation.
7. After you receive confirmation that your folder is shared, you should send a link to your shared files to the people you are sharing them with, so they know the files are shared and how to access them. Do one of the following:

- Click E mail Link to automatically open a Windows Mail e mail message with the link to your shared files.
- Manually copy and paste the link displayed on this screen into an e mail message. Right-click the link and click Copy Link. Then open a new e mail message and paste in the link. You might want to do this if you don't use Windows Mail as your e mail program.

8. If you don't want to send an e mail message to the person you are sharing files with, click Done. They won't be able to find the shared files, however, until you give them the network location of the files.

- You can give a shared folder a share name that makes it easier for someone else to find it on your computer. You can do this by using the Advanced Sharing dialog box for the folder. To access this dialog box, right-click a folder you have already shared, click Properties, click the Sharing tab, and then click Advanced Sharing. If you are prompted for an administrator password or confirmation, type the password or provide confirmation.

Share files from the Public folder

When you share files from the Public folder, you don't share them with specific people. Anyone with a user account on this computer can access the Public folder, but you decide whether to allow access to people on your network. You can only grant access to everyone or no one on the network.

You can also turn on password-protected sharing. This limits network access to the Public folder to only those people with a user account and password on your computer. By default, network access to the Public folder is turned off unless you enable it.

To share files from the public folder:

1. Copy or move whichever files you want to share to the Public folder or one of its subfolders, such as Public Documents or Public Music.
2. Your files in the Public folder are now shared with anyone who has access to the Public folder.

- You can't restrict access to some individual files and folders within the Public Folder but allow access to other files and folders there. If users have access to the Public folder, they will have access to everything in it.
- When you share files and folders with people using other computers, they can open and view those files and folders just as if they were stored on their own computers. Any changes you allow them to make to a shared file or folder will change the file or folder on your computer. However, you can restrict people to just viewing your shared files, without the ability to change them.

Notification Area Icons

If you choose to hide icons and notifications, you won't be notified about changes or updates. To view hidden icons at any time, click the arrow next to the notification area on the taskbar.

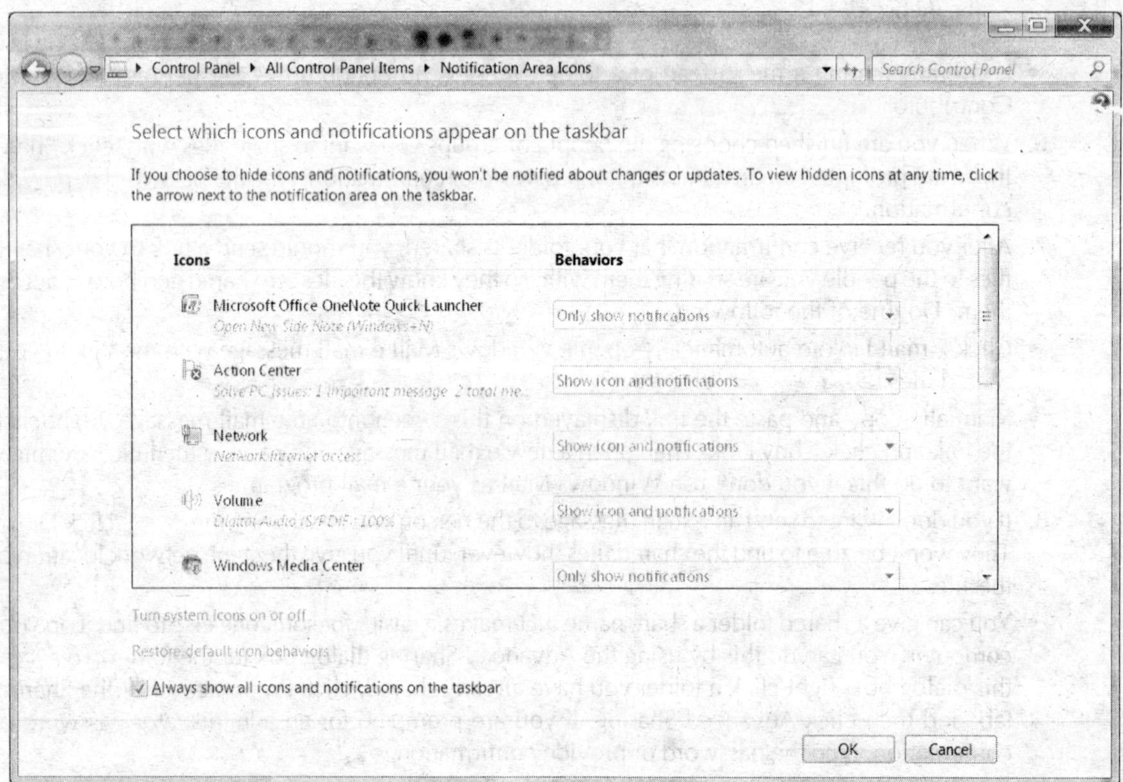

Parental Controls

You can use Parental Controls to help manage how your children use the computer. For example, you can set limits on your children's access to the web, the hours that they can log on to the computer, and which games they can play and programs they can run.

When Parental Controls blocks access to a webpage or game, a notification is displayed that the webpage or program has been blocked. Your child can click a link in the notification to request permission for access to that webpage or program. You can allow access by entering your account information.

Before you get started, make sure that each child that you want to set up Parental Controls for has a standard user account because Parental Controls can only be applied to standard user accounts. To set up Parental Controls for your child, you'll need an Administrator user account. Parental Controls cannot be applied to an Administrator user account.

To turn on Parental Controls for a standard user account

1. Click to open Parental Controls. If you are prompted for an administrator password or confirmation, type the password or provide confirmation.
2. Click the standard user account for which you want to set Parental Controls.
3. Under Parental Controls, click On.
4. Once you've turned on Parental Controls for your child's standard user account, you can adjust the individual settings that you want to control. You can control the following areas:

- Web restrictions. You can restrict the websites that children can visit, make sure children only visit age-appropriate websites, indicate whether you want to allow file downloads, and set up which content you want the content filters to block and allow. You can also block or allow specific websites.

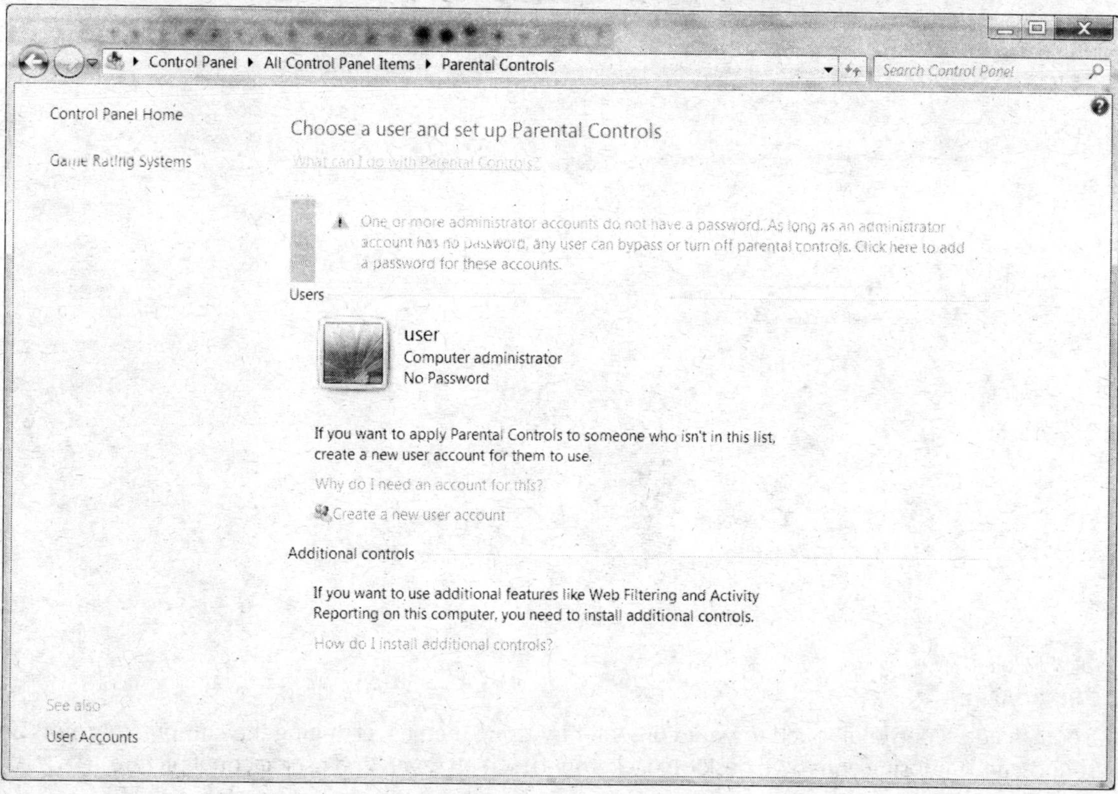

- Time limits. You can set time limits to control when children are allowed to log on to the computer. Time limits prevent children from logging on during the specified hours and, if they are already logged on, they will be automatically logged off. You can set different logon hours for every day of the week.
- Games. You can control access to games, choose an age rating level, choose the types of content you want to block, and decide whether you want to allow or block unrated or specific games.
- Allow or block specific programs. You can prevent children from running programs that you don't want them to run.

Performance Information

Performance Information and Tools lists your computer's Windows Experience [illegible]x base score, which indicates the performance and overall capability of your computer's hardware.

Click to open Performance Information and Tools.

The base score can help you buy programs that match your computer's performance level. The base score only pertains to the performance aspects of the computer that affect how well features in Windows and other programs will run on this computer, and does not reflect the overall quality of your computer.

Individual hardware components, such as your computer's central processing unit (CPU) and random access memory (RAM), are tested and receive a subscore. Your computer's base score is determined by the lowest subscore. For example, if the lowest subscore of an individual hardware component is 2.6, then the base score is 2.6. The base score is not an average of the various subscores.

If you install new hardware and want to see if your score has changed, click Update my score. To view additional details about your computer's hardware, click View and print details.

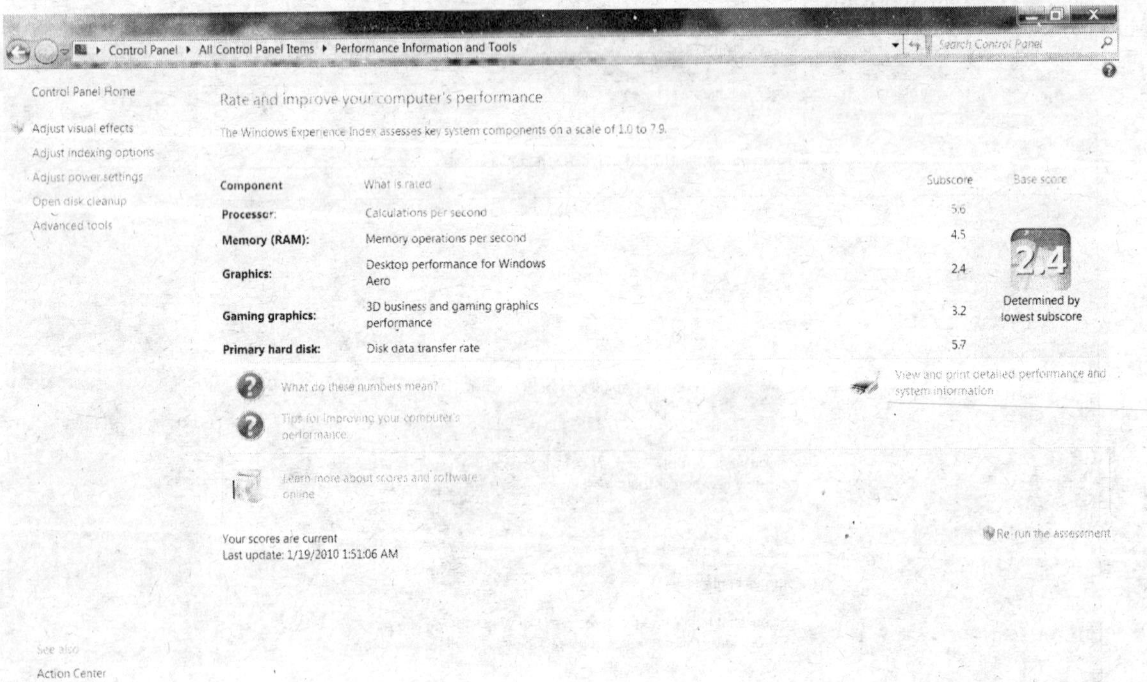

Personalize

You can add a personal touch to your computer by using themes, changing the computer's colors and sounds, and choosing your own desktop background, screen saver, and user account picture.

Themes

A theme is a collection of visual elements that can affect the style of windows, icons, fonts, colors, and sometime sounds. For example, a nature-based theme might include a desktop background with plants, a pointer that looks like a leaf, and system sounds that mimic bird chirps.

Color

Windows Aero is the premium visual experience of this version of Windows. It features a transparent glass design with subtle window animations and new window colors. Click the Start button, click Control Panel, click Appearance and Personalization, click Personalization, and then click Window Color and Appearance.

- If you see the Appearance Settings dialog box instead of the Window Color and Appearance window, the theme might not be set to Windows Vista, the color scheme might not be set to Windows Aero, or the computer might not meet the minimum hardware requirements for running Windows Aero.

Sound

You can change the sound your computer makes when you receive e mail, start Windows, or shut down your computer.

Desktop background

The desktop background, also called wallpaper, is a picture or design on the desktop. It provides a backdrop to your open windows.

Screen saver

A screen saver is a picture or animation that appears on the screen when you haven't used the mouse or keyboard for a set period of time. Windows includes a variety of screen savers to choose from. You can create a personalized screen saver by displaying selected pictures and videos as a slide show.

To use pictures as a slide show

1. Click to open Screen Saver Settings.
2. Click the Screen saver list, and then click Photos.
3. If you want to specify a location for the pictures you want to use in your screen saver, modify the slide show speed, or configure any other screen saver settings, click Settings. After you make your changes, click Save.
4. Click OK.

User account picture

A user account picture helps identify your account on a computer. The picture is displayed on the Welcome screen and on the Start menu. You can change your user account picture to one of the pictures included with Windows, or you can use your own picture.

Windows Sidebar

Windows Sidebar provides a way to organize the information, games, and tasks that you want to access quickly without cluttering your workspace. It's made up of gadgets, which are customizable mini-programs that can display continuously updated headlines, a picture slide show, contacts, and more, without having to open a new window.

Phone and Modem Options

The following are descriptions of the settings on the Dialing Rules, Modems, and Advanced tabs in Phone and Modem Options.

Click to open Phone and Modem Options.

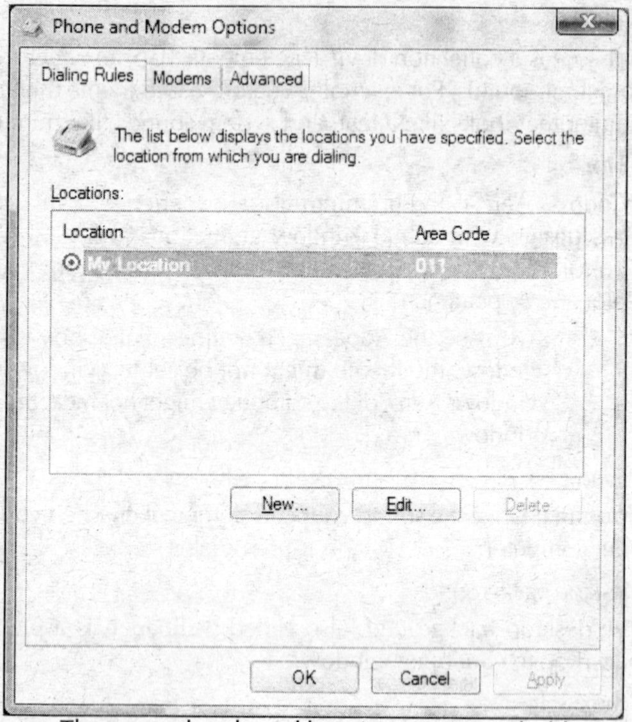

If you haven't opened Phone and Modem Options before, a dialog box will be displayed, prompting you to type your area code and other access codes.

Dialing Rules tab

The Dialing Rules tab lists all currently defined dialing locations (sets of rules applied to outgoing phone calls from your computer's modem). Use this tab to add, delete, or configure dialing locations. When you specify the destination phone number, the rules associated with the dialing location determine whether the area code must be included, whether a calling card should be used, and so on.

The following table describes the options on the Dialing Rules tab.

Control	***Description***
Locations	Lists all of the currently defined locations on your computer. The currently selected location appears in bold text, and its rules apply to any phone calls made from your computer. Double-clicking a location opens the Edit dialog box, where you can make changes to the rules associated with that location.
New	Allows you to create a new location and specify the rules associated with that location.
Edit	Allows you to edit the rules for the currently selected location.
Delete	Removes the currently selected location and all rules associated with it. It does not remove any existing calling card definitions.

Modems tab

The Modems tab lists all modems currently installed on your computer. Use this tab to add, remove, and configure modems.

The following table describes the options on the Modems tab.

Control	***Description***
The following modems are installed	Lists the modems currently installed on your computer, and the communications port your computer uses to communicate with each modem.
Add	Allows you to install a new modem on your computer. If the drivers for your new modem are not already installed on your computer, you will be asked to install the drivers provided by the modem manufacturer.
Remove	Uninstalls the currently selected modem from your computer. You should unplug or remove the modem from your computer after uninstalling it, or it could be detected and reinstalled the next time you start your computer.
Properties	Allows you to view or change the configuration of the currently selected modem. The options available depend on the make and model of the modem.

Advanced tab

The Advanced tab lists the telephony providers (software used to communicate with telephony hardware, such as modems) currently installed on your computer. Use this tab to add, remove, and configure providers.

The following table describes the options on the Advanced tab.

Control	***Description***
Providers	Lists the telephony providers currently installed on your computer.
Add	Allows you to add a Telephony Application Programming Interface (TAPI) service provider to the list and make it available to telephony programs. To do this, you must have the drivers for the TAPI-supported telephony hardware already installed on your computer.
Remove	Removes the selected TAPI service provider from the list. Removing a TAPI service provider makes it unavailable to telephony programs. It does not delete any files from your computer.
Configure	Allows you to view or change the properties of the selected TAPI service provider. If this is unavailable, there are no configurable properties for the service provider.

Power Options

The Power Options program manages the power consumption of your computer. That's a big deal when you are running off a laptop's battery, of course, but it's also important if you'd like to save money (and the environment) by cutting down on the juice consumed by your desktop PC. In Windows 7, Microsoft has tried to simplify the business of managing the electricity/speed tradeoff in two ways. First, it has abandoned the old name power scheme and adopted a new one: power plan.

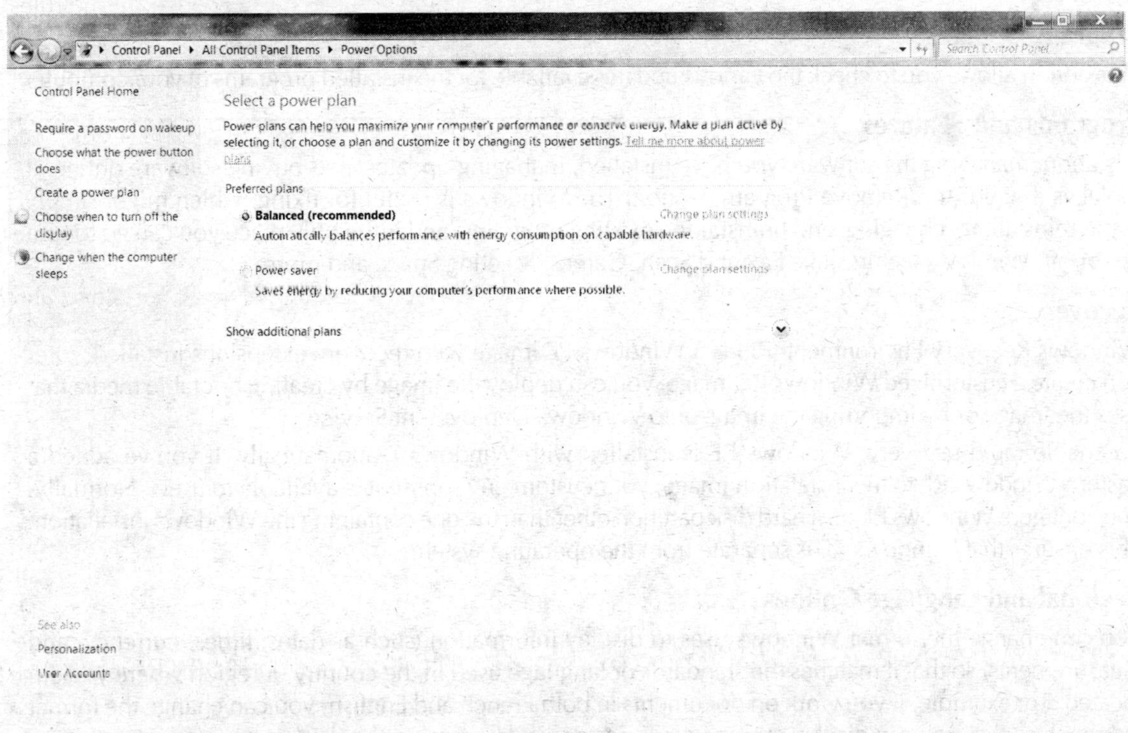

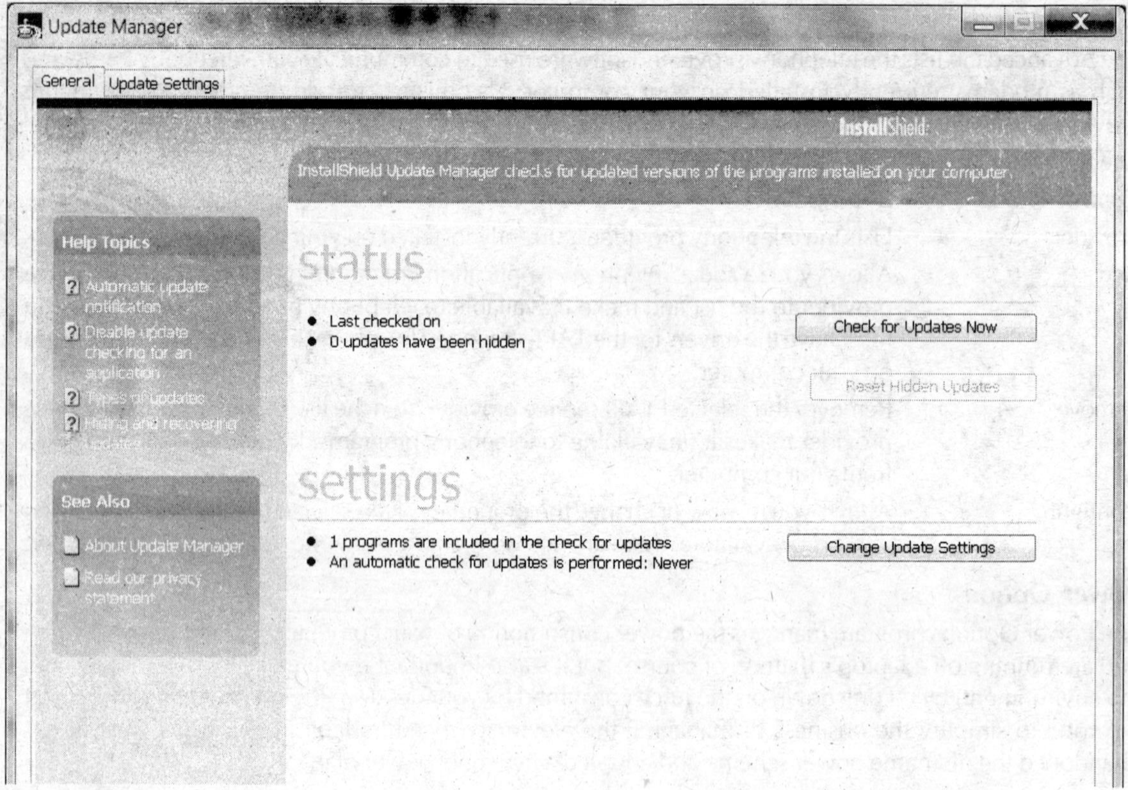

Program Updates

This option allows you to check the various updates available for the installed programs of your computer

Programs and Features

It is about managing the software you have installed, managing updates, and buying software online. It replaces the old Add/Remove Programs option. The Windows is useful for fixing, which might simply mean reinstalling, changing, and uninstalling existing programs, and is the only place you can go to turn on, or off, Windows features like Fax and Scan, Games, Meeting Space and more.

Recovery

Windows Recovery Environment (RE) is a Windows PE image with recovery extensions installed. After you create a customized Windows RE image, you can deploy the image by creating bootable media that uses the image or by importing the image into Windows Deployment Services.

To enable rapid recovery, Windows RE is installed with Windows 7 auomatically. If you've added a custom Windows RE to the instalation image, your custom environment is available to users. Normally, you configure Windows RE on a hard disk partition other than the one containing the Windows installation. This ensures that Windows RE is separate from the operating system.

Regional and Language Options

You can change the format Windows uses to display information (such as dates, times, currency, and measurements) so that it matches the standards or language used in the country or region where you are located. For example, if you work on documents in both French and English, you can change the format to French so that you can display currency in Euros or display dates in the day/month/year format.

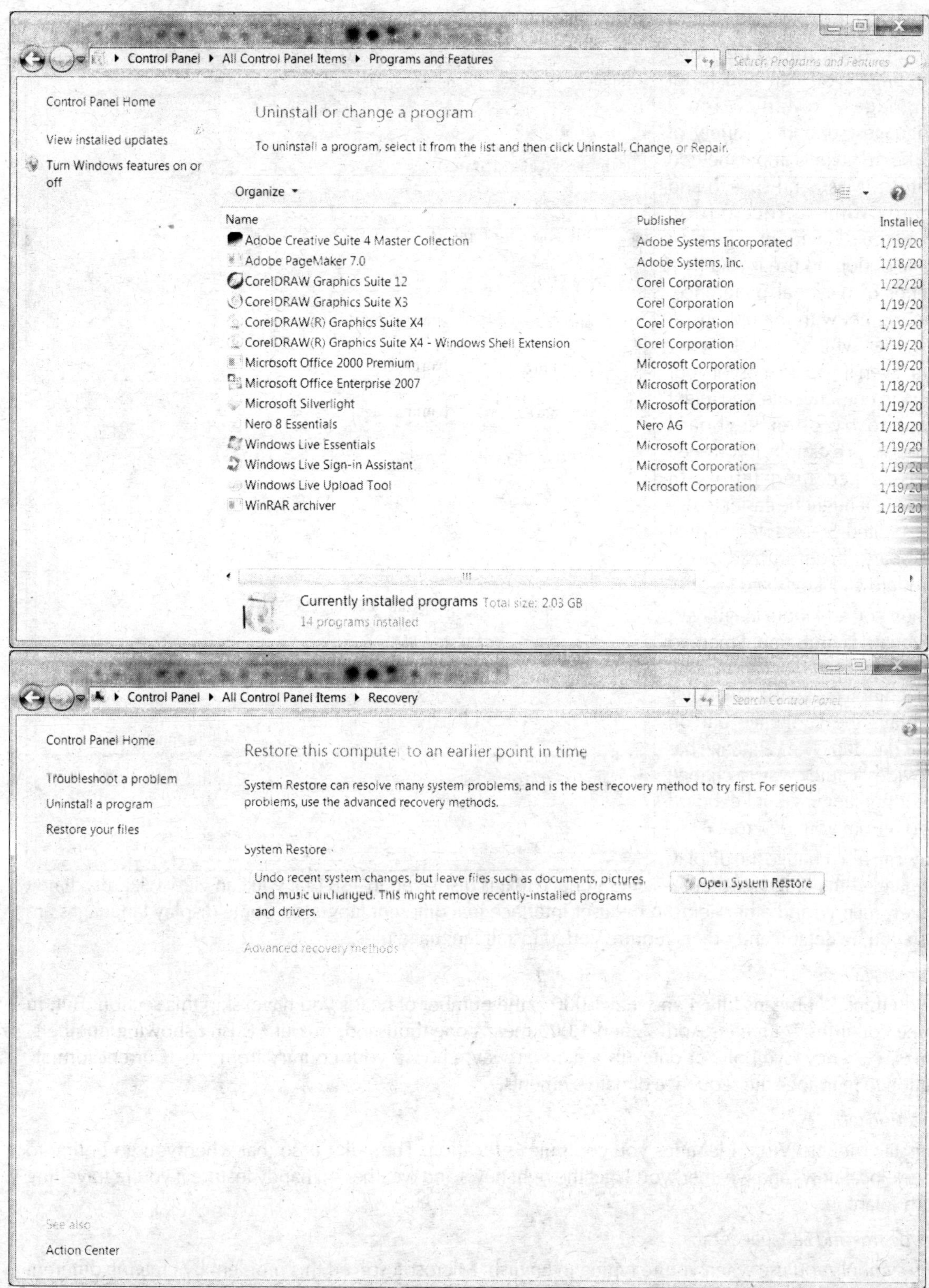
Control Panel ▸ All Control Panel Items ▸ Programs and Features
Search Programs and Features
Control Panel Home
View installed updates
Turn Windows features on or off
Uninstall or change a program
To uninstall a program, select it from the list and then click Uninstall, Change, or Repair.
Organize
Name
Publisher
Installed
Adobe Creative Suite 4 Master Collection
Adobe Systems Incorporated
Adobe PageMaker 7.0
Adobe Systems, Inc.
CorelDRAW Graphics Suite 12
Corel Corporation
CorelDRAW Graphics Suite X3
CorelDRAW(R) Graphics Suite X4
CorelDRAW(R) Graphics Suite X4 - Windows Shell Extension
Microsoft Office 2000 Premium
Microsoft Corporation
Microsoft Office Enterprise 2007
Microsoft Silverlight
Nero 8 Essentials
Nero AG
Windows Live Essentials
Windows Live Sign-in Assistant
Windows Live Upload Tool
WinRAR archiver
Currently installed programs Total size: 2.03 GB
14 programs installed
Control Panel ▸ All Control Panel Items ▸ Recovery
Search Control Panel
Control Panel Home
Troubleshoot a problem
Uninstall a program
Restore your files
Restore this computer to an earlier point in time
System Restore can resolve many system problems, and is the best recovery method to try first. For serious problems, use the advanced recovery methods.
System Restore
Undo recent system changes, but leave files such as documents, pictures, and music unchanged. This might remove recently-installed programs and drivers.
Open System Restore
Advanced recovery methods
See also
Action Center

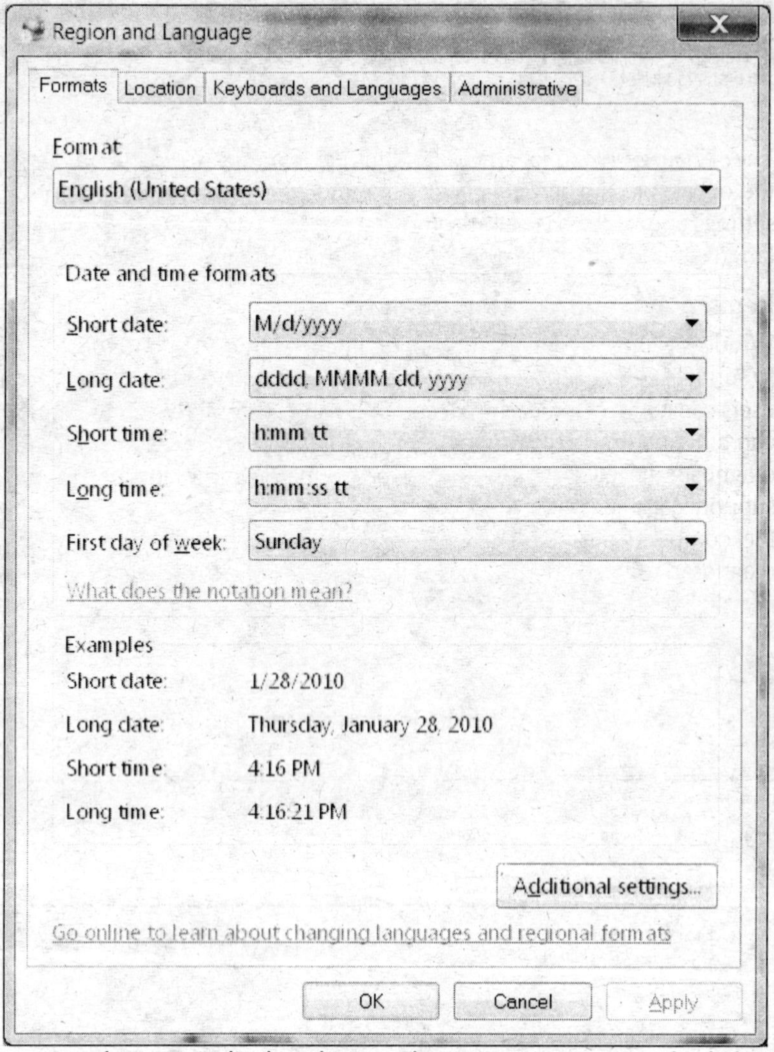

If you need to type and edit documents in more than one language, you can add input languages. Many input languages support a variety of keyboard layouts, input method editors (IMEs), and speech and handwriting recognition programs. Deciding which of these options to use is usually a matter of personal preference. Experiment with the options to discover which work best for you. Even if you do most of your work in one language, you might want to try other keyboard layouts. For example, if you need to type accented letters in English, it might be easier to use the United States-International keyboard layout instead of the standard U.S. keyboard layout.

When you add input languages, keyboard layouts, input method editors, or speech or handwriting recognition programs, Windows displays the Language bar on your desktop. The Language bar provides a quick way to change the input language or keyboard layout from your desktop.

You can also change the display language—the language that the user interface text is displayed in—so that you can view wizards, dialog boxes, menus, and other items in the user interface in a different language. Some display languages are installed by default and others require you to install language files.

Formats tab

If you think 7/4 means July 4 and that 1,000 is the number of heads you have, skip this section. But, in some countries 7/4 means April 7, and 1,000 means one thousand. If your PC isn't showing numbers, times, currency, symbols, or dates in a familiar way, choose your country from the "Current format" button to rearrange the sequence of date elements.

Location tab

This tab, new to Vista, identifies you computer's location. The point is so that when you go online to check local news and weather, you'll get the right news and weather—a handy feature if you're travelling with a laptop.

Keyboards and Languages tabs

The symbols you use when you're typing in English. Microsoft solved this problem by creating different keyboard layouts, one for each language, or more, like Qwerty or Dvorak for English. Each keyboard layout rearranges the letters that appear when you press the keys. For example, in the Swedish layout, pressing the semicolon key produces an Ö—not a simicolon(;).

Administrative tab

The "Change system locale" button this tab lets you specify—which language handles error messages and the occasional dialog box. The "Copy to reserved account" button lets the newly configured language settings apply to new user accounts, so anyone who gets a new account on this computer will have your language, format, and keyboard settings conveniently available to them.

Remote App and Desktop Connections

Windows 7 has several remote connectivity features. With Remote Assistance, users can send invitations to support technicians, enabling the technicians to service a computer remotely. With Remote Desktop, users can connect remotely to a computer and access it resources. Remote Assistance and Remote Desktop can function throught Network Address Translation (NAT) firewalls. Remote Assistance also has built-in diagnostic tools. To allow for easier troubleshooting and escalation of support issues, two different support staff can connect to a remote computer simultaneously. When troubleshooting requires restarting the computer, Remote Assistance sessions are reestablished automatically after the computer being diagnosed reboots.

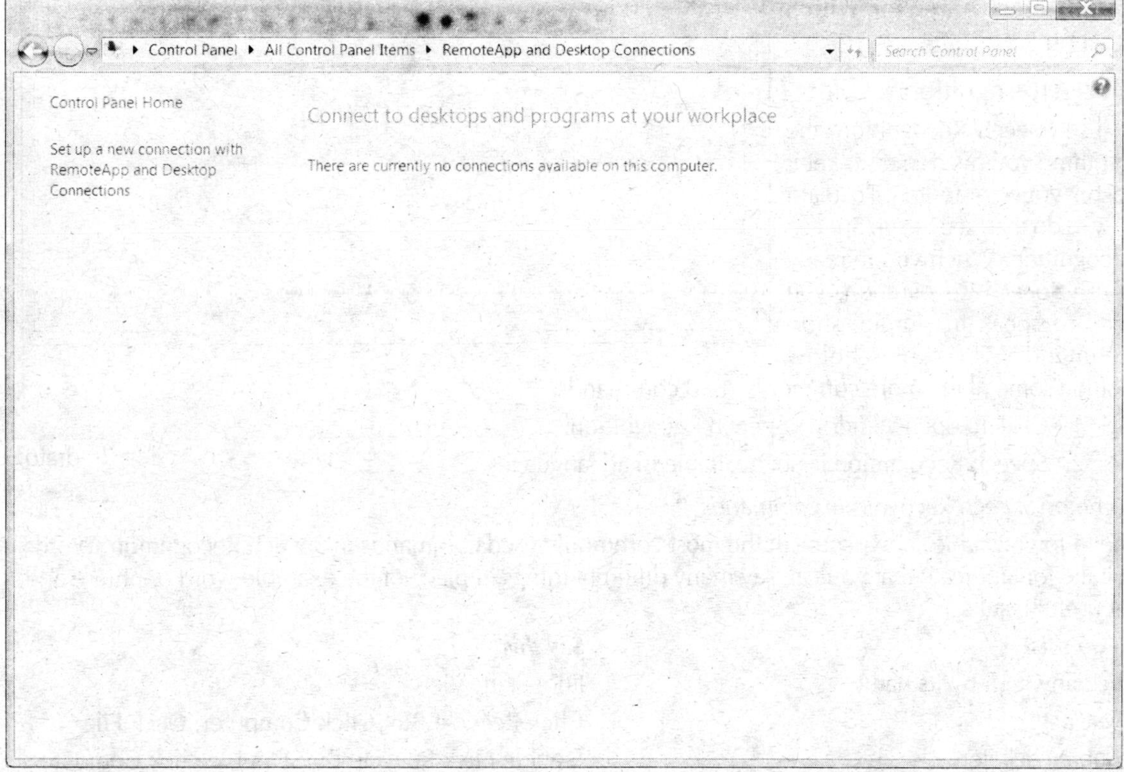

Sound

In Windows, the Sound dialog box has been simplified. It now contains only four tabs that control every aspect of your microphone and speakers: Playback, Recording, Sounds and Communications.

Playback and Recording tabs

These tabs simply contain the icon for each attached sound device. To change a device's settings, select it, and then click Configure.

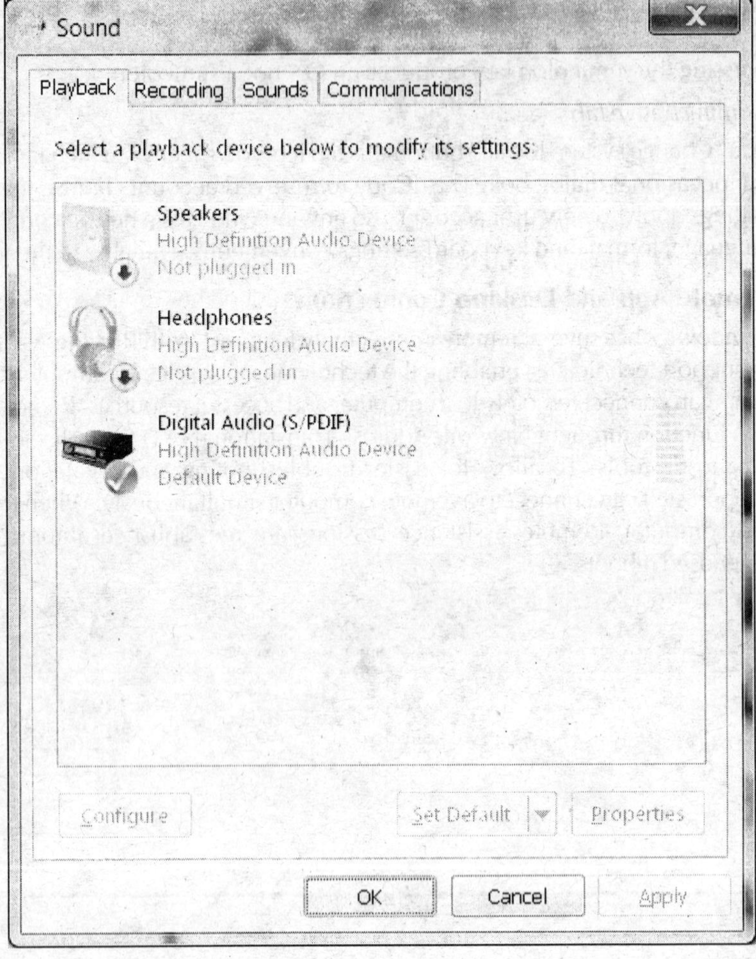

Sounds tab

Windows comes with a new, freshly composed suite of little sound effects—beeps, musical ripples, and chords—that play when you turn on the PC, trigger an error message, empty the Recycle Bin, and so on. And if you like, you can hear them on many other occasions, such as when you open or exit a program, open a menu, restore a window, and so on. The tab lets you specify which sound effect plays for which situation.

Speech Recognition

To use Speech Recognition, the first thing you need to do is set it up on your computer. To learn how to do that, see Set up Speech Recognition. When you're ready to use Speech Recognition, you need to speak in simple, short commands. The tables below include some of the more commonly used commands.

1. Click to open Windows Speech Recognition.
2. Speech Recognition is not available in all languages.

Common Speech Recognition commands

The following table shows some of the most commonly used commands in Speech Recognition. Words in italic font indicate that you can say many different things in place of the example word or phrase and get useful results.

To do this	***Say this***
Click any item by its name	File; Start; View
Click item	Click Recycle Bin; Click Computer; Click File
Double-click item	Double-click Recycle Bin; Double-click Computer; Double-click File
Switch to an open program	Switch to Paint; Switch to WordPad; Switch to program name; Switch application
Scroll direction	Scroll up; Scroll down; Scroll left; Scroll right

Insert a new paragraph or new line in a document	New paragraph; New line
Select a word in a document	Select word
Select a word and start to correct it	Correct word
Select and delete specific words	Delete word
Show a list of applicable commands	What can I say?
Update the list of speech commands that are currently available	Refresh speech commands
Make the computer listen to you	Start listening
Make the computer stop listening	Stop listening
Move the Speech Recognition microphone out of the way	Move speech recognition
Minimize the microphone bar	Minimize speech recognition

Dictation

The following table shows commands for using Speech Recognition to work with text. Words in italic font indicate that you can say many different things in place of the example word or phrase and get useful results.

To do this	***Say this***
Insert a new line in the document	New line
Insert a new paragraph in the document	New paragraph
Insert a tab	Tab
Insert the literal word for the next command; for example, you can insert the word "comma" instead of the punctuation mark	Literal word
Insert the numeral form of a number	Numeral number

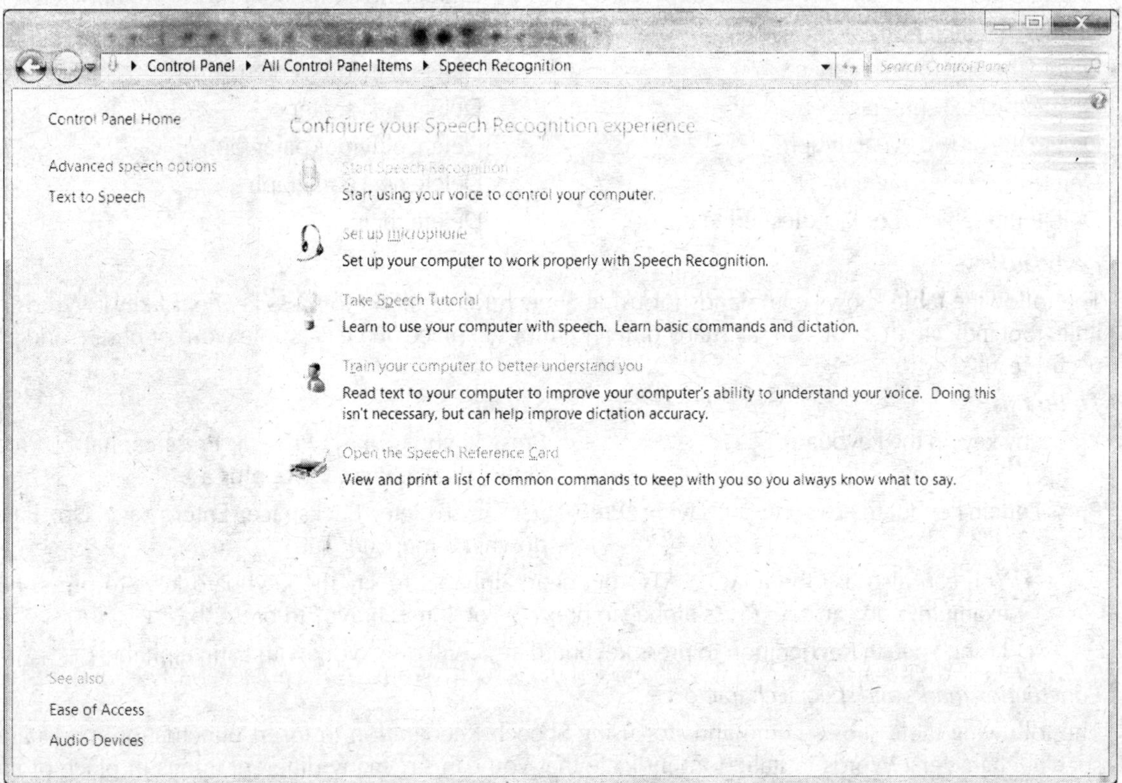

Put the cursor before a specific word	Go to word
Put the cursor after a specific word	Go after word
Do not insert a space before the next word	No space
Go to the start of the sentence that the cursor is in	Go to start of sentence
Go to the start of the paragraph the cursor is in	Go to start of paragraph
Go to the start of the document	Go to start of document
Go to the end of the sentence that the cursor is in	Go to end of sentence
Go to the end of the paragraph the cursor is in	Go to end of paragraph
Go to the end of the current document	Go to end of document
Select the word in the current document	Select word
Select the word range in the current document	Select word range; Select word through word
Select all text in the current document	Select all
Select the 1-20 words before the location of the cursor	Select previous 1-20 words; Select previous 10 words
Select the 1-20 words after the location of the cursor	Select next 1-20 words; Select next 10 words
Select the last text you dictated	Select that
Clear the selection on the screen	Clear selection
Capitalize the first letter of the word	Caps word
Capitalize all the letters of the word	All caps word
Make all the letters in the word lowercase	No caps word
Change the next number of words to uppercase	Change next number of words to uppercase
Change the next number of words to lowercase	Change next number of words to lowercase
Delete the previous sentence	Delete previous sentence
Delete the next sentence	Delete next sentence
Delete the previous paragraph	Delete previous paragraph
Delete the next paragraph	Delete next paragraph
Delete the selected or last dictated text	Delete that

Keyboard keys

The following table shows commands for using Speech Recognition to press keyboard keys. Words in italic font indicate that you can say many different things in place of the example word or phrase and get useful results.

To do this	***Say this***
Press any key on the keyboard	Press keyboard key; Press a; Press capital b; Press SHIFT plus a; Press CTRL plus a
Press certain keyboard keys without saying "Press" first	Delete; Backspace; Enter; Page Up; Page down; Home; End; Tab

- You can also use the ICAO\NATO phonetic alphabet to say the keyboard keys to press. For example, you can say "Press alpha" to press "a" or "Press bravo" to press "b."
- Using Speech Recognition to press keyboard keys will only work with Latin alphabets.

Punctuation marks and special characters

The following table shows commands for using Speech Recognition to insert punctuation marks and special characters. Words in italic font indicate that you can say many different things in place of the example word or phrase and get useful results.

To make this appear	***Say this***	***To make this appear***	***Say this***
,	Comma	;	Semicolon
.	Period; Dot; Full stop; Decimal point	:	Colon
“	Open double quote; Open quote; Open inverted commas		
”	Close double quote; Close quote; Close inverted commas		
‘	apostrophe	‘	Open single quote
’	Close single quote	>	Greater than sign
<	Less than sign	/	Forward slash
\	Backslash	~	Tilde
@	At sign	!	Exclamation mark; Exclamation point
?	Question mark	#	Number sign; Pound sign; Hash sign
$	Dollar sign	%	Percent sign
^	Caret	(	Open parenthesis; Open paren
)	Close parenthesis; Close paren	_	Underscore
-	Hyphen; Minus sign; Dash	–	En dash
—	Em dash; Double dash	=	Equal sign
+	Plus sign	{	Open brace; Open curly bracket
}	Close brace; Close curly bracket	[	Open bracket; Open square bracket
]	Close bracket; Close square bracket	|	Vertical bar
:-)	Press smiley face	:-(	Press frowny face
;-)	Press winky face	™	Trademark sign
¾	Three quarter sign	¼	One quarter sign
½	One half sign	£	Pound sterling sign; pound; pound sign
&	Ampersand; and sign	*	asterisk
//	Double slash	‘	Back quote
<	Open angle bracket	>	Close angle bracket
±	Plus or minus sign	«	Open angle quote
»	Close angle quote	×	Multiplication sign
÷	Division sign	¢	Cent sign
¥	Yen sign	§	Section sign
©	Copyright sign	®	Registered, Registered trademark sign
°	Degree sign	¶	Paragraph sign
...	Ellipsis; Dot dot dot	*f*	Function sign

Controls

The following table shows commands for using Speech Recognition to perform tasks in Windows. Words in italic font indicate that you can say many different things in place of the example word or phrase and get useful results.

To do this	***Say this***
Click any item by saying its name	File; Edit; View; Save; bold
Click any item	Click File; Click bold; Click Save; Click Close
Double-click any item	Double-click Computer; Double-click Recycle Bin; Double-click Folder name

Right-click any item	Right-click Computer; Right-click Recycle Bin; Right-click Folder name
Minimize all windows to show your desktop	Show Desktop
Click something you don't know the name of	Show numbers (Numbers will appear on the screen for every item in the active window)
Click a numbered item	19 OK; 5 OK
Double-click a numbered item	Double-click 19; Double-click 5
Right-click a numbered item	Right-click 19; Right-click 5

Windows

The following table shows commands for using Speech Recognition to work with windows and programs. Words in italic font indicate that you can say many different things in place of the example word or phrase and get useful results.

To do this	***Say this***
Open a program	Open Paint; Open WordPad; Open program name
Switch to an open program	Switch to Paint; Switch to WordPad; Switch to program name; Switch application
Close a program	Close that; Close Paint; Close Documents; Close Internet Explorer (only works with the active window)
Restore	Restore that; Restore Paint; Restore Internet Explorer (only works with the active window)
Minimize	Minimize that; Minimize Paint; Minimize Internet Explorer (only works with the active window)
Maximize	Maximize that; Maximize Paint; Maximize Internet Explorer (only works with the active window)
Cut	Cut that; Cut
Copy	Copy that; Copy
Paste	Paste
Delete	Delete that; Delete
Undo	Undo that; Scratch that; Undo
Scroll direction	Scroll up; Scroll down; Scroll right; Scroll left
Scroll an exact distance in pages	Scroll down 2 pages; Scroll up 10 pages
Scroll an exact distance in other units	Scroll up 5; Scroll down 7
Go to a field in a form or a program	Go to field name; Go to Subject; Go to Address; Go to Cc

Click anywhere on the screen

The following table shows commands for using Speech Recognition to click anywhere on the screen. Words in italic font indicate that you can say many different things in place of the example word or phrase and get useful results.

To do this	***Say this***
Show the mousegrid	Mousegrid
Move the mouse pointer to the center of any mousegrid square	number—or numbers—of the square; 1; 7; 9; 1, 7, 9
Click any mousegrid square	Click number of the square

Select an item to drag with the mousegrid	number—or numbers—of the square where the item appears; 3, 7, 9 (followed by) mark
Select an area where you want to drag the item with the mousegrid	number—or numbers—of the square where you want to drag; 4, 5, 6 (followed by) click

Sync Center

Sync is short for synchrônization. In Windows, sync is the process of keeping two or more versions of the same file stored in different locations matched with each other. If you add, change, or delete a file in one location, Windows can add, change, or delete the same file in the other locations that you choose to sync with, whenever you choose to sync.

Sync Center is a feature of Windows that allows you to keep information in sync between your computer and Mobile devices that you plug in to your computer or to which you connect wirelessly (such as portable music players, digital cameras, and mobile phones).

- Files stored in folders on network servers. (These are called offline files because you can access them even when your computer or the server is not connected to the network.)
- Programs that support Sync Center.

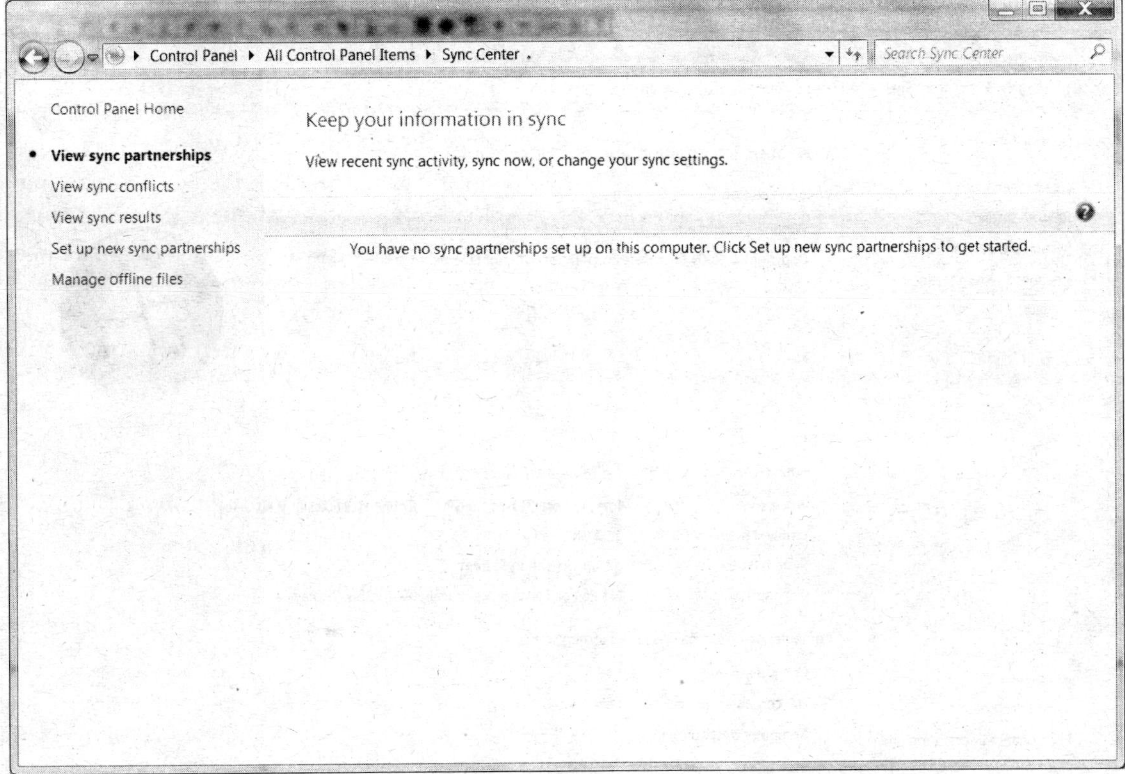

System

The system dialog box has the following information.

What edition of Windows 7 is installed on your computer?

As you know, Windows 7 comes in several editions. Not all editions are made equal; if you're failing to find some feature that you could have sworn is supposed to be in Windows 7, it's good to check here. You might find out that the feature you want is available only on higher-priced versions.

PC's performance in terms of Rating

Ratings are displayed in the Rating column in your library. By default, most items in your library are automatically given an auto rating. The auto rating is controlled by non-Microsoft data providers, such as AMG and some online stores. You can override an auto rating by explicitly choosing a new user rating. You can distinguish between the two types of ratings by the appearance of the stars, which are blue for auto ratings and bright yellow for user ratings.

The model name and speed of your PC's processor chip

Such as Intel Core Duo CPU E7400 @2.80 GHz.

How much memory your PC has?

That's a very helpful number to know, particularly if you need to improve your computer's speed.

Your computer's name, domain or workgroup

Remember, your computer name and description are primarily useful on a network, since that's how other people will identify your computer. Unless you tell it otherwise, Vista names your computer after you login name, somtheing like SUN-PC.

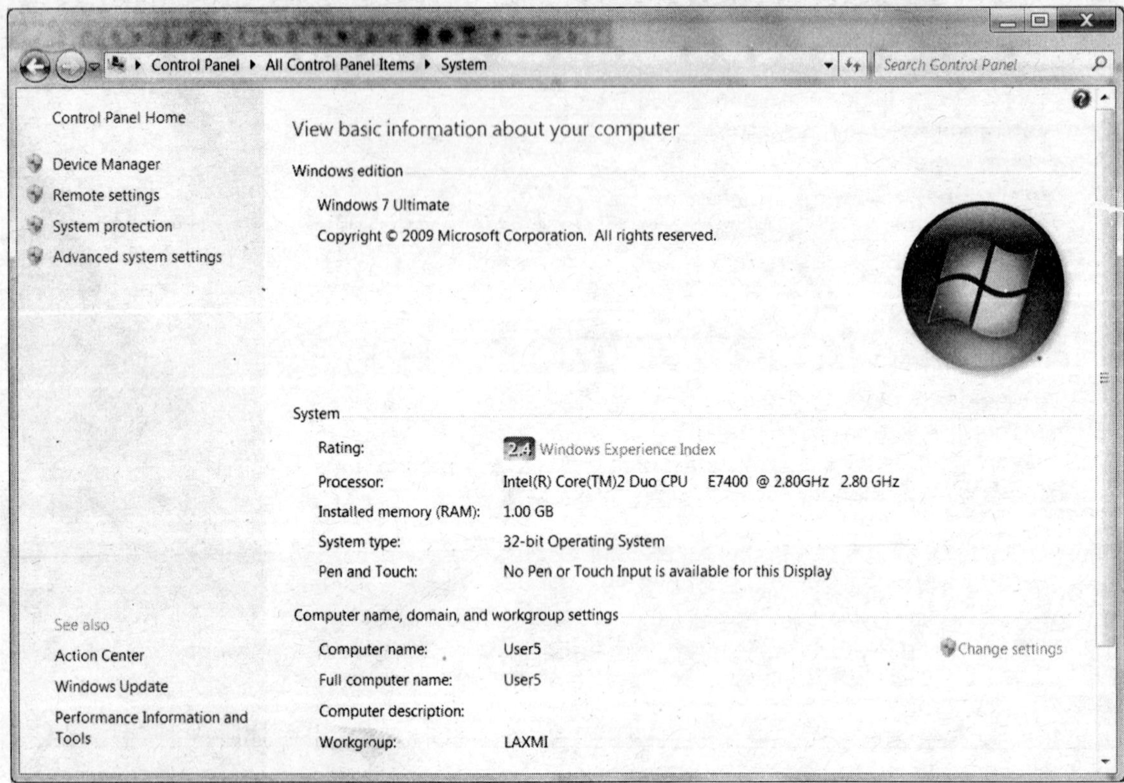

Taskbar and Start Menu

The Start menu is the main gateway to your computer's programs, folders, and settings. It's called a menu because it provides a list of choices, just as a restaurant menu does. And as "Start" implies, it's often the place that you'll go to start or open things.

Use the Start menu to do these common activities:

- Start programs
- Open commonly used folders
- Search for files, folders, and programs
- Adjust computer settings
- Get help with the Windows operating system
- Turn off the computer
- Log off from Windows or switch to a different user account

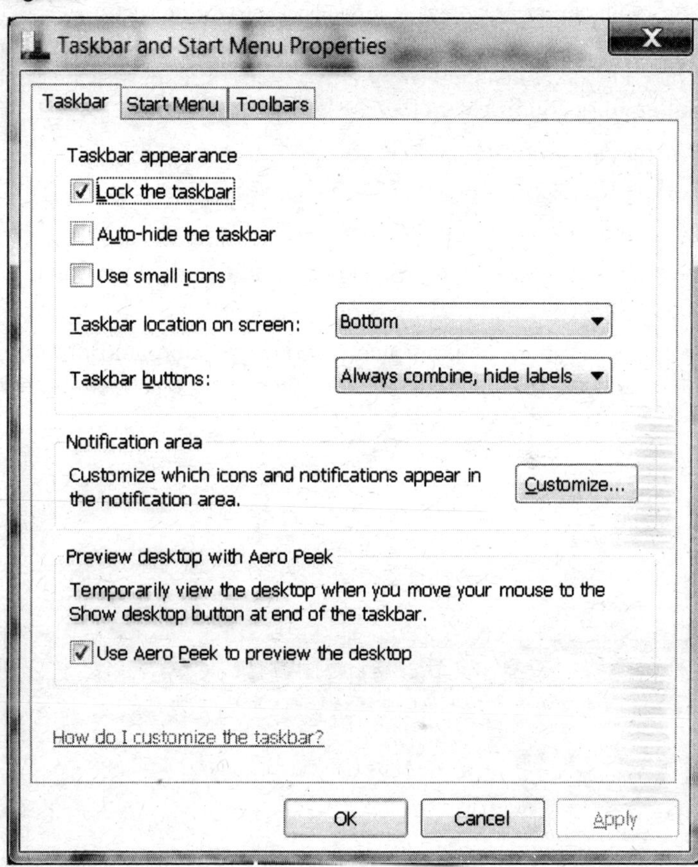

The taskbar is the long horizontal bar at the bottom of your screen. Unlike the desktop, which can get obscured by the windows on top of it, the taskbar is visible almost all the time. It has four main sections:

- The Start button, which opens the Start menu.
- The Quick Launch toolbar, which lets you start programs with one click.
- The middle section, which shows you which programs and documents you have open and allows you to quickly switch between them.
- The notification area, which includes a clock and icons (small pictures) that communicate the status of certain programs and computer settings.

Troubleshooting

It allows you to check your computer for minor problems before you call the engineer, for repairs. You can click on a task to automatically troubleshoot and fix common computer problems. To view more troubleshooters, click on a category or usee the Search box. Various category are: Programs, Hardware and Sound, Network and Internet, Appearance and Personalization, and System and Security.

User Accounts

User Account Control (UAC) is a new set of infrastructure technologies in this version of Windows that helps prevent malicious programs, sometimes called "malware," from damaging a system, while also helping organizations to deploy a better-managed desktop.

With UAC, applications and tasks always run in the security context of a non-administrator account, unless an administrator specifically authorizes administrator-level access to the system. UAC stops the automatic installation of unauthorized applications, and prevents inadvertent changes to system settings.

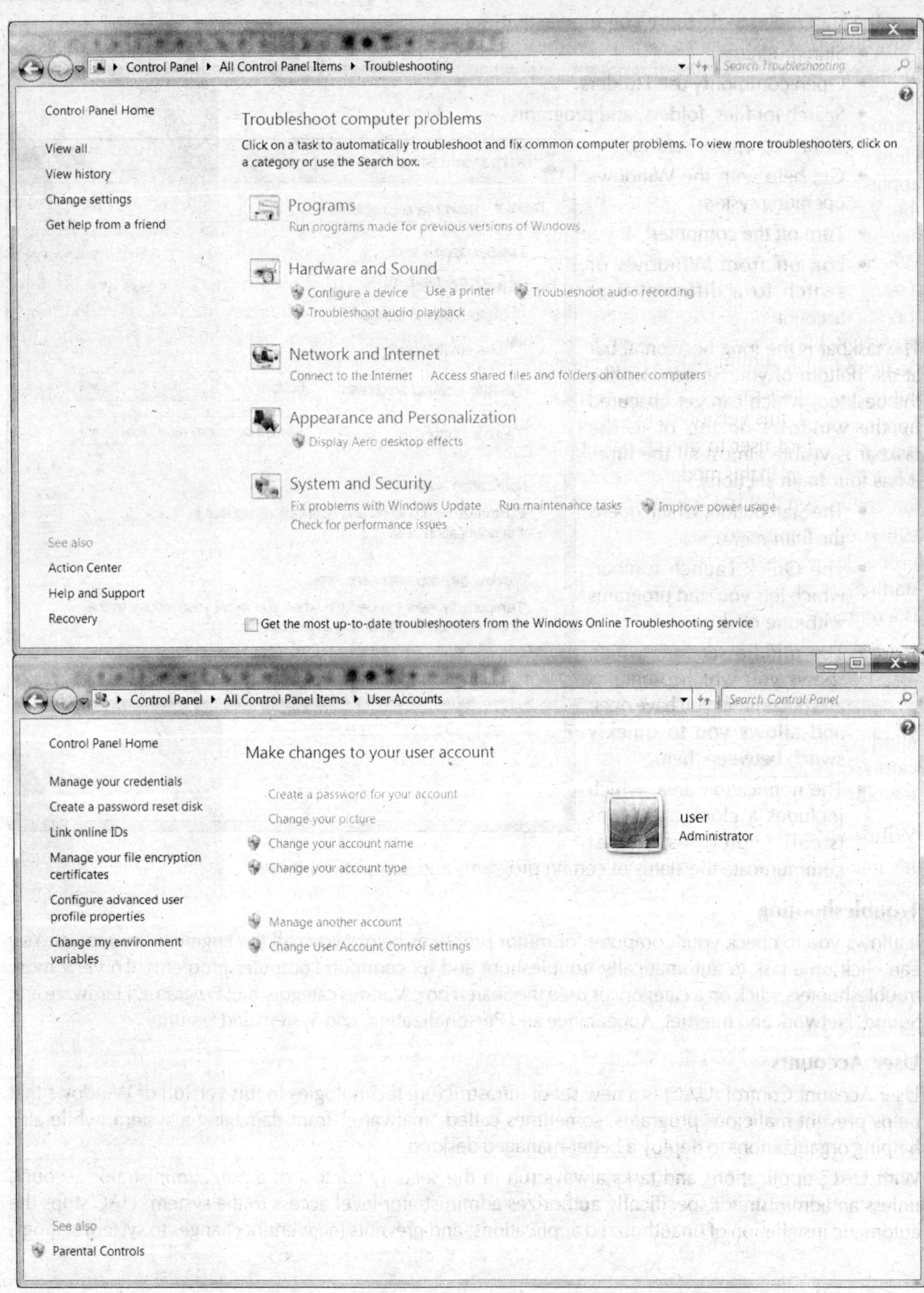

Control Panel ▸ All Control Panel Items ▸ Troubleshooting
Search Troubleshooting
Control Panel Home
View all
View history
Change settings
Get help from a friend
Troubleshoot computer problems
Click on a task to automatically troubleshoot and fix common computer problems. To view more troubleshooters, click on a category or use the Search box.
Programs
Run programs made for previous versions of Windows
Hardware and Sound
Configure a device
Use a printer
Troubleshoot audio recording
Troubleshoot audio playback
Network and Internet
Connect to the Internet
Access shared files and folders on other computers
Appearance and Personalization
Display Aero desktop effects
System and Security
Fix problems with Windows Update
Run maintenance tasks
Improve power usage
Check for performance issues
See also
Action Center
Help and Support
Recovery
Get the most up-to-date troubleshooters from the Windows Online Troubleshooting service
Control Panel ▸ All Control Panel Items ▸ User Accounts
Search Control Panel
Control Panel Home
Manage your credentials
Create a password reset disk
Link online IDs
Manage your file encryption certificates
Configure advanced user profile properties
Change my environment variables
Make changes to your user account
Create a password for your account
Change your picture
Change your account name
Change your account type
Manage another account
Change User Account Control settings
user
Administrator
See also
Parental Controls

How does UAC work?

In this version of Windows, there are two levels of users: standard users and administrators. Standard users are members of the Users group and administrators are members of the Administrators group on the computer.

Unlike previous versions of Windows, both standard users and administrators access resources and run applications in the security context of standard users by default. When any user logs on to a computer, the system creates an access token for the user. This access token contains information about the level of access that the user is granted, including specific security identifiers (SIDs) and Windows privileges. When an administrator logs on, this version of Windows creates two separate access tokens for the user: a standard user access token and an administrator access token. The standard user access token contains the same user-specific information as the administrator access token, but the administrative Windows privileges and SIDs have been removed. The standard user access token is used to start applications that do not perform administrative tasks ("standard user applications").

When the administrator needs to run applications that perform administrative tasks ("administrator applications"), this version of Windows prompts the users to change or "elevate" their security context from a standard user to an administrator. This default administrator user experience is called Admin Approval Mode. In this mode, applications require specific permission to run as an administrator application (an application that has the same access as an administrator).

When an administrator application is starting, by default a User Account Control message appears. If the user is an administrator, the message gives a choice to allow the application to start or to prevent it from starting. If the user is a standard user, the user can enter the user name and password of an account that is a member of the local Administrators group.

Windows CardSpace

Ever have to fill out a form on the Internet—name, address, email address—only to go to a differnt site that requests exactly the same information. CardSpace is Microsoft's attempt to solve that duplication-of-effort problem. You are supposed to create a profile containing this kind of information, like a digital ID card. You show your card at a site, and the site gest your information off the card, saving you all that retyping.

Windows Defender

It's important to run antispyware software whenever you're using your computer. Spyware and other potentially unwanted software can try to install itself on your computer any time you connect to the Internet. It can also infect your computer when you install some programs using a CD, DVD, or other removable media. Potentially unwanted or malicious software can also be programmed to run at unexpected times, not just when it is installed.

Windows Defender offers three ways to help keep spyware and other potentially unwanted software from infecting your computer:

- **Real-time protection.Windows** Defender alerts you when spyware or potentially unwanted software attempts to install itself or to run on your computer. It also alerts you when programs attempt to change important Windows settings.
- **SpyNet community**. The online Microsoft SpyNet community helps you see how other people respond to software that has not yet been classified for risks. Seeing if other members of the community allow software can help you choose whether to allow it on your computer. In turn, if you participate, your choices are added to the community ratings to help other people choose what to do.
- **Scanning options**. You can use Windows Defender to scan for spyware and other potentially

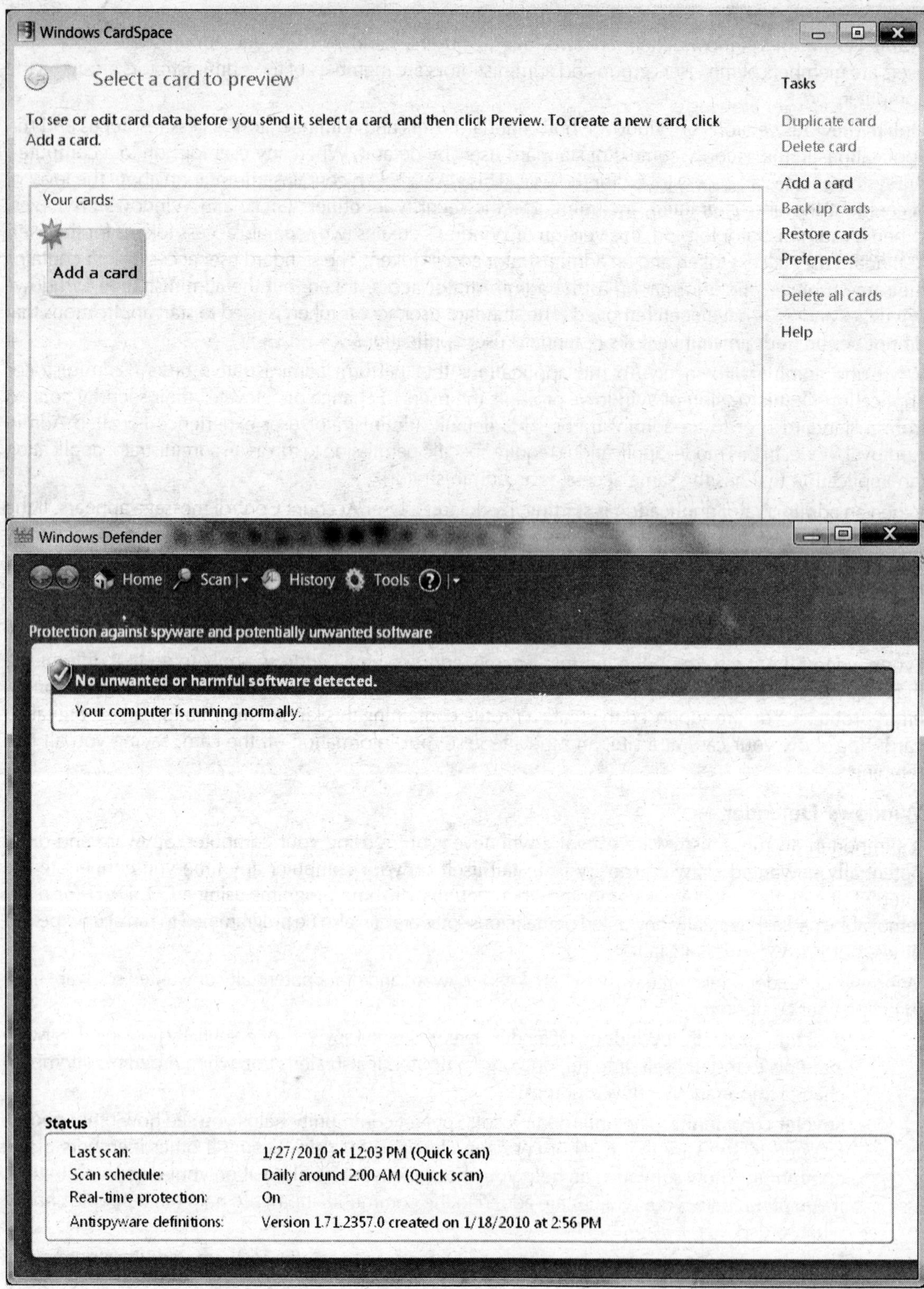
Windows CardSpace
Select a card to preview
To see or edit card data before you send it, select a card, and then click Preview. To create a new card, click Add a card.
Your cards:
Add a card
Tasks
Duplicate card
Delete card
Add a card
Back up cards
Restore cards
Preferences
Delete all cards
Help
Windows Defender
Home
Scan
History
Tools
Protection against spyware and potentially unwanted software
No unwanted or harmful software detected.
Your computer is running normally.
Status
Last scan: 1/27/2010 at 12:03 PM (Quick scan)
Scan schedule: Daily around 2:00 AM (Quick scan)
Real-time protection: On
Antispyware definitions: Version 1.71.2357.0 created on 1/18/2010 at 2:56 PM

unwanted software that might be installed on your computer, to schedule scans on a regular basis, and to automatically remove any malicious software that is detected during a scan.

When you use Windows Defender, it's important to have up-to-date definitions. Definitions are files that act like an ever-growing encyclopedia of potential software threats. Windows Defender uses definitions to determine if software that it detects is spyware or other potentially unwanted software, and then to alert you to potential risks. To help keep your definitions up to date, Windows Defender works with Windows Update to automatically install new definitions as they are released. You can also set Windows Defender to check online for updated definitions before scanning.

Windows Firewall

A firewall is software or hardware that checks information coming from the Internet or a network, and then either blocks it or allows it to pass through to your computer, depending on your firewall settings.

A firewall can help prevent hackers or malicious software (such as worms) from gaining access to your computer through a network or the Internet. A firewall can also help stop your computer from sending malicious software to other computers.

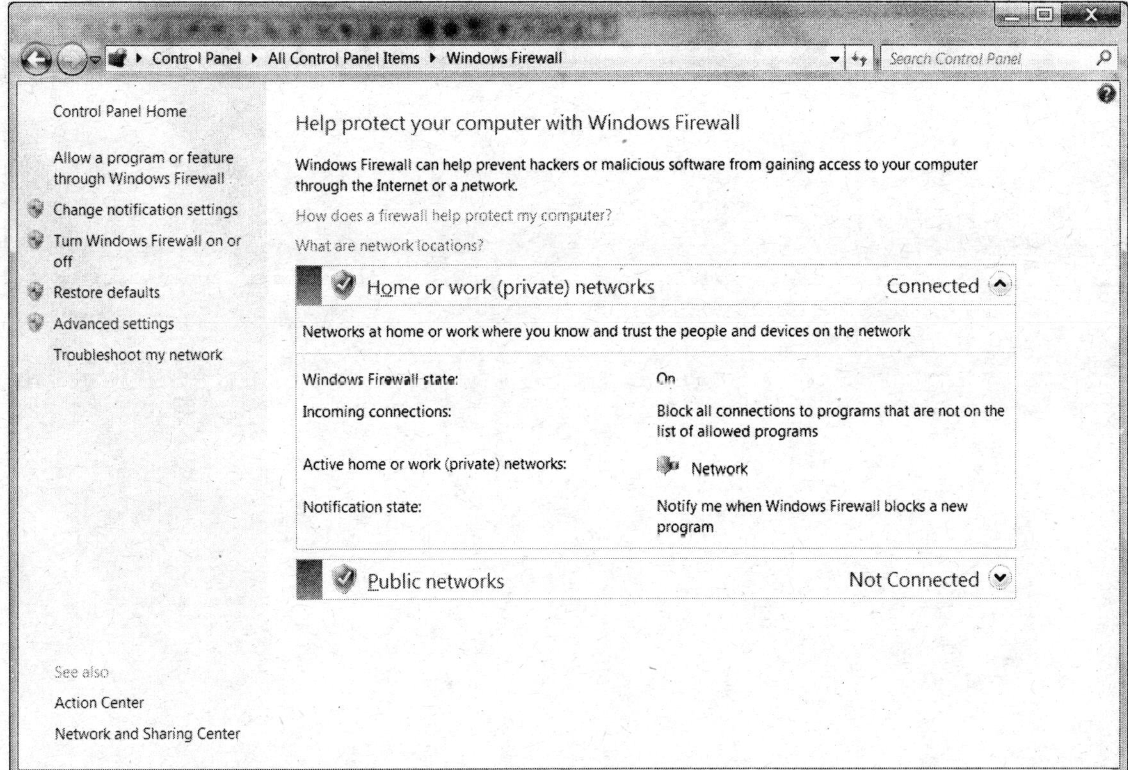

Windows Update

Because Windows is a constant work in progress, Microsoft frequently releases updates, fixes, patches, and drivers, in hope of constantly improving your computer's speed and security all the time.

CHAPTER 1

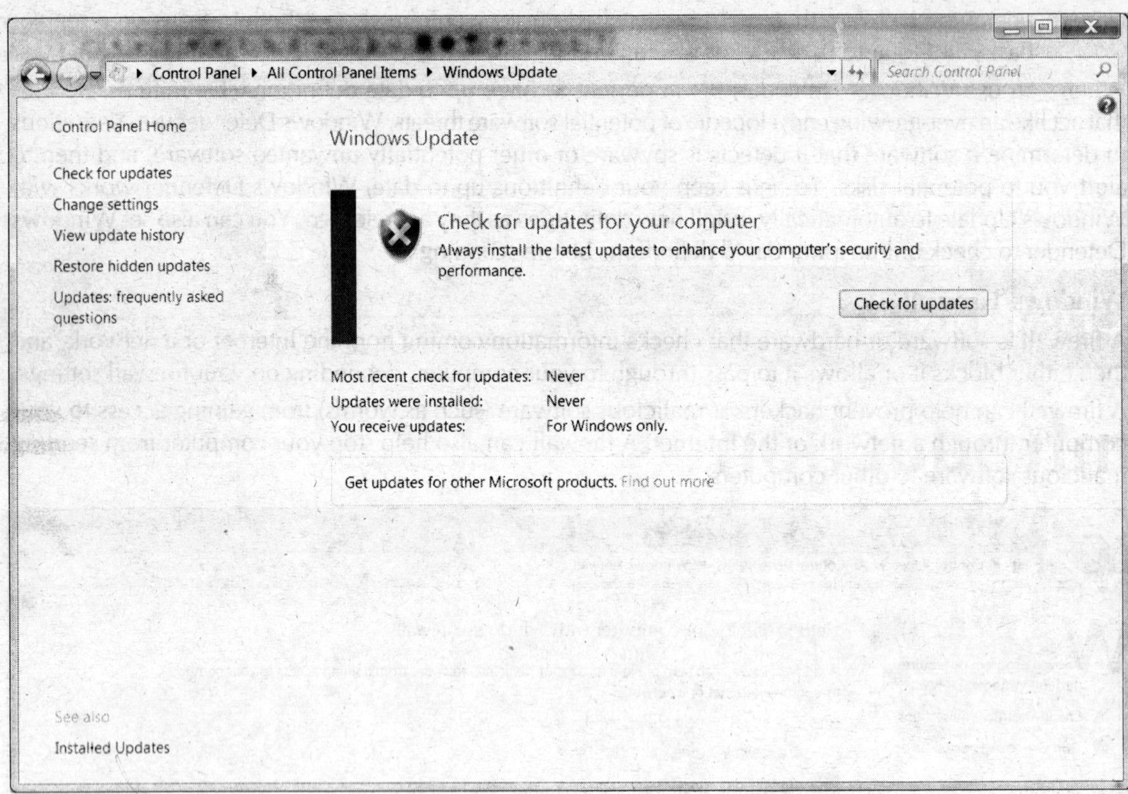
Control Panel ▸ All Control Panel Items ▸ Windows Update
Search Control Panel
Control Panel Home
Check for updates
Change settings
View update history
Restore hidden updates
Updates: frequently asked questions
Windows Update
Check for updates for your computer
Always install the latest updates to enhance your computer's security and performance.
Check for updates
Most recent check for updates: Never
Updates were installed: Never
You receive updates: For Windows only.
Get updates for other Microsoft products. Find out more
See also
Installed Updates

CHAPTER 2

Introduction to Microsoft Word 2010

Introduction

Microsoft Word 2010 is a word processing software which allows you to write letters, edit them and print them after formatting it according to your needs. It has all the possible options of a word processor in the form of font style and size; indents; line spacing; margins; spell checking and grammar checkers to name a few.

What's New in Microsoft Office Word 2010

Microsoft Office Word 2010 helps you produce professional-looking documents by providing a comprehensive set of tools for creating and formatting your document in a new interface. Rich review, commenting, and comparison capabilities help you quickly gather and manage feedback from colleagues. Advanced data integration ensures that documents stay connected to important sources of business information.

Introducing the new interface

There is a new look for Office Word 2010, the new Office Fluent user interface, which replaces menus, toolbars, and most of the task panes from earlier versions of Word with a single mechanism that is simple and discoverable. The new Fluent user interface is designed to help you be more productive in Word, more easily find the right features for various tasks, discover new functionality, and be more efficient.

This article is designed for experienced Word 2003 users — Help desk personnel, IT professionals, and others who are already familiar with the Word 2003 interface — who want to find familiar commands quickly in Office Word 2010.

Office Fluent user interface

The primary replacement for menus and toolbars in Office Word 2010 is the Ribbon, a component of the Office Fluent user interface. Designed for easy browsing, the Ribbon consists of tabs that are organized around specific scenarios or objects. The controls on each tab are further organized into several groups. The Office Fluent Ribbon can host richer content than menus and toolbars can, including buttons, galleries, and dialog box content.

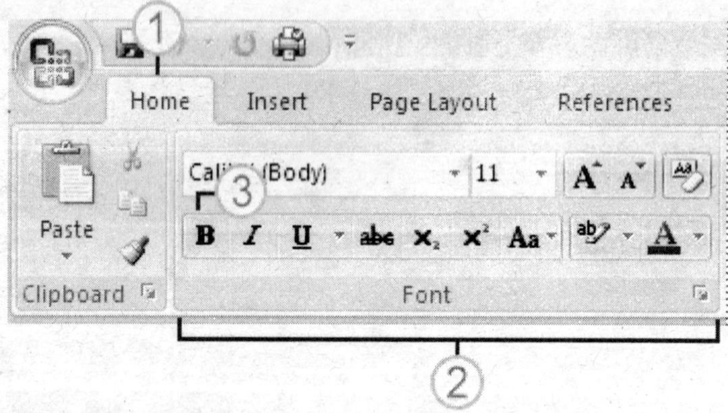

1. Tabs are designed to be task-oriented.
2. Groups within each tab break a task into subtasks.
3. Command buttons in each group carry out a command or display a menu of commands.

Tabs that appear only when you need them

In addition to the standard set of tabs that you see on the Ribbon whenever you start Office Word 2010, there are two other kinds of tabs, which appear in the interface only when they are useful for the type of task that you are currently performing.

Contextual tools Contextual tools enable you to work with an object that you select on the page, such as a table, picture, or drawing. When you click the object, the pertinent set of contextual tabs appear in an accent color next to the standard tabs.

1. Select an item in your document.

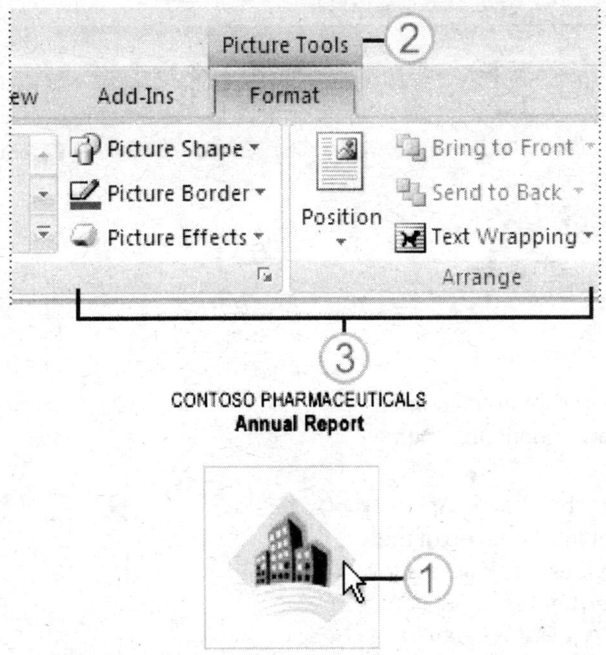

2. The name of the contextual tools appears in an accent color, and the contextual tabs appear next to the standard set of tabs.
3. The contextual tabs provide controls for working with the selected item.

Program tabs Program tabs replace the standard set of tabs when you switch to certain authoring modes or views, including Print Preview.

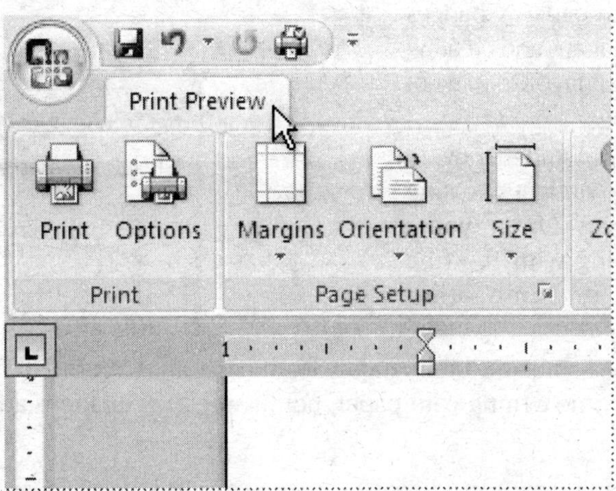

Menus, toolbars and other familiar elements

In addition to tabs, groups, and commands, Office Word 2010 uses other elements that also provide paths for accomplishing your tasks. The following elements are more like the menus and toolbars that you are already familiar with from earlier versions of Word.

CHAPTER 2

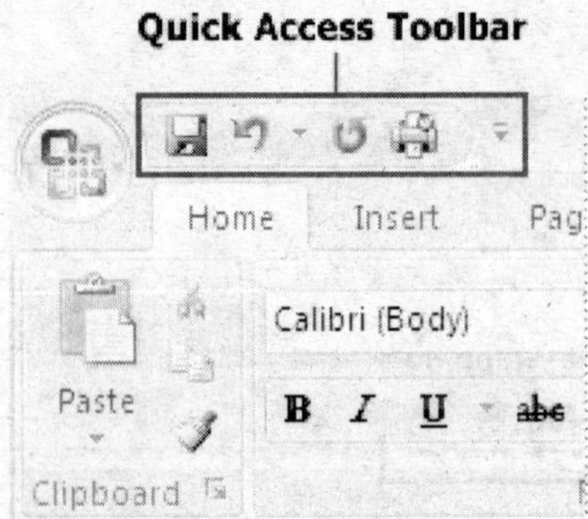

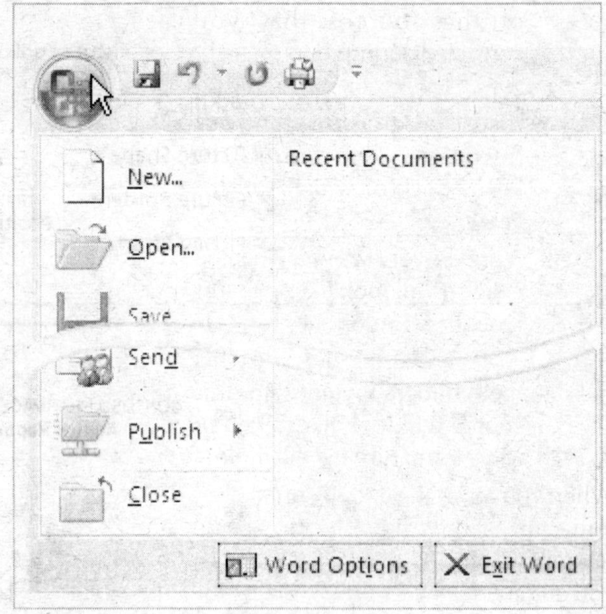

This button is located in the upper-left corner of the Word window and opens the menu shown here.

Quick Access Toolbar The Quick Access Toolbar is located by default at the top of the Word window and provides quick access to tools that you use frequently. You can customize the Quick Access Toolbar by adding commands to it.

Dialog Box Launchers Dialog Box Launchers are small icons that appear in some groups. Clicking a Dialog Box Launcher opens a related dialog box or task pane, providing more options related to that group.

Cite your sources

Are you writing a research paper? Chances are that keeping track of citations and creating a bibliography are not your favorite parts of the process.

Maybe you are a high school student new to bibliographies or a college student sweating the details of citing sources. Or are you a graduate student grappling with the fine points of MLA, APA, or some other publishing guideline?

If you create research papers, the new bibliography feature in Office Word 2010 does the heavy lifting for you. You can spend your time writing your paper, not fussing over citations and references.

Managing sources

As you conduct your research, you can add each source to a master list of sources that you consulted. You fill in information such as author, title, year of publication, and so on. Office Word 2010 automatically builds citations based on the information that you provide.

When you write your paper and you quote a source, you can easily insert a citation by selecting from the sources in your list, or you can add an entry for a new source. Citations are automatically formatted for the guidelines (such as Chicago or APA) that you specify.

1. Word 2010 stores a master list of the sources that you consulted during your research.
2. When you quote a source, you insert a citation in your document, and Word 2010 keeps track of which sources you cited.
3. A preview shows you what the citation will look like — in this case, in MLA format.
4. A preview also shows you what the bibliography entry for this source will look like, again in MLA format in this example.

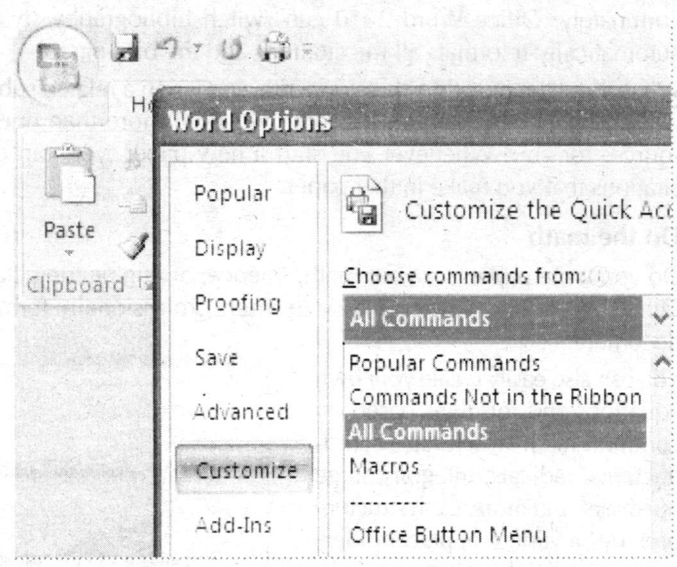

When you reach the end of your paper, you can easily assemble the list of references that you used. Just click a button to create the bibliography. Office Word 2010 formats it for you automatically according to the guidelines that you specify.

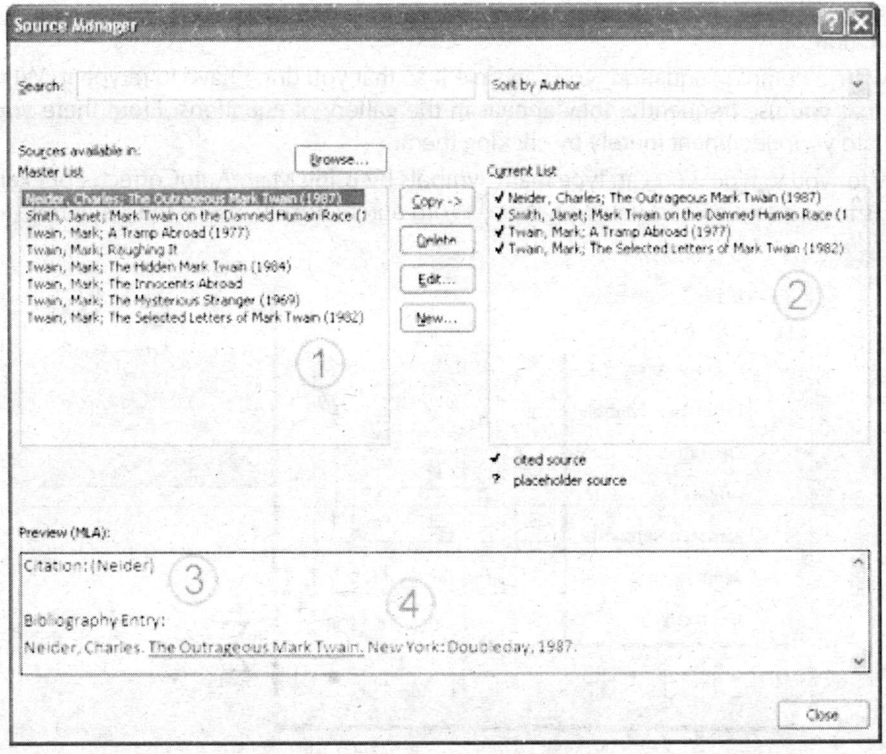

No need to start over

What if you write a paper for your literature class, but an educational journal wants to publish it? You used MLA style for formatting the citations and bibliography, but the journal uses APA style. It would be tedious to edit every citation and revise the bibliography to switch them from one style to the other.

Fortunately, Office Word 2010 can switch bibliography styles. Choose a different style, and Word automatically reformats all the citations and the bibliography.

What about the next time that you write a paper on a related subject? If your specialty is Mark Twain, you will probably cite many of his same works in more than one paper. Word stores your master list of sources for you. Whenever you start a new paper, you can choose from your list of sources for the citations that you make in that paper.

Do the math

Do you write papers for your math, science, or engineering class? The new equation writing feature in Office Word 2010 makes it easy to insert professionally formatted formulas and equations into your document.

You can also easily create your own equations and formulas based on common math structures, such as fractions, radicals, integrals, large operators, and more. Each structure provides a variety of placeholders for inserting mathematical symbols, which are organized in galleries. For example, you can choose from basic math, Greek letters, operators, arrows, and more.

When you solve the quadratic equation for x:

$$ax^2 + bx + c = 0$$

You end up with the following equation, which is the quadratic formula:

$$x = \frac{-b \pm \sqrt{b^2 - 4ac}}{2a}$$

After you write a complex equation, you can save it so that you don't have to retype it. When you save equations that you use frequently, they appear in the gallery of equations. From there you can insert equations into your document merely by clicking them.

If it is faster for you to type, you can type math symbols by using Math AutoCorrect. For example, when the cursor is in an equation and you type \beta, Word automatically inserts the ß symbol.

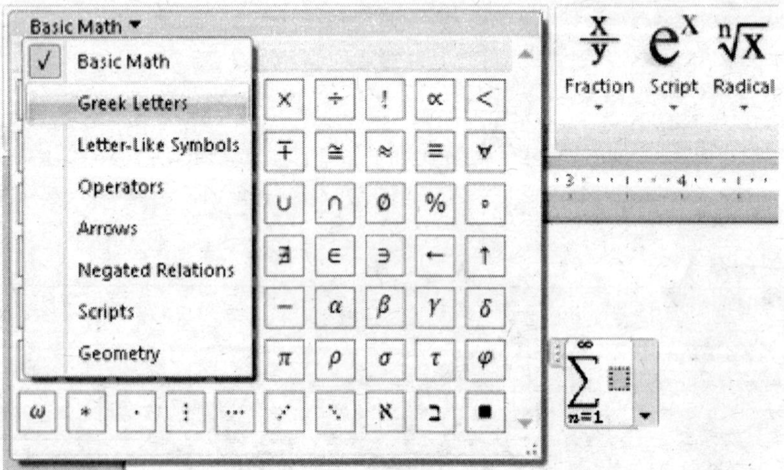

Rally your team

Is your paper a group project? If you write the introduction, Ben revises your work, and Susan writes additional content, but she makes some corrections to the introduction, how do you keep it all straight? Who did what, and who has the current version of this paper, anyway?

Improvements to the track changes feature in Office Word 2010 help you easily integrate revisions from multiple authors.

Keeping track of who did what

When you use the Track Changes command, Word keeps track of the revisions that you make in your document. Deletions are marked with a strikethrough, and additions are underlined. If you move content from one place to another, the change is marked as a move, which is an improvement over previous releases of Word. Previously, a move was marked as a deletion and an addition.

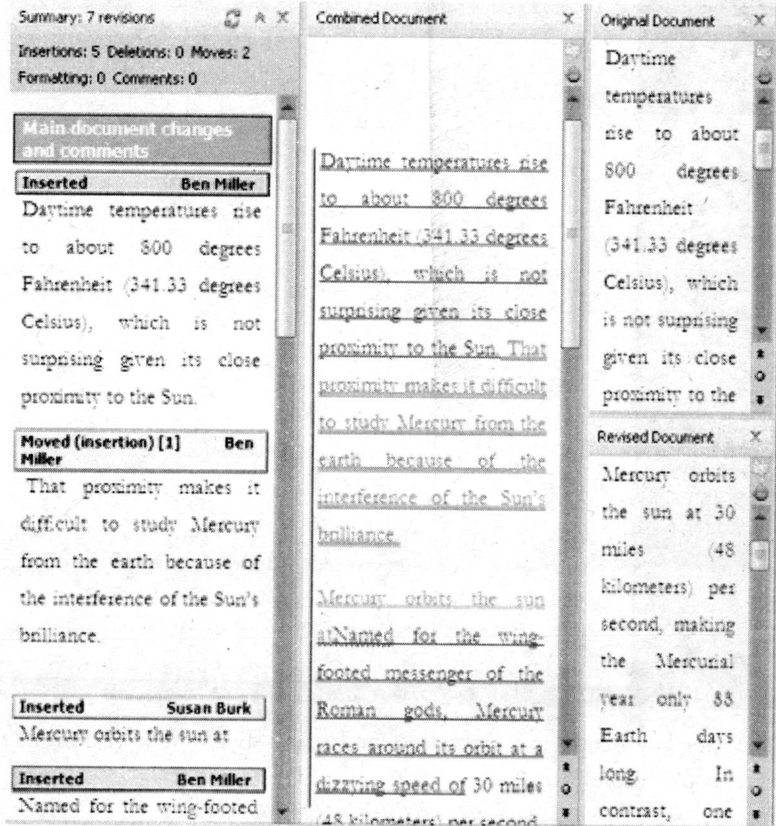

With your changes marked in the document, it is easy for you or someone else to review your revisions. If you review a paper for a colleague, you can make your changes with Track Changes turned on, save the document, and return it to the author. The author can then easily jump to each of your changes and accept or reject them.

Even if you don't use Track Changes, you can easily see the differences among versions of the same document.

The features for comparing and combining documents were improved in Office Word 2010, so you can see both documents being compared, and there is a summary pane that lists all the revisions in both documents. As you scroll through one document, the other document scrolls simultaneously so that you can see all the revisions in context.

Publish your work

Your paper is done, but everyone in your department posts their papers as PDF files, not Word documents. Office Word 2010 makes it easy to save your document in PDF format.

The first time that you use a 2010 Microsoft Office system program to save a file in PDF format, you need to install a free add-in. A link to the add-in is available when you click Save As. After you install the add-in, choose PDF when you use the Save As command.

Startup and settings

To change the author name and initials that are displayed in comments and tracked changes for new or existing documents, update the name in the User name box (Word options dialog box, Popular category) or the Author document property.

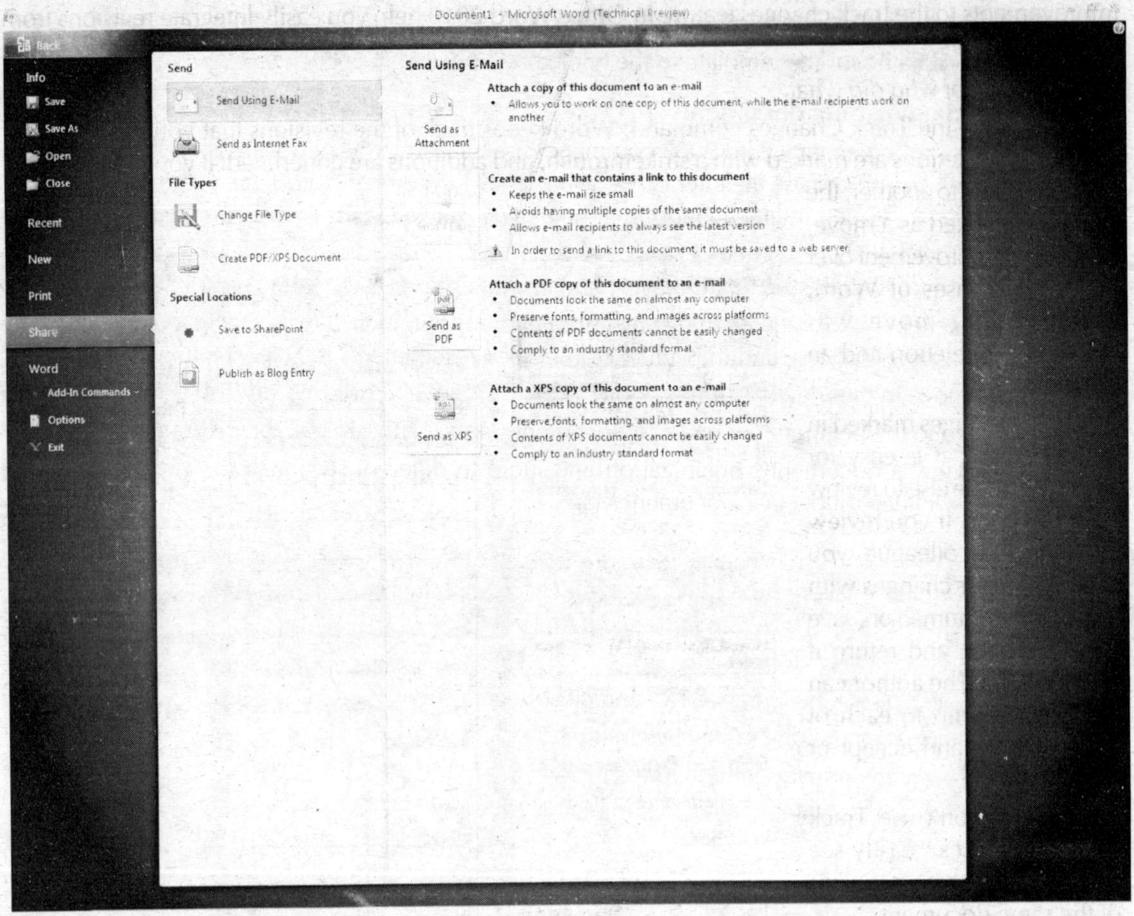

Document1 - Microsoft Word (Technical Preview)
Back
Info
Save
Save As
Open
Close
Recent
New
Print
Share
Word
Add-In Commands
Options
Exit
Send
Send Using E-Mail
Send as Internet Fax
File Types
Change File Type
Create PDF/XPS Document
Special Locations
Save to SharePoint
Publish as Blog Entry
Send Using E-Mail
Attach a copy of this document to an e-mail
Allows you to work on one copy of this document, while the e-mail recipients work on another
Send as Attachment
Create an e-mail that contains a link to this document
Keeps the e-mail size small
Avoids having multiple copies of the same document
Allows e-mail recipients to always see the latest version
In order to send a link to this document, it must be saved to a web server.
Attach a PDF copy of this document to an e-mail
Documents look the same on almost any computer
Preserve fonts, formatting, and images across platforms
Contents of PDF documents cannot be easily changed
Comply to an industry standard format
Send as PDF
Attach a XPS copy of this document to an e-mail
Documents look the same on almost any computer
Preserve fonts, formatting, and images across platforms
Contents of XPS documents cannot be easily changed
Comply to an industry standard format
Send as XPS

To assign keyboard shortcuts to frequently used styles, click Customize in the Customize category in the Word options dialog box.

Block users from changing the default Quick Style set

1. On the Home tab, in the Styles group, click the Styles Dialog Box Launcher.
2. In the Styles dialog box, click Manage Styles, and then click the Restrict tab.
3. Select the Block Quick Style Set switching check box.

AaBbCcDc
¶ Normal
AaBbCcDc
¶ No Spaci...
AaBbC
Heading 1
AaBbCc
Heading 2
AaB
Title
AaBbCc
Subtitle
Change Styles
Styles

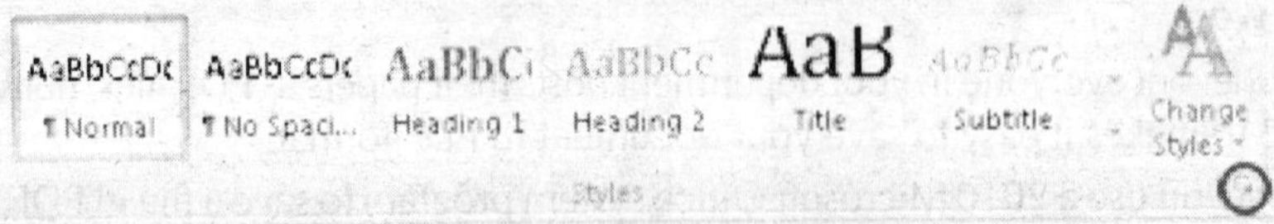

Restricting users from changing the Quick Style set does not prevent them from changing the font or color themes.

Save a template in the My templates folder

1. Click the Microsoft Office Button , and then click Save As.
2. In the Save As dialog box, click Trusted Templates (Microsoft Windows XP) or Templates (Windows Vista).

3. In the Save as type list, select Word Template.
4. Type a name for the template in the File name box, and then click Save.

Viewing and navigating documents

- To see where many Word 2003 commands are located in the new Microsoft Office Fluent user interface, you can use the Interactive: Word 2003 to Word 2010 command reference guide. The guide is a visual, interactive tool that helps you quickly learn where commands are in Office Word 2010
- To turn off Full Screen Reading view and return to Print Layout view, press ESC.
- To prevent Full Screen Reading view from opening automatically, in Full Screen Reading view, click View Options, and then click Don't Open Attachments in Full Screen.
- To move to the previous or next word, press CTRL + LEFT ARROW or CTRL + RIGHT ARROW.
- To go to the beginning or end of a document, press CTRL + HOME or CTRL + END.
- To view a document's organization and jump to different sections, on the View tab, in the Show/Hide group, click Document Map.

Formatting text

- To format a word without selecting it, click the word and apply the formatting that you want. For example, press CTRL + B to apply bold formatting.
- To select a word, double-click it.
- To select a sentence, press CTRL and click in the sentence.
- To select a paragraph, triple-click in the paragraph.
- To select an entire document, press CTRL + A.
- To paste only text and not formatting, paste the text, click Paste Options, and then select Keep Text Only.
- To preserve formatting when you move or copy a paragraph, include the paragraph mark ( ).
- To center, left-align, or right-align a selected paragraph, press CTRL + E, CTRL + L, or CTRL + R.
- To create a line, press the hyphen key three or more times, and then press ENTER. To create a thicker line, hold the SHIFT key down and press the hyphen key three or more times, and then press ENTER.
- To make text larger or smaller, select the text, and then press CTRL + SHIFT +] or CTRL + SHIFT + [.

Format text by using the Mini toolbar

The Mini toolbar appears automatically when you select text and when you right-click text.

1. Select the text that you want to format.
2. Move your pointer to the Mini toolbar, and then make the formatting changes that you want.

Reuse formatting

Use the Format Painter to copy the text formatting from one area of a document and apply it to another area.

1. Select the text that has the formatting that you want to apply to other areas.
2. On the Home tab, in the Clipboard group, click Format Painter..

To apply the text format to multiple areas, double-click Format Painter. When you finish applying formatting, click Format Painter again, or press ESC.

Display highlighting on screen and when you print

1. Click the Microsoft Office Button , and then click Word Options.

2. Click Display.
3. Under Page display options, select or clear the Show highlighter marks check box.

Formatting tables

- To clear the contents of a table, select the table, and then press DELETE.
- To remove a table and its contents, select the table, and then press BACKSPACE.
- To add a row at the end of a table, click in the last cell, and then press TAB.
- To insert a tab character in a table cell, click in the cell, and then press CTRL+TAB.
- To number rows in a table, select the left column, and then on the Home tab, in the Paragraph group, click Numbering.
- To number columns in a table, select the top row, and then on the Home tab, in the Paragraph group, click Numbering.
- To insert a blank line before a table, click before any text in the upper-left cell of the table, and then press ENTER.
- To move a table row and its contents up or down, select the row, and then press ALT+SHIFT+UP ARROW or ALT+SHIFT+DOWN ARROW.

Save frequently used tables in the Quick Tables gallery

1. Select the table.
2. On the Insert tab, in the Tables group, click Table, point to Quick Tables, and then click Save Selection to Quick Tables Gallery.

Editing and reviewing documents

- To compare two versions of a document to find out what has changed, use the legal blackline option. On the Review tab, in the Compare group, click Compare, and then click Compare.
- To merge comments and changes from several documents into one document, on the Review tab, in the Compare group, click Compare, and then click Combine.
- To compare documents side-by-side, open both of the documents that you want to view. On the View tab, in the Window group, click View Side by Side.
- To see two parts of a document simultaneously, on the View tab, in the Window group, click Split.
- To return to the location of the last edit, press SHIFT+F5.

Opening Screen of Microsoft Word Screen

Gone are the days of Menu, for example, File menu, Edit menu, etc. Now everything is there on the screen. You have to just click it and presto, you have the command available to you. But, first have a look at the opening screen, which is shown next. There are some main Tabs, which are basic substitutions for the menus. They are: Home, Insert, Page Layout, References, Mailings, Review, and View. Let us see what each one of them contains.

Home Panel

It has the various options of changing the style and type of text. Among the various important features are: Clipboard, Font, Paragraph, Styles, and Editing. Let us look at them one by one.

Clipboard

Most important commands here are: Cut, Copy, Paste and Format Painter.

The Format Painer is used for copying formattting from one place and applying it to another. Paste includes options like, Paste Special and Paste as Hyperlink.

Font

Various options of the font dialog box are all here. You can choose Font, Font size, Grow font, Lower font, Clear formatting in the first row. The second row contains options for Bold, Italics, Underline, Strikethrough, Subscript, Superscript, Change case, Text highlighting, and Text colour. The underlining option contains options for different type of lines which can be chosen for underlining and then choosing the colour of the same too. In Change case you have the option of changing the case to Sentence case, lowercase, UPPERCASE, Captalize Each Word and tOGGLE cASE. Text highlighting and colours have various options too.

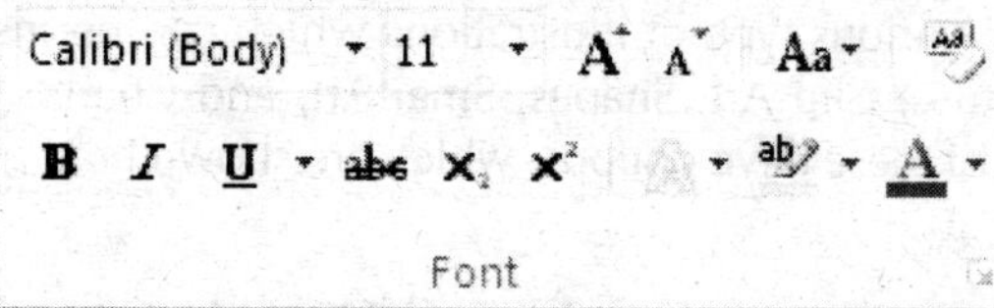

Paragraph

It has options for paragraph styling. The first row contains options for Bullets, Numbering, Multilevel numbering, Shifting text to left, Shifting text to right, Sort, Show/hide non printing characters. In the second row you have the options of making

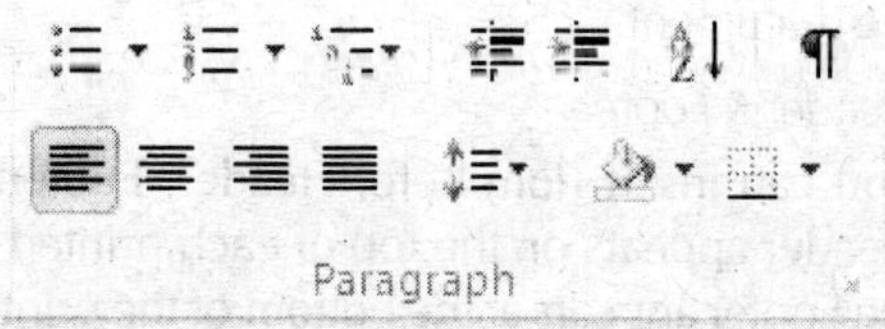

CHAPTER 2

paragraph, Left aligned, Centrally aligned, Right aligned, Box aligned, Line spacing, Shading, and Bottom border. Bullets have different options. Numering can be done in different styles too. So can be done in the case of Multilevel numbering.

Styles

It displays the various styles which you have created. Just click at the one you want to apply to your text and it will be done. You can also Change Styles and create your own style from it.

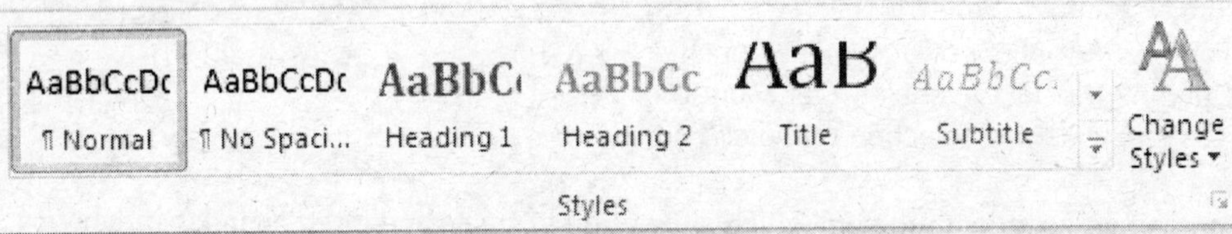

Editing

It has various other editing options, like, Find, Replace, and Select. Find allows you to find a particular word in the text. Replace allows you to find the word and replace it with another one. Select allows you to select text, select objects or the text with similar formatting.

Find
Replace
Select
Editing

The next panel is Insert.

Insert Panel

It has options like: Pages, Tables, Illustrations, Links, Header & Footer, Text, and Symbols.

Pages

It has options of Cover Page, Blank Page, Page Break. Blank page inserts a blank page in the text. Page break puts a page break in the text.

Cover Page
Blank Page
Page Break
Pages

Tables

Inserts table format in the text. If you click at the arrow, you will see the options shown here, which not only describe the type of table you are choosing but also draws the table in the text simultaneously. You can also insert as a table, an Excel Spreadsheet. There is option of Quick Tables too, which allows you to save a table format, which can be called later for quickly creating a table.

Table
Tables

Illustrations

The various type of illustrations which can be inserted into the text of the document are: Picture, Clip Art, Shapes, SmartArt, and Charts. All of these have options, which are shown here.

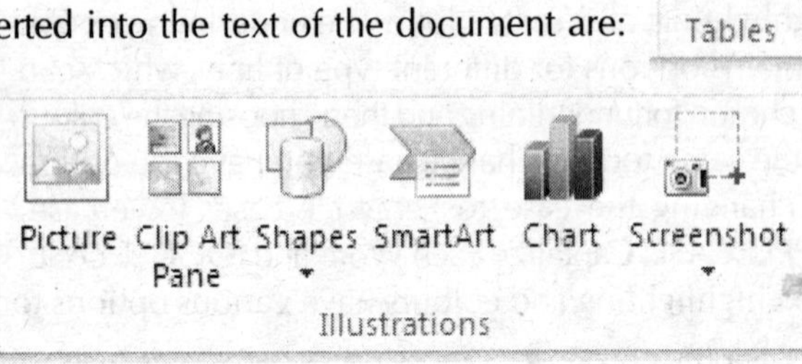

Links

Among the various options which are here are: Hyperlink, Bookmark, and Cross-reference. These can be used in inserting these links into the text of the document.

Header & Footer

You can insert from here, Header, Footer and Page Numbers. Header appears on the top of each printed page. The content of the Footer appears at the bottom of the printed page. Header and

Footer both of options of Editing and Removing them. Page number options are Top of Page, Bottom of Page, Page Margins, Current Position, Format Page Numbers and Remove Page Numbers.

Text

Various options here are: Text Box, Quick Parts, Word Art, Drop Cap, Signature Line, Date and Time, and Object. Text box creates a box which can be filled up with the text and is independent of the document text.

Quick Parts has the options of Document Property, Field, Building Blocks Organizer, Get More on Office Online, and Save Selection to Quick Part Gallery.

WordArt is an independent program which allows you to create and insert an independent text.

Drop Cap allows you to put a capital letter in the beginning of the text. It can cover 2-3 lines of the text to highlight the alphabet.

Signature Line allows you to insert a signature line.

Date and Time would insert date and time in the text, in the format selected by you.

Object allows you to insert objects in the text. It also allows you to insert text from another file.

Symbols

It has two options: Equation and Symbol. Equation allows you to enter equations in the text, after creating it using the various symbols available under it. It is quite a big topic and can be discussed in an advanced book. Symbol button allows you insert a symbol from the list shown here.

Now we come to Page Layout.

Page Layout Panel

It has the following options: Themes, Page Setup, Page Background, Paragraph, and Arrange.

Themes

Among the various option which you can choose here are: Colours, Fonts and Themes. Each one of them have their own set of options, as shown here.

Page Setup

Among the various options available here are: Margins, Orientation, Size, Columns, Breaks, Line Numbers and Hyphenation.

Margins allows you to set margins of the page, i.e., margins from the left and right of the page.

Orientation has two options: Portrait and Landscape.

Size allows you to choose from the various size of the paper normally used globally.

Columns allow you to set the page into various columns with line in-between or not.

Breaks inserts break into the text in the form of line, page, etc.

Line Numbers are inserted using this option.

Hyphenation allows to have hyphens in the paragraph or not.

Page Background

As shown here, it has three options in the form of Watermark, Page Color, Page Borders.

Watermark can be in the form of a picture or the text. As shown here, you can select the picture or create the text which will form the background of the page.

Page Color allows you to choose the color of the background.

Page Borders allows you place a border in the background of the page.

Watermark Page Color Page Borders
Page Background

Paragraph

It has two main options: Indent and Spacing.

Indent allows you to set the left and right indent.

Spacing allows you to set the Before and After paragraph space.

Indent
Left: 1.5"
Right: 1.5"
Spacing
Before: 0 pt
After: 0 pt
Paragraph

Arrange

It has the following options: Position, Bring to Front, Send to Back, Text Wrapping, Align, Group and Rotate.

Position allows you to position the picture/object as per the options available.

Bring to Front and Send to Back are used when you have to rearrange the picture/object with respect to the text.

Align allows you to align the text, as per the options shown here.

Group allows you to group two or more objects together.

Rotate allows you to rotate the inserted object as per the options shown here.

Position Wrap Text Bring Forward Send Backward Selection Pane Align Group Rotate
Arrange

References Panel

It has the following options: Table of Contents, Footnotes, Citations and Bibliography, Captions, Index, and Table of Authorities.

Table of Contents

It has the options: Table of Contents, Add Test and Update Table. Table of Contents allows you create table of contents of the text. Add Text allows you to set levels of the text. Update Table updates an existing table of contents.

Table of Contents
Add Text
Update Table
Table of Contents

Footnotes

It has the options: Insert Footnote, Insert Endnote, Next Footnote, and Show Notes. Insert Footnote allows you to insert a footnote in the text. Insert Endnote allows you to insert endnote. Next footnote allows to insert the next or prev footnote, endnote. Show notes shows all the notes in the text.

Insert Footnote
Insert Endnote
Next Footnote
Show Notes
Footnotes

Citations & Bibliography

It has the options of Inserting a Citation, Managing Sources, Style, and Bibliography. Citation allows you to cite a book, journal article, or other periodical as the source for a piece of information in the document.

Choose from the list of sources you have created or enter information for a new source. Word formats the citation according to the style you have selected. Manage Sources allow you to look into the source manager and manage it. Style allows you to choose from the various styles given. Bibliography allows you to maintain the various references.

Captions

This has the following options: Insert Caption, Insert Table of Figures, Update Table, and Cross-reference.

Insert Caption allows you to add a caption to a picture or other image. A caption is a line of text that appears below an object to describe it.

Insert Table of Figures inserts a Table of Figures into the document. A Table of Figures includes a list of all of the figures, table, or equations in the document.

Cross-reference refers to items such as headings, figures, and tables by inserting a cross reference such as, "See Table 6 below" or "Turn to page 8." Cross references are automatically updated if the content is moved to another location. By default, cross references are inserted as hyperlinks.

Index

It has the following commands: Mark Entry, Insert Index, and Update Index.

Mark Entry allows you to include the selected text in the index of the document.

Insert Index inserts an index into the document. An index is a list of keywords found in the document along with the page numbers the words appear on.

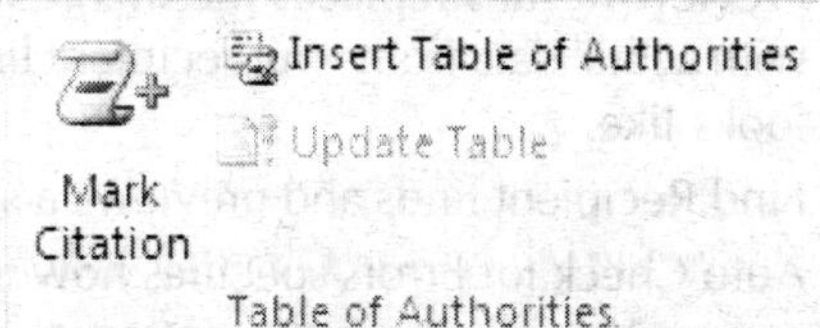

Table of Authorities

It has the option called Mark Citation, Insert Table of Authorities, and Update Table of Authorities. Mark Citation adds the selected text as an entry in the Table of Authorities.

Insert Table of Authorities
Update Table
Mark Citation
Table of Authorities

Mailings Panel

It has the following options: Create, Start Mail Merge, Write & Insert Fields, Preview Results, and Finish.

Create

It has the following options: Envelopes, and Labels. Each one of them gives rise to a dialog box, which allows you to create envelopes and labels.

Envelopes Labels
Create

Start Mail Merge

It has options to Start Mail Merge, Select Recipients and Edit Recipients List.

Start Mail Merge allows you to select the options of Letters, E-Mail Messages, Evelopes, Labels, Directory or start the Step by Step Mail Merge Wizard.

Select Recipients allows you to choose the list of people you intend to send the letter to. You can type you own list, use your Outlook contacts, or connect to a database. It also has options to Type New List, Use Existing List or Select from Outlook Contacts.

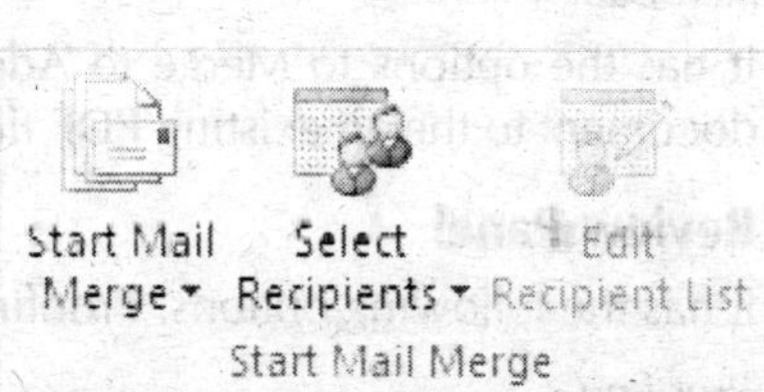

Write & Insert Fields

It has the options to Highlight Merge Fields, Address Block, Greeting Line, Insert Merge Field, Rules, Match Fields, and Update Labels.

Highlight Merge Fields highlights the fields you have inserted into the document. This makes it easy to see what part of your form letter will be replaced by information from the recipient list you have chosen.

Addresss Block adds an address to your letter. You specify the formatting and location, and Word will replace it with actual addresses from your recipient list when you finish the mail merge.

Greeting Line adds a greeting line such as "Dear< <First Name> >", to your document.

Insert Merge Field adds any field from your recipient list to the document, such as "Last Name," "Home Phone," "Company Name," or any other field.

When you finish the mail merge, Word will replace these fields with the actual information from the recipient list.

Rules specifies rules to be added decision-making ability to the mail merge. For instance, you could use If...Then...Else to check the address of recipient and show a local phone number to recipients near you and an international phone number for recipients outside of your country.

Match Fields allows you to tell Word the meaning of different fields in your recipient list. For example, you can indicate that your custom field "Home" is equivalent to normal built-in field "Home Phone."

Update Labels allow you to create labels, update all the labels in the document to use information from the recipient list. For a mail merge to a printed letter or e-mail, this command is not necessary.

Preview Results

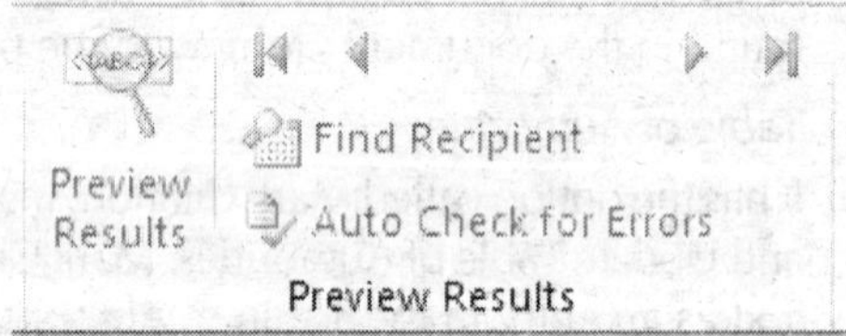

It has the options to Preview Results, Find Recipient, and Auto Check for Errors.

Preview Results replaces the merge fields in your document with acutal data from your recipient list so you can see what it looks like.

Find Recipient finds and previews a specific record in the recipient list by searching for text.

Auto Check for Errors specifies how to handle errors that occur when completing the mail merge. You also have the option of simulating the mail merge to see if any errors would occur.

Finish

It has the options to Finish & Merge. It completes the mail merge. You can create separate documents for each copy of the letter, send them all directly to the printer, or send them via e-mail.

Acrobat

It has the options to Merge to Adobe PDT, which in turn allows you to merge your document to the an existing PDF file.

Review Panel

It has the following options: Proofing, Comments, Tracking, Changes, Compare, and Protect.

Proofing

It has the following options: Spelling & Grammer, Research, Thesaurus, and Word Count.

Spelling & Grammar checks the spelling and grammar of text in the document.

Research opens the Research Task Pane to search through reference materials, such as dictionaries, encyclopedias, and translation services.

Thesaurus suggests other words with a similar meaning to the word you have selected.

Word Count finds out the number of words, characters, paragraphs, and lines in the document. You can also find the word count in the status bar at the bottom of the window.

Language

Translates the selected text into a different language. Translation ScreenTip enables a ScreenTip that translates words you pause your cursor over into another language.

Editing Language sets the language used to check the spelling and grammar of the selected text.

Comments

This has the following options: New Comment, Delete, Previous, and Next.

New Commnet adds a selection over the selection.

Delete command deletes an existing comment.

Previous locates the previous comment.

Tracking

This has the following options: Track Changes, Balloons, Final Showing Markup, Show Markup, and Reviewing Pane.

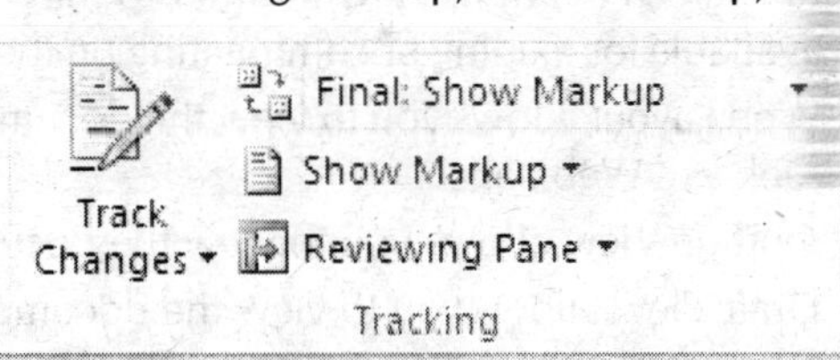

Track Changes trackes all changes made to the document, including insertions, deletions, and formatting changes. Change Tracking Options allows you to change the tracking options. Change User Name would allow you to change the user name.

Balloons allow you to choose how to show revisions to the document. You can show revisions as balloons in the margins of the coument or show them directly within the document itself.

Display for Review allows you to choose how to view the proposed changes to the document. Final shows the document with all proposed changes included; Original shows the document before any changes were made. The markup shows what changes have been proposed.

Show Markup allows you to choose what kind of markup to show in the document. You can hide or show comments, insertions and deletions, formatting changes, and other kinds of markup.

Reviewing Pane shows revisions in a separate window.

Changes

This has the following options: Accept, Reject, Previous, and Next.

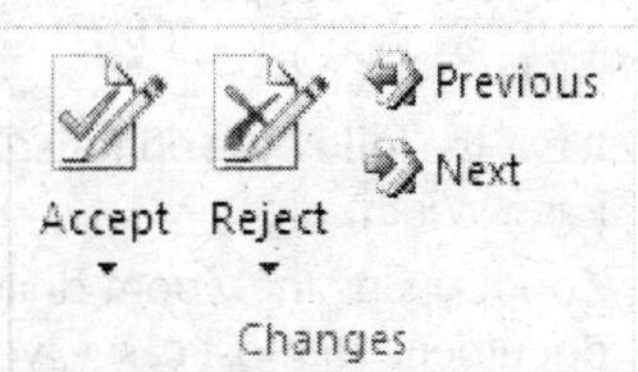

Accept and Move to Next allows you to access other options such as accepting all changes in the document.

Reject and Move to Next allows you to access other options such as rejecting all changes in the document.

Previous Change allows you to navigate to the previous revision in the document so that you can accept or reject it.

Next Change allows you to navigate to the next revision in the document so that you can accept or reject it.

Compare

This has the following options: Compare, and Show Source Documents.

Compare compares or combines multiple versions of a document.

Show Source Documents allows you to choose which source documents to show. You can show the original document, the revised document, or booth.

Protect

This has only one option: Protect Document.

It restricts how people can access the document.

View

It has the following options: Document Views, Show/Hide, Zoom, Window, and Macros.

Document Views

It has the following options: Print Layout, Full Screen Reading, Web Layout, Outline, and Draft.

Print Layout views the document as it will appear on the printed page.

Full Screen Reading allows you to view the document in full screen Reading View in order to maximize the space available for reading or commenting on the document.

Web Layout allows you to view the document as it would look as a Web page.

Outline View allows you to view the document as an outline and show the outlining tools.

Draft View allows you to view the document as a draft to quickly edit the text.

Show

It has the following options: Ruler, Gridlines, Message Bar, Document Map, and Thumbnails.

Ruler allows you to view the rulers, used to measure and line up objects in the document.

Gridlines turns on gridlines to which you can align objects in the document.

Message Bar opens the Message Bar to complete any required actions on the document.

Document Map opens the Document Map, which allows you to navigate through a structural view of the document.

Thumbnails opens the Thumbnails pane, which you can use to navigate a long document through small pictures of each page.

Zoom

It has the following options: Zoom, 100%, One Page, Two Pages, and Page Width.

Zoom opens the Zoom dialog box to specify the zoom level of the document. In most cases, you can alos use the zoom controls in the status bar at the bottom of the window to quickly zoom the document.

100% zooms the document to 100% of the normal size.

One Page zooms the document so that an entire page fits in the window.

Two Pages zooms the document so that two pages fit in the window.

Page Width zooms the document so that the width of the page matches the width of the window.

Window

It has the following options: New Window, Arrange All, Split, View Side by Side, Synchronous Scrolling, Reset Window Position, and Switch Windows.

New Window allows you to open a new window containing a view of the current document.

Arrange All tiles all open program windows side-by-side on the screen.

Split Window splits the current window into two parts so that you can view different sections of the document at the same time.

View Side by Side allows you to view two documents side-by-side so that you can compare their contents.

Synchronous Scrolling synchronizes the scrolling of two documents so that they scroll together. To enable this feature, turn View Side by Side.

Reset Window Position resets the window position of the documents being compared side-by-side so that they share the screen equally. To enable this feature, turn on View Side by Side.

Switch Windows allows you to switch to a different currently open window.

Macros

It has only one option, i.e., Macros.

Macros command allows you to view macros. Click here to record a macro or to access other macro options.

View

It has the following options: Document Views, Show/Hide, Zoom, Window, and Macros.

Create Adobe PDF

It has the options: Create PDF and Preferences.

Create PDF allows you to create PDF of the document.

Preferences allows you to set preferences for the PDF.

Create and Email

It has the options: Create and Attach to Email and Meil Merge.

Create and Attach to Email allows you to create an email or add the document to an existing email..

Mail Merge allows you to start the mail merge process.

Review and Comment

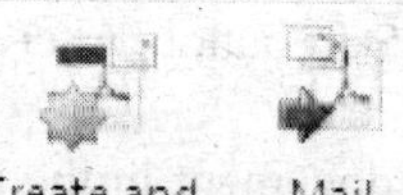

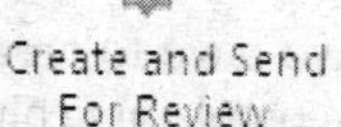

It has the options: Create and Send for Review and Acrobat Comments.

Create and Send For Review sends the document file for reviewing.

Acrobat Comments allows you to see the comments mentioned by Acrobat.

Connect .

It has the option of Starting a Meeting.

Start Meeting
Connect

Office Button

Besides, the commands mentioned till now, we have a set of commands, under the so called Office Button. These are the commands which can be used just by a clik. Given below are the various options available.

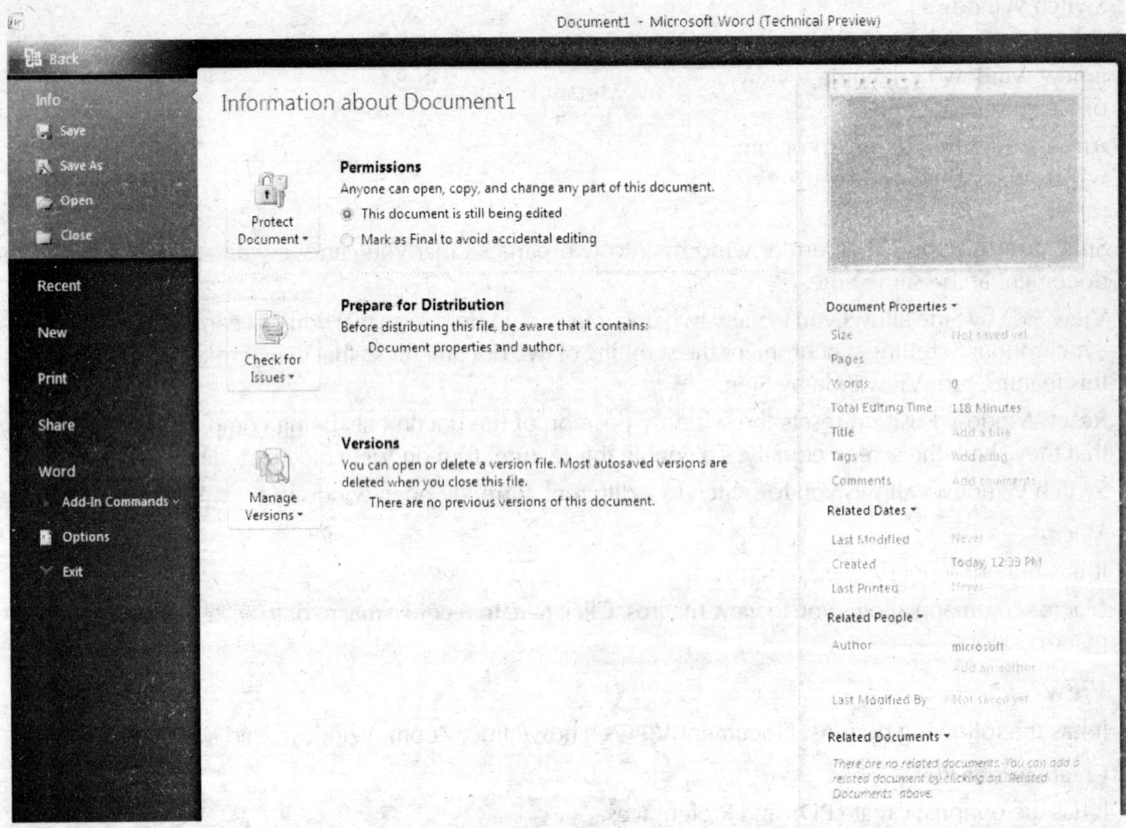

They are: Info, Save, Save As, Open, Close, Recent, New, Print, Share, Word, Add-in Commands, Options and Exit. Want to see what is there in each one of them. Go through the pages here to see them.

Working with Documents in Microsoft Word 2010

The best way to learn about a new software is to use it. It is like jumping into the swimming pool to learn swimming. What we will do here is that we will type our document and learn the various commands side by side. Starting Word 2010 is easy so I am not discussing that here. Let us start a new document here. This can again be done from the Start button. After you have opened Word 2010 you can either click at New from the Office button.

Supposing we have to create a document in the form of a letter written to the General Manager of Telephones complaining him of the inflated bills. The text of the letter is shown next. Now that you have opened a new document, do not worry about any typing mistakes or any formatting, just type the text as it is.

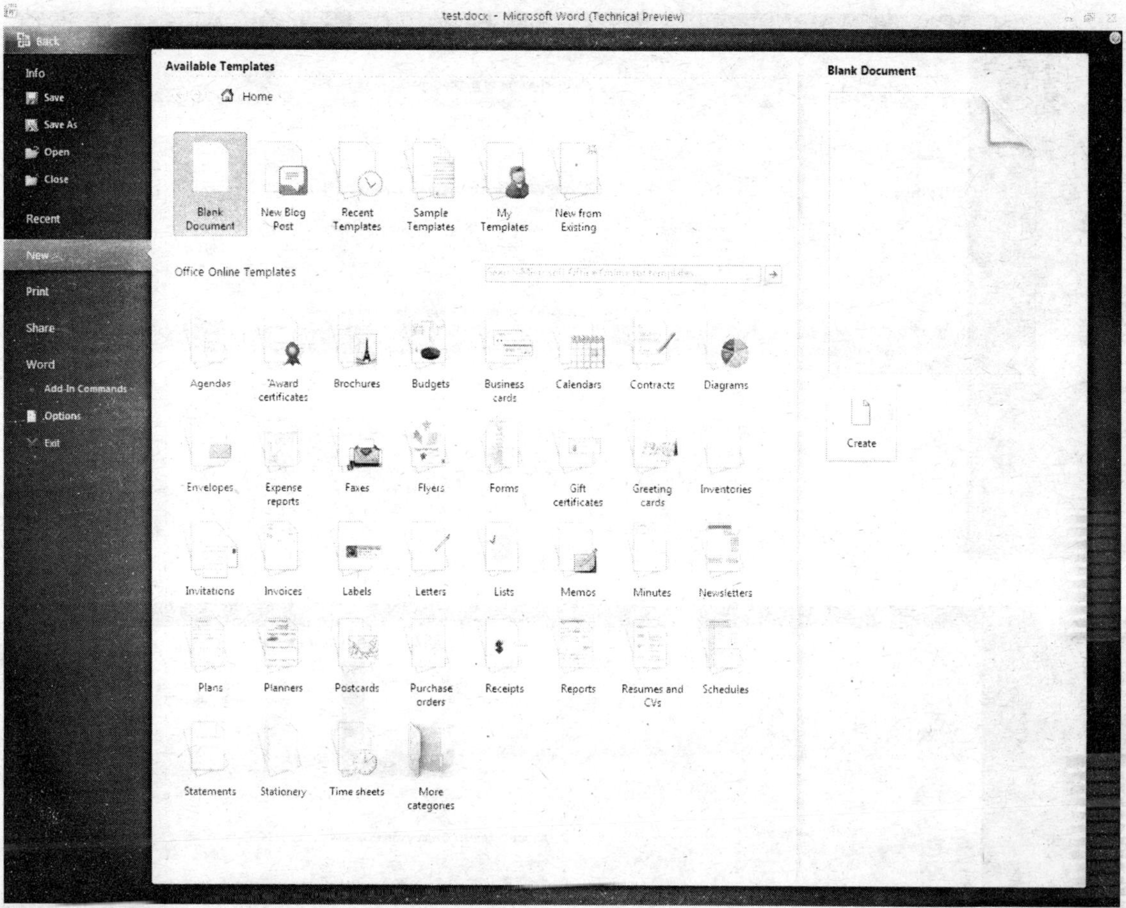

test.docx - Microsoft Word (Technical Preview)
Back
Info
Save
Save As
Open
Close
Recent
New
Print
Share
Word
Add-In Commands
Options
Exit
Available Templates
Home
Blank Document
New Blog Post
Recent Templates
Sample Templates
My Templates
New from Existing
Office Online Templates
Agendas
Award certificates
Brochures
Budgets
Business cards
Calendars
Contracts
Diagrams
Envelopes
Expense reports
Faxes
Flyers
Forms
Gift certificates
Greeting cards
Inventories
Invitations
Invoices
Labels
Letters
Lists
Memos
Minutes
Newsletters
Plans
Planners
Postcards
Purchase orders
Receipts
Reports
Resumes and CVs
Schedules
Statements
Stationery
Time sheets
More categories
Blank Document
Create

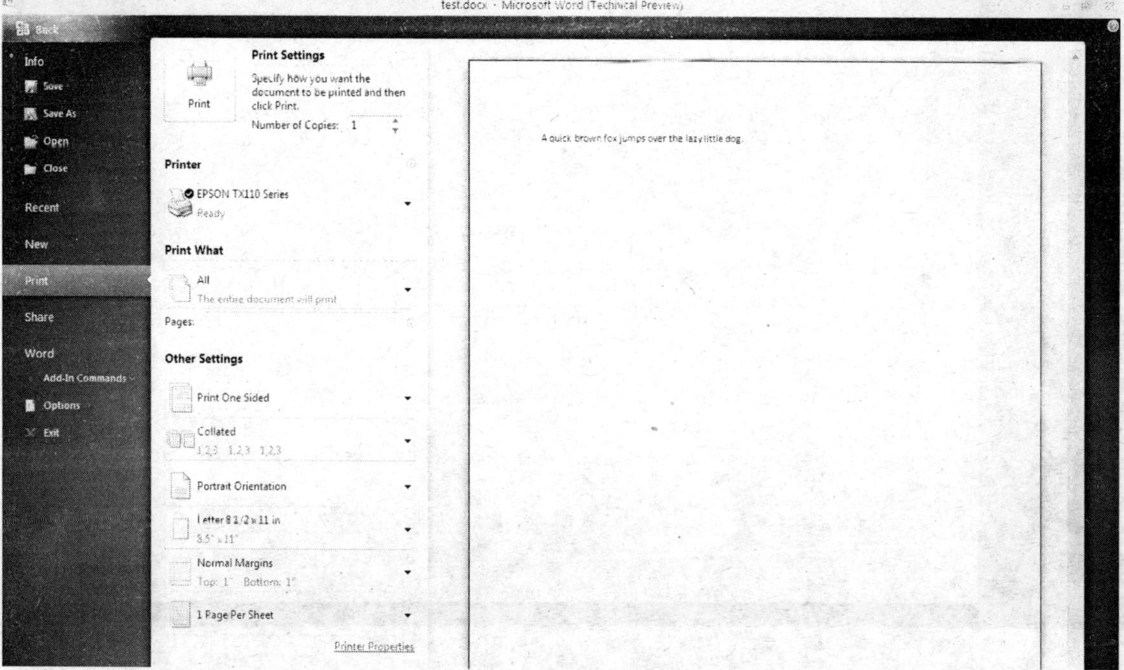
test.docx - Microsoft Word (Technical Preview)
Back
Info
Save
Save As
Open
Close
Recent
New
Print
Share
Word
Add-In Commands
Options
Exit
Print Settings
Specify how you want the document to be printed and then click Print.
Print
Number of Copies: 1
Printer
EPSON TX110 Series
Ready
Print What
All
The entire document will print
Pages:
Other Settings
Print One Sided
Collated
1,2,3 1,2,3 1,2,3
Portrait Orientation
Letter 8 1/2 x 11 in
8.5" x 11"
Normal Margins
Top: 1" Bottom: 1"
1 Page Per Sheet
Printer Properties
A quick brown fox jumps over the lazy little dog.

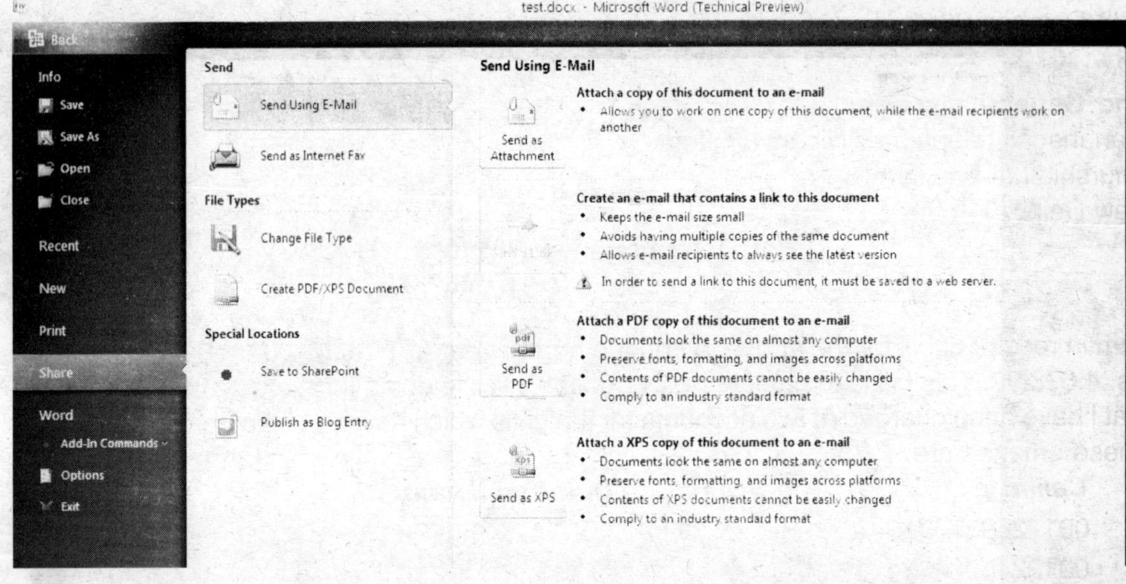

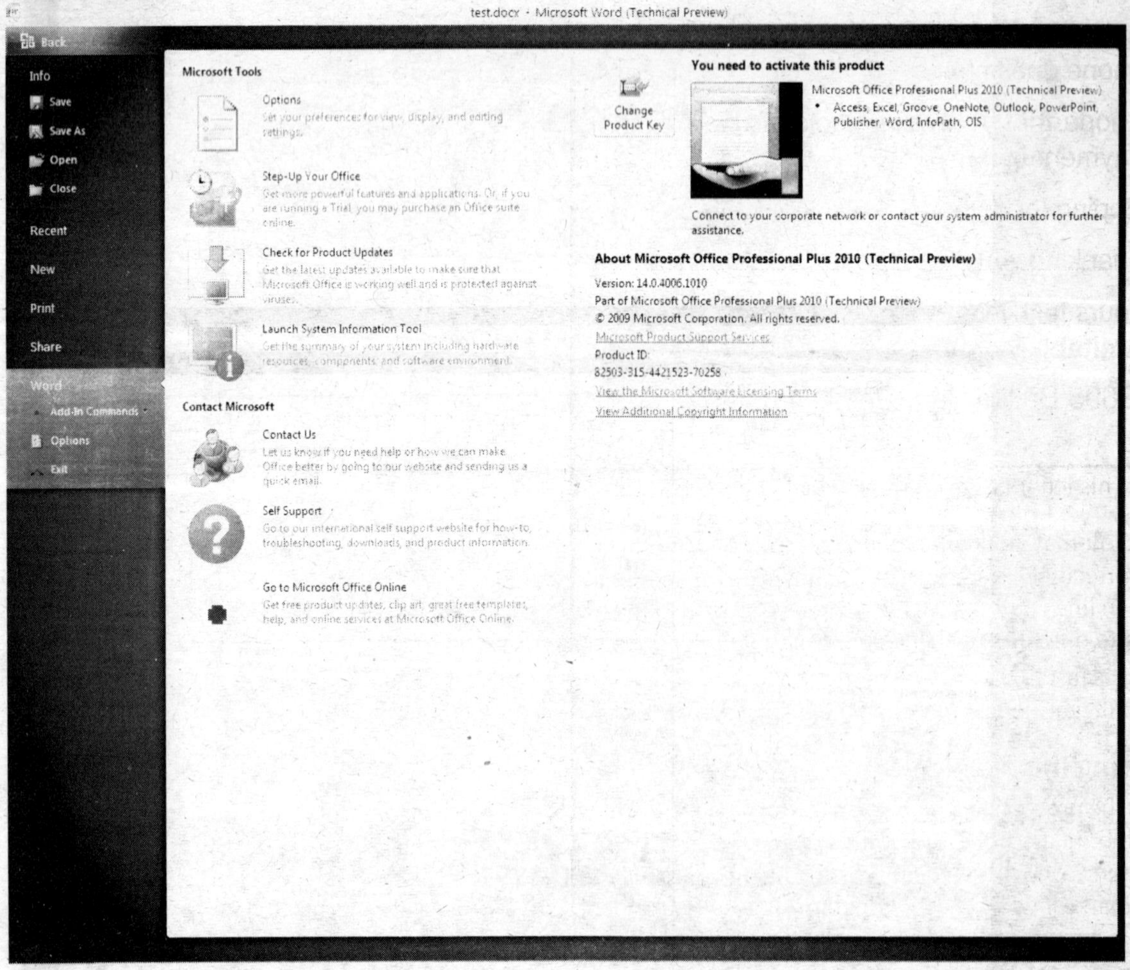

test.docx - Microsoft Word (Technical Preview)

Back
Info
Save
Save As
Open
Close
Recent
New
Print
Share
Word
Add-In Commands
Options
Exit

Microsoft Tools

Options
Set your preferences for view, display, and editing settings.

Step-Up Your Office
Get more powerful features and applications. Or, if you are running a Trial, you may purchase an Office suite online.

Check for Product Updates
Get the latest updates available to make sure that Microsoft Office is working well and is protected against viruses.

Launch System Information Tool
Get the summary of your system including hardware resources, components, and software environment.

Contact Microsoft

Contact Us
Let us know if you need help or how we can make Office better by going to our website and sending us a quick email.

Self Support
Go to our international self support website for how-to, troubleshooting, downloads, and product information.

Go to Microsoft Office Online
Get free product updates, clip art, great free templates, help, and online services at Microsoft Office Online.

Change Product Key

You need to activate this product

Microsoft Office Professional Plus 2010 (Technical Preview)
- Access, Excel, Groove, OneNote, Outlook, PowerPoint, Publisher, Word, InfoPath, OIS

Connect to your corporate network or contact your system administrator for further assistance.

About Microsoft Office Professional Plus 2010 (Technical Preview)

Version: 14.0.4006.1010
Part of Microsoft Office Professional Plus 2010 (Technical Preview)
© 2009 Microsoft Corporation. All rights reserved.
Microsoft Product Support Services
Product ID:
82503-315-4421523-70258
View the Microsoft Software Licensing Terms
View Additional Copyright Information

11th October, 2010

To,

The General Manager

Mahanagar Telephones Nigam Limited

Khurshid Lal Bhawan

New Delhi - 110 001

Ref: Telephone No. 4611098

Sir,

I am in receipt of bill for the above telephone number dated 1.10.2010 for an amount of Rs. 4,678.90. This bill is to be paid by 21.10.2010. While going through the bill, I notice that I have been charged at two accounts for the calls which have not been made by me. These enteries are:

Called Id	***Duration***	***Amount***
0017249873769	120	1,008.00
0013245934234	60	675.90

As you can notice that both these entries pertain to **International calls** and since my phone does not have this facility, these calls could not have been made from my phone.

I hope that you would look into and send me the revised bill, so that I can make the payment in time.

Hoping for an early action,

Thanking you,

Yours faithfully,

Amitabh Bachan

3695 Ballimaran, Delhi - 110 006

* This letter has few errors, which will be corrected in Word 2010

As you may notice that there are few red and green wavy lines. The red lines, show that the word is incorrectly typed as per the dictionary available with the system and the word/words under whom the green line is, show that the words are grammatically wrong. This is the opinion of the software, you may beg to differ from it. Since most of the proper names like Shah Rukh Khan, are shown as wrong.

This is just the raw text which has been typed. Now we have to do the formatting. But, before that, lest the file gets tangled in power failure or something, we must save the file.

Saving the file

It is the process by which you give the name to the file and save under that name. Since our letter pertains to the inflated bill, we will call our file as Bill. For saving, just select the Save option under Office button. You will get the following dialog box. Just type the name Bill in the space provided for typing the filename and click Save. Your file will be saved under this name and automatically the title bar will show the name of the file on the top of the Word 2010 screen.

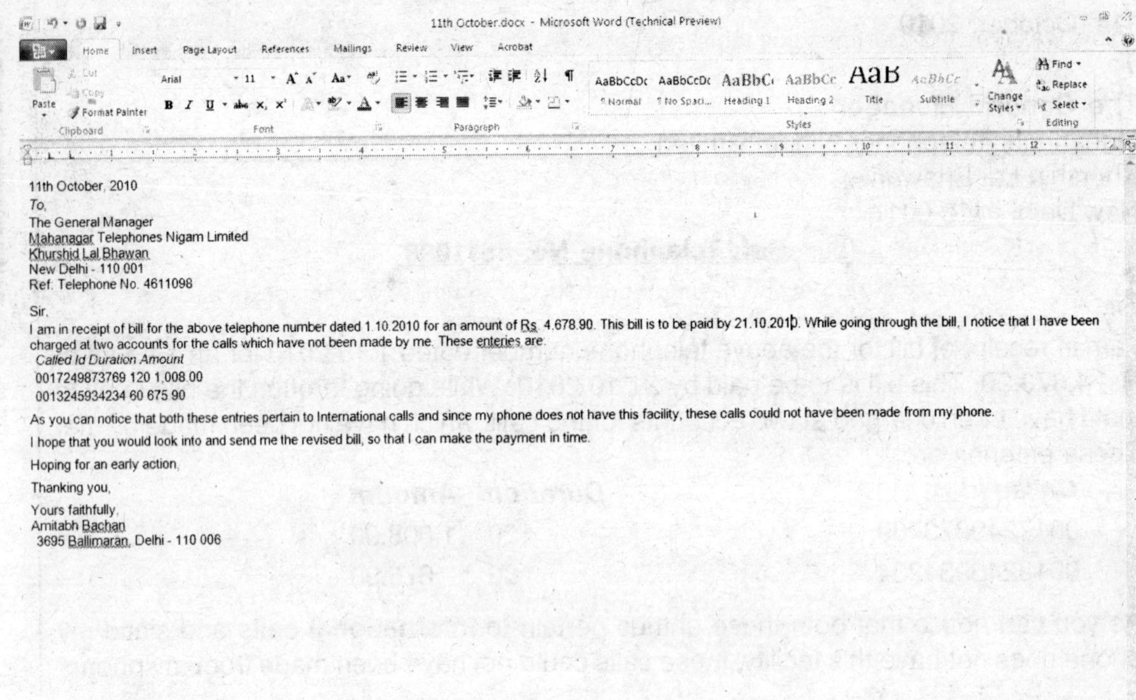

11th October, 2010

To,

The General Manager
Mahanagar Telephones Nigam Limited
Khurshid Lal Bhawan
New Delhi - 110 001
Ref: Telephone No. 4611098

Sir,

I am in receipt of bill for the above telephone number dated 1.10.2010 for an amount of Rs. 4,678.90. This bill is to be paid by 21.10.2010. While going through the bill, I notice that I have been charged at two accounts for the calls which have not been made by me. These enteries are:

Called Id Duration Amount
0017249873769 120 1,008.00
0013245934234 60 675.90

As you can notice that both these entries pertain to International calls and since my phone does not have this facility, these calls could not have been made from my phone.

I hope that you would look into and send me the revised bill, so that I can make the payment in time.

Hoping for an early action,

Thanking you,

Yours faithfully,
Amitabh Bachan
3695 Ballimaran, Delhi - 110 006

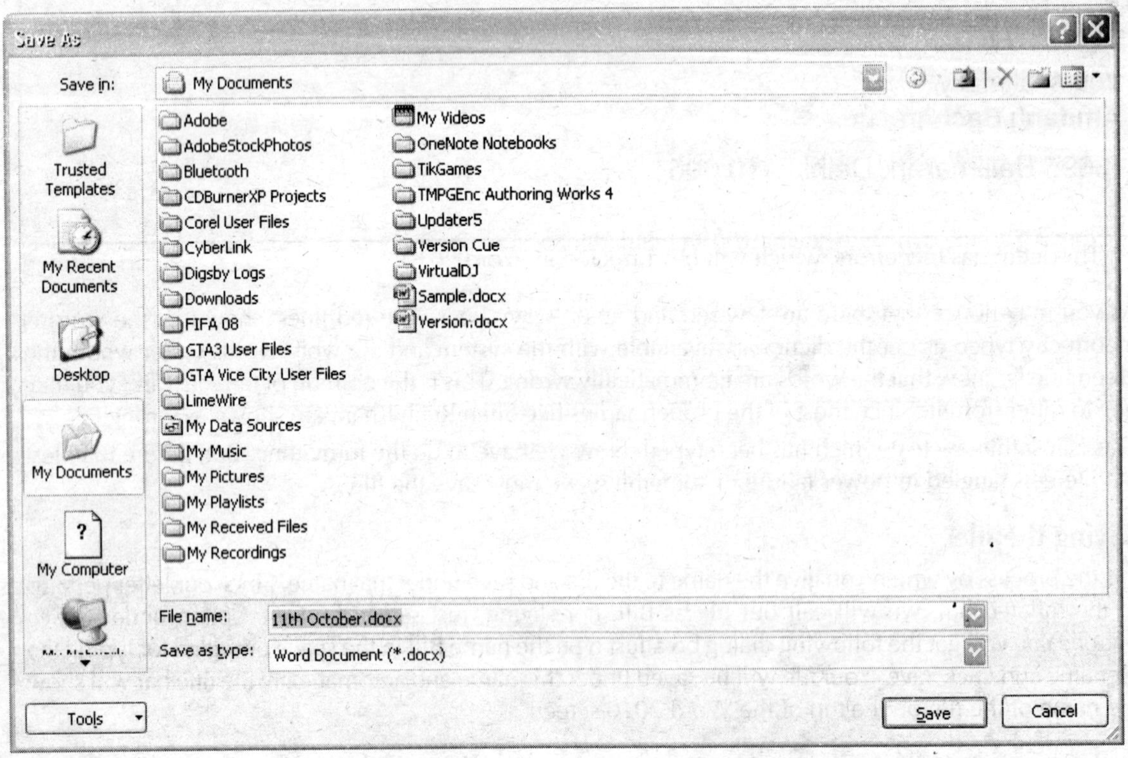

Save As

Save in: My Documents

Trusted Templates
My Recent Documents
Desktop
My Documents
My Computer
My Network

Adobe
AdobeStockPhotos
Bluetooth
CDBurnerXP Projects
Corel User Files
CyberLink
Digsby Logs
Downloads
FIFA 08
GTA3 User Files
GTA Vice City User Files
LimeWire
My Data Sources
My Music
My Pictures
My Playlists
My Received Files
My Recordings
My Videos
OneNote Notebooks
TikGames
TMPGEnc Authoring Works 4
Updater5
Version Cue
VirtualDJ
Sample.docx
Version.docx

File name: 11th October.docx
Save as type: Word Document (*.docx)

Tools | Save | Cancel

Now we come to other fomatting tools.

Formatting the text

Let us now start our formatting from the top. The first line containing address has nothing to be done. The second line containing To, has to be *italized.*

For this do the following:

1. Click the mouse button at the left of T of To.
2. Now drag the mouse, still having it pressed to the right so that the next character o also gets highlighted. At this stage both T and o are highlighted.
3. Now leave the mouse with To highlighted.
4. With the mouse, click at I in the formatting toolbar to make To as *To*.
5. See how To looks in the next figure.

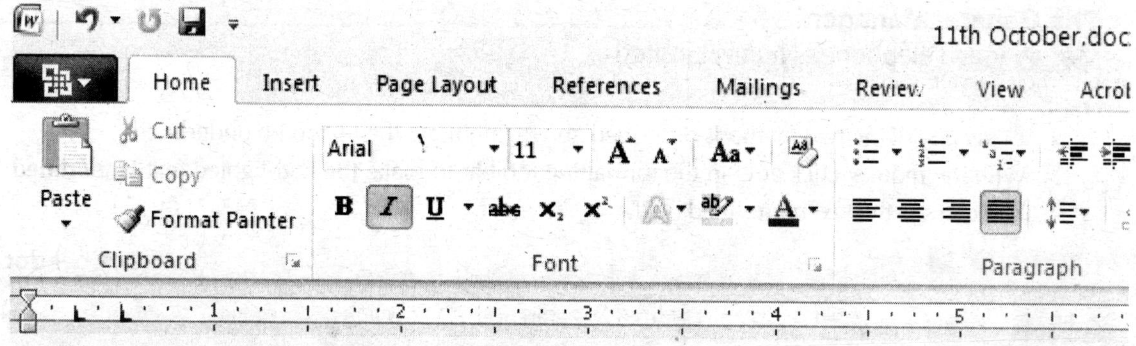

Now we come to the line having The General Manager. This line has to be made bold. This is how we do it.

1. Click the mouse button at the left of T of The General Manager.
2. Since we had highlighted the matter using mouse in the case of To, we will use a different approach here. Press Shift key and start pressing right arrow key ⇨. You will see that as the right arrow key is pressed the matter on the right gets highlighted. So highlight the matter till the point you want it to highlight. In this case highlight till r of Manager.
3. Now leave the shift key.
4. With the mouse, click at B in the formatting toolbar to make the highlighted text as **Bold**.
5. In the figure next, see how the text looks now.

Next in the line is the address, whose last line New Delhi - 110 001 has to be underlined. Word 2010 allows you the option of underlining the word with one or more lines. This option is available under Font. But for the time being, we will stick to single underline.

For this do the following:

1. Click the mouse button at the left of N of New Delhi - 110 001.

CHAPTER 2

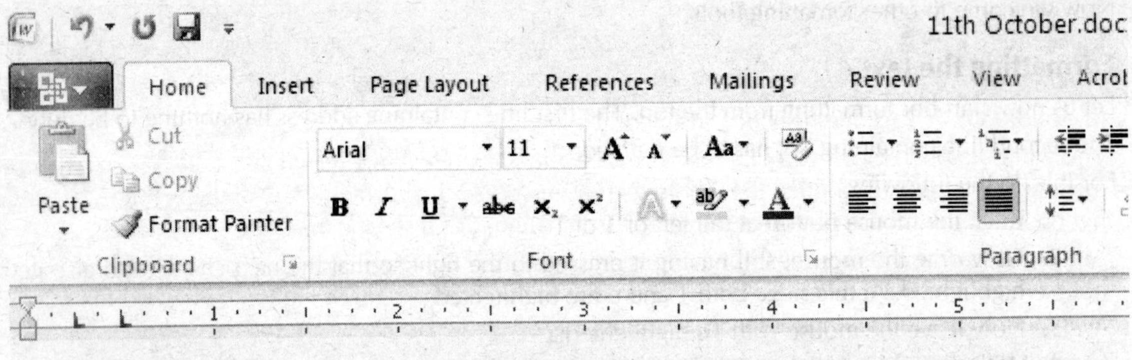

11th October, 2010

To,

The General Manager

Mahanagar Telephones Nigam Limited

2. Using any of the two methods described above, highlight the text to be underlined.
3. With the mouse, click at U in the formatting toolbar to make the highlighted text **Underlined**.
4. You can see the text underlined next.

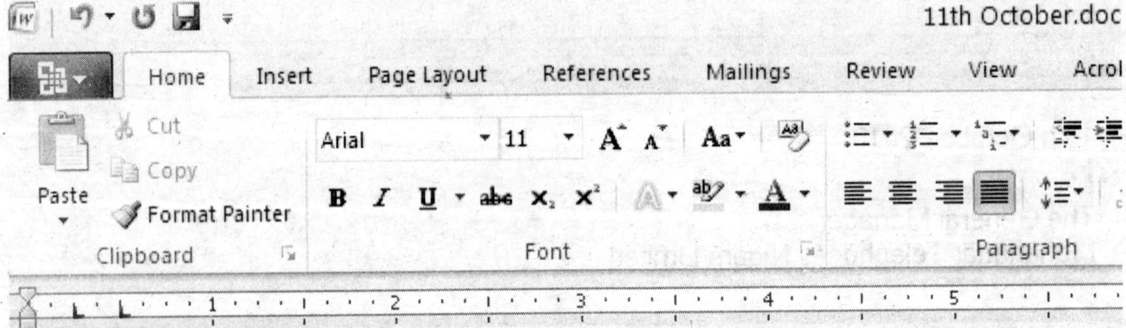

11th October, 2010

To,

The General Manager

Mahanagar Telephones Nigam Limited

Khurshid Lal Bhawan

New Delhi - 110 001

Ref: Telephone No. 4611098

Coming down now you see the line containing the telephone number. This line has to be underlined and centralized. I am not describing here the method to underline this line since it is similar to the one followed by you in the above case. I am sure you can do it yourself. Let us now concentrate on alignment. Let us see how it is done in Word 2010.

Alignment of Text

Word 2010 gives you the option of placing the text in four different alignments. These are:

Left aligned This line is left aligned.

Right aligned This line is right aligned.

Centralized This line is centrally aligned.

Justified This line has been justified.

You will not notice much of a difference here in left aligned text and justified text. This is so because the matter is small. Just notice the whole text of this book, it is justified, i.e., it aligns to the left and right both. Whereas this particular paragraph is left aligned and see the difference for yourself.

All the four alignments are there on the formatting toolbar. You can choose any one of them. (If you do not have all 4 of them, click at Add and Remove button on the right of the toolbar to add the missing alignment to the formatting toolbar.

Coming back to our text. We have to centrally align the line containing the telephone number.

For that do the following:

1. Click the mouse button at the left of R of Reference: Telephone No. 4611098.
2. Click at the icon which shows the centralized alignment.
3. Notice here that you do not have to highlight the text for alignment. This is so since the whole matter of the paragraph has to be aligned to the same alignment. It is not possible to align one word to one alignment and another word to another alignment.
4. You can see the text underlined and centralized aligned in the figure next.

Now that the next lines have nothing much to be done, expect that International calls and Amitabh Bachan have to be made bold. This I presume you will be able to do without any difficulty.

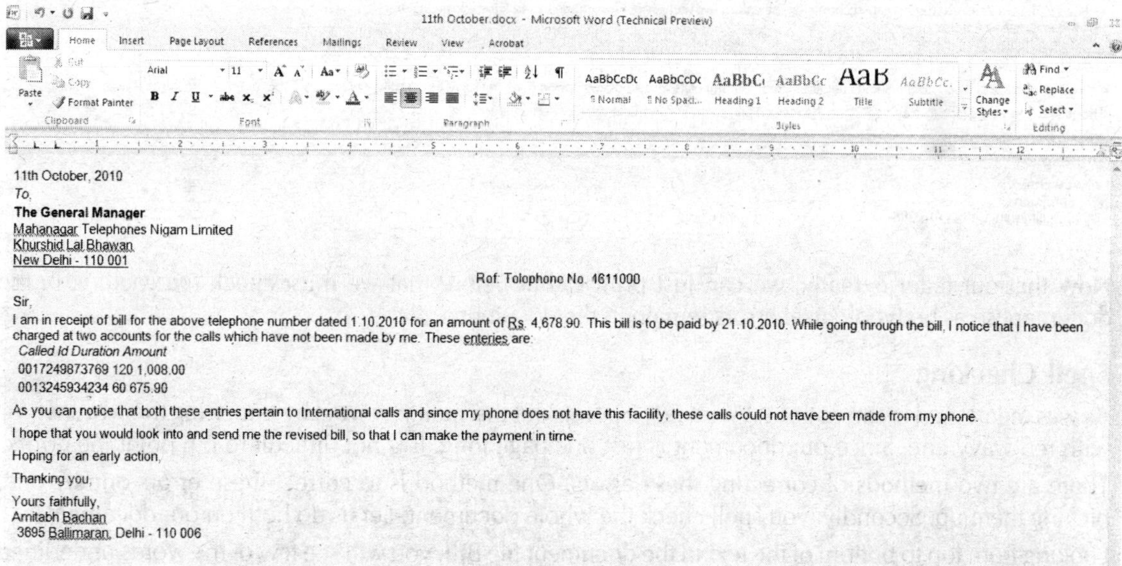

11th October, 2010

To,

The General Manager

Mahanagar Telephones Nigam Limited

Khurshid Lal Bhawan

New Delhi - 110 001

Rof: Tolophono No. 4611000

Sir,

I am in receipt of bill for the above telephone number dated 1.10.2010 for an amount of Rs. 4,678.90. This bill is to be paid by 21.10.2010. While going through the bill, I notice that I have been charged at two accounts for the calls which have not been made by me. These enteries are:

Called Id Duration Amount

0017249873769 120 1,008.00

0013245934234 60 675.90

As you can notice that both these entries pertain to International calls and since my phone does not have this facility, these calls could not have been made from my phone.

I hope that you would look into and send me the revised bill, so that I can make the payment in time.

Hoping for an early action,

Thanking you,

Yours faithfully,

Amitabh Bachan

3695 Ballimaran, Delhi - 110 006

It is time to save the document again so as to make sure that the changes made by you are stored in the hard disk.

Next, let us try to put some fancy things on the text. First among them is Font.

Applying fonts

It is upto you to select the same font for the whole text or have different fonts for different paragraphs. Let us see how it is done.

1. Click at any place in the text with the mouse.
2. Click at Select All in the Edit menu or simply press Ctrl and then A. This will highlight the whole text in the document.
3. Now you can select the font of your liking in the whole text. You can also change the size of the font too.
4. Select Arial for font and size 12 for the whole text in the Formatting toolbar.
5. This will make the whole text 12 points and will have Arial as the font.
6. The previous changes made by you in terms of **Bold**, *Italics* will remain intact and will not be disturbed by doing this.
7. Now if you want you can change the font of particular items like address, etc., to make it more decorative.

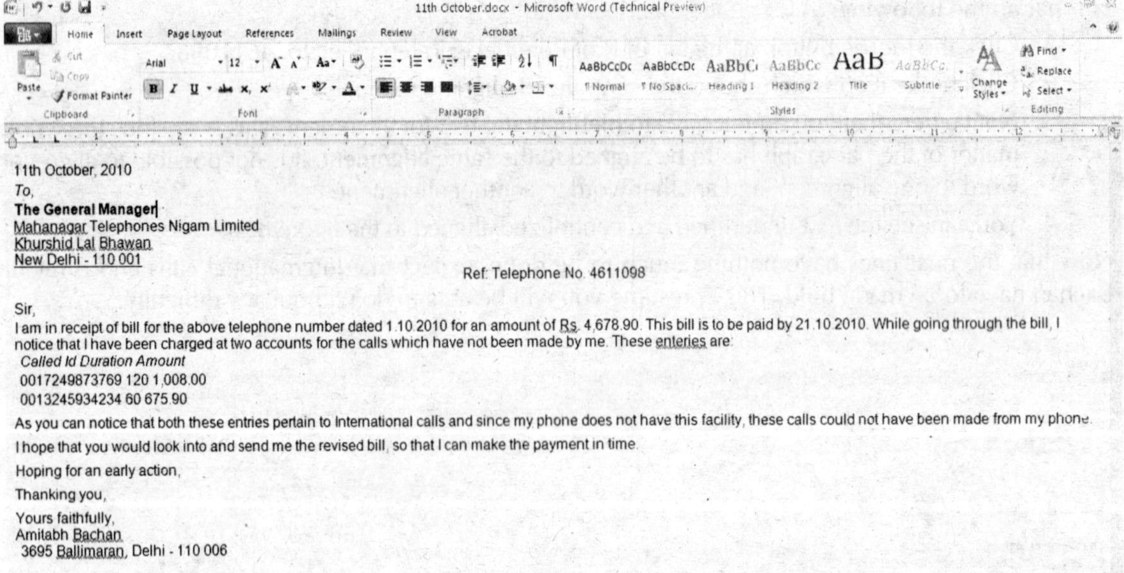

11th October, 2010
To,
The General Manager
Mahanagar Telephones Nigam Limited
Khurshid Lal Bhawan
New Delhi - 110 001

Ref: Telephone No. 4611098

Sir,
I am in receipt of bill for the above telephone number dated 1.10.2010 for an amount of Rs. 4,678.90. This bill is to be paid by 21.10.2010. While going through the bill, I notice that I have been charged at two accounts for the calls which have not been made by me. These enteries are:
Called Id Duration Amount
0017249873769 120 1,008.00
0013245934234 60 675.90
As you can notice that both these entries pertain to International calls and since my phone does not have this facility, these calls could not have been made from my phone.
I hope that you would look into and send me the revised bill, so that I can make the payment in time.
Hoping for an early action,
Thanking you,
Yours faithfully,
Amitabh Bachan
3695 Ballimaran, Delhi - 110 006

Now that our letter is ready, we can just print it, but before that we must check the spelling in the document so as no typological errors remain in the document.

Spell Checking

As was mentioned in the options, Word 2010 points out the spelling errors by underling the word/words with red wavy line. Since our document is just one page long. It is not difficult to pin point the errors. There are two methods of correcting these errors. One method is to correct these errors one by one, picking them up. Secondly, you spell check the whole document. Let us do both on our document.

Looking from top to bottom of the text in the document file Bill, you will see few of the words underlined by wavy red line. Few of them are the proper words and thus cannot be corrected.

Words like Mahanagar is basically a *Hindi* word, so it cannot be in the dictionary of Word 2010 and that is why it has been shown as an error. Similar is the case with enteries which is wrong and needs to be corrected. For this follow the following procedure:

1. Click with the mouse at any place within the word to be corrected, in this case enteries.
2. Now right click the mouse button.
3. A pop-menu will pop-up as shown next.

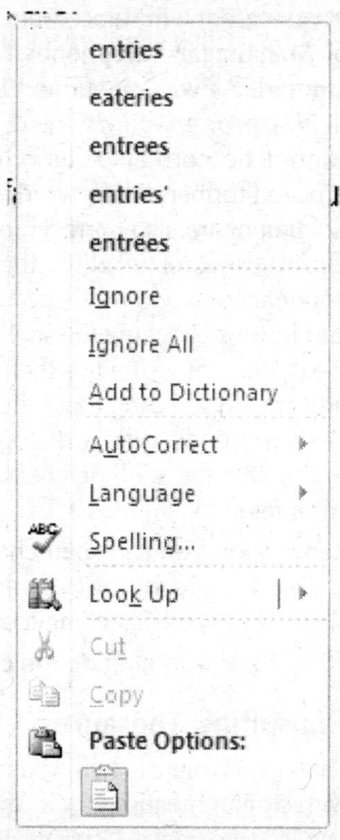

4. Among the various options are:

Alternative words: Word 2010 displays few words which are similar to the word in question with a hope that these may had been word in your mind while typing this word wrongly. You can choose any one of them, which you feel is the right word by just clicking and selecting that and leaving the mouse. The word will stand corrected with the new word and will replace the wrong word.

Ignore: It is like over ruling the dictionary and saying that whatever you have typed is right and would like the dictionary to ignore this not only at this place but also at all other places within the document.

Ignore All: This will allow you to ignore this error thoughout the document.

Add to Dictionary: You feel that this word is right and would like this word to be added to the dictionary so that it is not shown as an error in the future.

AutoCorrect: You will learn about AutoCorrect later. But, only thing to understand here is that it is a list of mostly misplaced word which can be corrected without referring to the dictionary. For example, you may have the bad habit of typing *the* as *teh*. You can add this to AutoCorrect to correct *teh* to *the* always without even telling you.

Language: You feel that this particular word which has been pointed as wrong by the current dictionary would be available in other language dictionary. So mention here the name of the other dictionary where this word could be found. If you do not have a second dictionary loaded, just ignore this.

Spelling: By clicking at this, you can start the spell checking of the whole document from this point onward.

Look Up: It looks for an alternative word in the Thesaurus.

Cut, Copy and Paste: These can be used for transferring the word to some other place in the document by cutting or copying it at this place and pasting it there.

5. In our case we will accept entries as the correct substitute for the wrong word enteries.

Since there is no other word which is to be corrected here. The corrected text would now look like the one shown next. Now we come to the second way of spell checking which is checking the whole document. In this case place the cursor at the beginning of the text in the document. In our case we will place the cursor at the left of 1 of 11th January.

From here do either of the following to start the spell checking.

1. Select Spelling and Grammar from the Tools menu.

   Or

2. Press F7

   Or

3. Click at Spell Grammar in Proofing panel of Review.

This will initiate the spell checking process and will start the spell checking of the document with each word of the document being searched with the similar word with the words available in the dictionary. If not found it will point out.

CHAPTER 2

In our case it will select *Mahanagar* of **Mahanagar Telephones Nigam Limited**. As was mentioned before it is a proper *Hindi* word, so it cannot be corrected. Ignore it to proceed further. Other words in the document are also correct. So keep clicking Ignore for all of them till you reach the end of the document and it stops checking the spelling of the document. After this there is no other word to correct and the spell checking ends with a dialog box, saying that the spelling checking is complete.

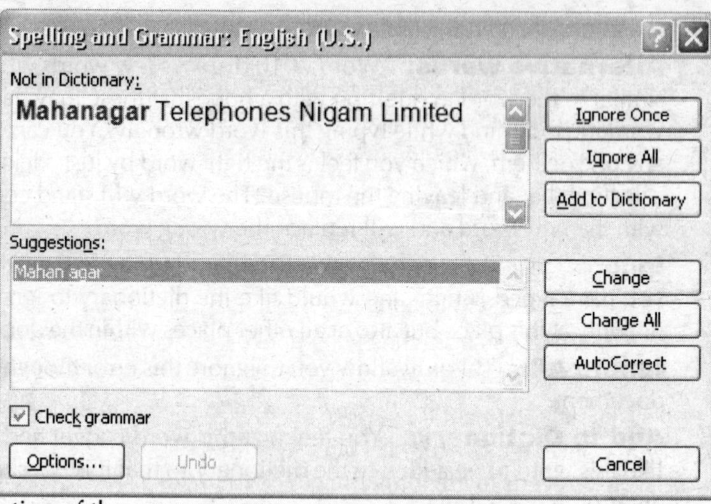

Remember, you can spell check a portion of the text or a word by just highlighting it and then clicking at Spell Checking Icon.

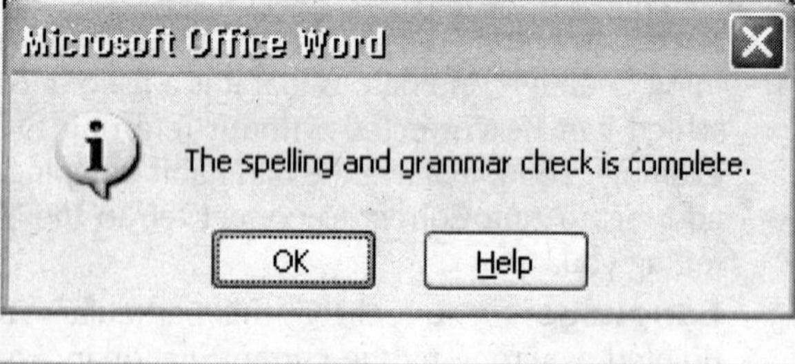

Then there is another option called Thesaurus.

Consulting Thesaurus

Thesaurus is there to help you find Synonym, words with similar meanings and Antonym, words with opposite meanings. Using the thesaurus not only helps your vocabulary, but gives you alternatives to using the same word over and over again throughout your text.

Let us try to use this option in our text. We would like to see the alternatives to the word Bill. For this we do the following:

1. Select the word bill in the second line of the paragraph.
2. Now select Thesaurus from the Proofing panel.
3. You will get the dialog box as shown here.
4. The options given here are Invoice as the main. But there are others too like statement, check, etc.
5. You have the option to select a new word Invoice or other or let the bill remain as it is.

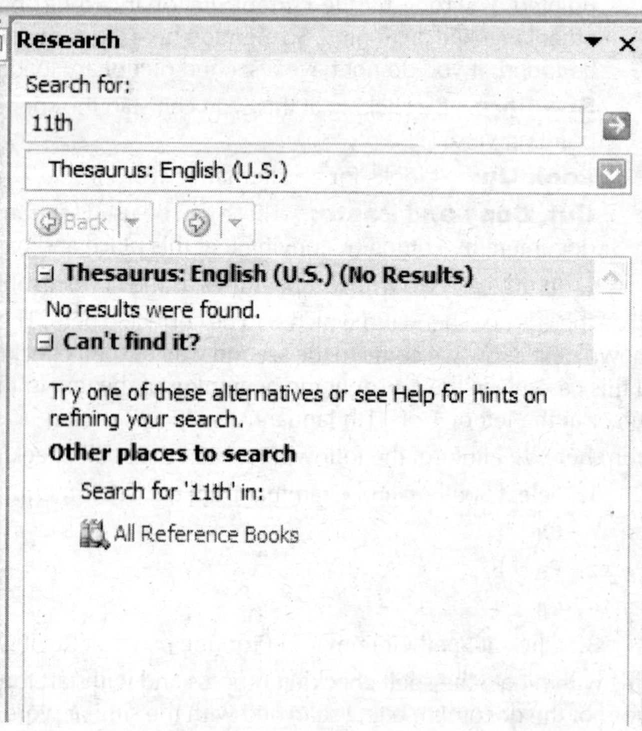

Assign Character Styles

Styles are sets of formatting attributes that you can apply to text in your document. Typically styles are applied to whole paragraphs and allow you to use preset formatting for headings, captions, numbered paragraphs, and so forth. However, Character styles are useful when you find yourself using the Format Painter over and over again to apply character formatting.

Character styles add to the current formatting of text. For example, if the text is 12 point Arial italics and your character style applies **bold** and **strikethrough**, the text to which you apply the character style will be 12 point **Arial bold**, *italic*, and ~~strikethrough~~.

Assign a Character Style

1. To apply a style to existing text, select the text to which you want to assign the style. If you want to apply a style as your are entering new text, place your insertion point where you want the newly styled text to appear.
2. Choose a style from the Style panel on the Home menu. When you click the Style box, you see each style name displayed in the style's font. An underlined "a" indicates a character style.
3. Click the name of the style you want to use to apply the style to the selected text.

When you want to remove the character style from selected text, apply the character style Default Paragraph Font. The text reverts to the formatting defined in the paragraph style assigned to the paragraph in which the selected text is located.

Create a Character Style

1. Open the Home menu and choose Styles. Click at the bottom right hand corner.
2. Choose New Style icon at the left hand bottom.
3. This will give you a dialog box, as shown next.
4. Type a name for the new style in the Name box.
5. Choose Paragraph from the Style Type box.
6. Choose Format then Font to set the style's attributes from the Font dialog box. Choose Ok.
7. To add a border or shading to the new character font, choose Format and then Border to open the Borders and Shading dialog box. Make your selections and then choose OK.

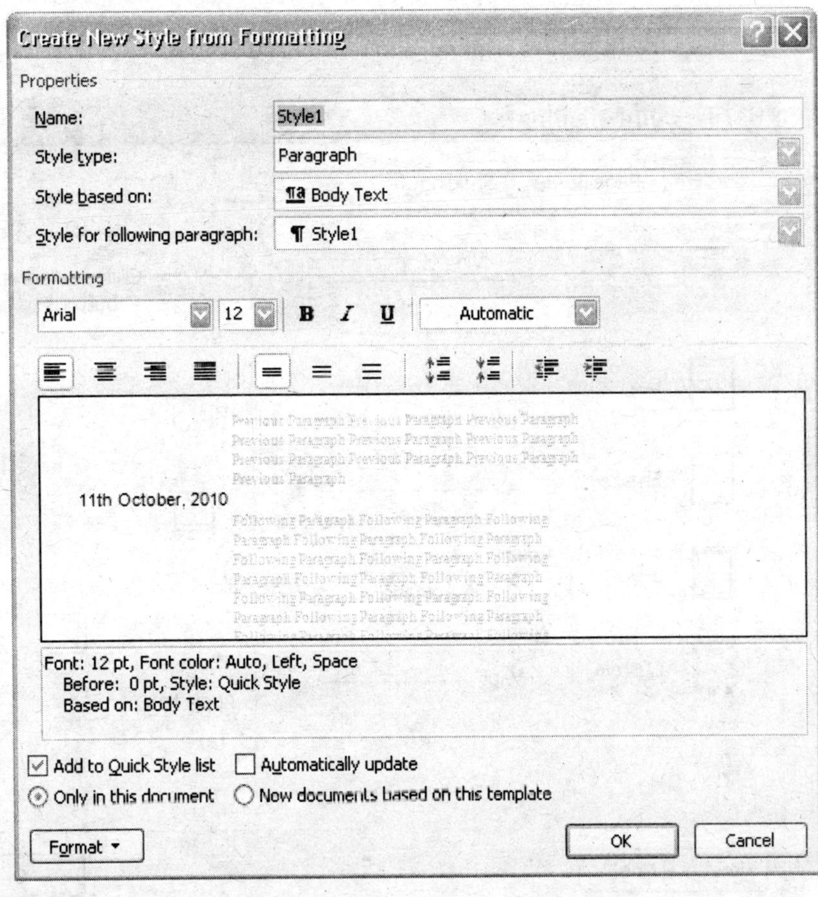

8. Choose Ok to close the New Style dialog box.
9. Choose Apply to apply the new style to current text. Choose Close to save the new style definition without assigning it to any text.

Creating a character style is easiest when you select text first, apply the font attributes you want in the new style, and then follow steps 1-5 above. You won't have to select any formatting, so skip to steps 7-8 to finish creating the style.

Borders and Shading

Word 2010 allows you to highlight headlines, captions, and other text of importance by applying a border or shading to that text. You can apply it to a piece of text or to the full text.

Apply Borders and Shading

1. Select the text on which you want to apply Borders or Shading. Basically the rules to follow this are:
   - If no text is selected, the paragraph where the cursor is, will be taken as the starting point.
   - If you select text within a single paragraph, but the paragraph mark itself is not included in the selection, the results affect only the selected text.
   - If you select text included in more than one paragraph (so that at lease one paragraph mark is included in the selection), the results affect all the paragraphs in which any of the selected text resides.
2. Open the Page Layout menu, and select Page Border.

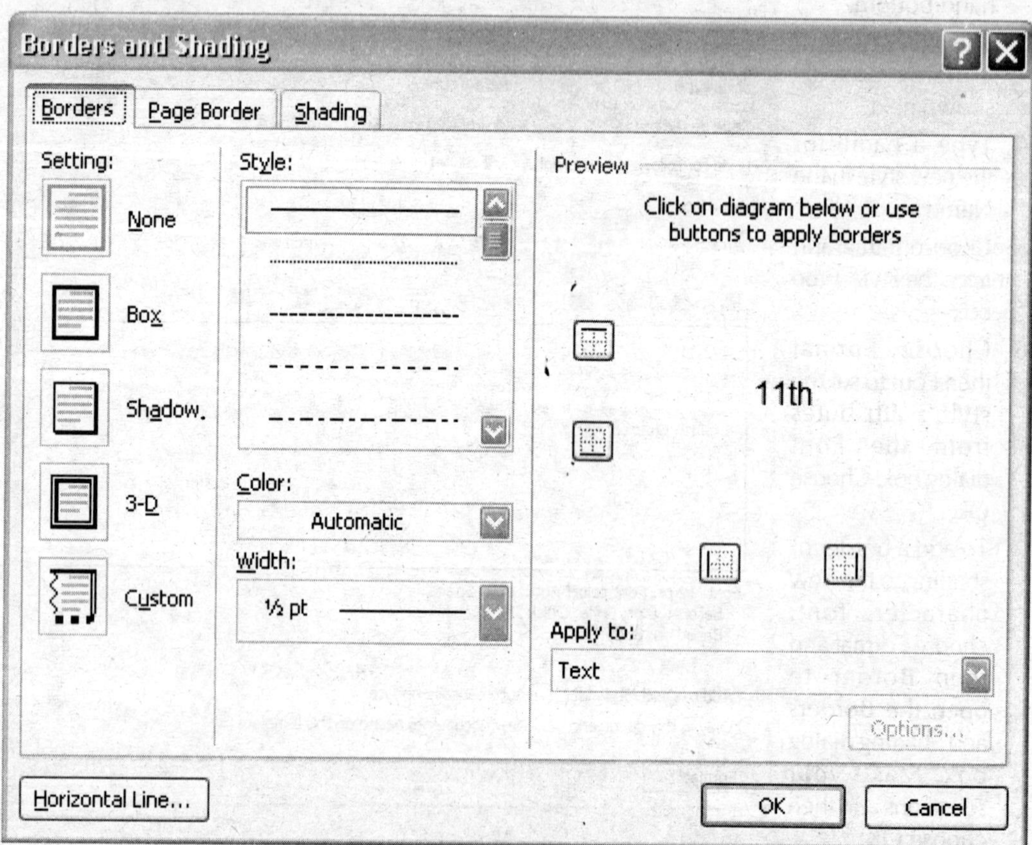

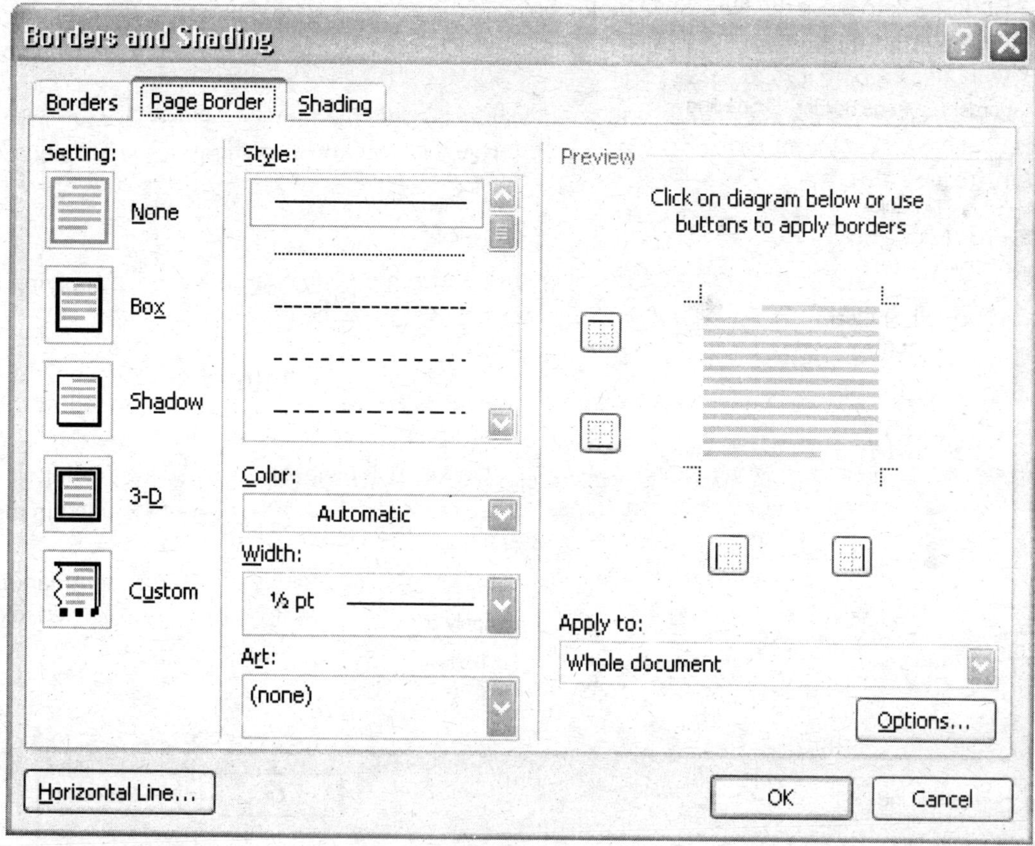

3. Click Borders to work with options available under it.

- Under Setting, click one of the preset border options.
- Select None to remove all borders from the selected paragraph(s), Box to insert a box border around the selected paragraph(s), and Shadow to insert a box border around the selected paragraph(s) and apply preset shadow formatting to the border.
- Select 3-D to insert a box border around the selection and apply preset 3D border formatting. Choose Custom to create a border using the options you click in the Preview window. When you choose any of these settings, the current selections in Style, Colour, and Width apply to the borders.
- From the Style list, select the type of line you want to use for the border, including *dotted, dashed*, and *wavy lines*.
- Click the Color drop-down list to select a colour to apply to the border.
- From the Width drop-down list, choose the thickness of the border line from ¼ point to 6 points.
- In the Preview box, click the individual border lines or use the border line buttons to apply or remove borders or change the attributes of a particular border (select the attributes first and then add the border).
- From the Apply To drop-down list, select whether to apply the border to just the selected text or to the whole paragraph(s).

4. Select Shading to choose shading options.

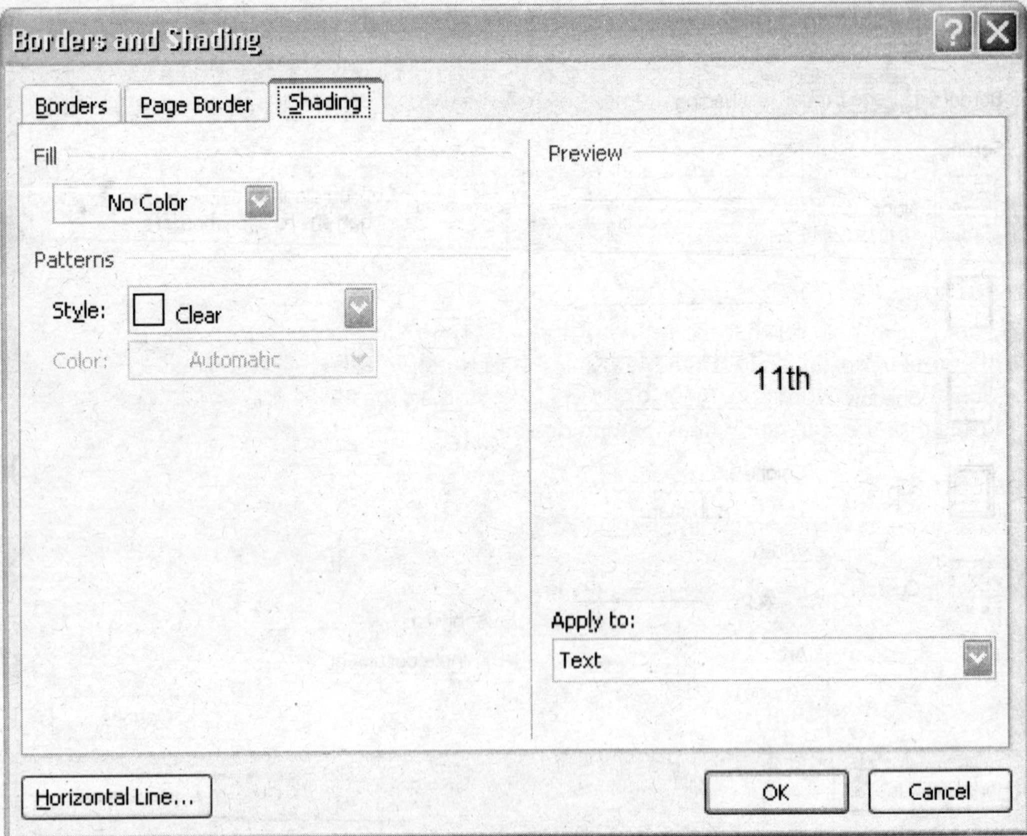

- Under Fill, select the colour or shade of gray with which you want to fill the selection. Click More Colors to see a larger selection of colours.
- From the Patterns Style drop-down list, choose a shading percentage for the colour you selected under Fill or a pattern of lines such as Lt Horizontal or Dk Trellis.
- If you selected a pattern of lines, select the Color of the lines from the drop-down list. The Fill colour then becomes the background colour for the pattern.
- From the Apply To drop-down list select whether to apply the shading options to just the selected text or to the whole paragraph(s).

5. Click Ok.

You can use all these options of Borders and Shading from the Tables and Border toolbar, which can be called from toolbar options.

This will allow you to select shading colours, border line styles, border line colours, and border line widths, etc.

Following are the button on the toolbar that apply to borders and shading.

Button	***Description***
Line Style	Sets the style of the border lines (dotted, dashed, wavy, double, and so on)
Line Weight	Sets the thickness of the border lines
Border Color	Sets the colour of the border lines
Borders	Specifies where the border appears (top, bottom, left, right, or box)

Shading Color	Sets the colour of the background shading for the paragraph (you cannot specify the percentage)

Since our letter is a formal one, we would not like to use any of these decorations. They have been told here so that they can be used at a later stage in another document.

Now that our letter is final. What we would do now is that we will close the file and then reopen and finally print. This is deliberately done so as to learn the concept of closing and opening of the file. If you want you can print the file as it is.

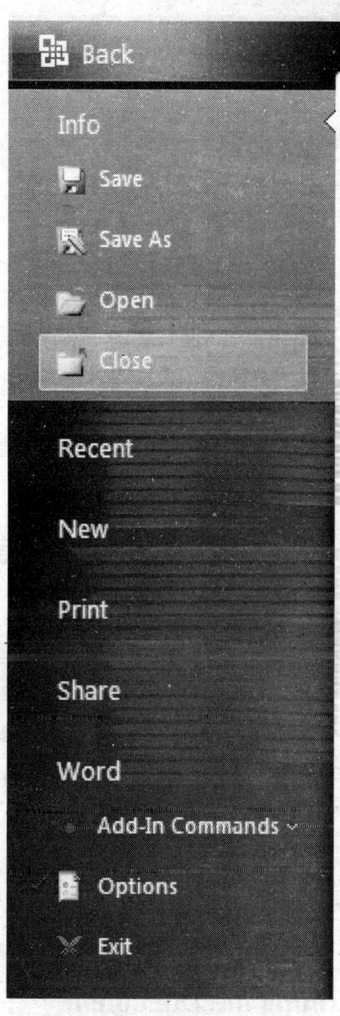

Closing of the File

As you would have noticed that there is no Close command in File menu. All you have to do is close the file using the ☒ button on the extreme right top of the word document. But don't forget to save the file before closing else the software will ask you to do so.

Save as option

Unlike the earlier options of Save As, this time in Word 2010 has different options for Save As. These can be seen here in the dialog box. The options are: Word Document, Word Template, Word 97-2003 Document, Find add-ins for other file formats, and Other Formats. These are self explanatory.

Printing Your Document

As mentioned earlier, no document preparation process is complete without printing it. For this we have the Print option under the File menu.

Once clicked it gives rise to a dialog box as shown here. The various options, which can differ depending upon the printer, which you are working on, of the dialog box are as follows:

Printer: Select the printer to which you want to send the printing. From the drop-down list, you can select one of the many printers which you may have installed under Windows.

Properties: Clicking at it would lead to a dialog box having the properties of the selected printer. If some adjustments are to be made in the properties of the selected printer, they can be done here.

Print to file: Sometimes it is possible that you may like to print the document to the printer which is not installed in your computer. In this case you will select this option and create a print file for that particular printer and copy the file and then print on that printer where it is installed.

Print range: You may like to print few selective pages instead of printing the whole document. So either click **All**, for printing all pages of the document or **Pages**, for defining the pages you want to print. You can even print the current page, i.e., page on the screen.

Copies: Word 2010 allows you to print multiple copies of the pages in the document. You can mention here the number of copies you want. What's more you can have the copies collated for you, if you select the **collate** option.

Print what: Various options available here are Document, Document properties, Comments, Styles, AutoText entries, Key assignments. But, most of the time you would be printing with Document option.

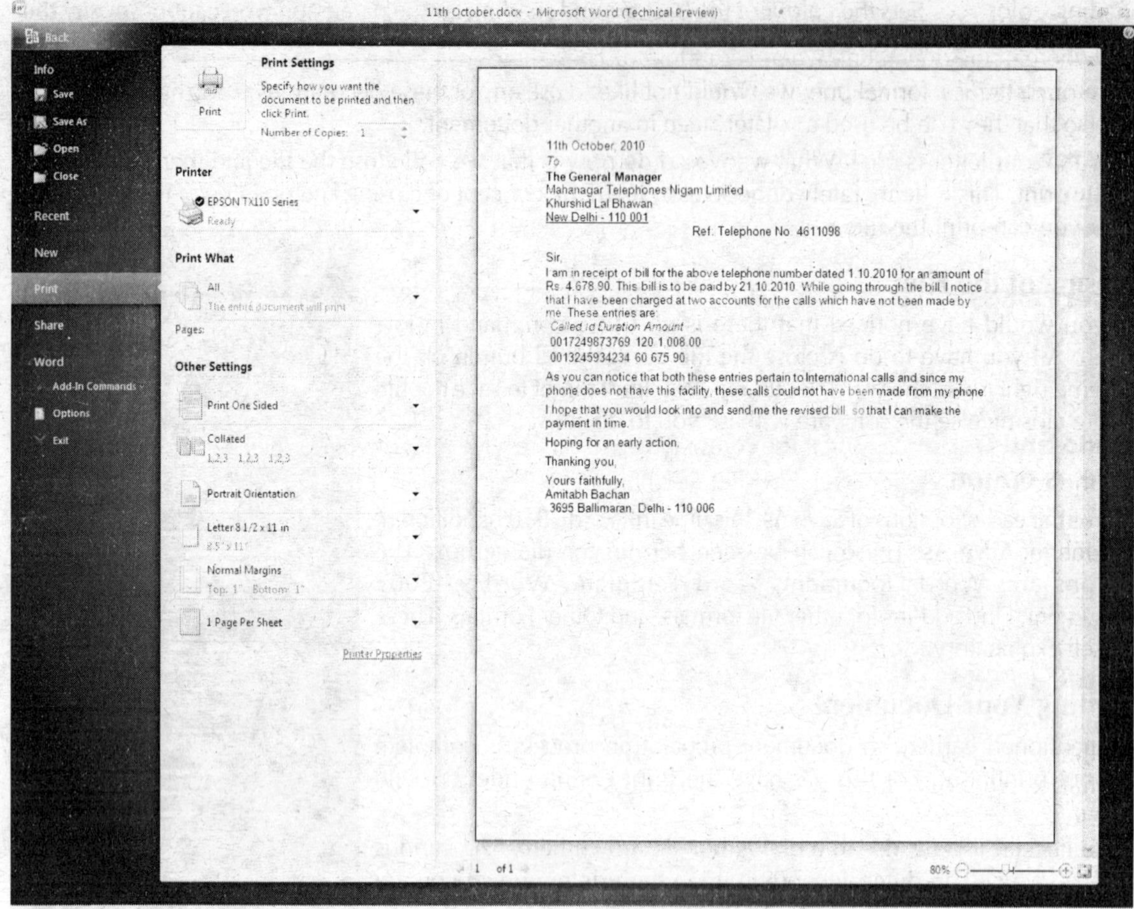

Print: You have the option of printing all pages or all **odd pages** or all **even pages**.

Zoom: Pages per sheet allows you to print 1 to 16 pages of the document on one sheet. Scaling allows you to scale your document to the various sizes of the paper.

Options: This will lead to the print options, already described under **Options** and select the option of your choice.

Once you are sure that you have selected all the options required by you, just click Ok to for document to start printing. However, do not forget to have the Printer ON before giving the final print command.

Editing the Document

Now that you have printed the document, you may want to either correct few words which you have realized that they do not look good in the letter. Even otherwise you may want to enhance the overall look of the letter. Besides this you would also learn how to do the tailor's job, i.e., Cut, Copy and Paste. There are other options too which may not be used in this letter but are quite useful overall for editing. Let us start with the proofing tools.

Editing Tools

Many editing functions are performed on selected text, such as cut, copy, move, and delete. There are various tools provided by Word to help you edit text:

Cut, Copy: Cutting and copying items places them on the Clipboard and you can paste these items anywhere in the document, wherever required. These items can be text, graphics, tables and any other object which is there in the word document. Cut and Copy can be performed using mouse and key strokes.

Paste: It is the command used to paste whatever is available on the Clipboard to paste it in the document. This is also done by the use of mouse and key strokes.

Move: It is an action associated with the mouse. However, if you cut and paste from one place to another, it can also be called move.

Insert Mode: It is the feature that adjusts spacing when you add new text to the document.

Overtype Mode: This option replaces the existing text with your new text.

Delete: It is an action you should reserve for text you want to permanently remove. Deleted text is not placed in the Clipboard. You can delete text with either mouse or key strokes.

Undo and Redo: Using these commands you can reverse the tasks performed earlier.

All these commands are available on the toolbar in the Home menu.

For either cutting or copying, you have to highlight the part of the text on which you want to perform this operation. All these commands have their keyboard strokes associated with them too.

Let us now learn few options of Word 2010 which help us in correcting our document with minimum efforts.

AutoCorrect

It is a handy feature of Word 2010 which automatically corrects common typing, capitalization, and spelling errors for you, as you type. It also enables you to type shortcuts that AutoCorrect replaces with the full text, such as typing BOMBAY and having AutoCorrect replace it with MUMBAI. This has been neccesiated due to the fact that the name of the city has been changed as thus. Although Word 2010 has a number of default AutoCorrect entries, you can add your own common misspellings and shortcuts.

It only checks whole words, so if you type TEH, Word won't replace it with THE until your press the spacebar, period, or some other key that indicates that the word is complete. It is also useful tool for applying formatting options. In a business letter, for example, you might want your company name to always appear in a certain font and size, regardless of the font you are using for the letter. By creating an AutoCorrect entry of your company name with formatting options, you eliminate the need to format while you type, or to run search and replace when you are finished with the letter.

Add AutoCorrect Entries Without Formatting

1. From the Office button, select Word Options, and then Proofing, AutoCorrect options.
2. Click Replace Text as You Type to place a check mark there, if it isn't already checked.
3. In the replace box, enter the text you want AutoCorrect to automatically replace for you, such as your initials or a word you commonly misspell.
4. Click Plain Text if it is not selected to inserted text without formatting options.
5. Choose Add. If the text in the Replace box is already listed, choose Replace to replace the existing replacement text with the text you entered in the With box.
6. Click Ok.

Text your new AutoCorrect entry by typing the word in a document and pressing the Spacebar.

Add New AutoCorrect Entries with Formatting

1. Type the text in your document and format it.

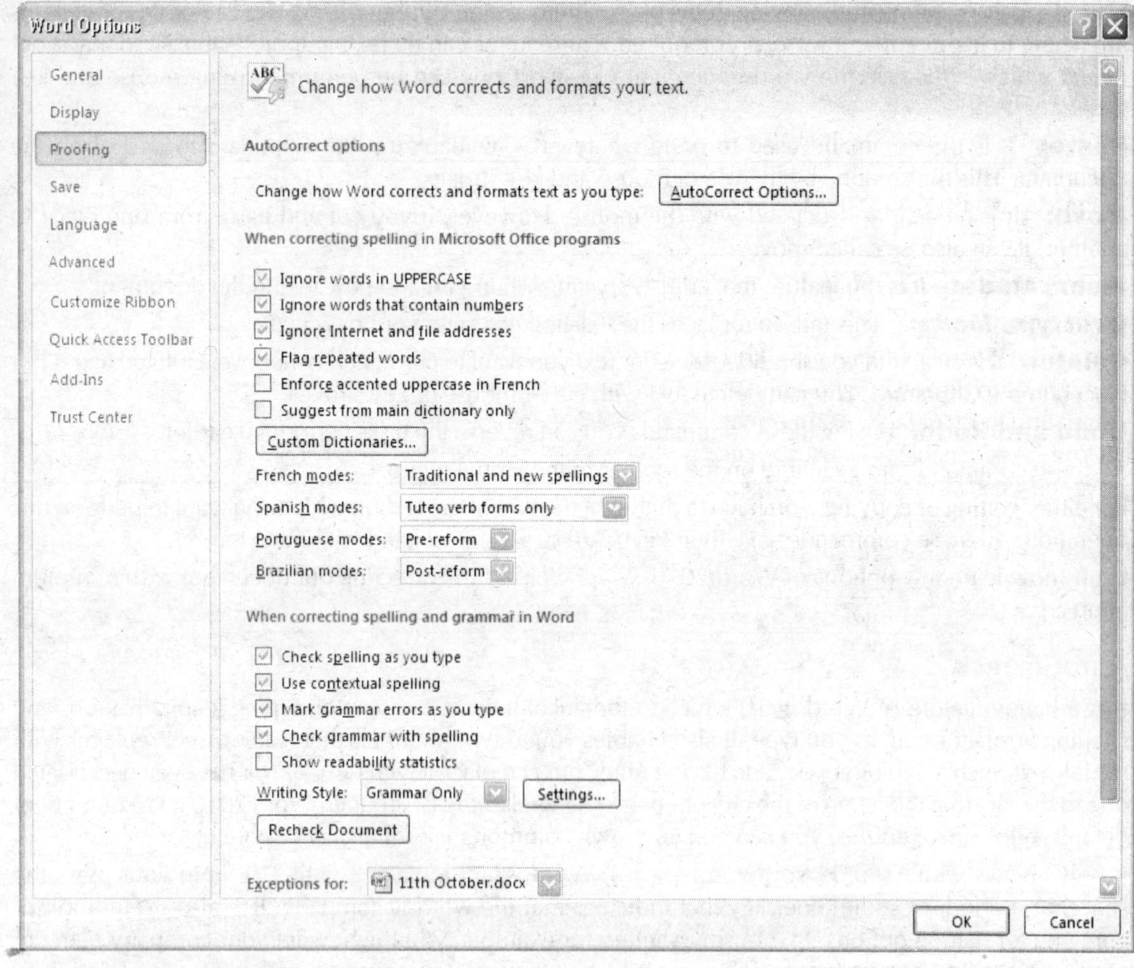

2. Select the text. To store paragraph formatting with your entry, include the paragraph mark at the end of the text, in your selection.
3. From the Office button, select Word Options and Proofing and AutoCorrect Options. The AutoCorrect dialog box appears.
4. In the Replace text box, type a name for the AutoCorrect entry (an abbreviation, or the entire word or phrase).
5. Click Formatted Text.
6. To save the entry and close the dialog box, click Add.

Here you have an option for Math AutoCorrect tool, which allows you to create mathematical characters, by just writing the english word for it.

AutoFormat

Word 2010 has automated a lot of small, tedious chores that we had to do manually in older word processing programs. Many of these are formatting chores, and Word collects them under the term AutoFormat. You can control what formatting chores Word 2010 performs automatically in the AutoFormat panels of the AutoCorrect dialog box. The benefit of using AutoFormat is that you can concentrate more on the content of your document and less on the details of formatting.

AutoFormat works on two different ways—as you type or on command.

AutoFormat as You Type

Automatically formats headings, bulleted and numbered lists, borders, numbers, symbols, and so on, as you type.

AutoFormat on Command

Automatically formats selected text or the entire document in one pass. You don't have to do anything to activate AutoFormat. By default, AutoFormat as You Type is enabled—you just enter text and Word formats it as you go. You can change the default to AutoFormat on Command, which allows you to manually run AutoFormat. This is similar to the way in which you can spell check a document—as you type, or manually, using the menu commands or toolbar icons.

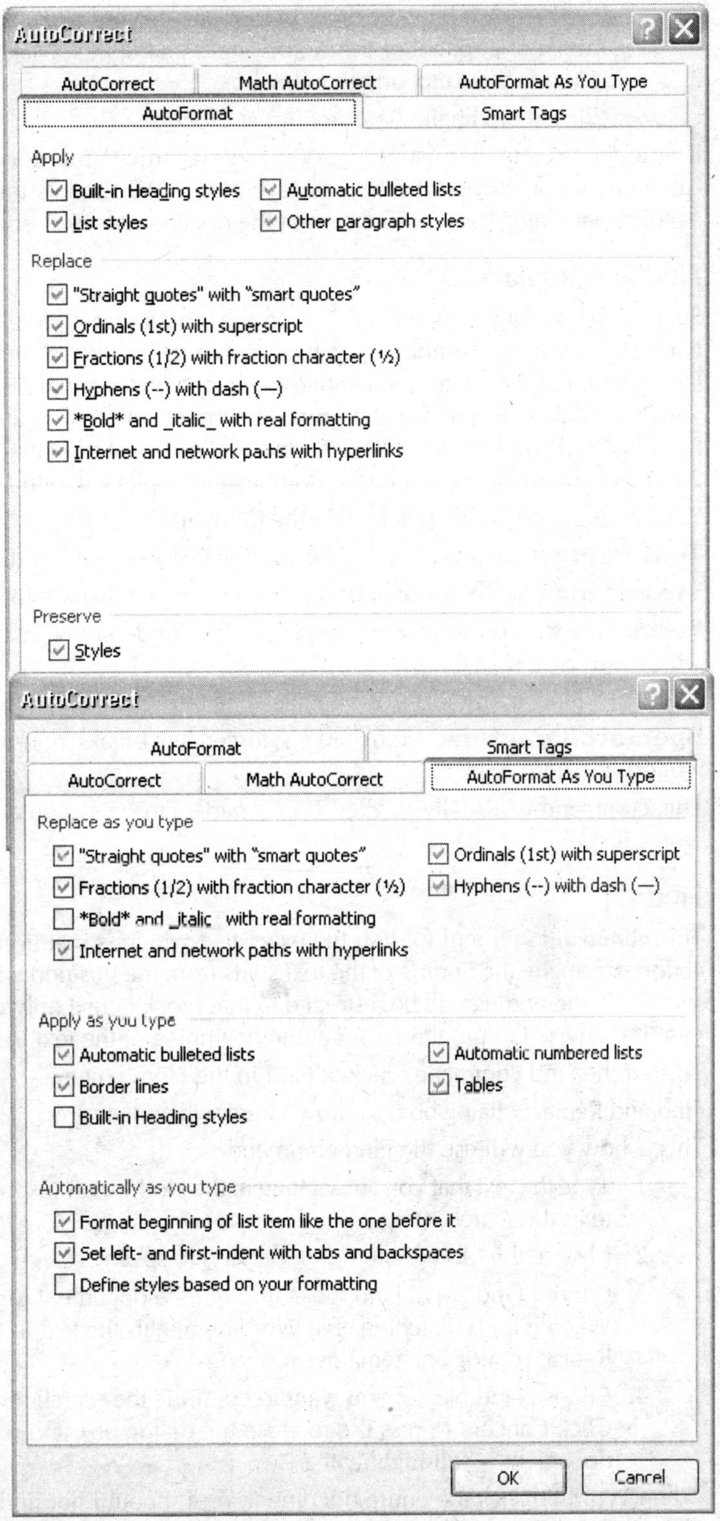

AutoFormatting Text

1. To AutoFormat a block of text, select it. To AutoFormat the entire document, make sure that no text is selected.
2. From the Office button, select Word Options followed by Proofing options. From here click at AutoCorrect options to get the dialog box.
3. Click AutoFormat.
4. Click AutoFormat and Review Each Change if you want the opportunity to accept or reject each change proposed by Word.
5. Choose the type of document you have created in the drop-down list labelled Please Select a Document Type to Help Improve the Formatting Process. This helps Word to AutoFormat the document properly.

AutoCorrect

AutoCorrect | Math AutoCorrect | AutoFormat As You Type | AutoFormat | Smart Tags

Apply
- [x] Built-in Heading styles
- [x] Automatic bulleted lists
- [x] List styles
- [x] Other paragraph styles

Replace
- [x] "Straight quotes" with "smart quotes"
- [x] Ordinals (1st) with superscript
- [x] Fractions (1/2) with fraction character (½)
- [x] Hyphens (--) with dash (—)
- [x] *Bold* and _italic_ with real formatting
- [x] Internet and network paths with hyperlinks

Preserve
- [x] Styles

AutoCorrect

AutoFormat | Smart Tags | AutoCorrect | Math AutoCorrect | AutoFormat As You Type

Replace as you type
- [x] "Straight quotes" with "smart quotes"
- [x] Ordinals (1st) with superscript
- [x] Fractions (1/2) with fraction character (½)
- [x] Hyphens (--) with dash (—)
- [ ] *Bold* and _italic_ with real formatting
- [x] Internet and network paths with hyperlinks

Apply as you type
- [x] Automatic bulleted lists
- [x] Automatic numbered lists
- [x] Border lines
- [x] Tables
- [ ] Built-in Heading styles

Automatically as you type
- [x] Format beginning of list item like the one before it
- [x] Set left- and first-indent with tabs and backspaces
- [ ] Define styles based on your formatting

OK | Cancel

6. If you want to limit the types of formatting Word does, choose the Options button to display the AutoFormat panel of the AutoCorrect dialog box. Make your selections and then click Ok to return to the AutoFormat dialog box.
7. Click Ok to begin the AutoFormat process.

If you choose AutoFormat Now, Word 2010 formats the document, and that's that. If you choose AutoFormat and Review Each Change, Word 2010 formats the document and then presents a new AutoFormat dialog box. This version of the document looks very different from the first version.

Find and Replace

Supposing you had prepared a thesis on the working of middle level managers in the city of Bombay. Naturally the word Bombay must have come in it quite a number of times. Then you hear that the Government of that State has decided to change the name of city from **Bombay** to **Mumbai**. What will you do? Will you be able to locate each occurrence of Bombay and physically change it to Mumbai? No! For this Word 2010 has an excellent option called Find and Replace. Once you give this command, Word 2010 will automatically search for Bombay and replace it with Mumbai.

You can use Find and Replace to do the following:

Text strings: Either strings of text embedded in words, or discrete words or whole phrases.

Text strings with formatting: Strings of text that are formatted a particular way, such as Bold.

Formatting: Font formatting options, such as underlining and bold, that are not necessarily associated with words or text.

Styles: Find all instances of a named style or replace one named style with another.

Special characters: Tab markers, forced line breaks, non-breaking spaces, non-breaking hyphens, whitespace, and so on.

This command is actually divided into 2 parts, Find and Replace. Let us see how the find command works first.

Find

This command will find for you the exact text which is mentioned in its box and will stop for further action. Normally the finding of the text starts from the position where the cursor is. If you have selected some text, the finding will be restricted to that block of text only. So if you have to select the entire text, then it is advised to put the cursor at the beginning of the text in the document.

To start the Find command, click at Find in the Home menu.

Find and Replace dialog box, as shown here will appear.

This is how you will use the Find command.

1. Type the text that you are seeking in the Find What? text box. This word or phrase is also referred to as the search string.
2. Choose the More button (if necessary) to specify search options.
3. Choose Find Next. Find looks through the document for text that matches your search strings. When it finds matching text, Word highlights the text in the document and stops. The Find and Replace dialog box remains on screen.
4. Choose Find Next if you want to continue the search for another instance of the search string. Click Cancel or press Esc to close the dialog box and return to the document. The text in the document is still highlighted.

When Word finishes the entire document, or if it could not find the search string in the document, a dialog box displays a message to that effect. Choose Ok to continue working in the document.

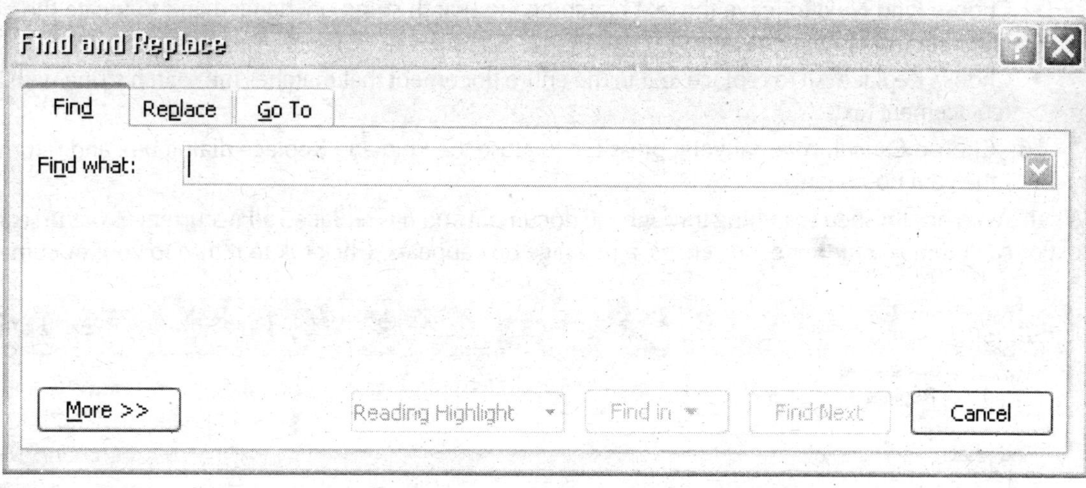

Replace Text

Next step after finding the required text is to replace it with some other text. For this we would call the command called Replace. To get the replace command click at Replace in the Home menu.

Now on the Find and Replace dialog box click at the Replace panel and do the following:

1. Type the text you want to replace in the Find What text box (in this case, *Bombay*). You can leave this field blank if you have to search for a formatting only. However, you have to search for something.
2. Type the text you want to replace it with in the Replace With text box (in this case, *Mumbai*). If you search for text and leave this field blank, you are in effect telling Word to delete all instances of the search strings, because they would be replaced by a blank.
3. Choose the More button (if necessary) to specify search options.
4. Choose Find Next to locate and highlight the first occurence of text that matches your search string.
5. Then do one of the following:

- Choose Replace to replace the text matching the search string with the replacement text and then locate the next occurrence of the search string in your document.

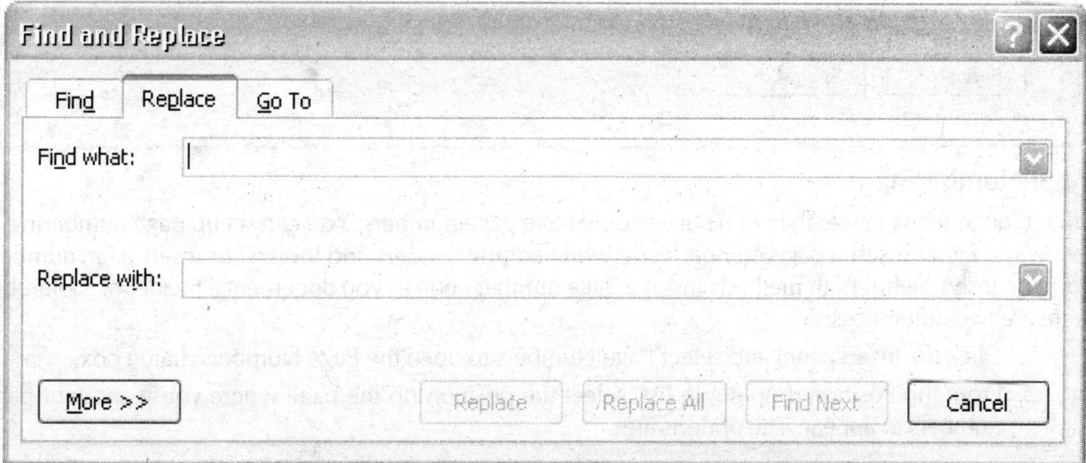

- Choose Find Next to leave the text matching the search string unchanged and to locate the next occurence of the search string.
- Choose Replace All to replace text in the entire document that matches the search string with the replacement text.

6. Choose Cancel. Alternatively, press Esc to close the Find and Replace dialog box and return to the your document.

When Word has finished searching through the document and has replaced all occurrences of the search text or can't find any further occurrences, a message box appears. Click Ok to return to your document.

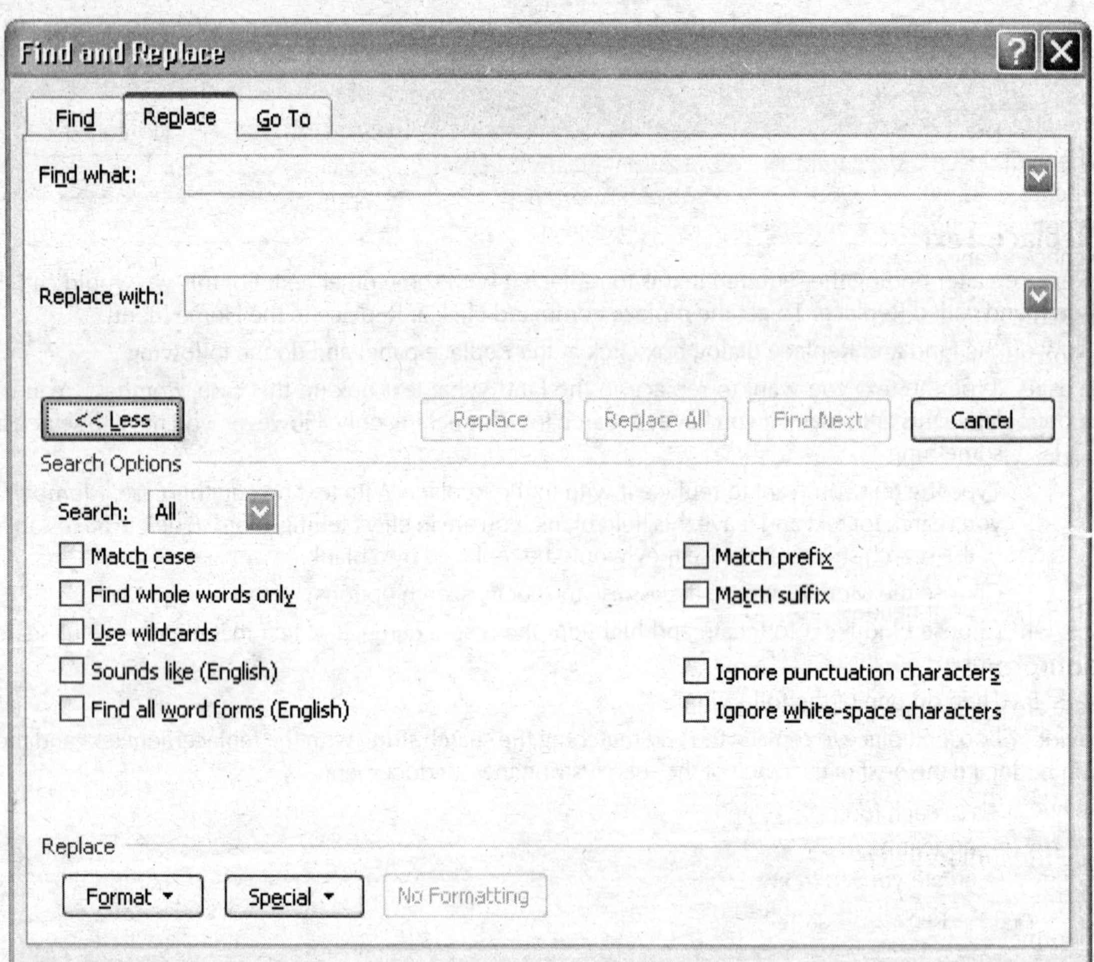

Page Numbering

Printed documents longer than one page should have page numbers. You can set up page numbering in two ways. Either insert a page number code while editing headers and footers, or insert page numbers from the Insert menu. Both methods insert a page number code in you documents' header or footer, but there are two differences.

1. Click the Insert panel and select Page Numbers to open the Page Numbers dialog box.
2. From the Position drop-down list, select the position on the page where you want your page numbers to appear. The options are:

Top of the Page (Header)
Bottom of the Page (Footer)

3. From the alignment drop-down list, select Left, Center, or Right to specify the horizontal position of the page number in relation to the right or left margins.
4. If you want the page number to appear on the first page, Show number on first page to place check mark there. Deselecting this option creates a separate header or footer for the first page.
5. Click Ok.

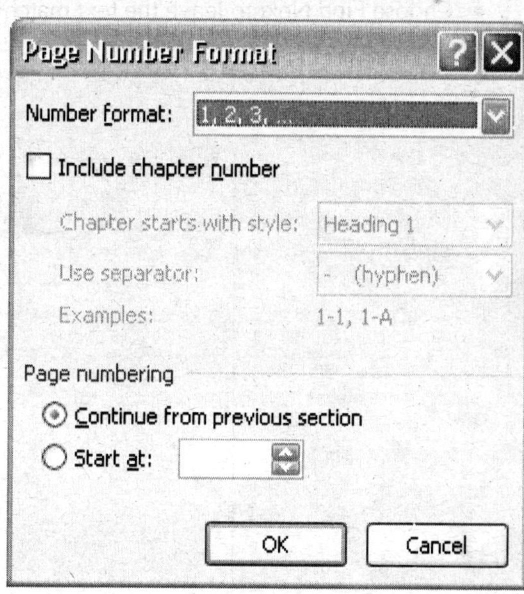

When you insert a page number, Word automatically switches you to Print Layout view so you can scroll to the portion of the page where the page number appears to check its appearance.

Header and Footer

As you must be knowing that Header appears on the top of the page and Footer appears on the bottom of the page. Word 2010 allows you to put both of them on the document pages. Once clicked they give you the options to choose from.

Headers and footers can vary within a document. Choices include:

1. The same header and footer on every page.
2. A different header and footer for the first page only
3. Different headers and footers for odd numbered pages than those on even numbered pages.
4. Different headers and footers for each section of the document.

Footnotes and Endnotes

These are used in the documents to provide references to the source documents for the document text, to provide more detailed explanations and definitions that might otherwise distract the reader if left in the main body of the document.

The two parts to each footnote or endnote are the reference mark—a number, character, or combination of characters appearing in the body of the document—and the note text. You may automatically number the marks or create your own custom marks. If you use the automatic numbering, Word renumbers the note reference marks if you add, delete, or move notes. The note can be of any length and format, and you can format the line that separates the notes from the body of the document.

To view the note text, rest the mouse pointer on the note reference mark. The note text appears in a pop-up box above the mark. Double-click the note reference mark to display the note text in a note pane at the bottom of the screen. If you are using Print Layout view, footnotes display at the bottom of the page, endnotes at the end of the document.

Add a Footnote or Endnote

1. Place curosr where you want the note reference mark to appear.
2. Choose the Reference menu and select Insert Footnote. The Footnote dialog box appears.
3. Select Footnote or Endnote.

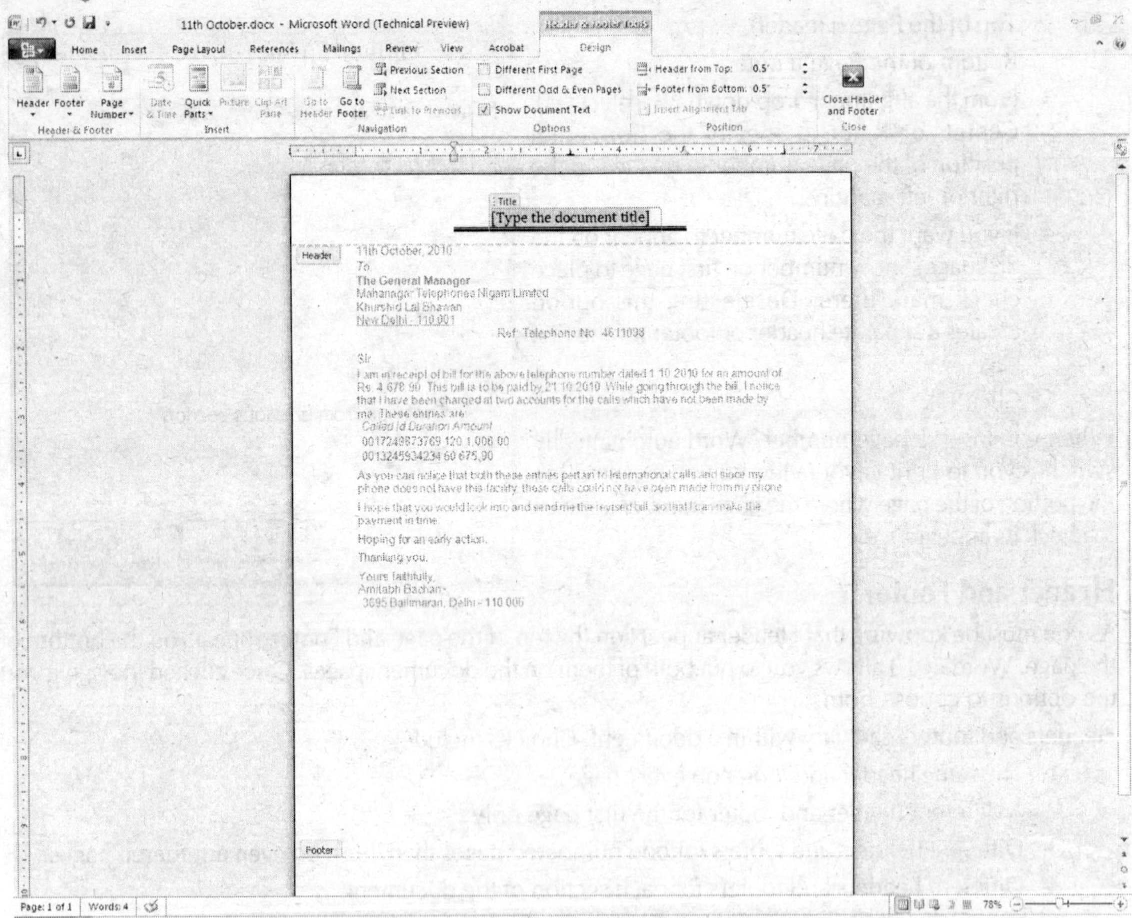

4. Under Numbering, select AutoNumber or Custom Mark. If you choose Custom Mark, insert the symbol or symbols for the reference mark or choose Symbol to open the Symbol dialog box. Choose a font, click the symbol you want to use, and then click Ok.
5. Choose Ok to close the Footnote and Endnote dialog box.
6. Type the note text in the footnote pane. Apply formatting as desired or, better yet, reformat the Footnote text style (which automatically appears in the Style list when you insert your first footnote).
7. Choose Close to close the footnote pane or click in the document to continue typing.

Splitting Panes

You can split a document window into two panes. Then, you can display different portions of the same document at the same time. This lets you compare two portions of a single document. It also makes it easier for you to move or copy text from one portion of a document to another. When you make a change to the document from either pane, the change is applied to the same document. As a result, the change can be found in both panes.

Splitting Document into Two Panes

1. Choose the New window command from the View panel, drag the separator bar to where you want to split the window, and click the left mouse button.

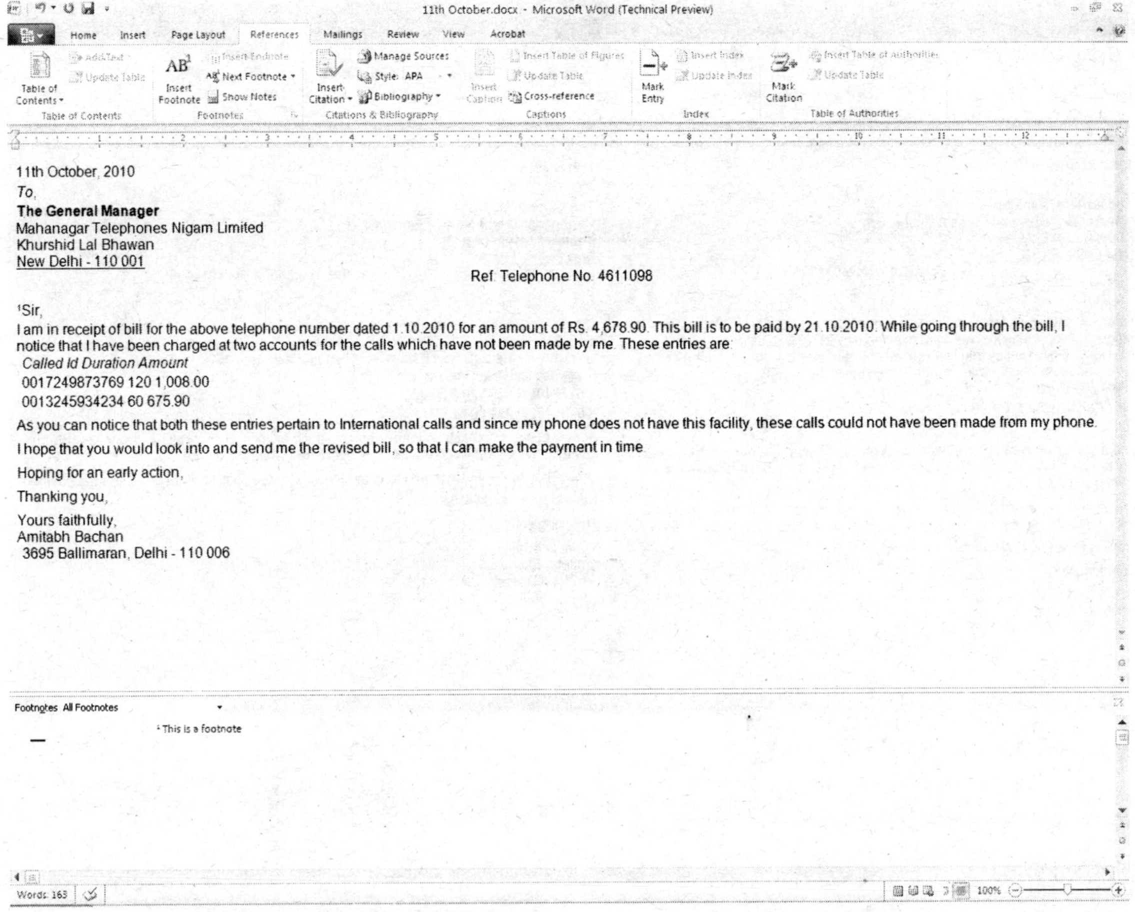

11th October, 2010

To,

The General Manager
Mahanagar Telephones Nigam Limited
Khurshid Lal Bhawan
New Delhi - 110 001

Ref. Telephone No. 4611098

[1]Sir,

I am in receipt of bill for the above telephone number dated 1.10.2010 for an amount of Rs. 4,678.90. This bill is to be paid by 21.10.2010. While going through the bill, I notice that I have been charged at two accounts for the calls which have not been made by me. These entries are:

Called Id Duration Amount
0017249873769 120 1,008.00
0013245934234 60 675.90

As you can notice that both these entries pertain to International calls and since my phone does not have this facility, these calls could not have been made from my phone.

I hope that you would look into and send me the revised bill, so that I can make the payment in time.

Hoping for an early action,

Thanking you,

Yours faithfully,
Amitabh Bachan
3695 Ballimaran, Delhi - 110 006

[1] This is a footnote

2. Use Remove Split to remove the split.

Tiling of the Documents

With tiling you can display two or more different documents at the same time. This makes it easy for you to compare two or more documents, or to move and copy text from one document to another. However, this works best when only two documents are open. Otherwise, the windows get too small for effective use. To return the display so only one window shows, just maximize the window that you want dispalyed.

To Tile Open Document Window

1. Choose the Arrange All command from the View menu.
2. The Arrange All command sizes the open documents windows so they are all the same height and so they are as wide as possible within Word's application window.
3. You can use standard Windows techniques to move, size and maximize the document windows and to switch between them.

Using MailMerge in Word 2010

MailMerge is one of the very important application of any word processing software. It has been given an important panel in the Word 2010. Word has indeed made it very easy to operate. In MailMerge you have the variable data coming from a data source which can be either a database file, spreadsheet, or even a

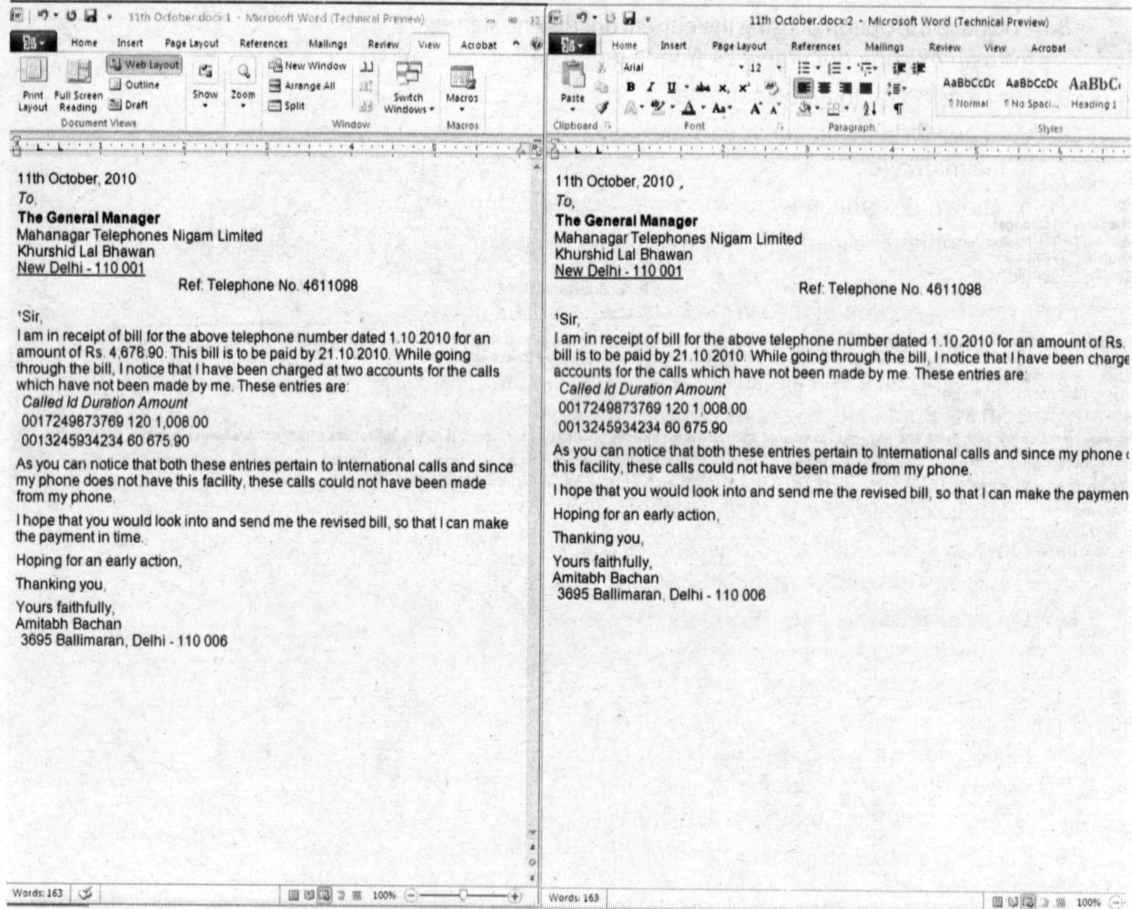

text file with fields marked in it. Then you have the document file whose text remains the same for all the subsequent merged files changing only the data which has been received from the source. So in fact you create multiple documents having the same text but having different fields depending upon the source.

Well, one can think of various usages of the MailMerge. The most important being sending the same letter to various parties. Sending the same invitation to various guests. Sending payment reminders to various creditors. Calling all the directors to the same board meeting. In all these cases, the text would remain more or less the same but the name and address of the receiver would change. You can even change the salutation too, for example, Dear Mr. so and so, picking the name from the data source.

MailMerge in Word is done in steps. Creating document (text), data source and then merging them before printing. Let us see how it is done. For your information, here I am creating a appreciation letter for the various members of the victories Indian Cricket Team. So, lets start.

1. Start Word 2010.
2. On the Panels menu, select Mailings.
3. From here on the Start Mail Merge, click at Step by Step Mail Merge Wizard.
4. As shown here, the first step is to select the document type.
5. Select Letters as shown here.
6. Click at Next to start document.
7. The second step as mentioned is to select the document.

8. You have the option of using the current document, starting from an existing document or from a template.
9. Step 3 asks you to type your letter.
10. We have written a letter to various people inviting them to the marriage.
11. As shown next the letter for the same has been type.
12. Now comes the part of selecting the recipients of the letter.
13. In the top portion of the Wizard, choose the Type a new list option and click at Create.
14. You would be given a blank dialog box to create a New Address Book. Here various options of filling the name, address, company's name, etc are given. Type the ones you want to use and ignore others. When you have types one, click at New Entry to go for the next entry.
15. Once you have typed all the entries, click at Ok. You would be asked to save the address list with a name.
16. Once again the same list would be shown to you for making the last minute correction, addition, deletion, etc. You can even change the sequence by sorting it.
17. In the next step, you would insert the field name at the place where it would be displayed. For this choose the option of Insert Merge Field, and then the field name, where it would be replaced with the actual data.
18. You will notice that the fields are shown within << and >>.
19. Next step would show you the preview of the letter by inserting the actual data from first entry into the letter.
20. Next step is to complete the merge.
21. This will create a file of all letters to be sent, one by one.

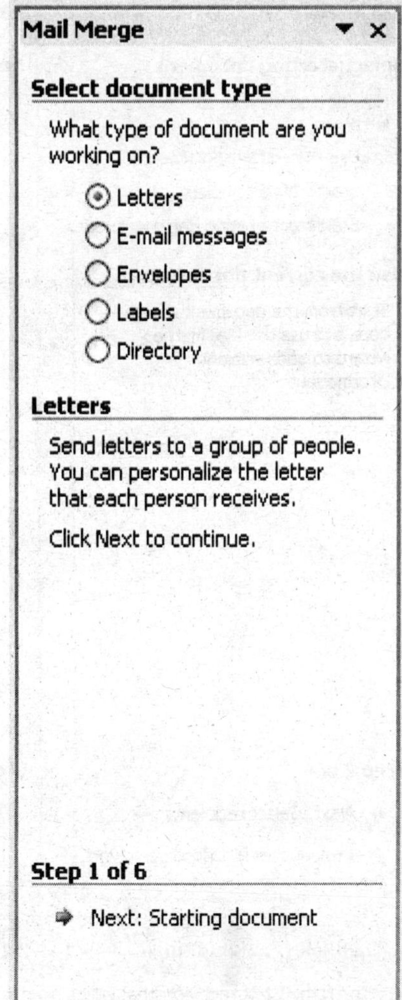

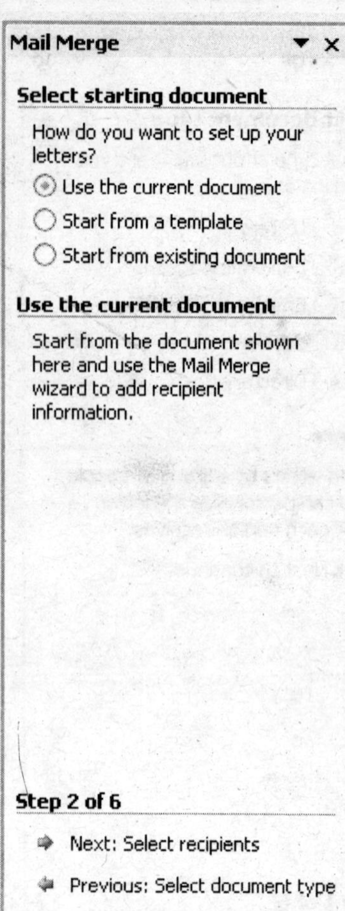
Mail Merge
Select starting document
How do you want to set up your letters?
Use the current document
Start from a template
Start from existing document
Use the current document
Start from the document shown here and use the Mail Merge wizard to add recipient information.
Step 2 of 6
Next: Select recipients
Previous: Select document type

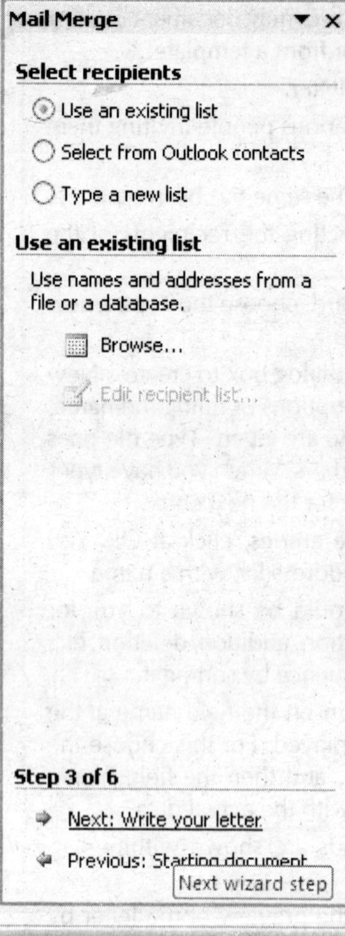
Mail Merge
Select recipients
Use an existing list
Select from Outlook contacts
Type a new list
Use an existing list
Use names and addresses from a file or a database.
Browse...
Edit recipient list...
Step 3 of 6
Next: Write your letter
Previous: Starting document
Next wizard step

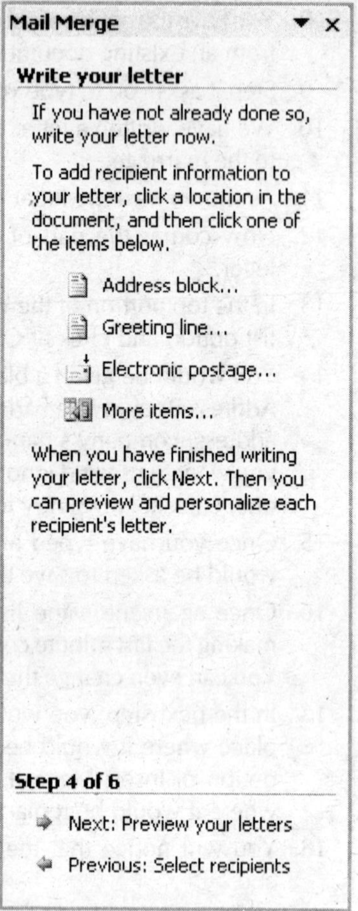
Mail Merge
Write your letter
If you have not already done so, write your letter now.
To add recipient information to your letter, click a location in the document, and then click one of the items below.
Address block...
Greeting line...
Electronic postage...
More items...
When you have finished writing your letter, click Next. Then you can preview and personalize each recipient's letter.
Step 4 of 6
Next: Preview your letters
Previous: Select recipients

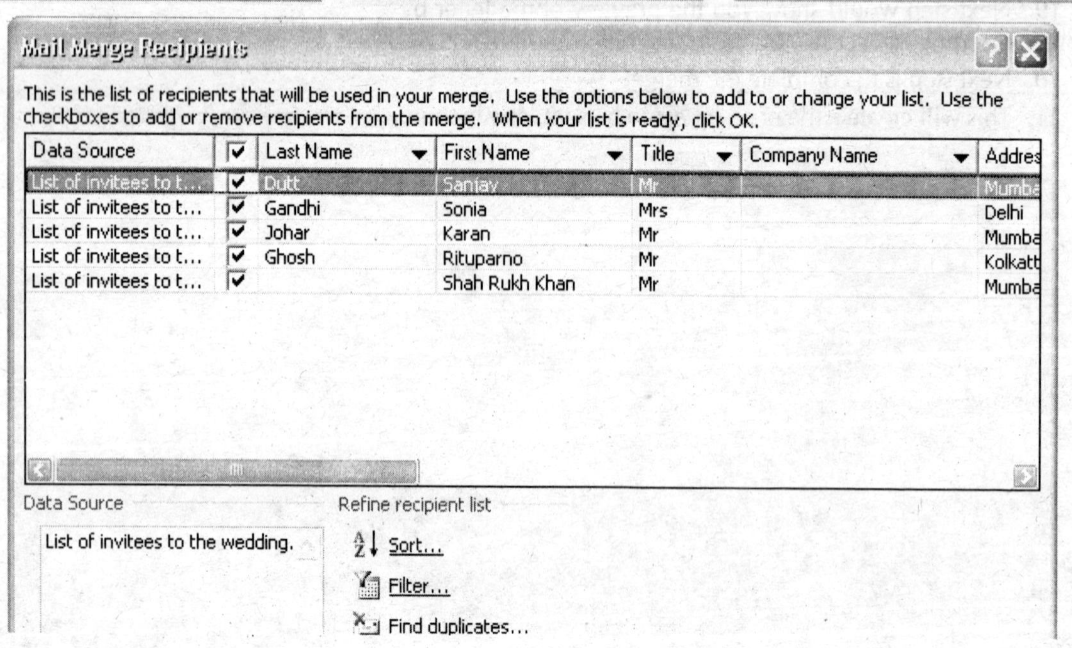
Mail Merge Recipients
This is the list of recipients that will be used in your merge. Use the options below to add to or change your list. Use the checkboxes to add or remove recipients from the merge. When your list is ready, click OK.
Data Source
Last Name
First Name
Title
Company Name
Addres
List of invitees to t... Dutt Sanjay Mr Mumba
List of invitees to t... Gandhi Sonia Mrs Delhi
List of invitees to t... Johar Karan Mr Mumba
List of invitees to t... Ghosh Rituparno Mr Kolkatt
List of invitees to t... Shah Rukh Khan Mr Mumba
Data Source
List of invitees to the wedding.
Refine recipient list
Sort...
Filter...
Find duplicates...

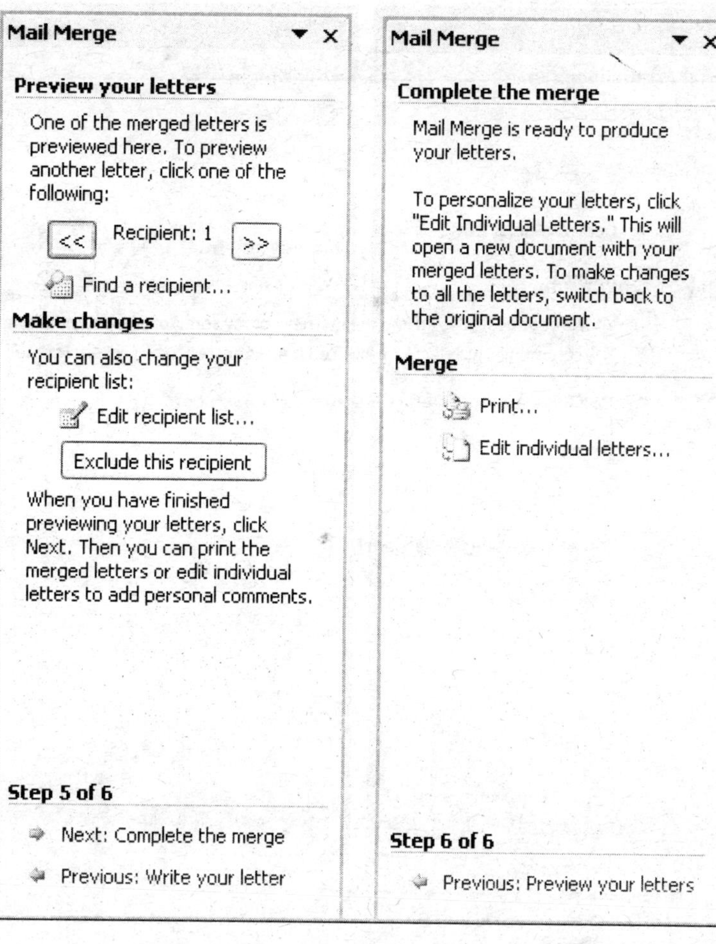

Dear Mr. Name

Addres1

Address 2

Address 3

Your are requested to attend the marriage of my son, Abhishek with Aishwarya on 20th of April, 2007. The ceremonies will start at 8 PM. You are requested to be present in time.

No gifts please. Your mere presence would be sufficient.

Yours truly,

Amitabh Bachchan

On behalf of the Bachchan family

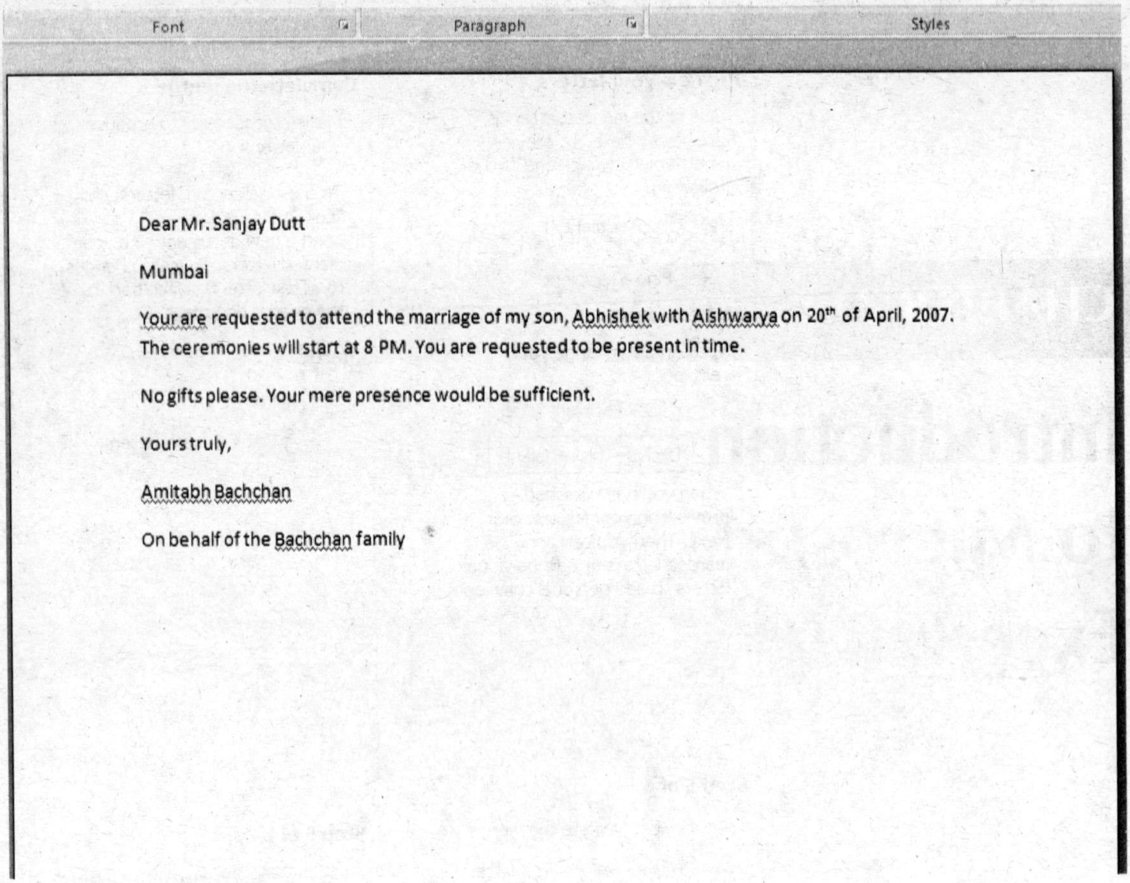

Font Paragraph Styles

Dear Mr. Sanjay Dutt

Mumbai

Your are requested to attend the marriage of my son, Abhishek with Aishwarya on 20th of April, 2007. The ceremonies will start at 8 PM. You are requested to be present in time.

No gifts please. Your mere presence would be sufficient.

Yours truly,

Amitabh Bachchan

On behalf of the Bachchan family

CHAPTER 3

Introduction to Microsoft Excel 2010

Introduction

This spreadsheet program allows you to manipulate and present your data in almost any way you choose. It allows you to work on a tabular pad consisting of columns and rows where you can perform all your mathematical, financial and statistical calculations. These calculations can be as simple as totalling a row or column of values or as complex as figuring the rate of return on an investment under varying circumstances. It also allows you to make a graphical representation of all your data in the form of 2-dimensional or 3-dimensional graph or pie chart.

Understanding Spreadsheets

Before we go into understanding the various commands of Excel, let us first understand the working of a spreadsheet. A spreadsheet as the name suggests is a sheet which is spread in such a way that it divides itself into the various horizontal rows and vertical columns. Rows are numbered from 1 onwards and Columns are numbered from A onwards. Graphically they can be represented as:

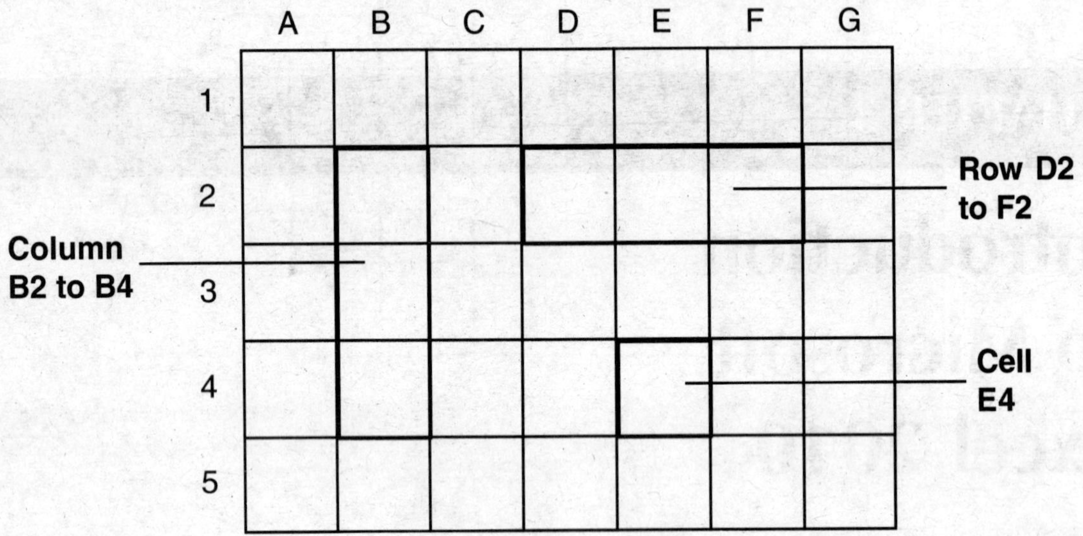

When we take this to the computer and see it electronically using our software Excel, this becomes Electronic Spreadsheet, also called Worksheet. The main features of the worksheets are:

Rows	These are the horizontal cells which can contain any information.
Columns	These are vertical cells which can also contain information.
Cell	It is the interaction of a row with a column. Each cell is identified with its position.

Naming Conventions

It is not that I have named rows from 1 onwards and columns A onwards on my own but they are so numbered by the software itself. These are the standard way of expressing these columns and rows.

If we have to name a large number of cell or columns, for that too we have the convention which asks us to call them with starting cell address and last cell address with colon in between. For example, see the following addressed cells, shown below.

Another convention is of the sheets in the worksheet.

Sheets

These are like pages in a book. Initially there are 16 worksheets in the file. But, you can add more. However, there may be only 6 of them visible on the screen. These sheets are independent but you can transfer data from one sheet to another. These sheets are very helpful. For example, for a salary spreadsheet, one sheet may belong to one month and there may be a sheet for the total of the year.

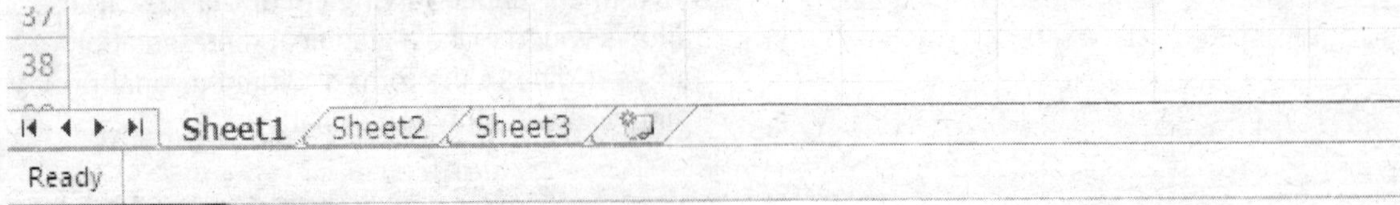

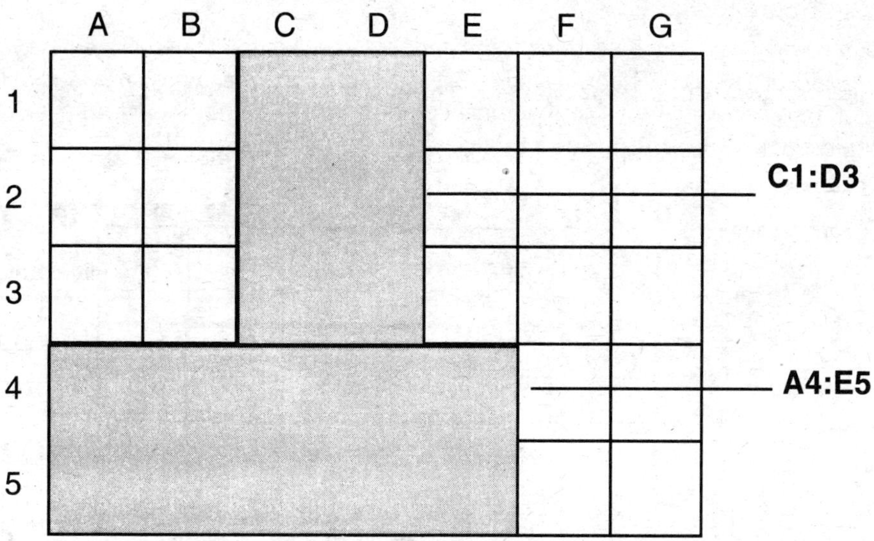

To understand the software better, let us create a worksheet in Excel 2010 and apply the various options/ commands on it to see the working of the software. This will give you an idea about creating a workshett and applying the commands.

Creating a Worksheet in Excel 2010

We have learn' ,uite a number of commands and naturally would like to use them in a worksheet. So let us create a worksheet and use these commands side-by-side to see how they work out. Supposing we have the financial highlights of a company as given below:

Year	Total Income (A)	Interest Paid (B)	Profit (C)	Tax (D)	Profit After Tax (E)
1999	4,500	To be	To be	To be	To be
2000	5,500	Calculated	Calculated	Calculated	Calculated
2001	7,000	as 15%	as Income	as 12% of	as Profit
2002	8,000	of the	minus	the Profit	minus Tax
2003	9,000	Total	Interest		(C) - (D)
2004	12,000	Income	(A) - (B)		
2005	15,000				
2006	20,000				

As you can see that there are quite a number of fields which have to be calculated. This will act as a good exercise for you to do. Let us start from the very beginning, i.e., start the software Microsoft Excel 2003. You will end up with a blank worksheet, ready for you to take action, with the first cell **A1**, totally at your command to do something, as shown in the figure next.

So what we have to do here. We have to type "Year". So just type the word Year and press **Enter**. You will see the word being shown in the formula bar too. This will also take you to the cell **A2**. But, for typing the next heading, you have to go to the cell **B1**. So use the arrow keys right and up to reach **B1**. Next we have to type "Total Income". (Please note that for the sake of convenience I had shown this

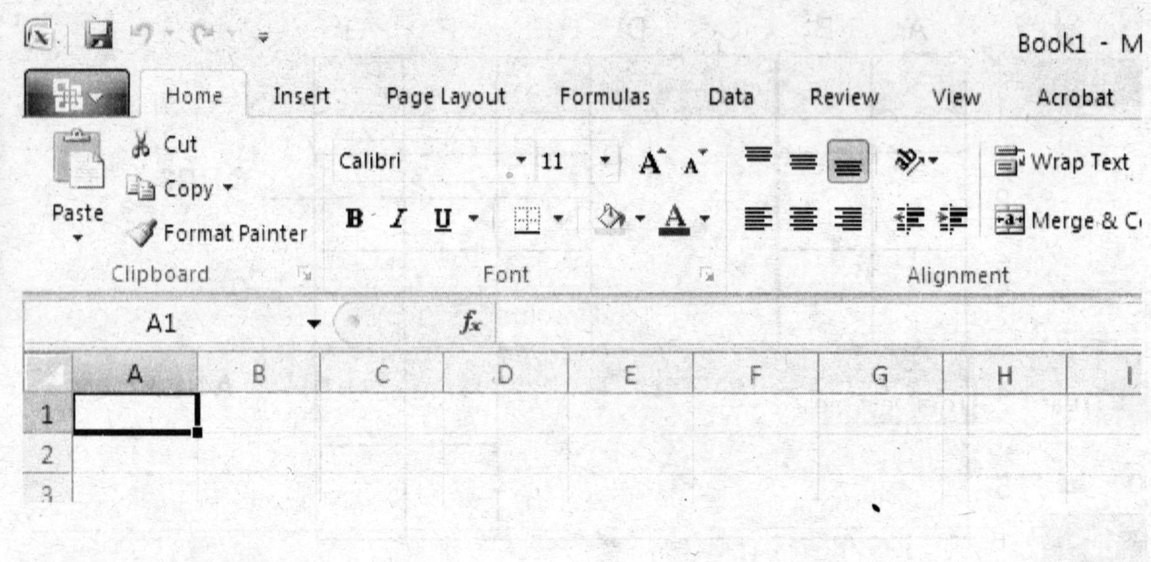

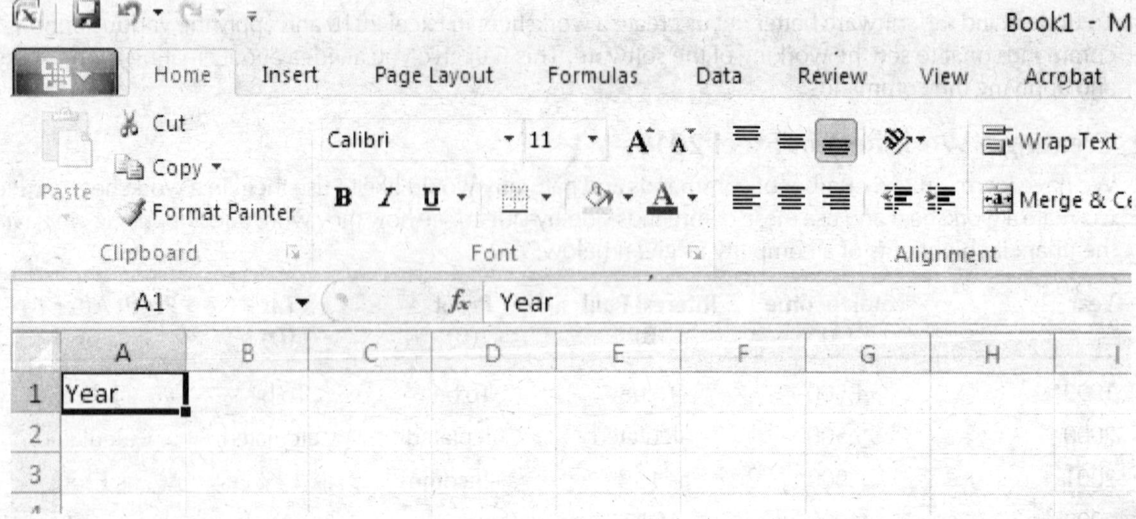

heading in 2 lines, but, if permitted we will type it in one line. Also (A), (B), etc., in the table are just symbolic and are not to be typed).

So for type the next heading, "Total Income" in the cell **B1**, as shown next.

Did you notice anything wrong here? Well, the cell is not big enough to carry your heading. So what will we do? We will increase the width of the column **B**, by using one of the methods mentioned earlier in the chapter, i.e., by using the Cells command under Tools.

This way now we will type the complete headings, i.e., all of them, as shown next.

But, since these are headings, and are to be highlighted. We will make them **Bold** and put them in the centre of the cells. This way they will look good.

Highlight all the cells by just clicking at cell **A1** and then while pressing **Shift** key click mouse in the cell **F1**, the whole row gets highlighted.

Now click at B in the formatting bar to make the whole text as Bold.

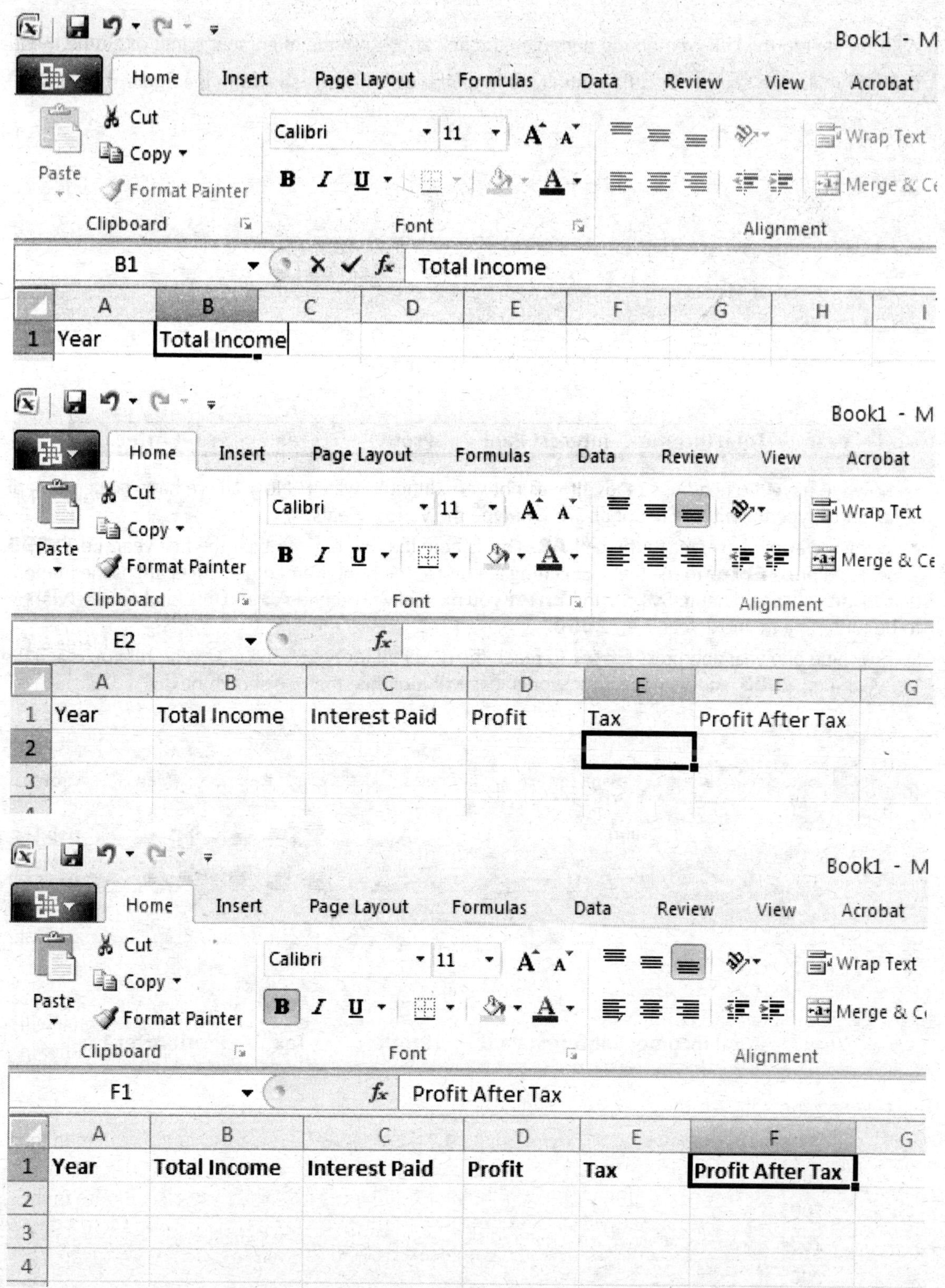
Book1 - M
Home
Insert
Page Layout
Formulas
Data
Review
View
Acrobat
Cut
Copy
Paste
Format Painter
Clipboard
Calibri
11
Font
Wrap Text
Merge & Ce
Alignment
B1
Total Income
Year
Total Income
E2
Year
Total Income
Interest Paid
Profit
Tax
Profit After Tax
F1
Profit After Tax
Year
Total Income
Interest Paid
Profit
Tax
Profit After Tax

With the text in the cells remaining highlighted, click at [center-align icon] in the alignment panel of Home menu. This will make the text in the cells centralized in all the cells. This is shown in the figure shown next.

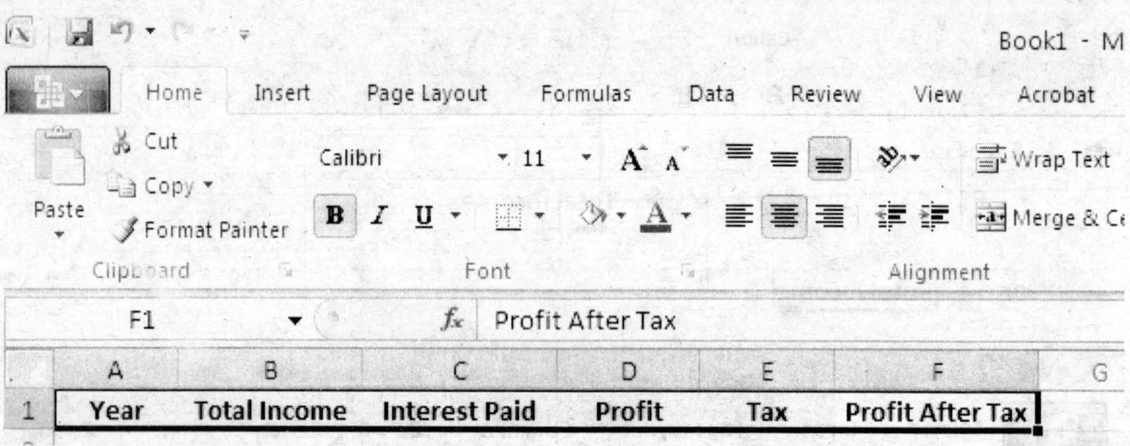

So now we have the headings ready. It was not very difficult, was it? Now all we have is the numeric data. Let us type them too. First of all we will type the various years.

By using the arrow keys, reach the cell **A2**. This is here that we have to type the first year, i.e., **1999**. Type it and press **Enter** to see the data getting aligned to the right. Remember, Excel aligns the numeric data to the right as a default. By pressing **Enter** you must have reached **A3** and this is where you wanted to be for typing the next year, i.e., **2000**.

So now type one year and press **Enter** to reach the next cell for typing the next year, till you reach the last year, i.e., **2006**. At this stage your worksheet will look like the one shown next .

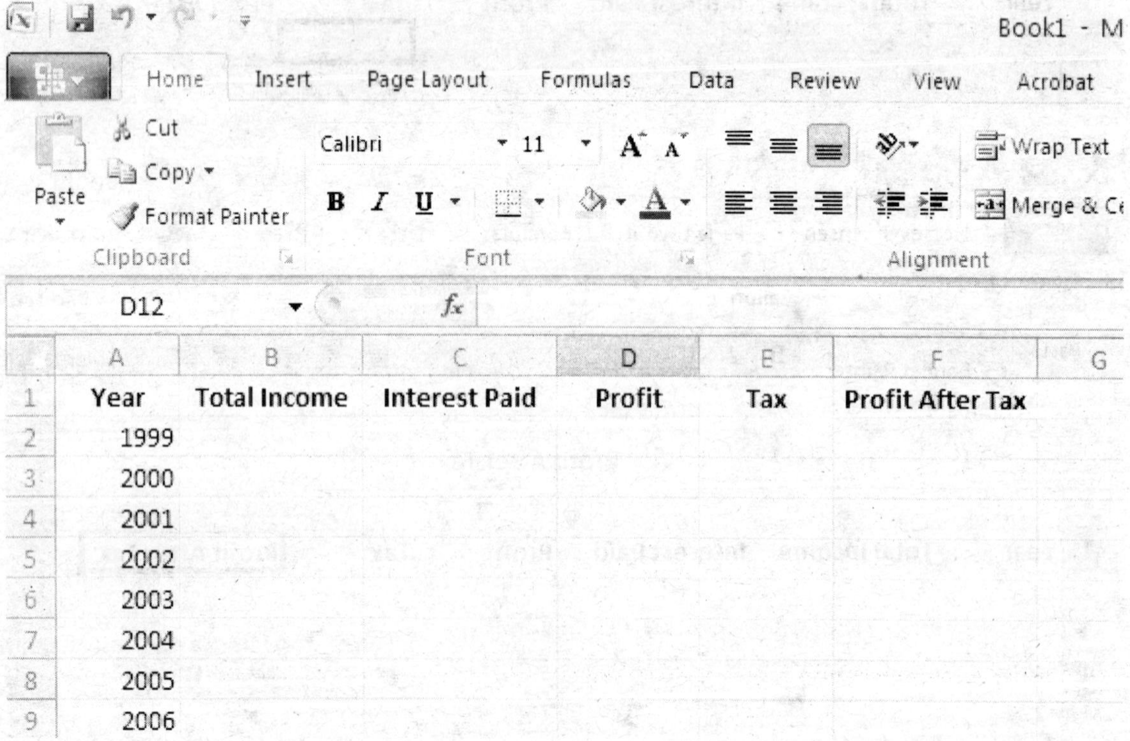

Next step is also easy. You have to just type the numbers in the cells **B2** to **B9**. All these figures are available with you. Just type one figure and press **Enter** to reach the next cell and so on till you reach the last cell in the column. After doing this your worksheet will look like the one shown next.

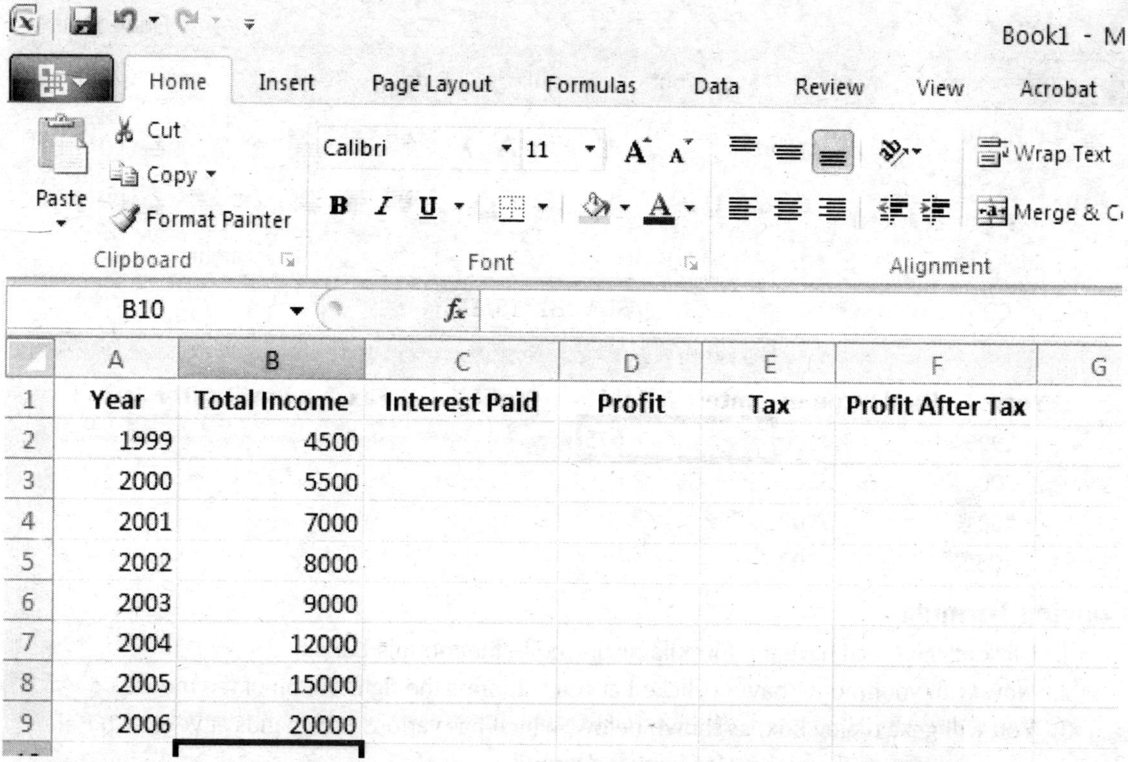

Book1 - M

Home Insert Page Layout Formulas Data Review View Acrobat

Cut Copy Format Painter Paste Clipboard | Calibri 11 Font | Wrap Text Merge & C Alignment

B10

	A	B	C	D	E	F	G
1	Year	Total Income	Interest Paid	Profit	Tax	Profit After Tax	
2	1999	4500					
3	2000	5500					
4	2001	7000					
5	2002	8000					
6	2003	9000					
7	2004	12000					
8	2005	15000					
9	2006	20000					

It would not be a bad idea to save this worksheet at this stage. For god forbid, if something happens, like power cut or so. So just press **Ctrl+S** to give the save command, as you would give in any other software. Now all you have to do it to give it a name and decide where you want to save this worksheet. Let us give the name **Finance** to it.

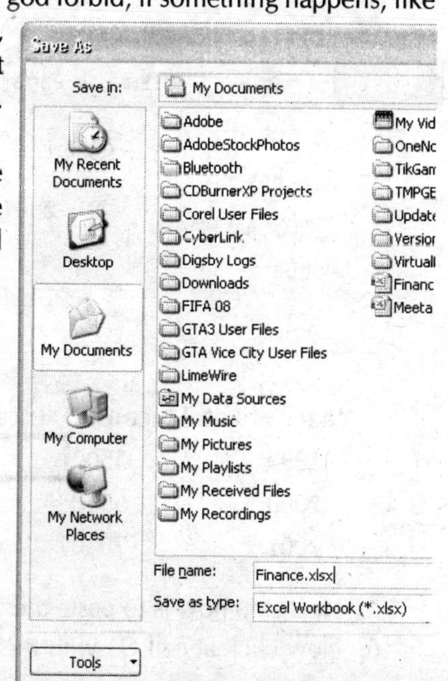

Now we come to the interesting part of this worksheet. So far we have typed whatever was available. Now we have to generate the figures. The column **C** is of Interest Paid which is to be calculated by using the formula.

$$\text{Interest Paid} = \frac{\text{Total Income} \times 15}{100}$$

Transformed to the computer language it will become:

Interest Paid = (Total Income x 15)/100

If we put this in Cell **C2**, it will become:

C2 = SUM(B2*15/100)

Try putting this in the cell **C2** and see the result. It will be as shown below. It has given a figure of 675. Calculate the amount manually to see whether the result is Ok or not. It is correct, isn't it? Now we have to apply this formula to all the cells from **C3** to **C9**. Do you have to put the formula for each cell or there is a method in Excel which allows you to copy the formula in each of the cell. Well, fortunately there is. So this is how you will do it.

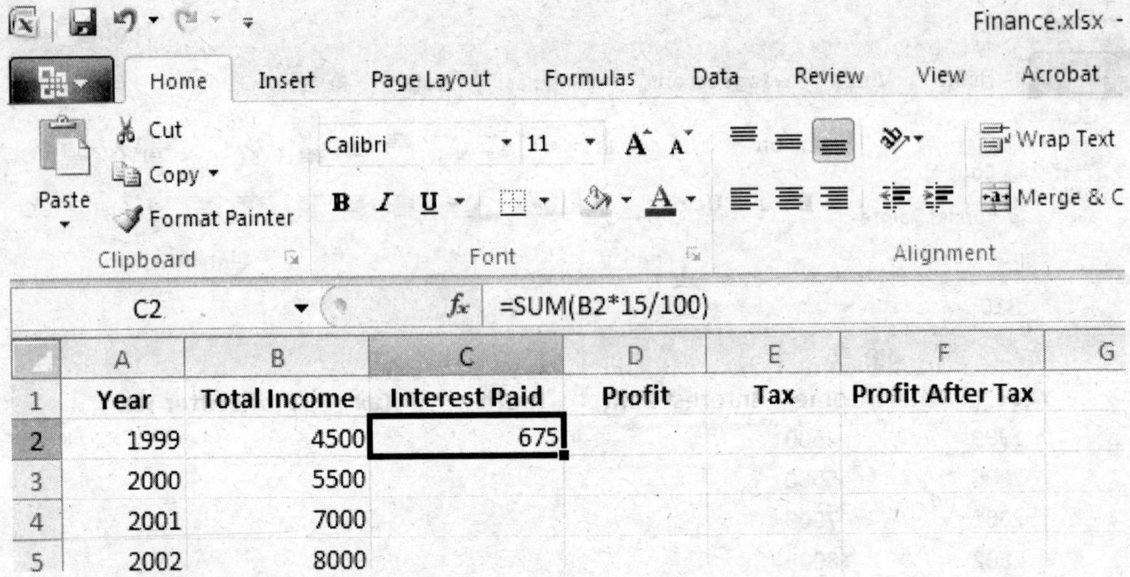

Copying Formula

1. Click at cell C2 to have the formula displayed in the formula bar.
2. Now with your mouse having clicked at cell C2, press the right button of the mouse.
3. You will get a dialog box, as shown below, which has various commands at your disposal.
4. Choose copy, as shown here, to copy the formula.

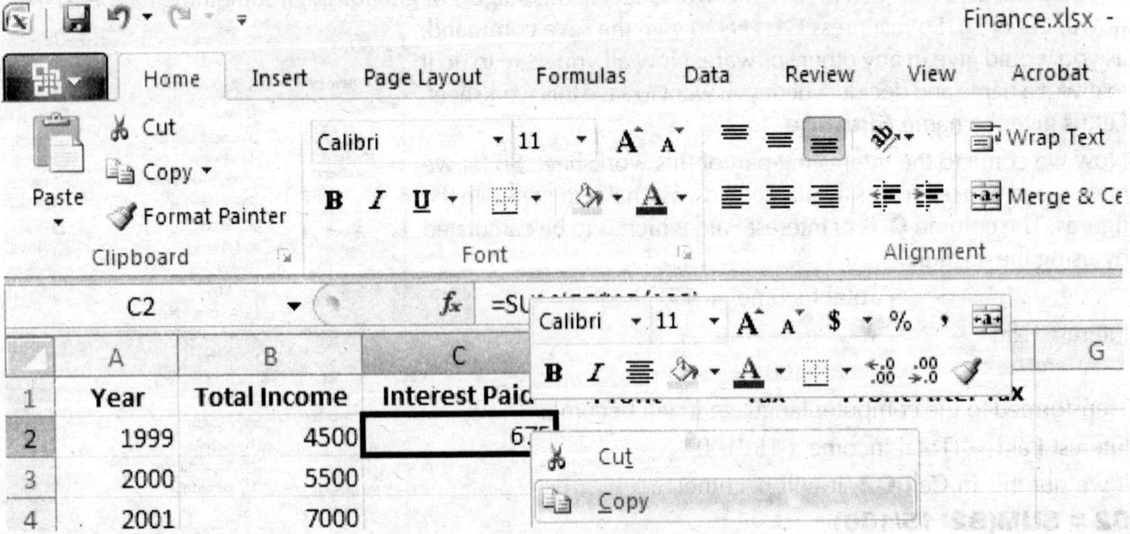

5. Next step now is to paste the formula in their respective cells.
6. Now click at cell C3 with the mouse (left button).

7. Click the right button again to get the dialog box.
8. This time click at Paste instead, as shown next.

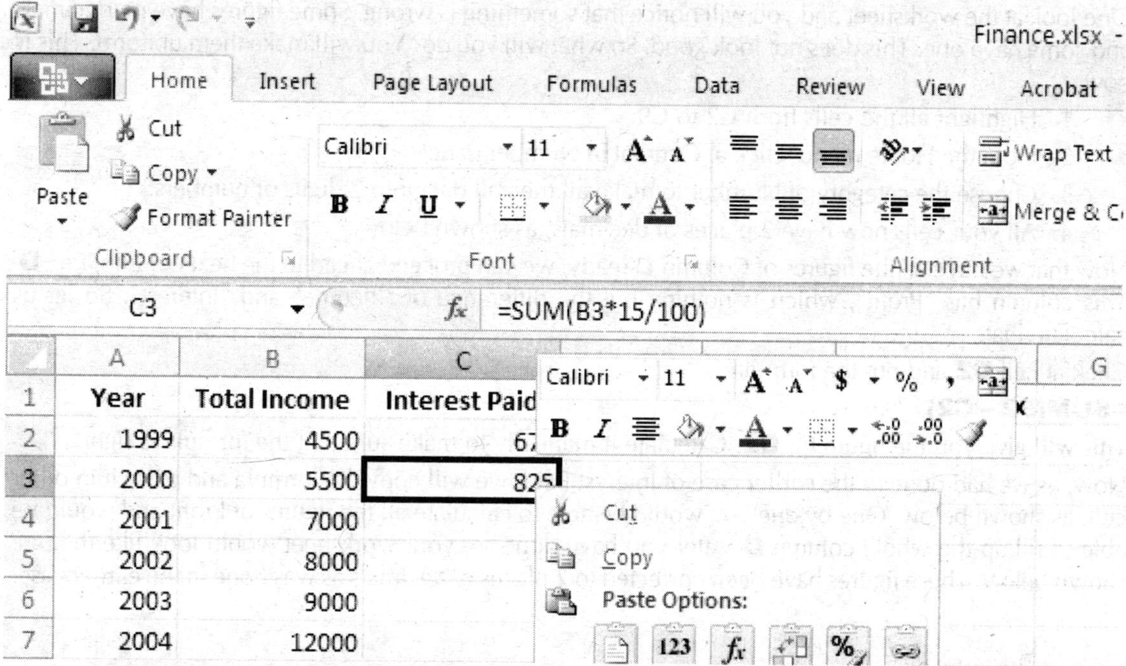

9. Immediately you will get the figure in cell C3.
   This calculation has been based on B3 (see the formula bar) and not B2 which had been copied in our formula. Is it not great? Excel has changed the cell address for you. This is called relative addressing and is a very useful feature of Excel.
10. Similar pasting in the cells from C4 to C9 can also be done.
11. Once done your worksheet should look like the one shown next.

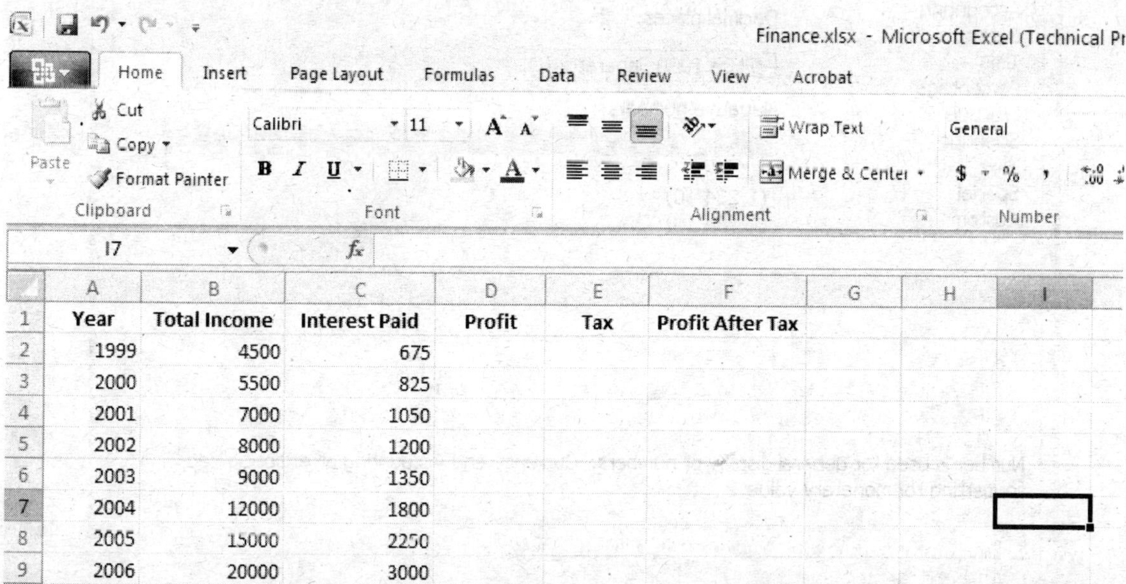

	A	B	C	D	E	F	G	H	I
1	Year	Total Income	Interest Paid	Profit	Tax	Profit After Tax			
2	1999	4500	675						
3	2000	5500	825						
4	2001	7000	1050						
5	2002	8000	1200						
6	2003	9000	1350						
7	2004	12000	1800						
8	2005	15000	2250						
9	2006	20000	3000						

Remember

1. You can take out the dotted lines blinking around the cell C2 by pressing the Esc key.

One look at the worksheet and you will notice that something is wrong. Some figures have no decimals and some have one. This does not look good. So what will you do? You will make them uniform. This is how:

1. Highlight all the cells from C2 to C9.
2. From the Home menu, click at General in Number panel.
3. Choose the category of Number to make all the cell data into 2 digits of numbers.
4. All your cells now have 2 places of decimals, as shown below.

Now that we have all the figures of Column **C** ready, we can proceed ahead to the next column, i.e., **D**. This column has "Profit", which is nothing but the difference of "Income" and "Interest". So let us calculate that.

Click at cell **D2** and put the formula

=SUM(B2 – C2)

This will give you the figure for **D2**. Calculate it manually to make sure that the formula is right.

Now, as we had done in the earlier case of Interest Paid, we will copy the formula and paste it in other cell, as shown below. One by one you would be able to calculate all the figures of Profit and would be able to fill up the whole column **D**. After you have done so, your worksheet would look like the one shown below. These figures have been corrected to 2 places of decimals as was done in the earlier case.

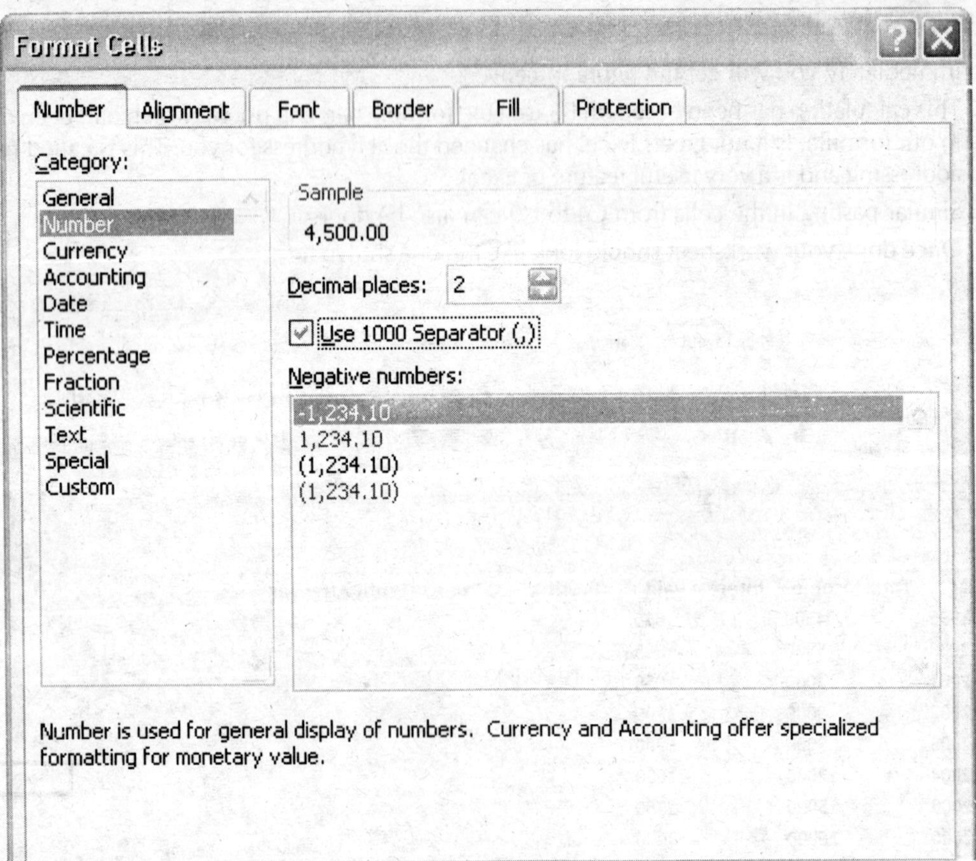

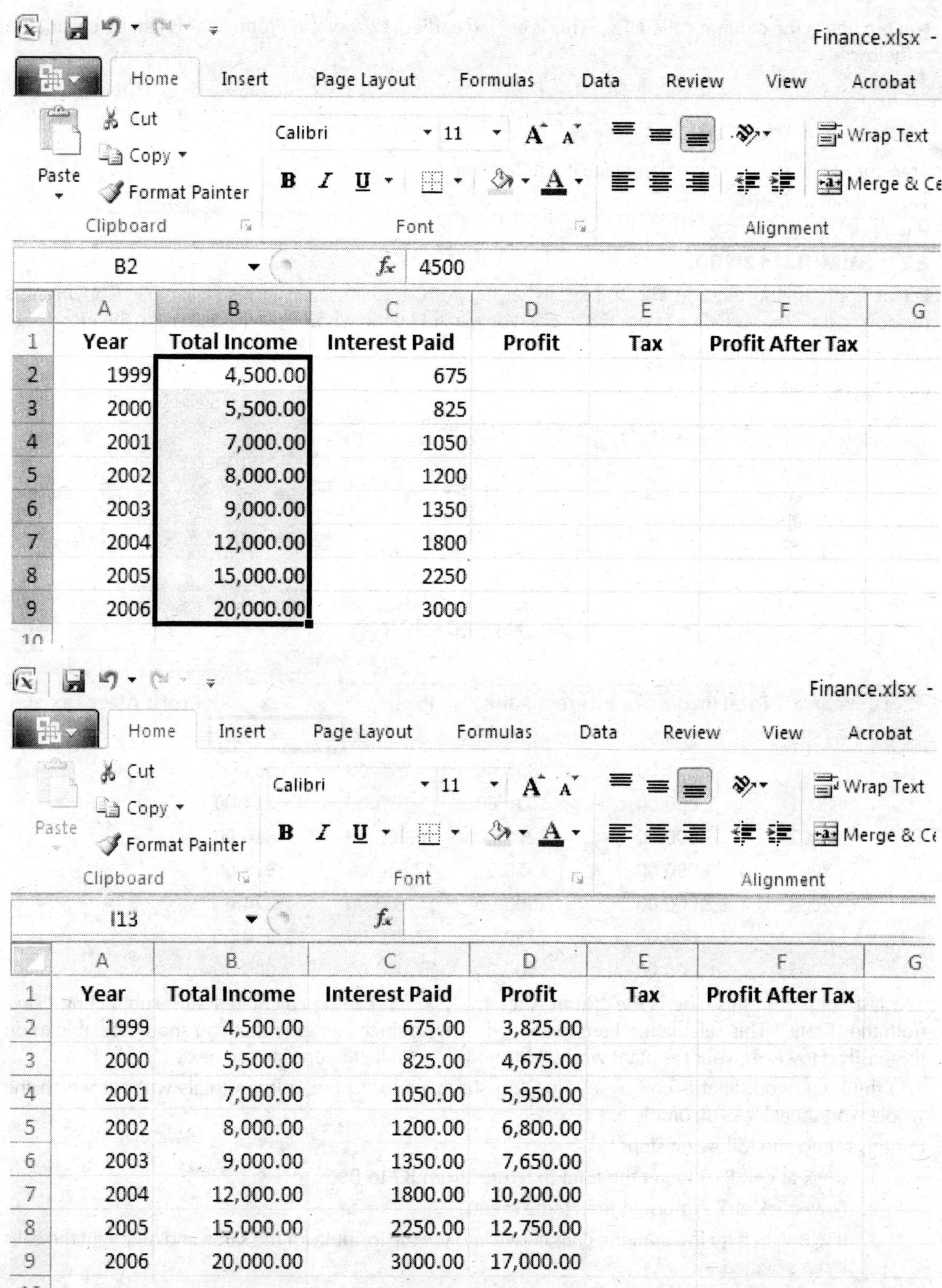

	A	B	C	D	E	F
1	Year	Total Income	Interest Paid	Profit	Tax	Profit After Tax
2	1999	4,500.00	675			
3	2000	5,500.00	825			
4	2001	7,000.00	1050			
5	2002	8,000.00	1200			
6	2003	9,000.00	1350			
7	2004	12,000.00	1800			
8	2005	15,000.00	2250			
9	2006	20,000.00	3000			

	A	B	C	D	E	F
1	Year	Total Income	Interest Paid	Profit	Tax	Profit After Tax
2	1999	4,500.00	675.00	3,825.00		
3	2000	5,500.00	825.00	4,675.00		
4	2001	7,000.00	1050.00	5,950.00		
5	2002	8,000.00	1200.00	6,800.00		
6	2003	9,000.00	1350.00	7,650.00		
7	2004	12,000.00	1800.00	10,200.00		
8	2005	15,000.00	2250.00	12,750.00		
9	2006	20,000.00	3000.00	17,000.00		

Next in line is the column called Tax. This is as said earlier, 12% of the Profit. So this can be calculated as below:

$$\text{Tax} = \frac{\text{Profit} \times 12}{100}$$

Transformed to the computer language it will become:

Tax= (Profit x 12)/100

If we put this in Cell **E2**, it will become:

E2 = SUM(D2*12/100)

Let us apply this formula in **E2** and see what happens. It gives you the result as 459. Copying this formula to the other cells, i.e., from **E3** to **E9**, you can fill up the whole column and make the worksheet look like the one shown next.

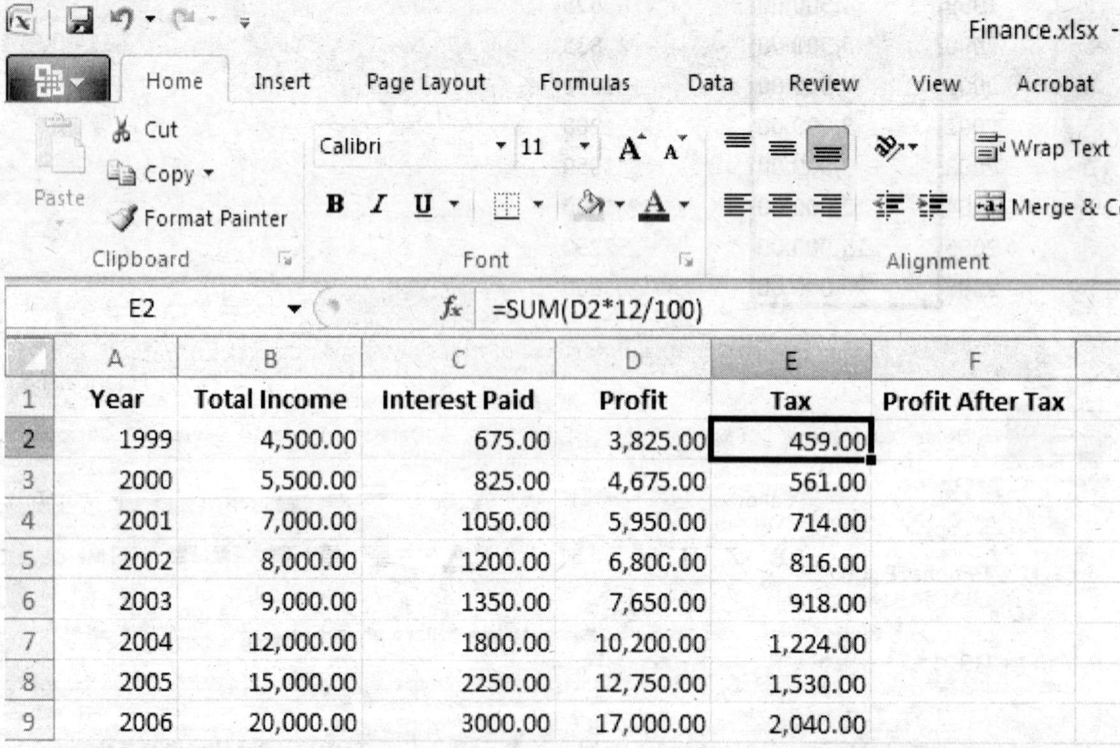

	A	B	C	D	E	F
1	Year	Total Income	Interest Paid	Profit	Tax	Profit After Tax
2	1999	4,500.00	675.00	3,825.00	459.00	
3	2000	5,500.00	825.00	4,675.00	561.00	
4	2001	7,000.00	1050.00	5,950.00	714.00	
5	2002	8,000.00	1200.00	6,800.00	816.00	
6	2003	9,000.00	1350.00	7,650.00	918.00	
7	2004	12,000.00	1800.00	10,200.00	1,224.00	
8	2005	15,000.00	2250.00	12,750.00	1,530.00	
9	2006	20,000.00	3000.00	17,000.00	2,040.00	

The last column in this case is the "Profit After Tax", which can be calculated after subtracting "Tax" from the "Profit". This calculation I am not showing here, since I assume that you should be able to do this easily. However, your resultant worksheet should look like the one shown next.

You think the worksheet is complete. No. You still have to do the column totals without which the whole worksheet looks incomplete.

For this follow the following steps.

1. Click at cell B10 to get the total of figures from B2 to B9.
2. Now click at Σ symbol in the Home menu.
3. It will search for the numeric cells above and put the formula for the same and highlight the cells it has selected.
4. It will wait for your Ok in the form of Enter to put the result.

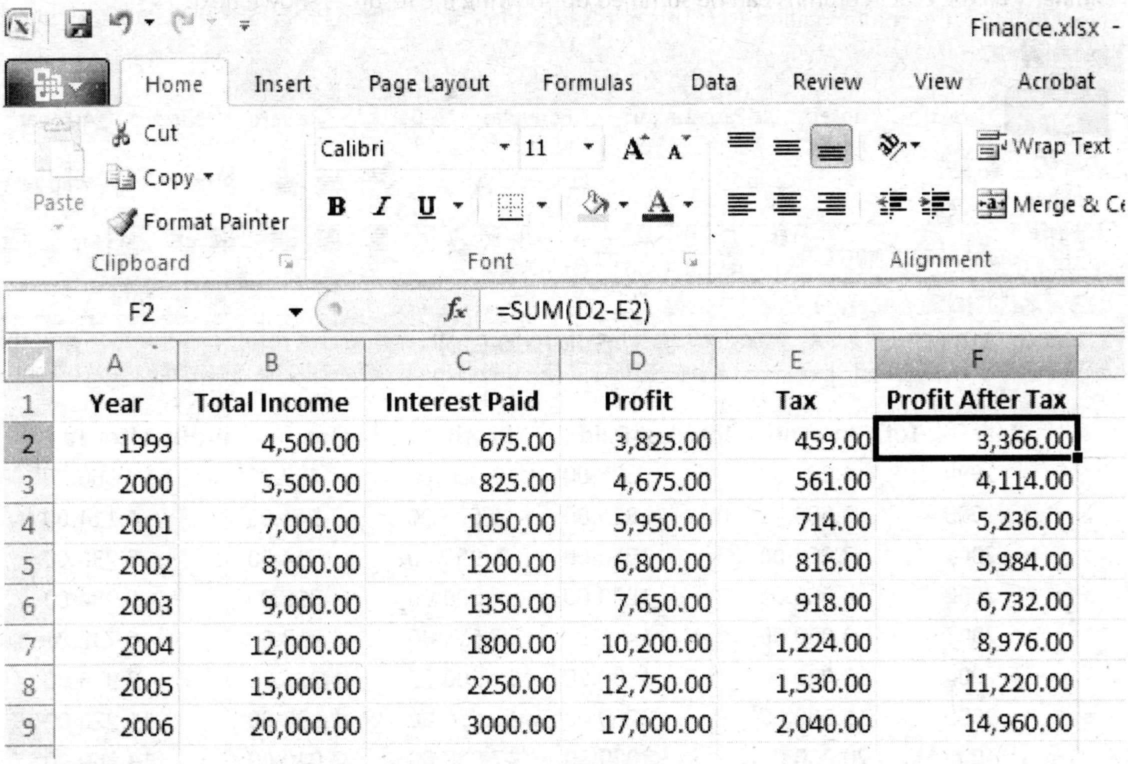

Finance.xlsx -

Home | Insert | Page Layout | Formulas | Data | Review | View | Acrobat

Cut | Copy | Format Painter | Paste | Clipboard | Calibri | 11 | Font | Wrap Text | Merge & Ce | Alignment

F2 | f_x =SUM(D2-E2)

	A	B	C	D	E	F
1	Year	Total Income	Interest Paid	Profit	Tax	Profit After Tax
2	1999	4,500.00	675.00	3,825.00	459.00	3,366.00
3	2000	5,500.00	825.00	4,675.00	561.00	4,114.00
4	2001	7,000.00	1050.00	5,950.00	714.00	5,236.00
5	2002	8,000.00	1200.00	6,800.00	816.00	5,984.00
6	2003	9,000.00	1350.00	7,650.00	918.00	6,732.00
7	2004	12,000.00	1800.00	10,200.00	1,224.00	8,976.00
8	2005	15,000.00	2250.00	12,750.00	1,530.00	11,220.00
9	2006	20,000.00	3000.00	17,000.00	2,040.00	14,960.00

5. Press Enter to get the total in the cell B10, as shown below.

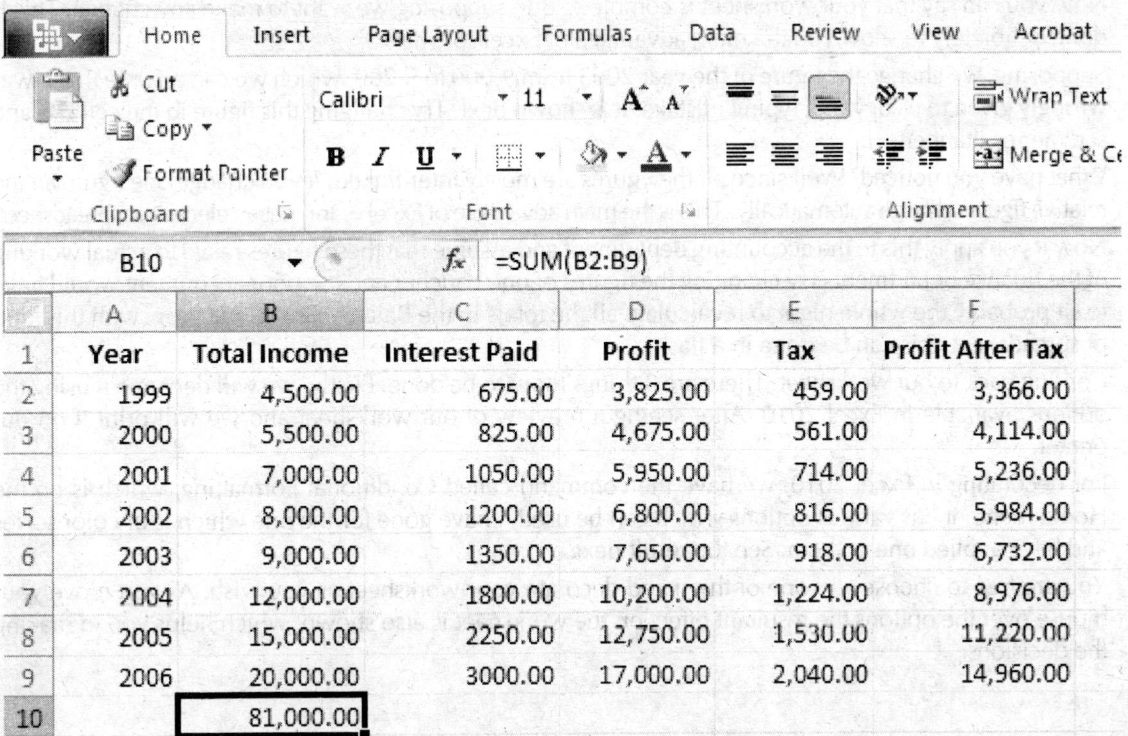

Finance.xlsx -

Home | Insert | Page Layout | Formulas | Data | Review | View | Acrobat

Cut | Copy | Format Painter | Paste | Clipboard | Calibri | 11 | Font | Wrap Text | Merge & Ce | Alignment

B10 | f_x =SUM(B2:B9)

	A	B	C	D	E	F
1	Year	Total Income	Interest Paid	Profit	Tax	Profit After Tax
2	1999	4,500.00	675.00	3,825.00	459.00	3,366.00
3	2000	5,500.00	825.00	4,675.00	561.00	4,114.00
4	2001	7,000.00	1050.00	5,950.00	714.00	5,236.00
5	2002	8,000.00	1200.00	6,800.00	816.00	5,984.00
6	2003	9,000.00	1350.00	7,650.00	918.00	6,732.00
7	2004	12,000.00	1800.00	10,200.00	1,224.00	8,976.00
8	2005	15,000.00	2250.00	12,750.00	1,530.00	11,220.00
9	2006	20,000.00	3000.00	17,000.00	2,040.00	14,960.00
10		81,000.00				

Similarly all the other columns can be summed up showing the result as shown next.

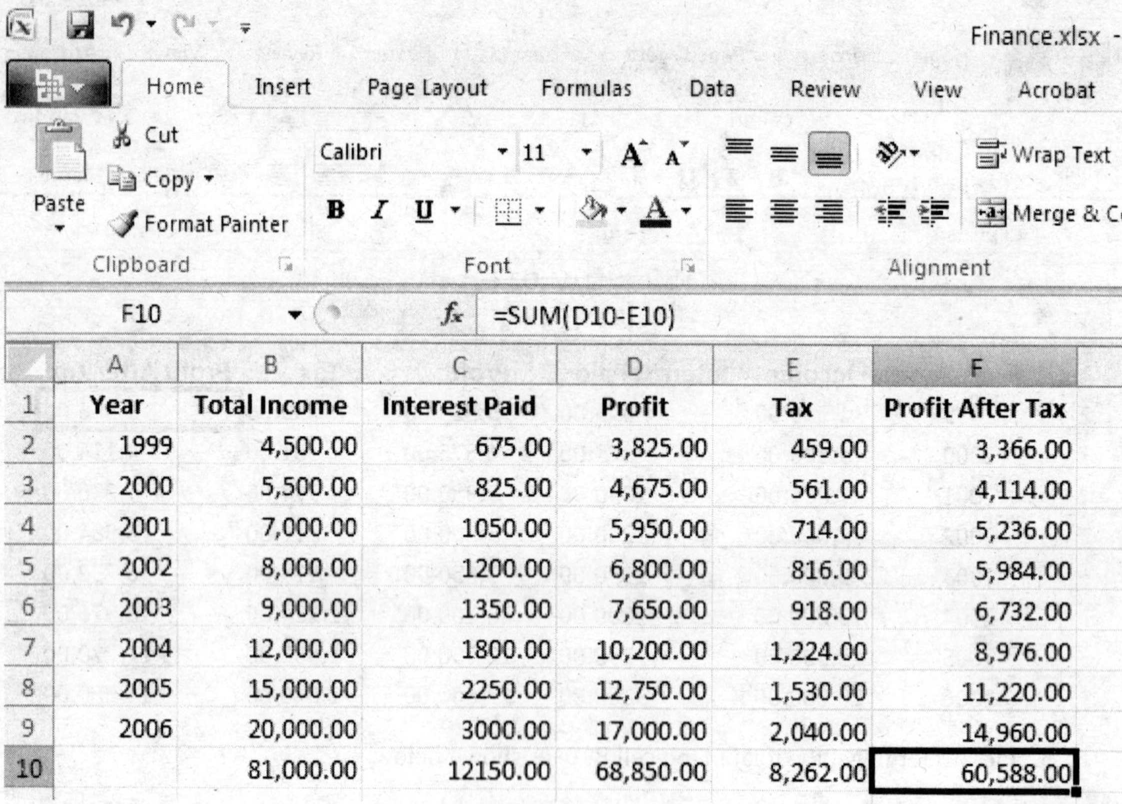

	A	B	C	D	E	F
1	Year	Total Income	Interest Paid	Profit	Tax	Profit After Tax
2	1999	4,500.00	675.00	3,825.00	459.00	3,366.00
3	2000	5,500.00	825.00	4,675.00	561.00	4,114.00
4	2001	7,000.00	1050.00	5,950.00	714.00	5,236.00
5	2002	8,000.00	1200.00	6,800.00	816.00	5,984.00
6	2003	9,000.00	1350.00	7,650.00	918.00	6,732.00
7	2004	12,000.00	1800.00	10,200.00	1,224.00	8,976.00
8	2005	15,000.00	2250.00	12,750.00	1,530.00	11,220.00
9	2006	20,000.00	3000.00	17,000.00	2,040.00	14,960.00
10		81,000.00	12150.00	68,850.00	8,262.00	60,588.00

Now you can say that your worksheet is complete. But, supposing we want to make any change. This is done deliberately to show you the main advantage of Excel software.

Supposing, we change the figure of the year 2003 from 9,000 to 9,200, which we can assume that it was wrongly given to us or was a typing mistake. It is shown next. Try changing this figure in the cell **B6** and see the resultant effect.

What have you noticed? Well since all the figures are mostly inter-linked, if you change one figure all the relative figures change automatically. This is the main advantage of Excel or for that an electronic spreadsheet. Now if you apply this to the accounting department and assume that these figures relate to actual working of the finance department. Try changing the figures of one voucher and the poor accountant would have to sit probably the whole night to recalculate all the totals in the Balance Sheet. But, now with this kind of spreadsheet, this can be done in a flash.

Coming back to our worksheet. There are 3 things more to be done. Firstly, we will decorate it using the options available in Excel 2010. After seeing a preview of our worksheet and we will print it on our printer.

For decorating in Excel 2010, we have the command called Conditional Formatting, which is on the Home menu. It has various options which can be used. I have gone for the one which is of color scales and have applied one of them. See the result next.

You are free to choose any one of them and decorate your worksheet as you wish. As you move your mouse over the options the resultant effect on the worksheet is also shown, which helps you in making the decisions.

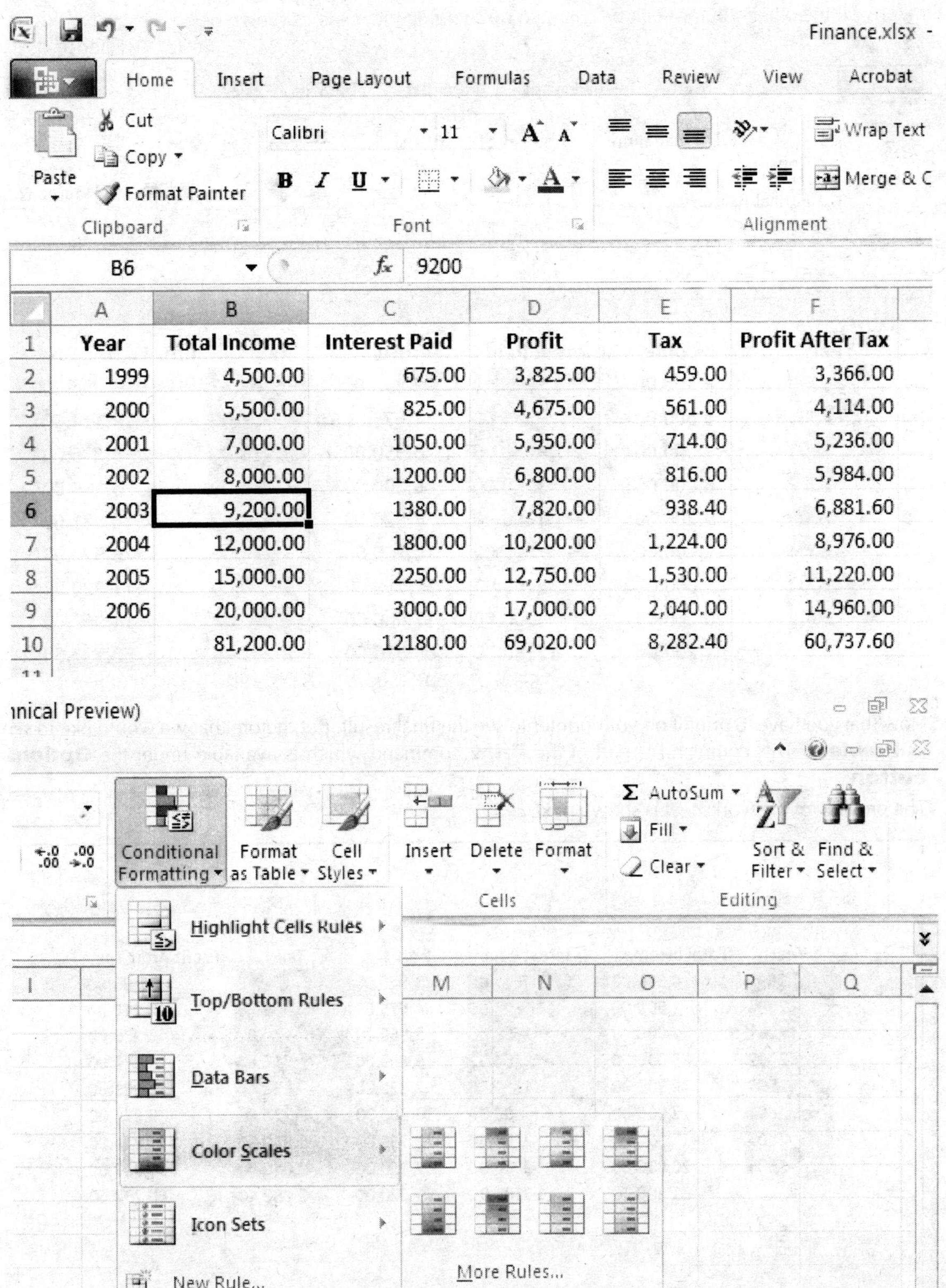

	A	B	C	D	E	F
1	Year	Total Income	Interest Paid	Profit	Tax	Profit After Tax
2	1999	4,500.00	675.00	3,825.00	459.00	3,366.00
3	2000	5,500.00	825.00	4,675.00	561.00	4,114.00
4	2001	7,000.00	1050.00	5,950.00	714.00	5,236.00
5	2002	8,000.00	1200.00	6,800.00	816.00	5,984.00
6	2003	9,200.00	1380.00	7,820.00	938.40	6,881.60
7	2004	12,000.00	1800.00	10,200.00	1,224.00	8,976.00
8	2005	15,000.00	2250.00	12,750.00	1,530.00	11,220.00
9	2006	20,000.00	3000.00	17,000.00	2,040.00	14,960.00
10		81,200.00	12180.00	69,020.00	8,282.40	60,737.60

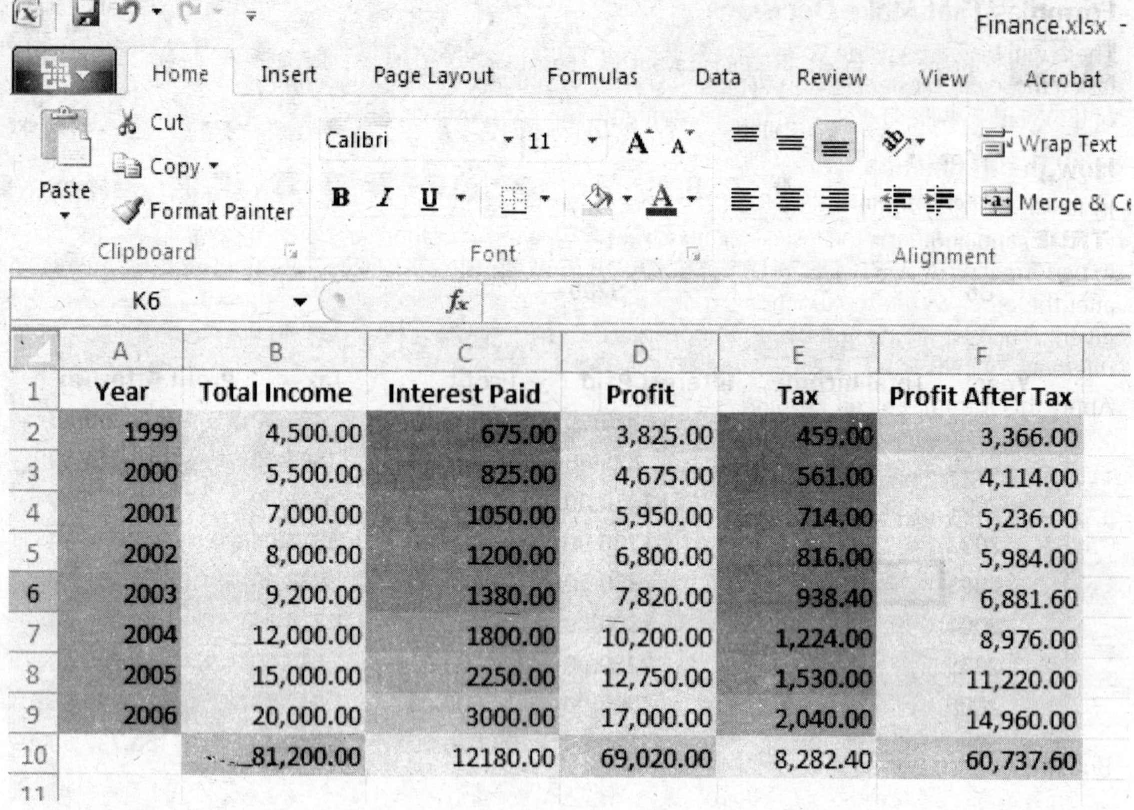

	A	B	C	D	E	F
1	Year	Total Income	Interest Paid	Profit	Tax	Profit After Tax
2	1999	4,500.00	675.00	3,825.00	459.00	3,366.00
3	2000	5,500.00	825.00	4,675.00	561.00	4,114.00
4	2001	7,000.00	1050.00	5,950.00	714.00	5,236.00
5	2002	8,000.00	1200.00	6,800.00	816.00	5,984.00
6	2003	9,200.00	1380.00	7,820.00	938.40	6,881.60
7	2004	12,000.00	1800.00	10,200.00	1,224.00	8,976.00
8	2005	15,000.00	2250.00	12,750.00	1,530.00	11,220.00
9	2006	20,000.00	3000.00	17,000.00	2,040.00	14,960.00
10		81,200.00	12180.00	69,020.00	8,282.40	60,737.60
11						

Now that you have to print it on your printer to see the final result. But, before that we would like to see its **Preview**. This command is part of the **Print** command which is available under the **Options button**.

The preview of the worksheet is shown next.

Year	Total Income	Interest Paid	Profit	Tax	Profit After Tax
1999	4,500.00	675.00	3,825.00	459.00	3,366.00
2000	5,500.00	825.00	4,675.00	561.00	4,114.00
2001	7,000.00	1050.00	5,950.00	714.00	5,236.00
2002	8,000.00	1200.00	6,800.00	816.00	5,984.00
2003	9,200.00	1380.00	7,820.00	938.40	6,881.60
2004	12,000.00	1800.00	10,200.00	1,224.00	8,976.00
2005	15,000.00	2250.00	12,750.00	1,530.00	11,220.00
2006	20,000.00	3000.00	17,000.00	2,040.00	14,960.00
	81,200.00	12180.00	69,020.00	8,282.40	60,737.60

Formulas That Make Decisions

There will be a time when you want Excel to carry out one task under certain circumstances and another task if those circumstances don't apply. If you are familiar with any programming language, it is the case of IF, WHEN or IF, THEN. You have a similar IF function in Excel.

How the IF function works

In its simplest form, the IF function tests the value of a cell and does one thing if the test is positive (**TRUE**) and another if the test is negative (**FALSE**). It requires three arguments: the test data, the action to perform if the test is TRUE and the action to perform if the test is FALSE. You supply the arguments one after the other within the function's parentheses, separating them with commas (no spaces are to be given). The text which you want to appear as it is, i.e., TRUE or FALSE should be given under quotes, reference of cells like **C5**, etc., should be as it is.

Apply this formula in cell **B6** and see the result:

1. Select cell B6, type the following in place of formula and press Enter:

   = IF(B2=0, TRUE, FALSE)

   Excel checks whether the value in cell B2 is zero (the test), and because it isn't zero, it ignores TRUE (the action to perform if the test is TRUE) and displays FALSE (the action to perform if the test is FALSE) in cell B6.
2. Double-click cell B6, change formula to

   = IF(B2>1000, TRUE, FALSE)

   and press Enter. The entry in cell B6 instantly changes from FALSE to TRUE because the value in cell B2 is greater than one thousand; that is, the test is TRUE.

Both the options can be seen next.

Finance.xlsx - Micrc

Home | Insert | Page Layout | Formulas | Data | Review | View | Acrobat

Cut | Copy | Format Painter | Paste | Clipboard | Calibri | 11 | B I U | Font | Wrap Text | Merge & Center | Alignment

B6 | =IF(B2=0, TRUE, FALSE)

	A	B	C	D	E	F	G
1	Year	Total Income	Interest Paid	Profit	Tax	Profit After Tax	
2	1999	4,500.00	675.00	3,825.00	459.00	3,366.00	
3	2000	5,500.00	825.00	4,675.00	561.00	4,114.00	
4	2001	7,000.00	1050.00	5,950.00	714.00	5,236.00	
5	2002	8,000.00	1200.00	6,800.00	816.00	5,984.00	
6	2003	FALSE	0.00	0.00	0.00	0.00	
7	2004	12,000.00	1800.00	10,200.00	1,224.00	8,976.00	
8	2005	15,000.00	2250.00	12,750.00	1,530.00	11,220.00	
9	2006	20,000.00	3000.00	17,000.00	2,040.00	14,960.00	
10		72,000.00	10800.00	61,200.00	7,344.00	53,856.00	

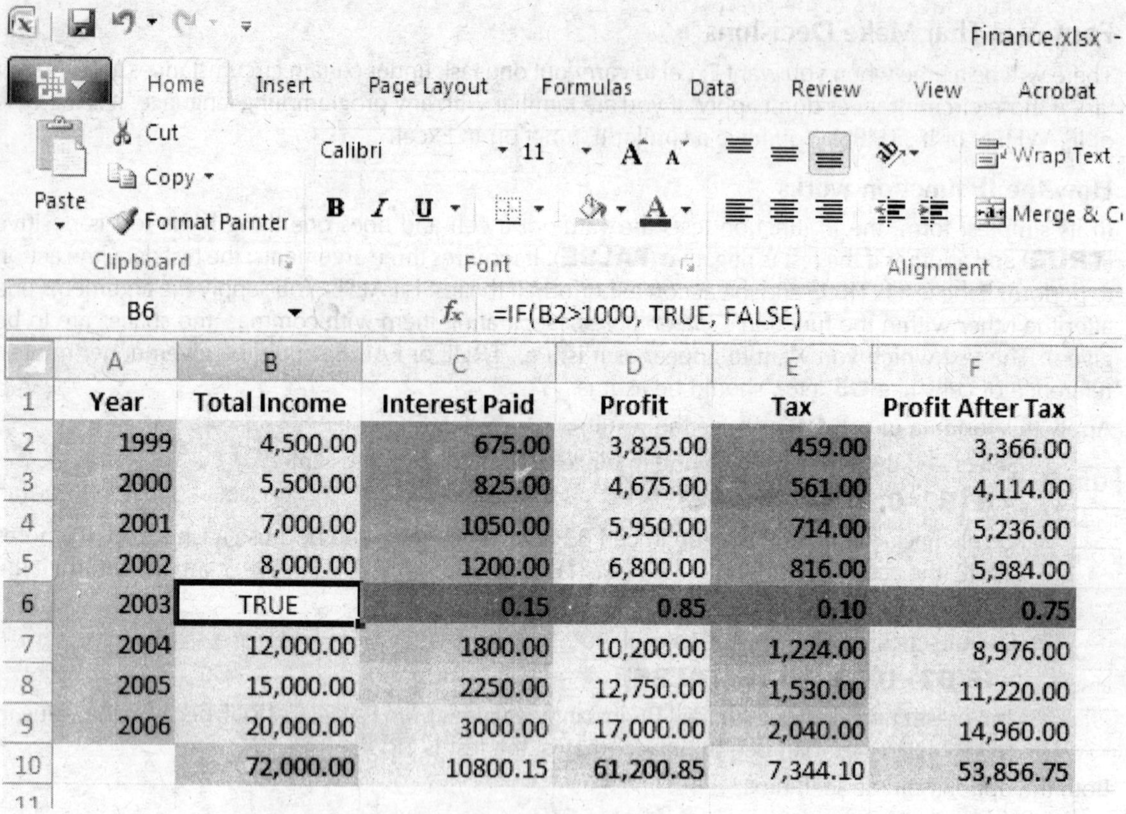

Finance.xlsx -

Home Insert Page Layout Formulas Data Review View Acrobat

Cut Copy Paste Format Painter Clipboard Calibri 11 B I U Font Wrap Text Merge & C Alignment

B6 fx =IF(B2>1000, TRUE, FALSE)

	A	B	C	D	E	F
1	Year	Total Income	Interest Paid	Profit	Tax	Profit After Tax
2	1999	4,500.00	675.00	3,825.00	459.00	3,366.00
3	2000	5,500.00	825.00	4,675.00	561.00	4,114.00
4	2001	7,000.00	1050.00	5,950.00	714.00	5,236.00
5	2002	8,000.00	1200.00	6,800.00	816.00	5,984.00
6	2003	TRUE	0.15	0.85	0.10	0.75
7	2004	12,000.00	1800.00	10,200.00	1,224.00	8,976.00
8	2005	15,000.00	2250.00	12,750.00	1,530.00	11,220.00
9	2006	20,000.00	3000.00	17,000.00	2,040.00	14,960.00
10		72,000.00	10800.15	61,200.85	7,344.10	53,856.75
11						

Now this was very simple. Isn't it. However, you can also build tests that involve other functions. Suppose that in our Finance worksheet, we say that the Tax has to be a minimum of 1000, which means that if the Tax is less than 1000 it has to be put as 1000 and if it more that 1000, then the figure will stand as it is.

For this perform the following steps.

1. Click at any entry in E and select to insert a column from Insert Menu.
2. Use the Cut, Paste and Format buttons to restore the entries now in E2:E9 to F2:F9.
3. Click at F2 and apply the formula

   =IF(E2>1000, E2, 1000)

   This means that you are asking the system to check if it is above 1000, One of the two possibilities will arise:

TRUE This means that the figure in cell is more than 1000, then the column will be replaced by the figure in **E2**, which means that it is not changed.

FALSE This means that the figure in the cell **E2** is less than 1000, then the second condition will be met, i.e., figure in cell **F2** will be replaced with the figure of 1000.

Repeat this for all the other cells of column **F**. The easiest way out to repeat the formula in each column.

Next we work with various commands of Excel 2010.

Styles

Create a Style by Example

1. Select cell containing desired formats

2. Click Cell Styles in the Home Panel.
3. It will show the various style sheet options available.
4. In the end there is an option of Create New Style which allows you to create one of your own.
3. Type a name for style in Style Name: The style's formats in Style includes box.

Exclude formats of selected cell from style:

1. Deselect Style Includes (by example) options: Number, Alignment, Font, Border, Fill, Protection
2. Click Ok.

Functions in Excel

They establish relationships between two or more cells. If you want to add the values in cells A3 and A4 and put the result in cell A5, move to the cell A5 and type =A3+A4 and press Enter. The result is displayed immediately in cell A5. Another way to achieve the same result is to move to cell A5 and type +, point to cell A3, type +, then point to A4, and press Enter. The easiest way to achieve this operation is to point to A5, pick up the AutoSum button Σ on the toolbar.

The following symbols have their specific meaning in the formulae which are used in Excel.

Symbol	Description	Symbol	Description
:	Reference operator	,	Argument operator
	Negation	%	Percentage sign
^	Exponent	*	Multiplication
/	Division	+	Addition
–	Subtraction	&	Text concatenation
>	Greater than	<	Less than
>=	Greater than or equal to	<=	Less than or equal to
<>	Not equal to		

While working with the formulae you would come across the various errors too, which could happen due to wrong use of formula or wrong typing. The following are the common type of errors.

Error Type	Description
####	the column is not wide enough to display the number so either widen the column, or reduce the font size or change the numeric format.
# DIV/0!	Dividing by zero is invalid
# N/A	Data is not available. It happens usually when you refer to a function or value where data is not available

# NAME?	The formula references a name that is unknown to Excel
# NUM !	The formula is using an invalid number
# REF !	A cell reference is not available may be because you deleted that cell or moved another cell onto it.
# VALUE !	The formula contains an invalid operator or argument, for example, adding a text value to a numeric value

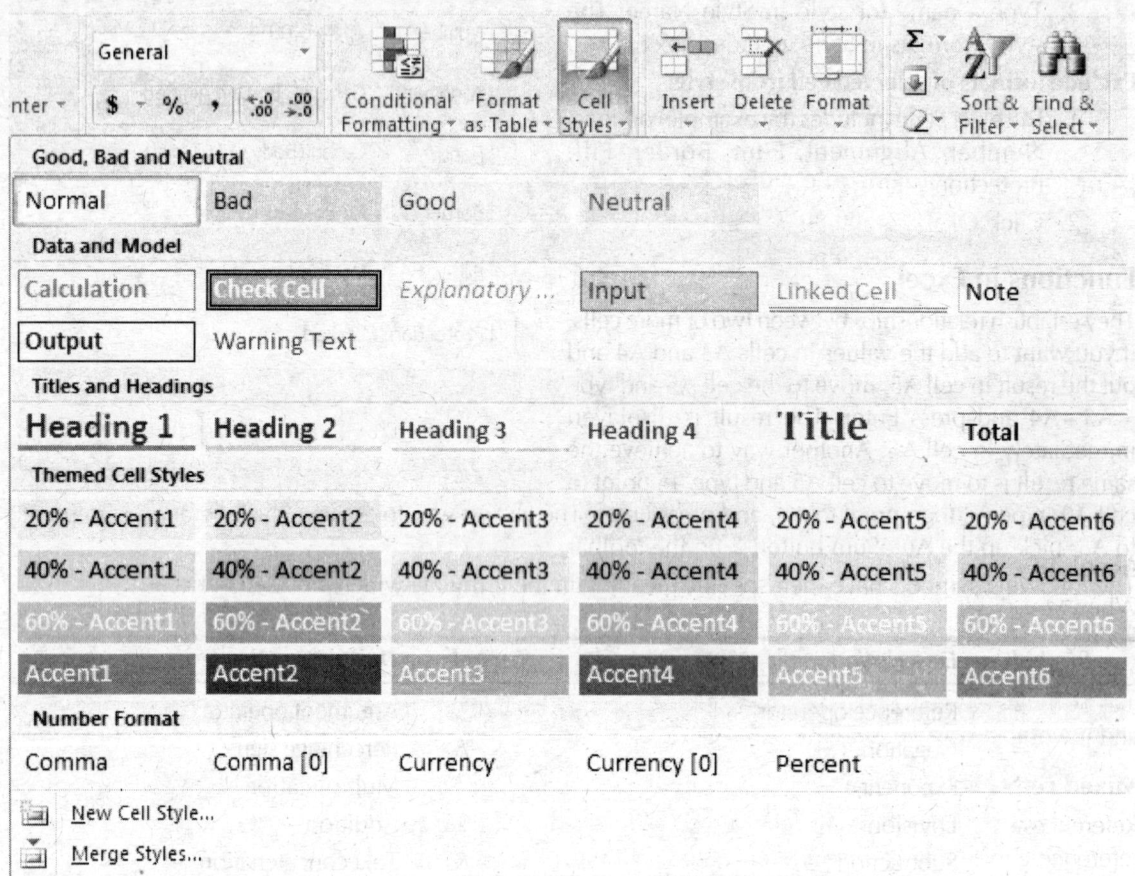

Using Autocalculate

It is very useful when you just want to total a number of columns but have the total in a particular field. The result will be displayed in Excel status bar and not in any cell. You can just view the sum. Perform the following steps to see the result.

1. Select the range whose total you want.
2. Right click at Status bar of the worksheet.
3. From the sub menu that appears, click at Sum.
4. The sum total would be displayed on the Status bar alongwith the sub menu, as shown next.

References

By default, Excel uses relative references in its formulae. Relative references refer to cells by their position in relation to the cell containing the formula. So when you copy the formula in cell F5 to cell F6, Excel changes the reference from E5 to E6.

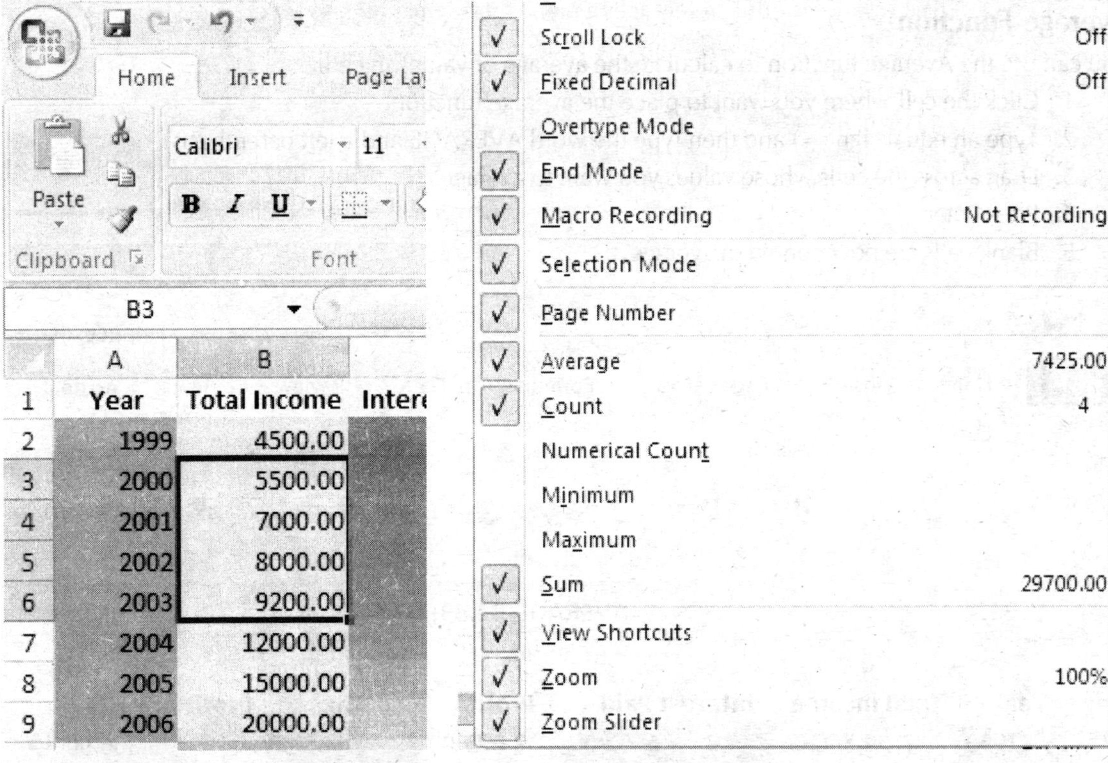

Absolute references

When you don't want a reference to be copied as a relative reference, you need to use an absolute reference. Absolute references refer to cells by their fixed position in the worksheet. To make a reference absolute, you add dollar signs before its column letter and now number. For example, you would enter it as $C$4:$C$9. You could then copy formula that contained this reference anywhere on the worksheet and it would always refer to the range C4:C9.

Mixed references

References can also be partially relative and partially absolute. For example, $C3 has an absolute column reference and a relative row reference and C$3 has a relative column reference and an absolute row reference.

Sum Function

The Sum function is perhaps the most commonly used of the Excel functions that carry out mathematical, statistical, financial, date, time, and other calculations.

1. Click the destination cell for the formula.
2. Type an equal sign to start the formula and then type the word SUM and a left parenthesis.
3. Drag down the column of numbers to sum.
4. Press Enter.

Points to Remember

1. You do not need to type the close (right) parenthesis before you press Enter—Excel will do it for you.
2. Use this technique instead of AutoSum to sum ranges of cells that contain blanks.

Average Function

You can use the Average function to calculate the average of values in cells.

1. Click the cell where you want to place the average function.
2. Type an equal sign (=) and then type the word AVERAGE and a left parenthesis.
3. Drag across the cells whose values you want to average.
4. Press Enter.
5. Blank cells are not counted in average.

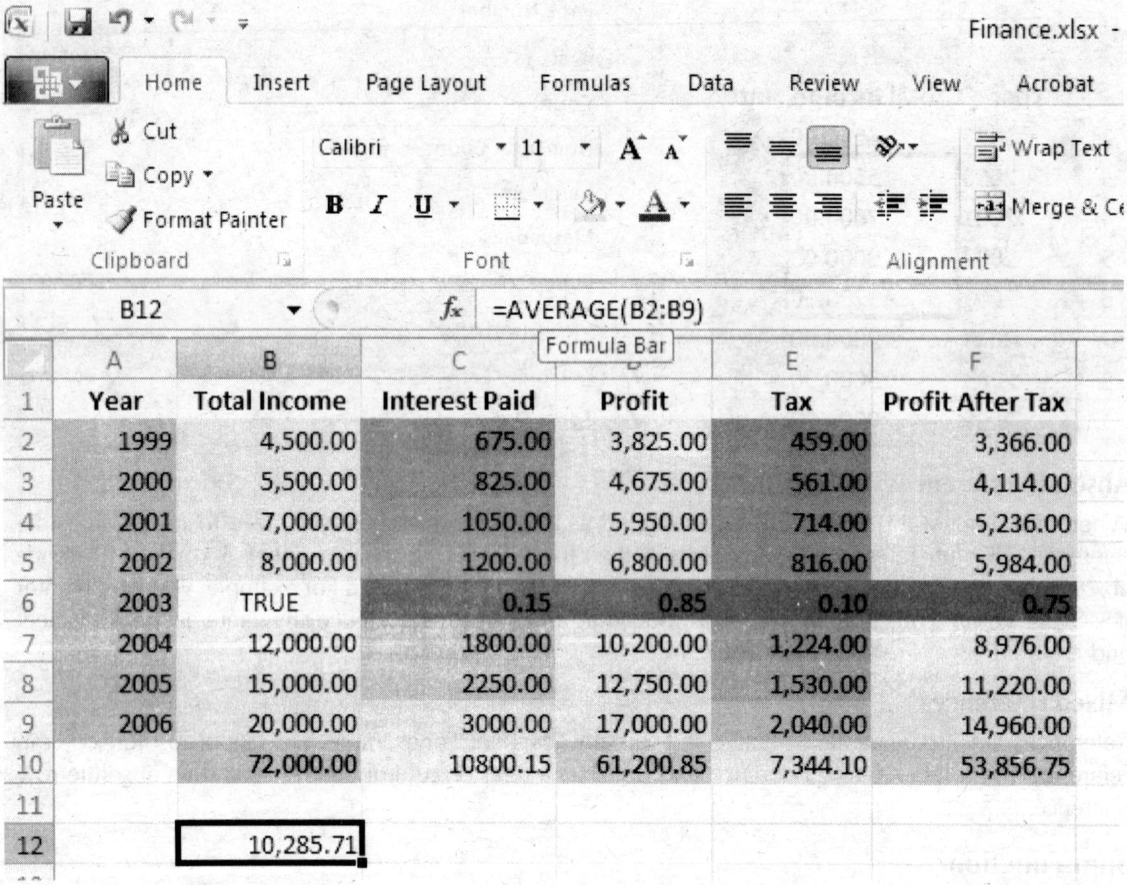

Finance.xlsx -
Home
Insert
Page Layout
Formulas
Data
Review
View
Acrobat
Cut
Copy
Paste
Format Painter
Clipboard
Calibri
11
Font
Wrap Text
Merge & Ce
Alignment
B12
=AVERAGE(B2:B9)
Formula Bar

	A	B	C	D	E	F
1	Year	Total Income	Interest Paid	Profit	Tax	Profit After Tax
2	1999	4,500.00	675.00	3,825.00	459.00	3,366.00
3	2000	5,500.00	825.00	4,675.00	561.00	4,114.00
4	2001	7,000.00	1050.00	5,950.00	714.00	5,236.00
5	2002	8,000.00	1200.00	6,800.00	816.00	5,984.00
6	2003	TRUE	0.15	0.85	0.10	0.75
7	2004	12,000.00	1800.00	10,200.00	1,224.00	8,976.00
8	2005	15,000.00	2250.00	12,750.00	1,530.00	11,220.00
9	2006	20,000.00	3000.00	17,000.00	2,040.00	14,960.00
10		72,000.00	10800.15	61,200.85	7,344.10	53,856.75
11						
12		10,285.71				

Creating Charts in Excel

In the earlier chapter we had created a worksheet and decorated it. There is another method of presenting this worksheet and that is by converting it into graphics and specially in the form of **Charts** in Excel. Let us use the same worksheet to make charts of the same. Different type of charts which can be created using Excel 2010 are shown here. Each one of them has various options underneath which can be chosen. For example, the 3-D column chart of the worksheet created earlier would be as shown below.

Column
Line
Pie
Bar
Area
Scatter
Other Charts
Charts

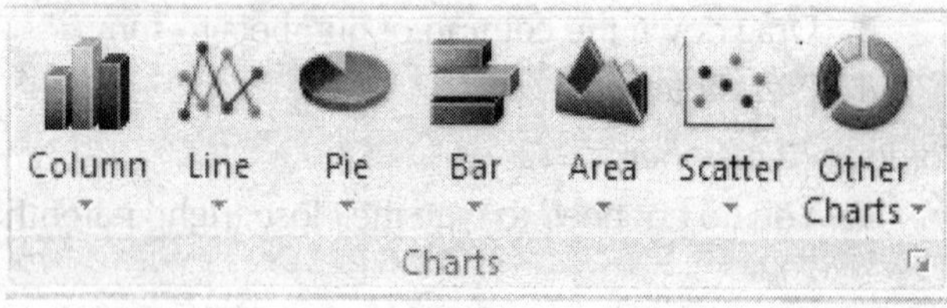

Similary you can create other type of charts. All these charts with their options can also be seen under All Chart Types under Other Charts.

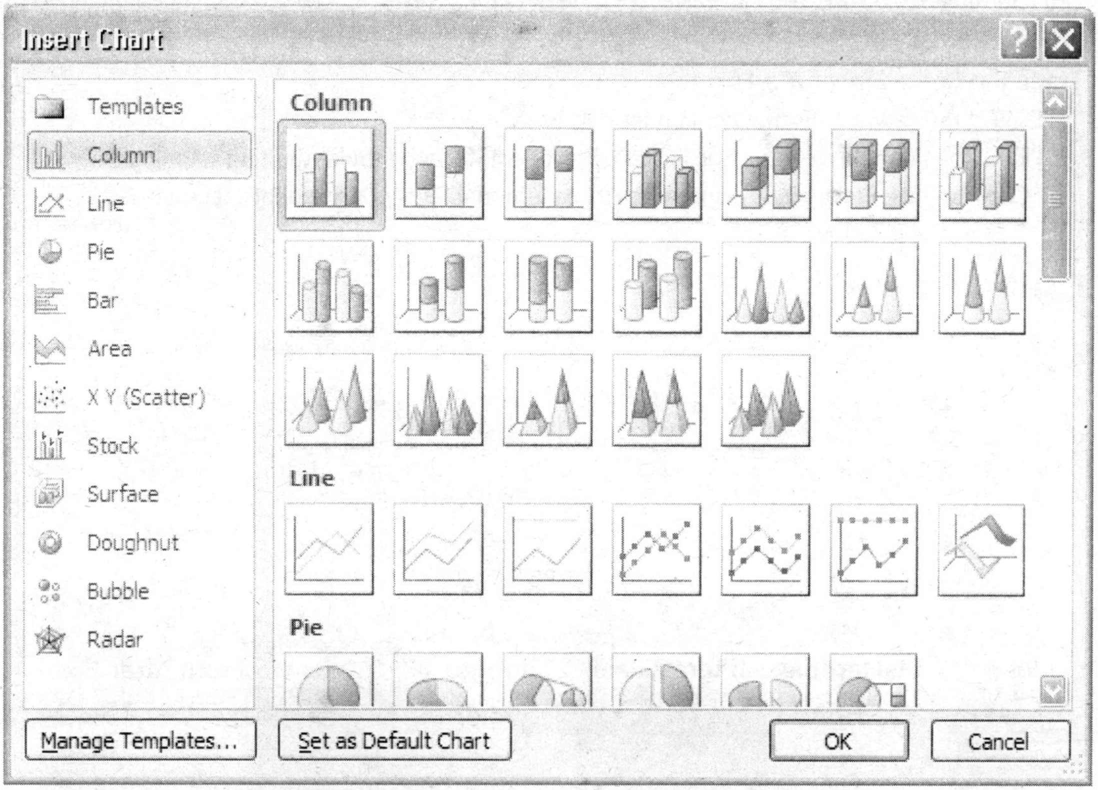

Insert Chart

Templates
Column
Line
Pie
Bar
Area
X Y (Scatter)
Stock
Surface
Doughnut
Bubble
Radar

Column

Line

Pie

Manage Templates... Set as Default Chart OK Cancel

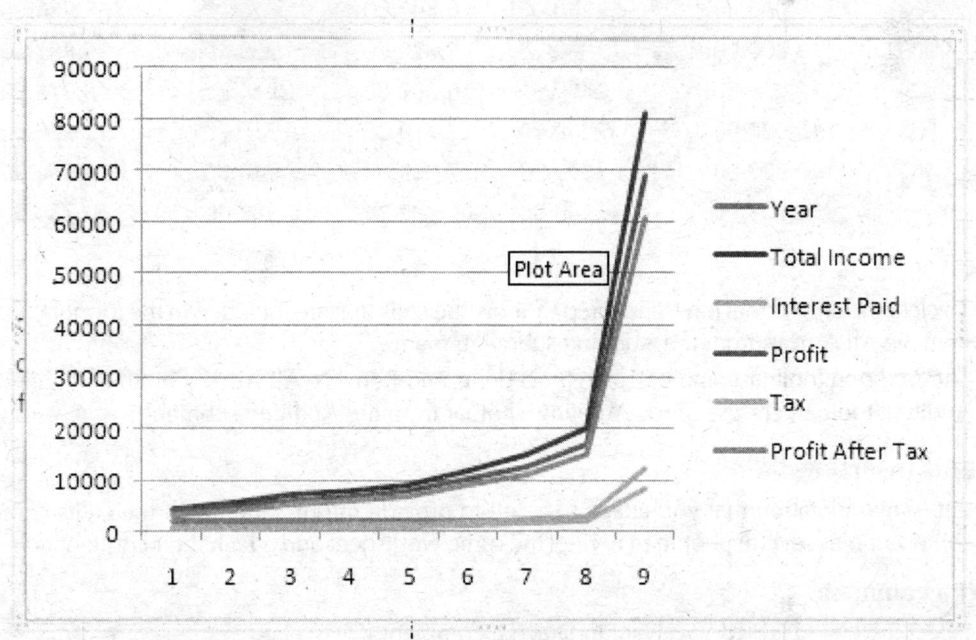

Auditing a Workbook

To avoid bogus results from incorrect formulas, you can have Excel identify the cells that have supplied data for a formula. That way, you can easily see whether all the cells you wanted have been included in the calculation.

To Trace the Precedents for a Formula:

1. Select the cell or cells that contain the formulas.
2. From the Formulas menu, choose Trace Precedents from Formula Auditing submenu.
3. Choose Trace Precedents again to view an additional level of precedents, if one exists.
4. This is shown below.

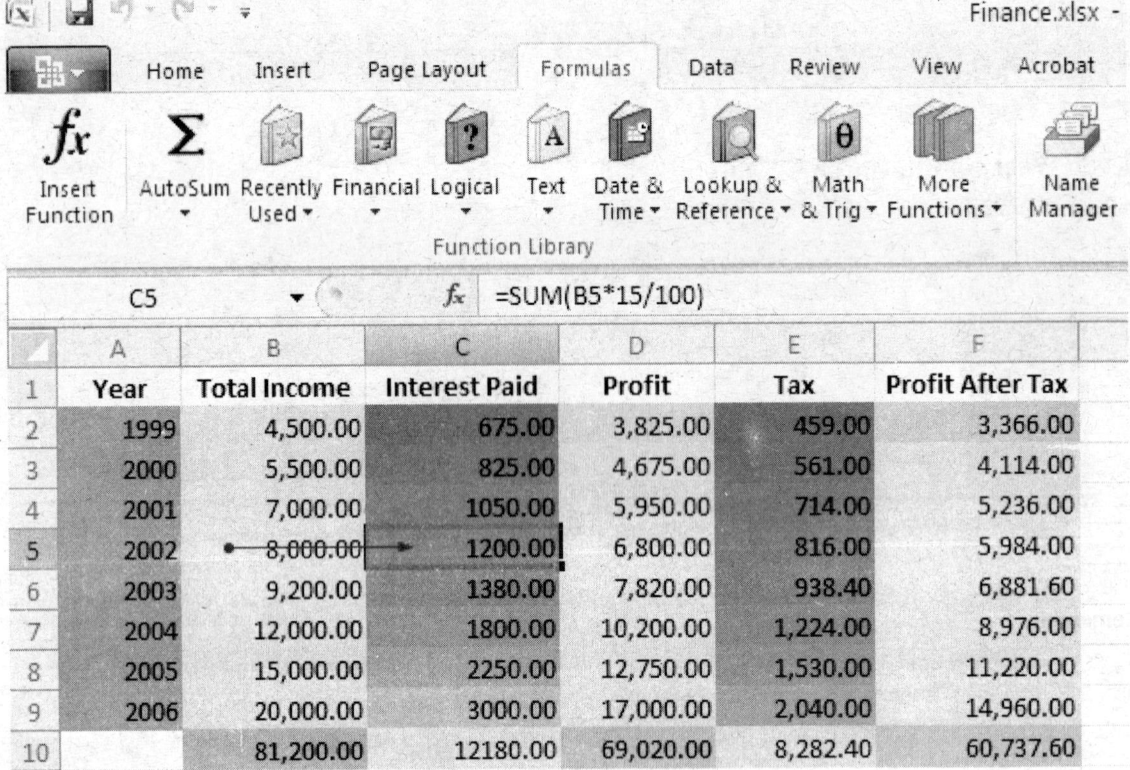

	A	B	C	D	E	F
1	Year	Total Income	Interest Paid	Profit	Tax	Profit After Tax
2	1999	4,500.00	675.00	3,825.00	459.00	3,366.00
3	2000	5,500.00	825.00	4,675.00	561.00	4,114.00
4	2001	7,000.00	1050.00	5,950.00	714.00	5,236.00
5	2002	8,000.00	1200.00	6,800.00	816.00	5,984.00
6	2003	9,200.00	1380.00	7,820.00	938.40	6,881.60
7	2004	12,000.00	1800.00	10,200.00	1,224.00	8,976.00
8	2005	15,000.00	2250.00	12,750.00	1,530.00	11,220.00
9	2006	20,000.00	3000.00	17,000.00	2,040.00	14,960.00
10		81,200.00	12180.00	69,020.00	8,282.40	60,737.60

Remember

1. To clear the arrows that have appeared to show the cells that are inciuded in the formula, choose Remove All Arrows from the Auditing submenu menu.
2. The Auditing toolbar contains Trace Precedents and Remove All Arrows buttons. To view the Auditing toolbar, choose Show Auditing Toolbar from the Auditing submenu.

Comments Inserting

A comment is an annotation that you attach to a cell to provide information about the cell's contents. This capability enables several people to review the same worksheet and attach their comments.

To insert a comment:

1. Select the cell to which you want to attach a comment.

2. From the Review menu, choose New Comment from Comments panel.
3. In the yellow text box that opens and displays the text for the comment.
4. Click in another cell to close the text box.

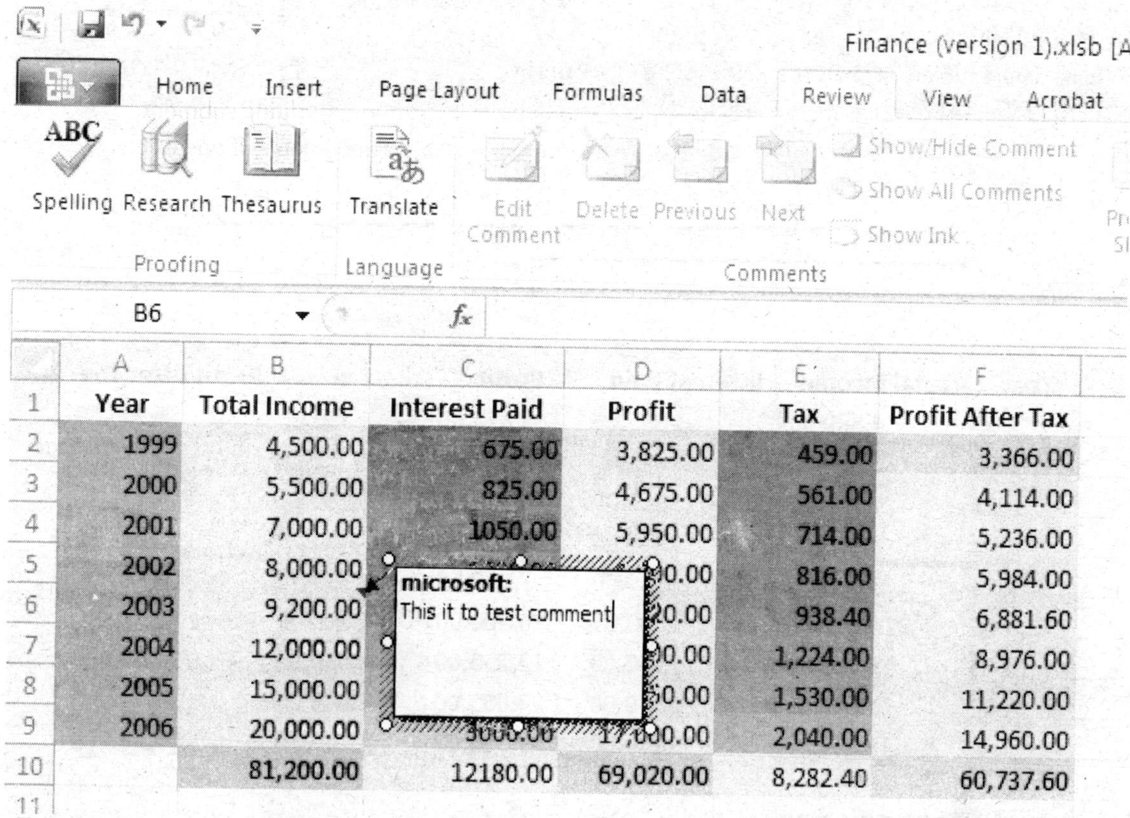

	A	B	C	D	E	F
1	Year	Total Income	Interest Paid	Profit	Tax	Profit After Tax
2	1999	4,500.00	675.00	3,825.00	459.00	3,366.00
3	2000	5,500.00	825.00	4,675.00	561.00	4,114.00
4	2001	7,000.00	1050.00	5,950.00	714.00	5,236.00
5	2002	8,000.00		0.00	816.00	5,984.00
6	2003	9,200.00		20.00	938.40	6,881.60
7	2004	12,000.00		0.00	1,224.00	8,976.00
8	2005	15,000.00		50.00	1,530.00	11,220.00
9	2006	20,000.00	3000.00	17,000.00	2,040.00	14,960.00
10		81,200.00	12180.00	69,020.00	8,282.40	60,737.60
11						

Remember

1. A comment is indicated by a comment marker (a small red triangle) at the upper right corner of the cell. To view the comment, pass the cursor over the cell.
2. To remove a comment, right-click in the cell, and choose Delete Comment from the shortcut menu.

Outlines

Outline a Worksheet Automatically

1. Select a single cell to outline or the entire worksheet
2. Select a range of cells to outline
3. Click Data menu, Group and Outline command, and click at Group.

An outline created with outline symbols to the left of the row heading and/or above column headings.

Clear Entire Outline

1. Select any cell in outline
2. Click at Data menu, Outline and Ungroup command, and Clear Outline.

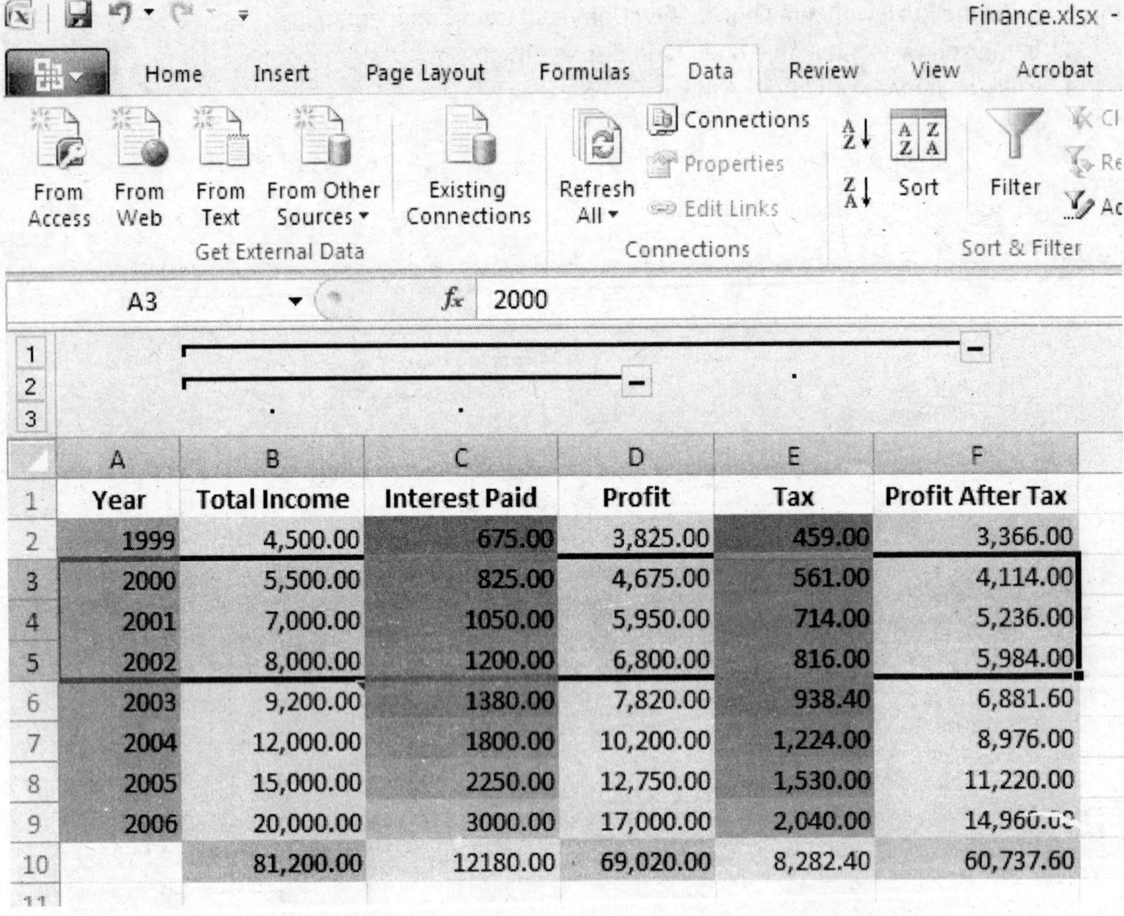

	A	B	C	D	E	F
1	Year	Total Income	Interest Paid	Profit	Tax	Profit After Tax
2	1999	4,500.00	675.00	3,825.00	459.00	3,366.00
3	2000	5,500.00	825.00	4,675.00	561.00	4,114.00
4	2001	7,000.00	1050.00	5,950.00	714.00	5,236.00
5	2002	8,000.00	1200.00	6,800.00	816.00	5,984.00
6	2003	9,200.00	1380.00	7,820.00	938.40	6,881.60
7	2004	12,000.00	1800.00	10,200.00	1,224.00	8,976.00
8	2005	15,000.00	2250.00	12,750.00	1,530.00	11,220.00
9	2006	20,000.00	3000.00	17,000.00	2,040.00	14,960.00
10		81,200.00	12180.00	69,020.00	8,282.40	60,737.60

Worksheet Fitting on a Page

If your worksheet is too large to print on one page even after you change the orientation and margins, you might consider using the Fit to option.

This option shrinks the worksheet to make it fit on the specified number of pages. You can specify the document's width and height.

Follow these steps to scale a worksheet to fit on a page:

1. Open the Page Setup menu and choose Page Setup and Print Area. The Page Setup dialog box appears.
2. Click the Page tab to display the Page options.
3. In the Fit to XX page wide by XX tall text boxes, enter the number of pages in which you want Excel to fit your data.
4. Click Ok to close the Page Setup dialog box and return to your worksheet. Or click the Print button in the Page Setup dialog box to display the Print dialog box, and then click Ok to print your worksheet.

Function Wizard

Sum and Average are just two of the most commonly used functions whereas there are lots of them in Excel. You can use them to get the desired results in a flash.

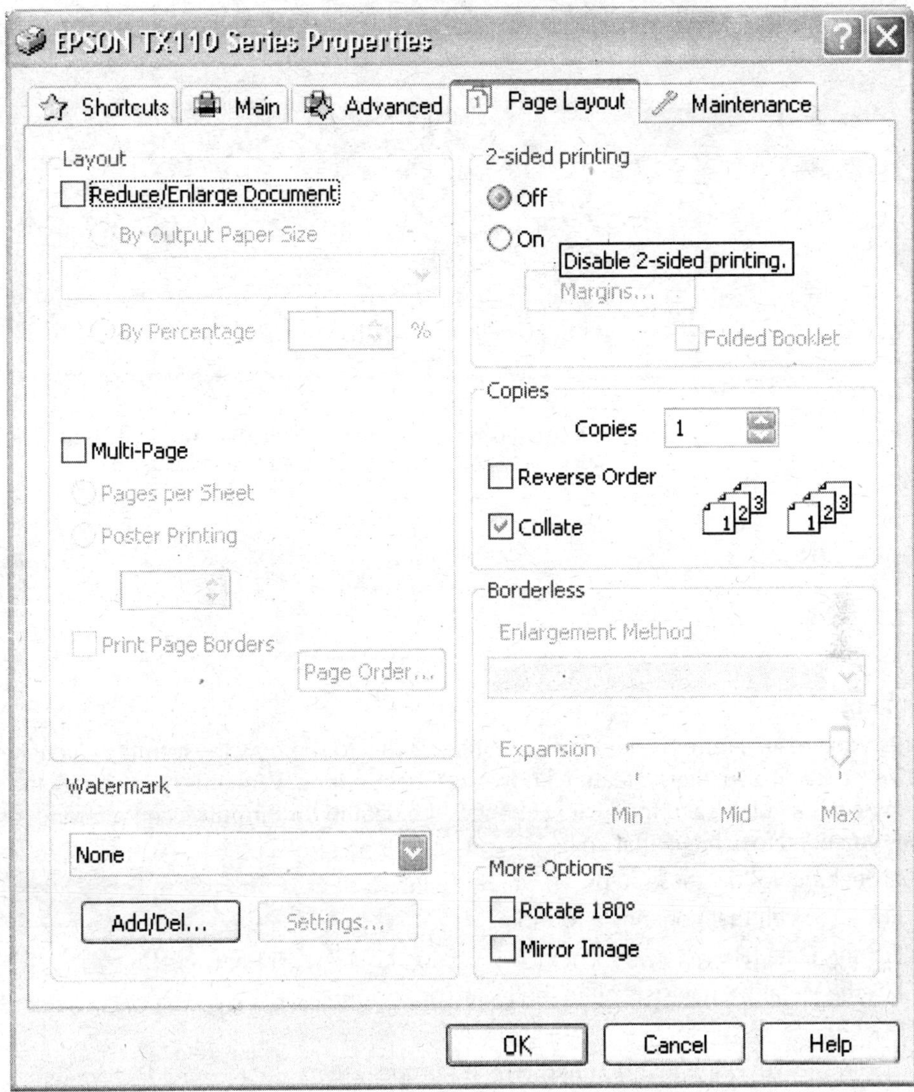

To get them click at the Formulas menu and then Function Library. Here you have the various options of the functions which you can choose from.

Insert Function

The Insert Function button is the option for building the formula. The Insert Function wizard takes you through the steps of building a formula.

1. Click the destination cell for the formula.
2. Click the Insert Function button.
3. In the Insert Function dialog box, select the category and then the function.
4. Click Ok.
5. Use the Insert Function Wizard to guide you in completing the formula.
6. Click Ok when you have finished.

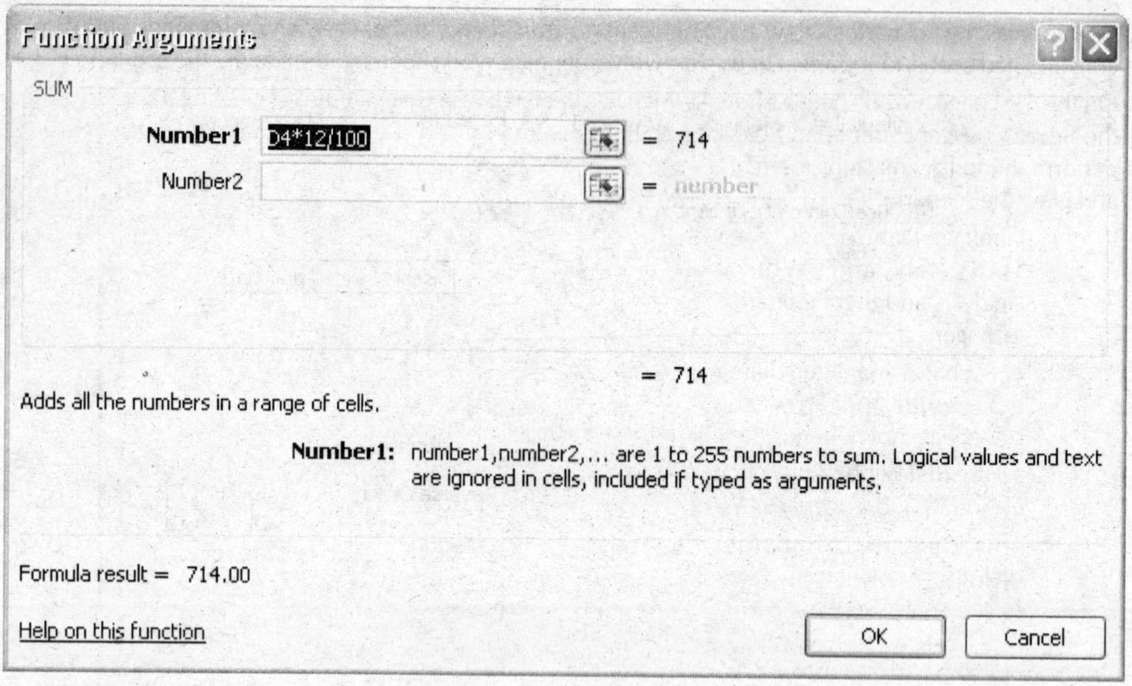

Function Arguments

SUM

Number1 D4*12/100 = 714

Number2 = number

= 714

Adds all the numbers in a range of cells.

Number1: number1,number2,... are 1 to 255 numbers to sum. Logical values and text are ignored in cells, included if typed as arguments.

Formula result = 714.00

Help on this function

OK Cancel

Goal Seeking

Usually after you create a formula, you can type in new data to see how the formula calculates the new result. However, Excel also offers a feature known as Goal Seeking. With this, you specify the value you want a formula to calculate, and then Excel changes the data in thr formula's cell references to tell you what values you need to achieve that goal.

To use Goal Seeking, follow these steps.

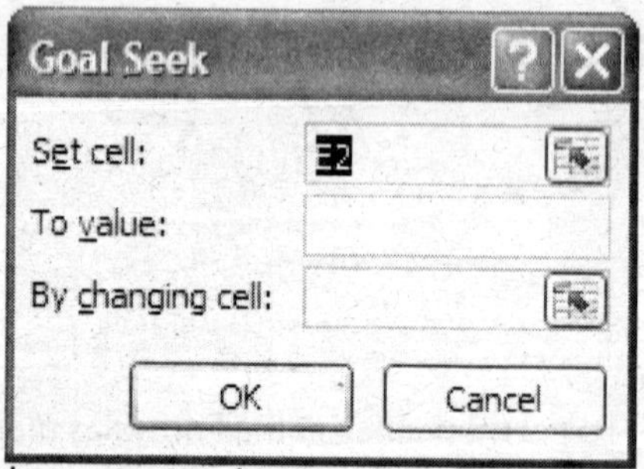

1. Click a the cell that contains a formula.
2. Click the Data tab.
3. Click the What-If Analysis Icon in the Data Tools group.
4. Click Goal Seek.
5. Click in the To Value text box and type a number that you want to appear in the formula stored in the cell that you clicked in Step 1.
6. Click in the By Changing Cell text box and click one cell that contains data used by the formula you choose in Step 1.
7. Click Ok.
8. Click Ok (to keep the changes) or click Cancel (to display the origianl vlaue your spreadsheet had before you choose the Goal Seek command)

Goal Seek

Set cell: E2

To value:

By changing cell:

OK Cancel

Scenarios Manager

Human mind is made of What-if situations. The same what-if can be applied to your worksheet to see if the results of the selection displays the good or bad results.

Each time you change the data, the previous solution is lost. To address this limitation, the Scenario Manager helps you keep track of multiple what-if models. Using the Scenarios manager, you can create new forecasting scenarios, view existing scenario, run scenario management commands and display consolidated scenario reports. Let us start with creating a worksheet and then apply the scenario to it.

On the next page a worksheet is shown which has been taken as an example for creating a scenario. Here the figures are very simple and calculated. If you want you can use the constant figures too. Next we perform the following steps to create and view the scenario.

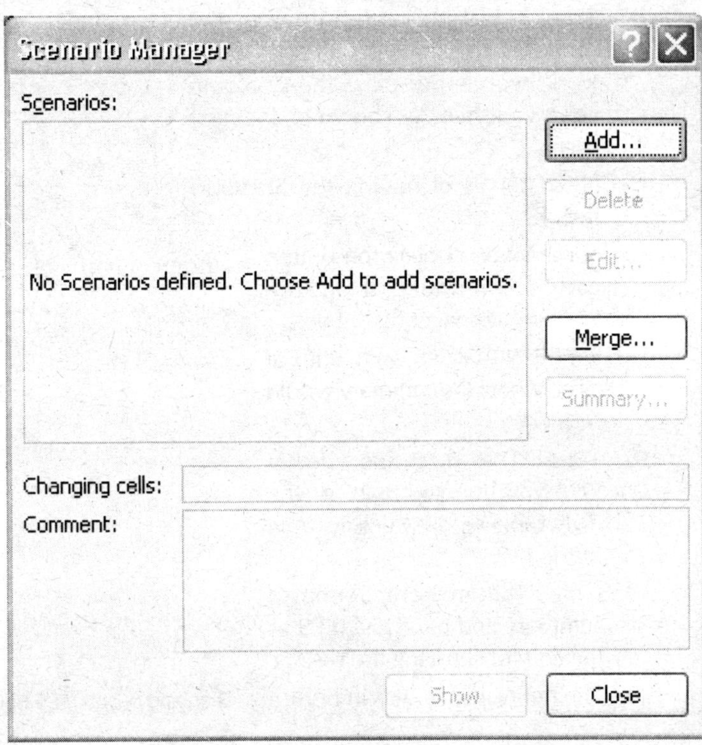

1. Click at Data panel, Data Tools tab and What-If Analysis and then Scenarios manager.
2. A Scenario manager dialog box would appear on the screen, as shown here.
3. As the dialog box says, click at Add to add a scenario.
4. This gives rise to another dialog box, which is called Add scenario.
5. In this dialog box, you have to firstly name the screnario.
6. I have named it as Good.
7. You can type the cell names or choose them by clicking at those cells. I have chosen cells from E2 to E4.
8. Click OK to add your scenario to the Scenario Manager. You'll see the Scenario Values dialog box, which asks you for your model's variables. The default values are the numbers that were already in the cells.
9. Type the various values which you want to see in the scenario.
10. Click Add to create a second scenario. If you do not want another set, just click at Ok.
11. This will return you to the scenario manager with your scenario added to it.

12. As mentioned you can add another scenario to it.
13. Now we will see how this scenario works. For this click at Show.
14. Excel substitutes the values in the scenario for the variables in your worksheet and displays the results in your worksheet, as shown on the next page.
15. Next step is of having the Scenario Reports.
16. For this you choose the button called Summary from the Scenario Manager dialog box.
17. For this you will have to click at a cell where the summary would be placed.
18. You also have to define whether you want the summary or the PivtoTable report. Click any one of the two.
19. I have taken here Scenario summary and have given E9 as the cell for showing the results.
20. The net results is shown here.

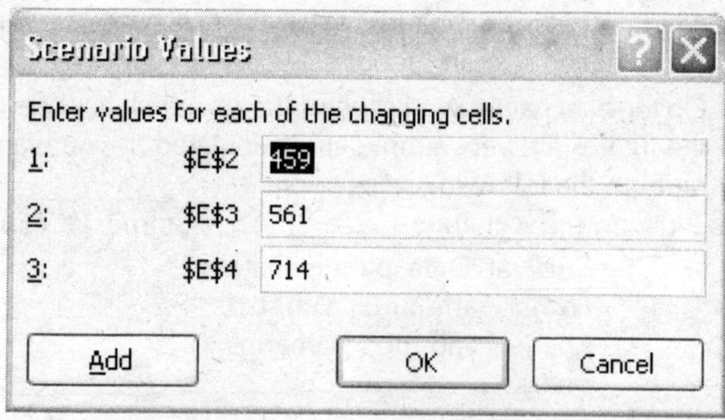

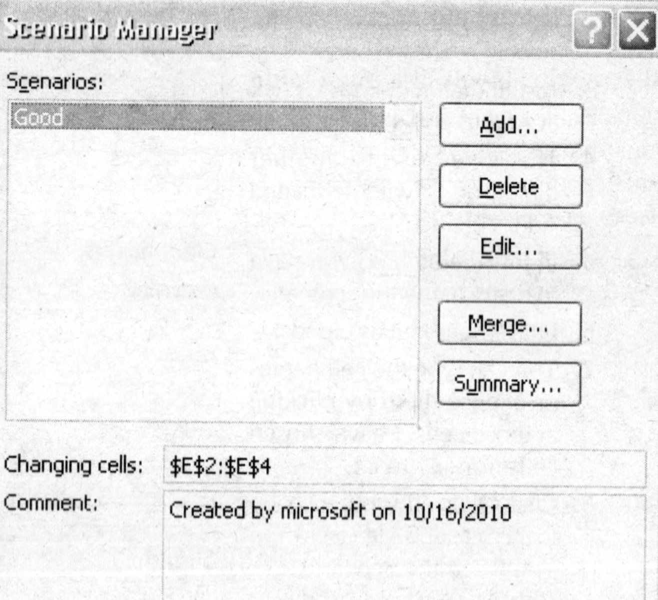

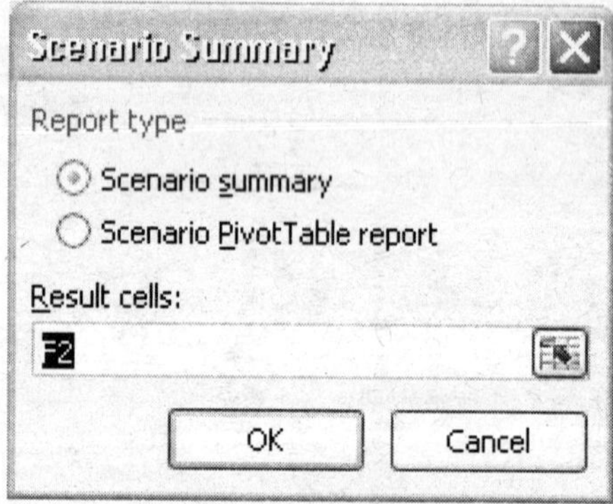

Scenario Summary		
	Current Values:	Good
Changing Cells:		
$E$2	459.00	459.00
$E$3	561.00	561.00
$E$4	714.00	714.00
Result Cells:		
$F$2	3,366.00	3,366.00

Creating a Pivot Table Report

PivotTable reports can help you look at data in different ways. Once the reports are created, you can swap rows with columns for different views.

1. Click in the selected data area.
2. From the Insert menu, choose PivotTable in the Tables group.
3. Select the cells that contain the data yu want to use in your pivot table. This is optional.

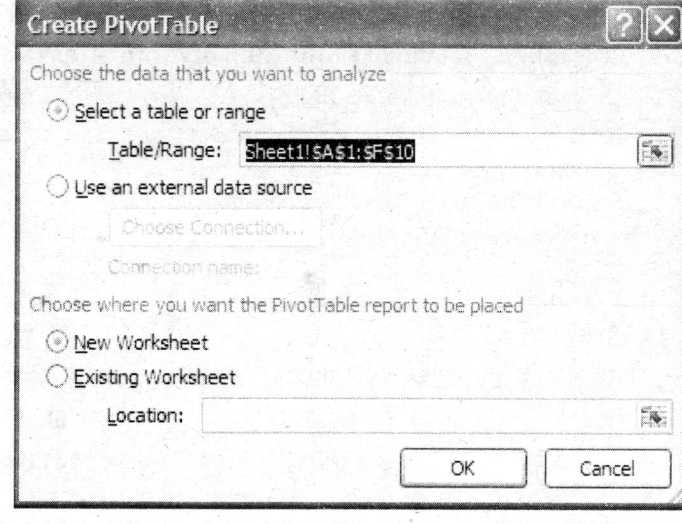

4. Select one of the following radio buttons:
   - New Worksheet: Puts the pivot table on a new worksheet.
   - Existing Worksheet: Puts the pivot table on an existing worksheet.
5. Click Ok, Excel displays a Pivot Table Fiel List pane.
6. Mark one or more check boxes inside the PivotTable Field List pane.

Rearranging labels in a pivot table

A pivot table organizesdata according to your spreadsheet's columns headings, which appear in a pivot table as row labels. To rearrange column headings in a pivot table, follow these steps:

1. Click the pivot table you want to rearrange.
2. Click the downward-pointing arrow of a lable that appears under the Row Labels group.

   Select one of the following:

   Move Up: Moves the lable one level closer to the beginning.

   Move Down: Moves the lable one level down to the end.

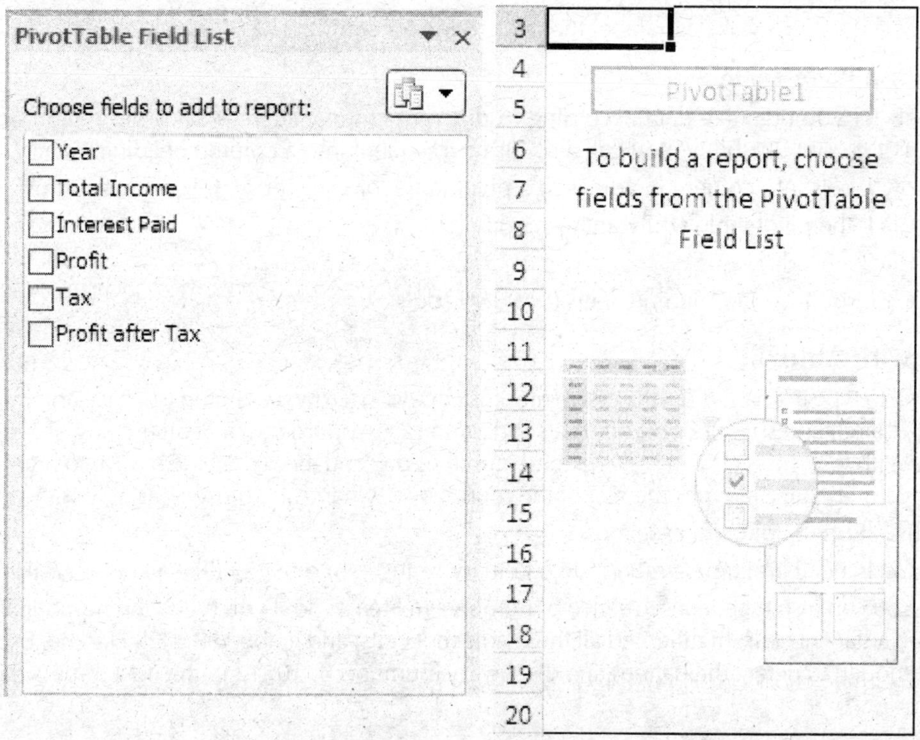

3		Values	
4	Row Labels	Sum of Profit	Sum of Profit after Tax
5	1999	3825	3366
6	2000	4675	4114
7	2001	5950	5236
8	2002	6800	5984
9	2003	7650	6732
10	2004	10200	8976
11	2005	12750	11220
12	2006	17000	14960
13	(blank)	68850	60588
14	**Grand Total**	**137700**	**121176**
15			
16			
17			
18			
19			
20			
21			

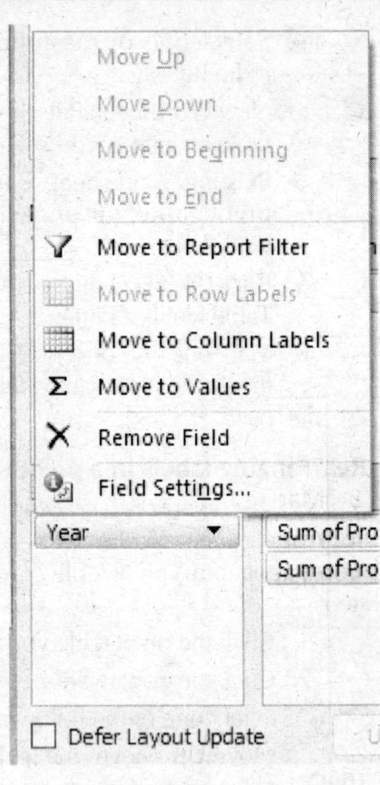

Move to Beginning: Makes the label the dominant criteria for sorting data.

Move to End: Makes the label the last criteria for sorting data.

Modifying a Pivot Table

Row labels let you organize data according to different criteria, such as sales per region and then by product. For greater flexibility, you can also turn a row label into a column heading.

To turn row labels into column headings in a pivot table (or vice versa), follow these steps:

1. Click the pivot table you want to modify.
2. Click a heading.
3. Choose Move to Column Labels (or Row Labels).

Typing with AutoFill

If you need to type the names of successive months or days in a row or column (such as January, February, February, March and so on). Excel offers a shortcut to save you from typing all the day or month names yourself. With this shortcut, you just type one month or day and them drag the mouse to highlight all the adjacent cell. Then Excel types the rest of the month or day names in those cells automatically.

To use this shortcut, follow these steps:

1. Click a cell and type a month (like January or just Jan) or a day (like Monday or just Mon).

   You can also type in a sequence of numbers in Step 1. So if you typed the numbers 2, 4, and 6 in adjacent cells, highlighted all these adjacent cells, and grabbed the Fill Handle, Excel is smart enough to detect the pattern and display the numbers 8, 10, 12 in the next three adjacent cells.

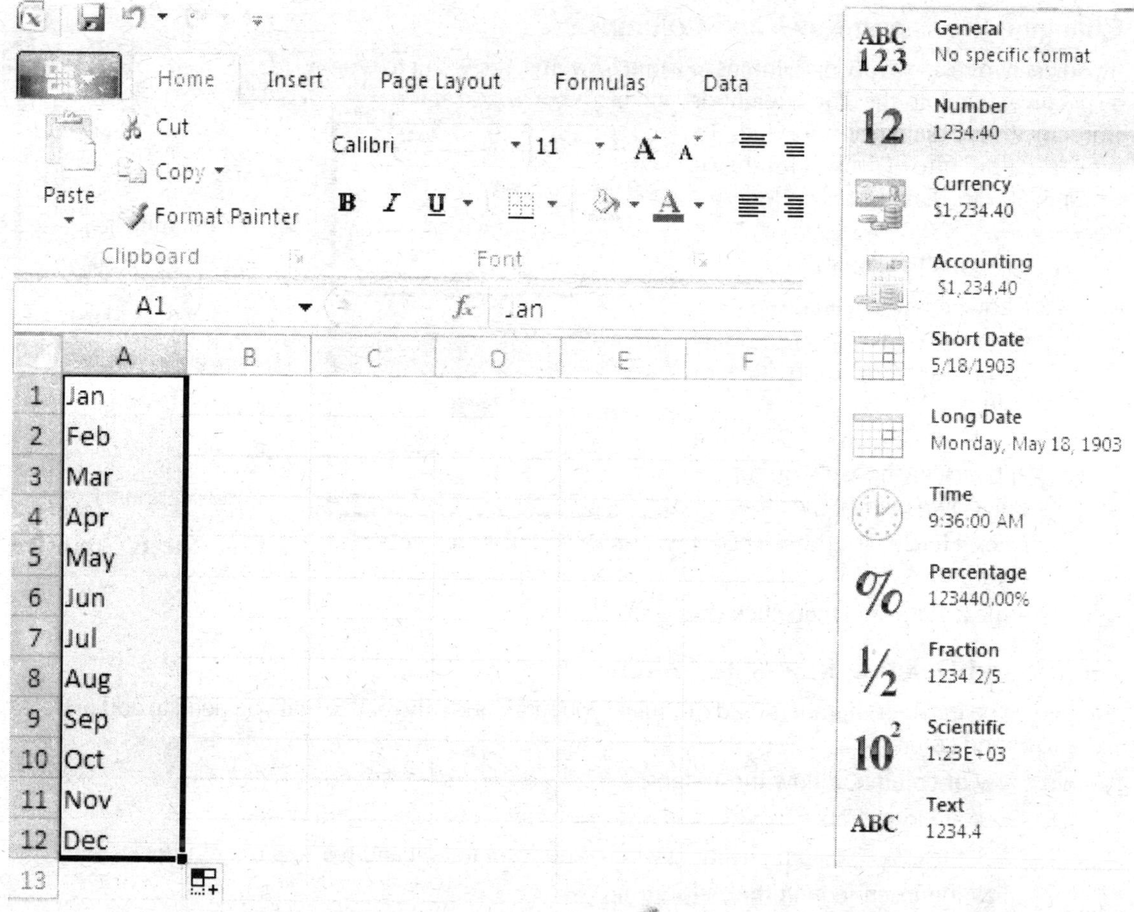

2. Move the mouse pointer over the Fill Handle until the mouse pointer turns into a black corosshair icon.
3. Hold down the left mouse button and drag the mouse down a column or across the row. As you drag the mouse, Excel automatically types in the remaining month or day names.

Formatting Numbers and Labels

When you first create a spreadsheet, numbers and labels appear as plain text. Plain labels might look boring, but plain numbers, such as 8495 or 0.29, can be difficult to read and understand it the numbers are supposed to represent currency amounts ($8,495) or percentage (29%). To make labels visually intersesting and numbers appear more description of what they actually represent, you need to format your data after you type it into a spreadsheet.

Formatting Numbers

To format the appearance of numbers, follow these steps:

1. Select one or more cells using the mouse or keyboard.
2. Click the Home tab.
3. Click the Number Format list box in the Number group.

Changing the size of Rows and Columns

If you need to resize a row or columns to a precise value, it's easier to type a specific value into the Row Height or Column Width dialog box instead. To type a value into a Row Height or Column Width dialog box, follow hes steps:

1. Click the Home tab.
2. Click the row or column heading that you want to resize. Excel highlights your entire row or column.
3. Click the Format icon that appears in the Cells group. A pull-down menu appears.
4. Click Height, if you select a row, or Width, if you selected a column.
5. Type a vlaue and then click Ok.

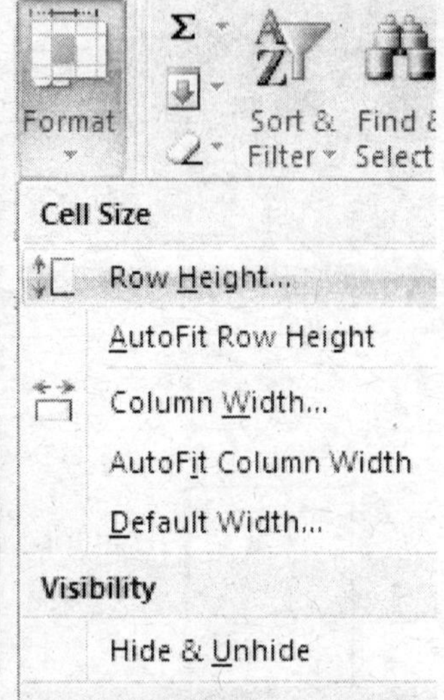

Adding and Deleting Rows and Columns

After you type in labels, numbers, and formulas, you may suddenly realize that you need to add or delete extra rows and columns.

To add a row or column, follow these steps:

1. Click at Home Tab.
2. Click the row or column heading where you want to add another row or column.
3. Click the Insert icon in the Cells group.

   Inserting a row adds a new row above the selected row. Inserting a column adds a new column to the left of the selected column.

To delete a row or column, follow these steps:

1. Click at Home tab.
2. Click the row or column heading that you want to delete.
3. Click the Delete icon in the Cells group.

   Deleting a row or colun deletes any data stored in that row or column.

Inserting (and Removing) Page Breaks

One problem with large spreadsheets is that when you print them out, parts may get cut off when printed on separate pages. To correct this problem, you can tell Excel exactly where page breaks should occur.

To insert page breaks, follow these steps:

1. Move the cursor in the cell to define where the vertical and horizontal page breaks will appear.
2. Click the Page Layout tab.
3. Click the Breaks icon in the Page Setup group.
4. Choose Insert Page Break.

   Excfel inserts a horizontal page directly above the cell you selected in Step 1 and a vertical page break to the left of that cell, too.

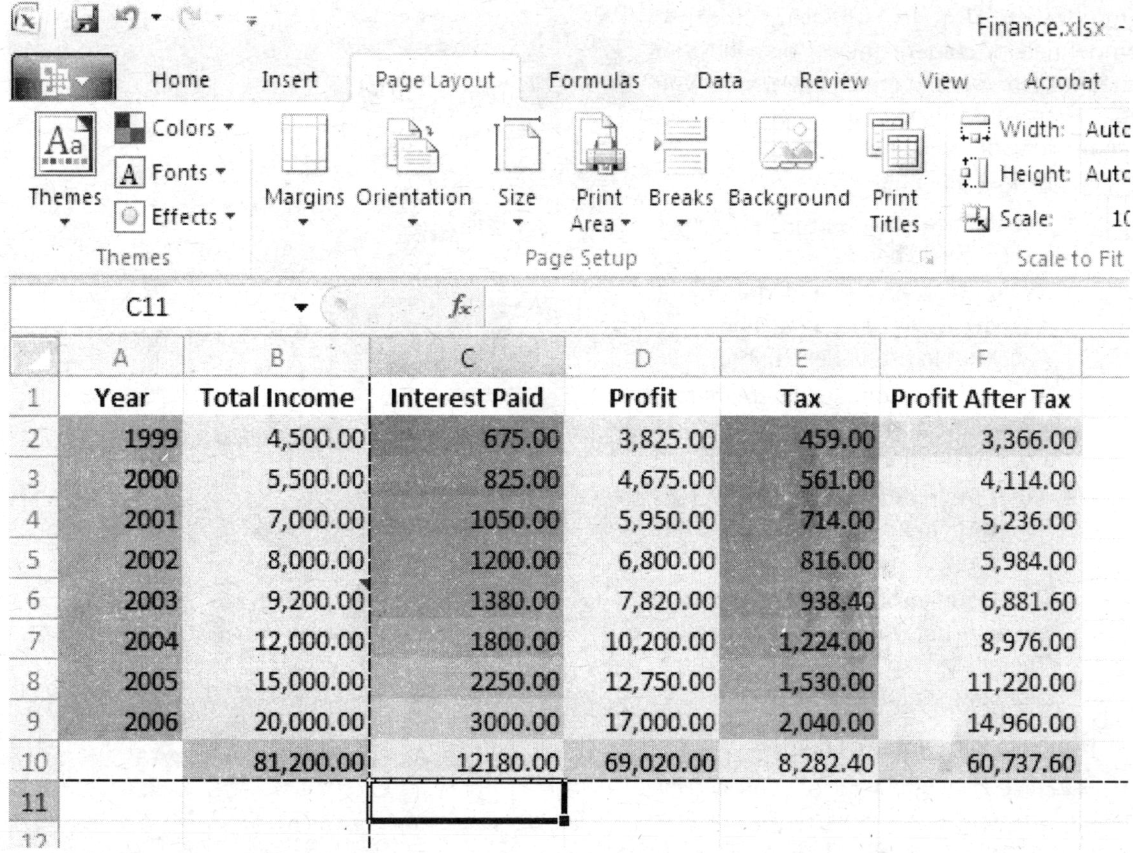

	A	B	C	D	E	F
1	Year	Total Income	Interest Paid	Profit	Tax	Profit After Tax
2	1999	4,500.00	675.00	3,825.00	459.00	3,366.00
3	2000	5,500.00	825.00	4,675.00	561.00	4,114.00
4	2001	7,000.00	1050.00	5,950.00	714.00	5,236.00
5	2002	8,000.00	1200.00	6,800.00	816.00	5,984.00
6	2003	9,200.00	1380.00	7,820.00	938.40	6,881.60
7	2004	12,000.00	1800.00	10,200.00	1,224.00	8,976.00
8	2005	15,000.00	2250.00	12,750.00	1,530.00	11,220.00
9	2006	20,000.00	3000.00	17,000.00	2,040.00	14,960.00
10		81,200.00	12180.00	69,020.00	8,282.40	60,737.60
11						
12						

To remove a page break, follow these steps:

1. Choose one of the following:
   - To remove a horizontal page break: Click in any cell that appears directly below that horizontal page break.
   - To remove a vertical page break: Click in any cell that appears directly to the right of the vertical page break and directly underneath the horizontal page break.
   - To remove both a vertical and horizontal page break: Click in the cell that appears to the right of the vertical page break and directly underneath the horizontal page break.
2. Click the Page Layout tab.
3. Click the Breaks icon in the Page Setup group.
4. Choose Remove Page Break. Excel removes your chosen page break.

Applying Themes

You can quickly and easily format an entire document to give it a professional and modern look by applying a document theme. A document theme is a set of formatting choices that include a set of theme colors, a set of theme fonts (including heading and body text fonts), and a set of theme effects (including lines and fill effects).

Apply a Document Theme

You can change the document theme that is applied by default in Office programs, such as Word, Excel, and PowerPoint, by selecting another predefined document theme or a custom document theme. Document themes that you apply immediately affect the styles that you can use in your document.

Do one of the following:

- On the Page Layout tab, in the Themes group, click Themes.
- To apply a predefined document theme, click the document theme that you want to use under Built-In.
- To apply a custom document theme, click the document theme that you want to use under Custom.
- Custom is available only if you created one or more custom document themes.
- If a document theme that you want to use is not listed, click Browse for Themes to find it on your computer or a network location.

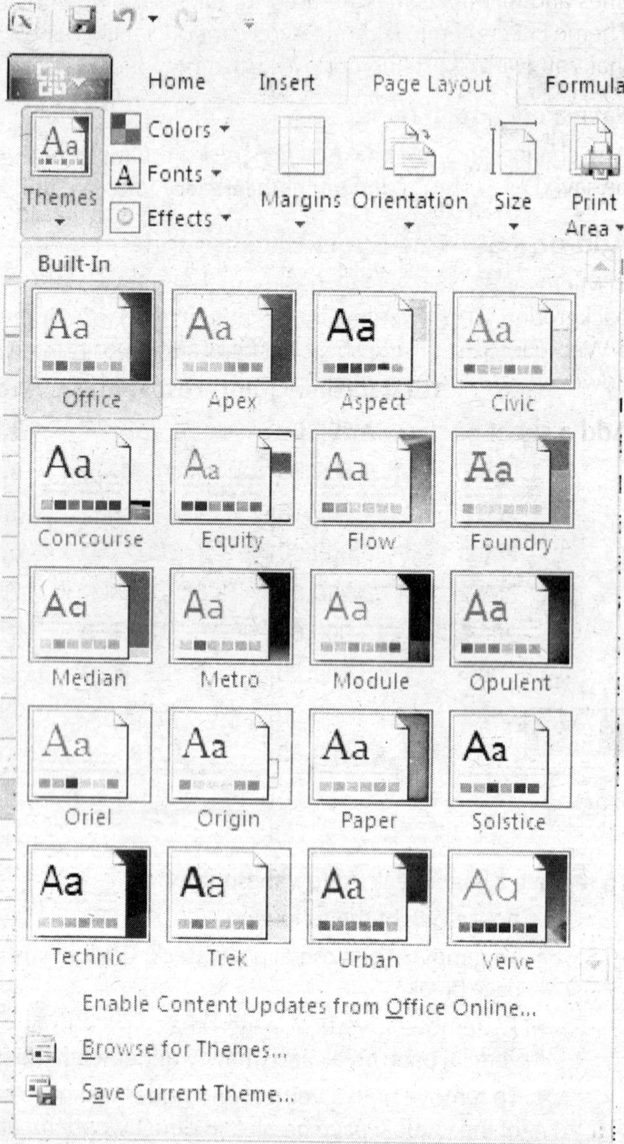

Customize a Document Theme

To customize a document theme, you start by changing the colors, the fonts, or the line and fill effects that are used. Changes that you make to one or more of these theme components immediately affect the styles that you have applied in the active document. If you want to apply these changes to new documents, you can save them as a custom document theme.

Customize the theme colors

Theme colors contain four text and background colors, six accent colors, and two hyperlink colors. The colors in the Theme Colors button represent the current text and background colors. The set of colors that you see next to the Theme Colors name after you click the Theme Colors button represent the accent and hyperlink colors for that theme. When you change any of these colors to create your own set of theme colors, the colors that are shown in the Theme Colors button and next to the Theme Colors name will change accordingly.

Customize the theme fonts

Theme fonts contain a heading font and a body text font. When you click the Theme Fonts button, you can see the name of the heading font and body text font that is used for each theme font below the Theme Fonts name. You can change both of these fonts to create your own set of theme fonts.

Select a set of theme effects

Theme effects are sets of lines and fill effects. When you click the Theme Effects button , you can see the lines and fill effects that are used for each set of theme effects in the graphic that is displayed with the Theme Effects name. Although you cannot create your own set of theme effects, you can choose the one that you want to use in your own document theme.

Save a document theme

Any changes that you make to the colors, the fonts, or the line and fill effects of a document theme can be saved as a custom document theme that you can apply to other documents.

Add or Remove a Sheet Background

In Microsoft Office Excel, you can use a picture as a sheet background for display purposes only. A sheet background is not printed, and it is not retained in an individual worksheet or in an item that you save as a Web page. Because a sheet background is not printed, it cannot be used as a watermark. You can, however, mimic a watermark by inserting a graphic in a header or footer.

Add a sheet background

1. Click the worksheet that you want to display with a sheet background. Make sure that only one worksheet is selected.
2. On the Page Layout tab, in the Page Setup group, click Background.
3. Select the picture that you want to use for the sheet background, and then click Insert.
4. The selected picture is repeated to fill the sheet.

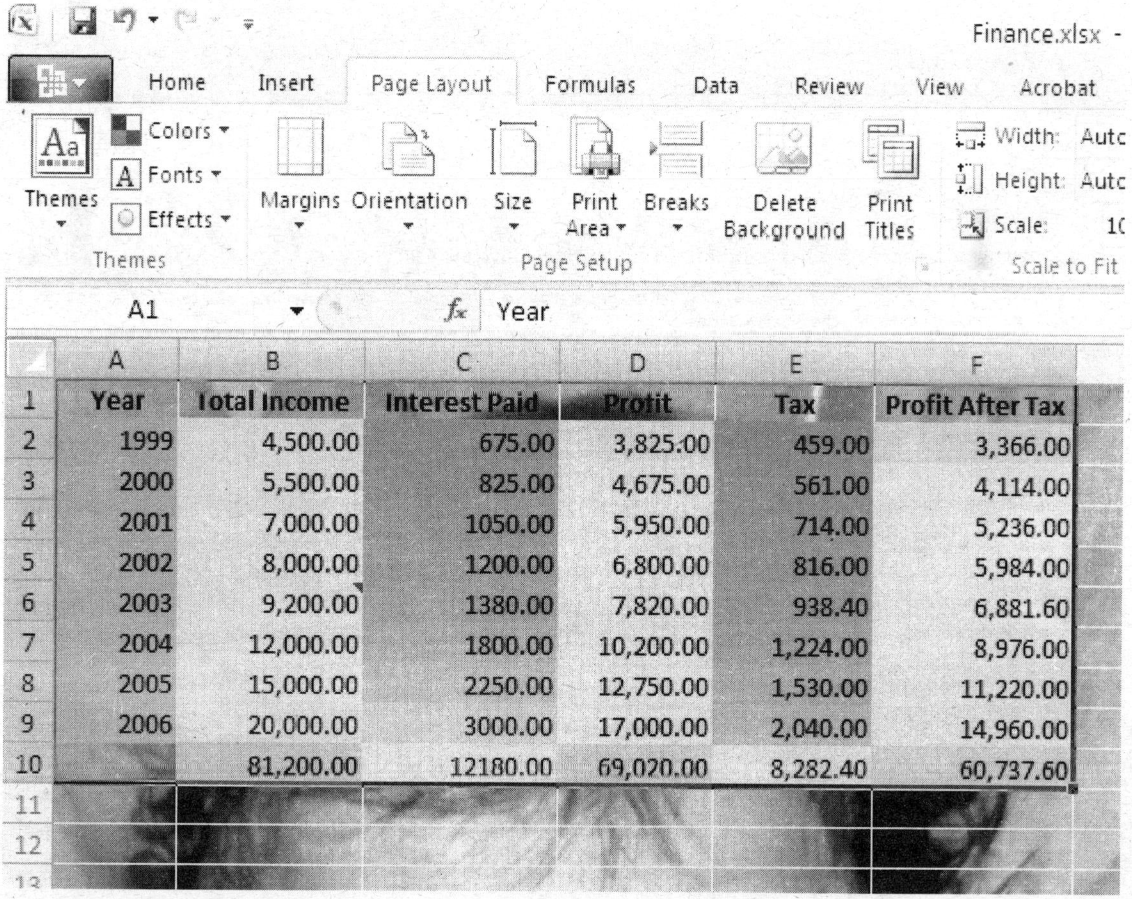

Finance.xlsx -

Home | Insert | Page Layout | Formulas | Data | Review | View | Acrobat

Themes: Themes, Colors, Fonts, Effects
Page Setup: Margins, Orientation, Size, Print Area, Breaks, Delete Background, Print Titles
Scale to Fit: Width: Autc, Height: Autc, Scale: 1(

A1 | fx Year

	A	B	C	D	E	F
1	Year	Total Income	Interest Paid	Profit	Tax	Profit After Tax
2	1999	4,500.00	675.00	3,825.00	459.00	3,366.00
3	2000	5,500.00	825.00	4,675.00	561.00	4,114.00
4	2001	7,000.00	1050.00	5,950.00	714.00	5,236.00
5	2002	8,000.00	1200.00	6,800.00	816.00	5,984.00
6	2003	9,200.00	1380.00	7,820.00	938.40	6,881.60
7	2004	12,000.00	1800.00	10,200.00	1,224.00	8,976.00
8	2005	15,000.00	2250.00	12,750.00	1,530.00	11,220.00
9	2006	20,000.00	3000.00	17,000.00	2,040.00	14,960.00
10		81,200.00	12180.00	69,020.00	8,282.40	60,737.60
11						
12						
13						

Remove a sheet background

1. Click the worksheet that is displayed with a sheet background. Make sure that only one worksheet is selected.
2. On the Page Layout tab, in the Page Setup group, click Background.

Convert Text to Columns

You can convert text to columns in Excel by using the Wizard called Convet Text to Columns. For this select the text which you want to convert and select the wizard from Data menu and Text to Columns from Data Tools tab. Rest is easy. Just follow the three steps shown here.

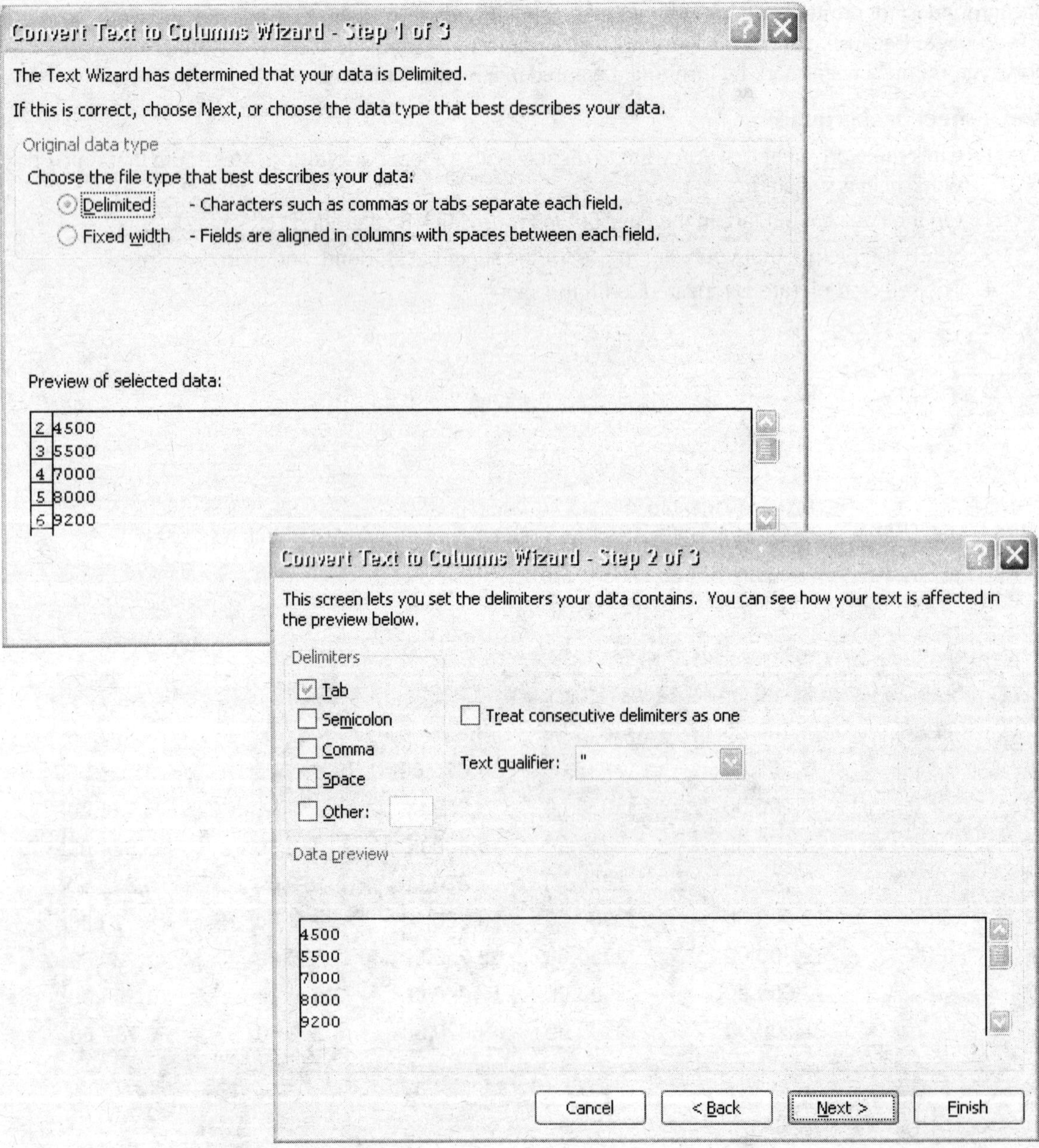

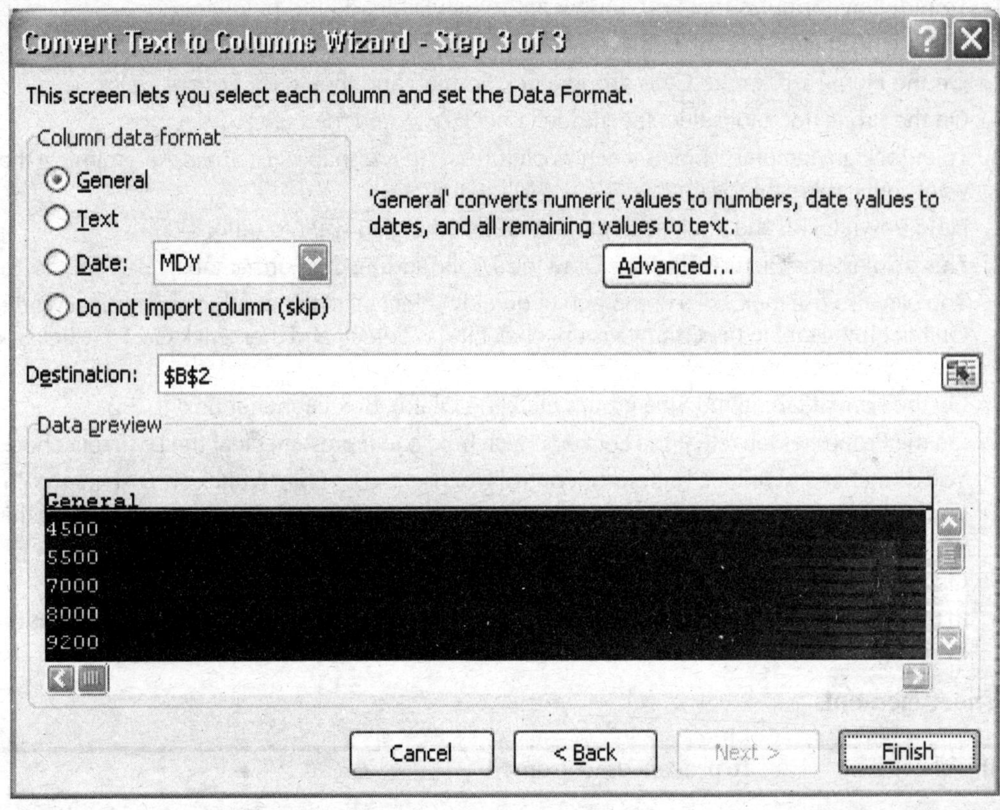

Protect Worksheet or Workbook Elements

To prevent a user from accidentally or deliberately changing, moving, or deleting important data, you can protect certain worksheet (worksheet: The primary document that you use in Excel to store and work with data. Also called a spreadsheet. A worksheet consists of cells that are organized into columns and rows; a worksheet is always stored in a workbook.) or workbook elements, with or without a password.

Workbook and worksheet element protection should not be confused with workbook-level password security. Element protection cannot protect a workbook from users who have malicious intent.

Protect Worksheet Elements

1. Select the worksheet that you want to protect.
2. To unlock any cells or ranges that you want other users to be able to change, do the following:
1. Select each cell or range that you want to unlock.
2. On the Home tab, in the Cells group, click Format, and then click Format Cells.
3. On the Protection tab, clear the Locked check box, and then click OK.

3. To hide any formulas that you don't want to be visible, do the following:
1. In the worksheet, select the cells that contain the formulas that you want to hide.
2. On the Home tab, in the Cells group, click Format, and then click Format Cells.
3. On the Protection tab, select the Hidden check box, and then click OK.
4. To unlock any graphic objects (such as pictures, clip art, shapes, or Smart Art graphics) that you want users to be able to change, do the following:
1. Hold down CTRL and click each graphic object that you want to unlock.
2. This displays the Picture Tools or Drawing Tools, adding the Format tab.

   You can also use the Go To command to quickly select all of the graphic objects in a worksheet. On the Home tab, in the Editing group, click Find & Select, and then click Go To. Click Special, and then click Objects.
3. On the Format tab, in the Size group, click the Dialog Box Launcher next to Size.
4. On the Properties tab, clear the Locked check box, and if present, clear the Lock text check box.

   You don't need to unlock buttons or controls for users to be able to click and use them. You can unlock embedded charts, text boxes, and other objects created with the drawing tools that you want users to be able to modify.
5. On the Review tab, in the Changes group, click Protect Sheet.
6. In the Allow all users of this worksheet to list, select the elements that you want users to be able to change.

Worksheet elements

Clear this check box	To prevent users from
Select locked cells	Moving the pointer to cells for which the Locked check box is selected on the Protection tab of the Format Cells dialog box. By default, users are allowed to select locked cells.
Select unlocked cells	Moving the pointer to cells for which the Locked check box is cleared on the Protection tab of the Format Cells dialog box. By default, users are allowed to select unlocked cells, and they can press the TAB key to move between the unlocked cells on a protected worksheet.
Format cells	Changing any of the options in the Format Cells or Conditional Formatting dialog boxes. If you applied conditional formats before you protected the worksheet, the formatting continues to change when a user enters a value that satisfies a different condition.
Format columns	Using any of the column formatting commands, including changing column width or hiding columns (Home tab, Cells group, Format button).
Format rows	Using any of the row formatting commands, including changing row height or hiding rows (Home tab, Cells group, Format button).
Insert columns	Inserting columns.
Insert rows	Inserting rows.
Insert hyperlinks	Inserting new hyperlinks (hyperlink: Colored and underlined text or a graphic that you click to go to a file, a location in a file, a Web page on the World Wide Web, or a Web page on an intranet. Hyperlinks can also go to newsgroups and to Gopher, Telnet, and FTP sites.), even in unlocked cells.

Delete columns	Deleting columns. Note If Delete columns is protected and Insert columns is not also protected, a user can insert columns that he or she cannot delete.
Delete rows	Deleting rows. Note If Delete rows is protected and Insert rows is not also protected, a user can insert rows that he or she cannot delete.
Sort	Using any commands to sort data (Data tab, Sort & Filter group). Note Users can't sort ranges that contain locked cells on a protected worksheet, regardless of this setting.
Use AutoFilter	Using the drop-down arrows to change the filter on ranges when AutoFilters are applied. Note Users cannot apply or remove AutoFilters on a protected worksheet, regardless of this setting.
Use PivotTable reports	Formatting, changing the layout, refreshing, or otherwise modifying PivotTable reports or creating new reports. Edit objects Doing the any of the following: • Making changes to graphic objects—including maps, embedded charts, shapes, text boxes, and controls—that you did not unlock before you protected the worksheet. For example, if a worksheet has a button that runs a macro, you can click the button to run the macro, but you cannot delete the button. • Making any changes, such as formatting, to an embedded chart. The chart continues to be updated when you change its source data. • Adding or editing comments.
Edit scenarios	Viewing scenarios that you have hidden, making changes to scenarios that you have prevented changes to, and deleting these scenarios. Users can change the values in the changing cells, if the cells are not protected, and add new scenarios.

Functions in Excel

As mentioned earlier, functions are ready-made formulas which can be recalled and used while working in Excel. Here is the complete list of functions, alongwith some examples.

Financial Functions

DB	Returns the depreciation of an asset for a specified period using the fixed-declining balance method.
DDB	Returns the depreciation of an asset for a specified period using the double-declining balance method or some other method you specify.
FV	Returns the future value of an investment.
IPMT	Returns the interest payment for an investment for a given period.
IRR	Returns the internal rate of return for a series of cash flows.
ISPMT	Returns the straight-loan payment interest.
MIRR	Returns the internal rate of return where positive and negative cash flows are financed at different rates.
NPER	Returns the number of periods for an investment.
NPV	Returns the net present value of an investment based on a series of periodic cash flows and a discount rate.

PMT	Returns the periodic payment for an annuity.
PPMT	Returns the payment on the principal for an investment for a given period.
PV	Returns the present value of an investment.
RATE	Returns the interest rate per period of an annuity.
SLN	Returns the straight-line depreciation of an asset for one period.
SYD	Returns the sum-of-years digits depreciation of an asset for a specified period.
VDB	Returns the depreciation of an asset for a specified or partial period using a declining balance method.

Logical Functions

AND	Returns TRUE if all its arguments are TRUE.
FALSE	Returns the logical value FALSE.
IF	Specifies a logical test to perform.
NOT	Reverses the logic of its argument.
OR	Returns TRUE if any argument is TRUE.
TRUE	Returns the logical value TRUE.

Text Functions

BAHTTEXT	Converts a number to text (bath).
CHAR	Returns the character specified by the code number.
CLEAN	Removes all nonprintable characters from text.
CODE	Returns a numeric code for the first character in a text string.
CONCATENATE	Joins several text items into one text item.
DOLLAR	Converts a number to text, using currency format.
EXACT	Checks to see if two text values are identical.
FIND	Finds one text value within another (case-sensitive).
FIXED	Formats a number as text values are identical.
LEFT	Returns the leftmost characters from a text value.
LEN	Returns the number of characters in a text string.
LOWER	Converts text to lowercase.
MID	Returns a specific number of characters from a text string starting at the position you specify.
PROPER	Capitalizes the first letter in each word of a text value.
REPLACE	Replaces characters within text.
REPT	Repeats text a given number of times.
RIGHT	Returns the rightmost characters from a text value.
SEARCH	Finds one text value within another (not case-sensitive).
SUBSTITUTE	Substitutes new text for old text in a text string.
T	Converts its arguments to text.
TEXT	Formats a number and converts it to text.
TRIM	Removes spaces from text.
UPPER	Converts text to uppercase.

VALUE	Converts a text argument to a number.

Date and Time Functions

DATE	Returns the serial number of a particular date.
DATEVALUE	Converts a date in the form of text to a serial number.
DAY	Converts a serial number to a day of the month.
DAYS360	Calculates the number of days between two dates based on a 360-day year.
HOUR	Converts a serial number to an hour.
MINUTE	Converts a serial number to a minute.
MONTH	Converts a serial number to a month.
NOW	Returns the serial number of the current date and time.
SECOND	Converts a serial number to a second.
TIME	Returns the serial number of a particular time.
TIMEVALUE	Converts a time in the form of text to a serial number.
TODAY	Returns the serial number of today's date.
WEEKDAY	Converts a serial number to a number that represents a day of the week.
YEAR	Converts a serial number to a year.

Lookup and Reference Functions

ADDRESS	Returns the number of areas in a reference.
AREAS	Chooses a value from a list of values.
CHOOSE	Chooses a value or action to perform from a list of values, based on an index number.
COLUMN	Returns data stored in a PivotTable.
COLUMNS	Returns the number of columns in an array or reference.
GETPIVOTDATA	Extracts data stored in a PivotTable
HLOOKUP	Looks in the top row of an array and returns the value of a cell in the same column, in the row that you specify.
HYPERLINK	Creates a shortcut or jump that opens a document stored on a network server, an intranet, or the internet.
INDEX	Uses an index to choose a value from a reference or array.
INDIRECT	Returns a reference indicated by a text value.
LOOKUP	Looks up values in a one-row or one-column vector or array.
MATCH	Looks up values in a reference or array and returns its relative position in the array.
OFFSET	Returns a reference offset from a given reference.
ROW	Returns the row number of a reference.
ROWS	Returns the number of rows in a reference.
RTD	Retrieves real-time data from a program that supports COM automation.
TRANSPOSE	Returns the transpose of an array.
VLOOKUP	Looks in the first column of an array and moves across the row to return the value of a cell in the column you specify.

Math and Trigonometric Functions

Function	Description
ABS	Returns the absolute value of a number.
ACOS	Returns the arccosine of a number.
ACOSH	Returns the inverse hyperbolic cosine of a number.
ASIN	Returns the arcsine of a number.
ASINH	Returns the inverse hyperbolic sine of a number.
ATAN	Returns the arctangent of a number.
ATAN2	Returns the arctangent from x- and y- coordinates.
ATANH	Returns the inverse hyperbolic tangent of a number.
CEILING	Rounds a number up to the nearest integer or to the nearest multiple of significance.
COMBIN	Returns the number of combinations for a given number of objects.
COS	Returns the cosine of a number.
COSH	Returns the hyperbolic cosine of a number.
DEGREES	Converts radians to degrees.
EVEN	Rounds a number up to the nearest even integer.
EXP	Returns e raised to the power of a given number.
FACT	Returns the factorial of a number.
FLOOR	Rounds a number down, toward zero.
INT	Rounds a number down to the nearest integer.
LN	Returns the natural logarithm of a number.
LOG	Returns the logarithm of a number to a specified base.
LOG10	Returns the base-10 logarithm of a number.
MDETERM	Returns the matrix determinant of an array.
MINVERSE	Returns the matrix inverse of an array.
MMULT	Returns the matrix product of two arrays.
MOD	Returns the remainder from division.
ODD	Rounds a number up to the nearest odd integer.
PI	Returns the value of p (pi) to 15 digits.
POWER	Returns the result of a number raised to a power.
PRODUCT	Multiplies its arguments.
RADIANS	Converts degrees to radians.
RAND	Returns a random number between 0 and 1.
ROMAN	Converts an arabic numeral to roman, as text.
ROUND	Rounds a number to a specified number of digits.
ROUNDDOWN	Rounds a number down, toward zero.
ROUNDUP	Rounds a number up, away from zero.
SIGN	Returns the sign of a number.

SIN	Returns the sine of the given angle.
SINH	Returns the hyperbolic sine of a number.
SQRT	Returns a positive square root.
SUBTOTAL	Returns a subtotal in a list or database.
SUM	Adds its arguments.
SUMIF	Adds the cells specified by a given criteria.
SUMPRODUCT	Returns the sum of the products of corresponding array components.
SUMSQ	Returns the sum of the squares of the arguments.
SUMX2MY2	Returns the sum of the difference of squares of corresponding values in two arrays.
SUMX2PY2	Returns the sum of the sum of squares of corresponding values in two arrays.
SUMXMY2	Returns the sum of squares of differences of corresponding values in two arrays.
TAN	Returns the tangent of a number.
TANH	Returns the hyperbolic tangent of a number.
TRUNC	Truncates a number to an integer.

Statistical Functions

AVEDEV	Returns the average of the absolute deviations of data points from their mean.
AVERAGE	Returns the average of its arguments.
AVERAGEA	Returns the average of its arguments, including numbers, text, and logical values.
BETADIST	Returns the cumulative beta probability density function.
BETAINV	Returns the inverse of the cumulative beta probability density function.
BINOMDIST	Returns the individual term binomial distribution probability.
CHIDIST	Returns the one-tailed probability of the chi-squared distribution.
CHIINV	Returns the inverse of the one-tailed probability of the chi-squared distribution.
CHITEST	Returns the test for independence.
CONFIDENCE	Returns the confidence interval for a population mean.
CORREL	Returns the correlation coefficient between two data sets.
COUNT	Counts how many numbers are in the list of arguments.
COUNTA	Counts how many values are in the list of arguments.
COUNTBLANK	Counts the number of blank cells within a range.
COUNTIF	Counts the number of non blank cells within a range that meet the given criteria.
COVAR	Returns covariance, the average of the products of paired deviations.
CRITBINOM	Returns the smallest value for which the cumulative binomial distribution is less than or equal to a criterion value.
DEVSQ	Returns the sum of squared of deviations.
EXPONDIST	Returns the exponential distribution.
FDIST	Returns the F probability distribution.
FINV	Returns the inverse of the F probability distribution.
FISHER	Returns the Fisher transformation.

FISHERINV	Returns the inverse of the Fisher transformation.
FORECAST	Returns a value along a linear trend.
FREQUENCY	Returns a frequency distribution as a vertical array.
FTEST	Returns the result of an F-test.
GAMMADIST	Returns the gamma distribution.
GAMMAINV	Returns the inverse of the gamma cumulative distribution.
GAMMALN	Returns the natural logarithm of the gamma function, G(x).
GEOMEAN	Returns the geometric mean.
GROWTH	Returns values along an exponential trend.
HARMEAN	Returns the harmonic mean.
HYPGEOMDIST	Returns the hypergeometric distribution.
INTERCEPT	Returns the intercept of the linear regression line.
KURT	Returns the kurtosis of a data set.
LARGE	Returns the kth largest value in a data set.
LINEST	Returns the parameters of a linear trend.
LOGEST	Returns the parameters of an exponential trend.
LOGINV	Returns the inverse of the lognormal distribution.
LOGNORMDIST	Returns the cumulative lognormal distribution.
MAX	Returns the maximum value in a list of arguments.
MAXA	Returns the maximum value in a list of arguments, including numbers, text, and logical values.
MEDIAN	Returns the median of the given numbers.
MIN	Returns the minimum value in a list of arguments.
MINA	Returns the smallest value in a list of arguments, including numbers, text, and logical values.
MODE	Returns the most common value in a data set.
NEGBINOMDIST	Returns the negative binomial distribution.
NORMDIST	Returns the normal cumulative distribution.
NORMSINV	Returns the inverse of the standard normal cumulative distribution.
PEARSON	Returns the Pearson product moment correlation coefficient.
PERCENTILE	Returns the kth percentile of values in a range.
PERCENTRANK	Returns the percentage rank of a value in a data set.
PERMUT	Returns the number of permutations for a given number of objects.
POISSON	Returns the Poisson distribution.
PROB	Returns the probability that values in a range are between two limits.
QUARTILE	Returns the quartile of a data set.
RANK	Returns the rank of a number in a list of numbers.
RSQ	Returns the square of the Pearson product moment correlation coefficient.
SKEW	Returns the skewness of a distribution.
SLOPE	Returns the slope of the linear regression line.
SMALL	Returns the kth smallest value in a data set.

STANDARDIZE	Returns a normalized value.
STDEV	Estimates standard deviation based on a sample.
STDEVA	Estimates standard deviation based on a sample, including numbers, text, and logical values.
STDEVP	Calculates standard deviation based on the entire population.
STDEVPA	Calculates standard deviation based on the entire population, including numbers, text, and logical values.
STEYX	Returns the standard error of the predicted y- value for each x in the regression.
TDIST	Returns the Student's t-distribution.
TINV	Returns the inverse of the Student's t-distribution.
TREND	Returns values along a linear trend.
TRIMMEAN	Returns the mean of the interior of a data set.
TTEST	Returns the probability associated with a Student's t-test.
VAR	Estimates variance based on a sample.
VARA	Estimates variance based on a sample, including numbers, text, and logical values.
VARP	Calculates variance based on the entire population.
VARPA	Calculates variance based on the entire population, including numbers, text, and logical values.
WEIBULL	Returns the Weibull distribution.
ZTEST	Returns the two-tailed P-value of a z-test.

Database Functions

DAVERAGE	Returns the average of selected database entries.
DCOUNT	Counts the cells that contain numbers in a particular field of records that match specified criteria in a database.
DCOUNTA	Counts non blank cells in a particular field of records that match specified criteria in a database.
DGET	Extracts a single record from a database that matches the specified criteria.
DMAX	Returns the maximum value from selected database entries.
DMIN	Returns the minimum value from selected database entries.
DPRODUCT	Multiplies the values in a particular field of records that match the criteria in a database.
DSTDEV	Estimates the standard deviation based on a sample of selected database entries.
DSTDEVP	Calculates the standard deviation based on the entire population of selected database entries.
DSUM	Sums the values in a particular field for all records that match the specified criteria.
DVAR	Estimates variance based on a sample from selected database entries.
DVARP	Calculates variance based on the entire population of selected database entries.

Information Functions

CELL	Returns information about the formatting, location, or contents of a cell.
ERRORTYPE	Returns a number corresponding to an error type.

INFO Returns information about the current operating environment.

ISBLANK Returns TRUE if the value is blank.

ISERR Returns TRUE if the value is any error value expect #N/A.

ISERROR Returns TRUE if the value is any error value.

ISLOGICAL Returns TRUE if the value is a logical value.

ISNA Returns TRUE if the value is the #N/A error value.

ISNONTEXT Returns TRUE if the value is non text.

ISNUMBER Returns TRUE if the value is a number.

ISREF Returns TRUE if the value is reference.

ISTEXT Returns TRUE if the value is text.

N Returns a value converted to a number.

NA Returns the error value #N/A.

TYPE Returns a number indicating the data type of a value.

CHAPTER 4

Introduction to Microsoft PowerPoint 2010

Introduction

Want to make a presentation in a hurry! This is an ideal program of the same. Make sophisticated slide shows and professional looking electronic presentations. It also allows you to add charts, tables and pictures for make the presentation look alive.

Creating Presentation from Template

Most of the office 2010 software have ready made outputs called Templates. This is true in the case of PowerPoint 2010 too. Let us see how it can be used to create a presentation.

1. Select New from the Office button.
2. Select Installed Themes and then select any one of the available templates. I have chosen Introduction to PowerPoint 2010.

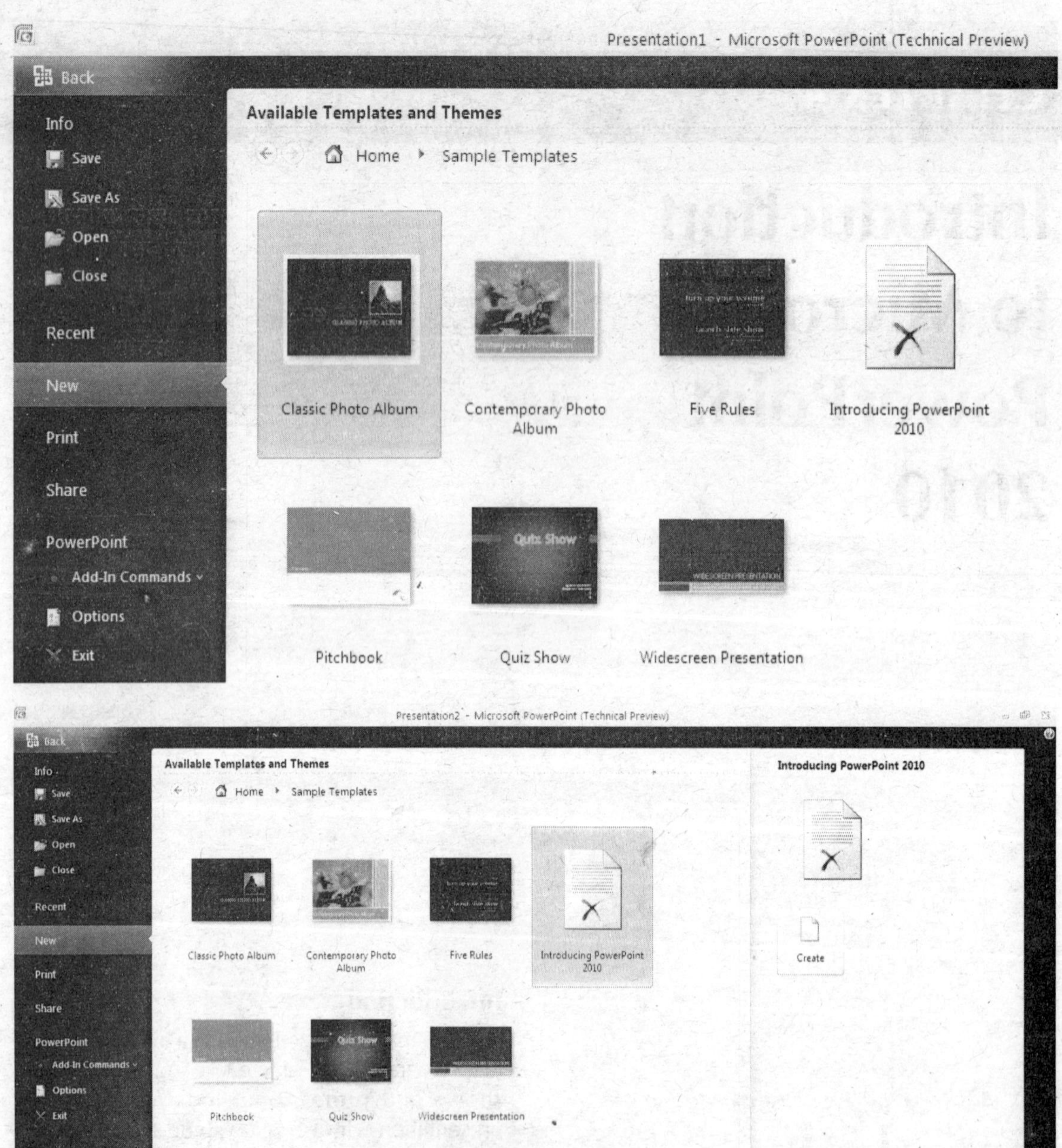

3. Click at Create to start with the presentation.
4. The first slide with the Introduction to PowerPoint 2010 appears on the screen.

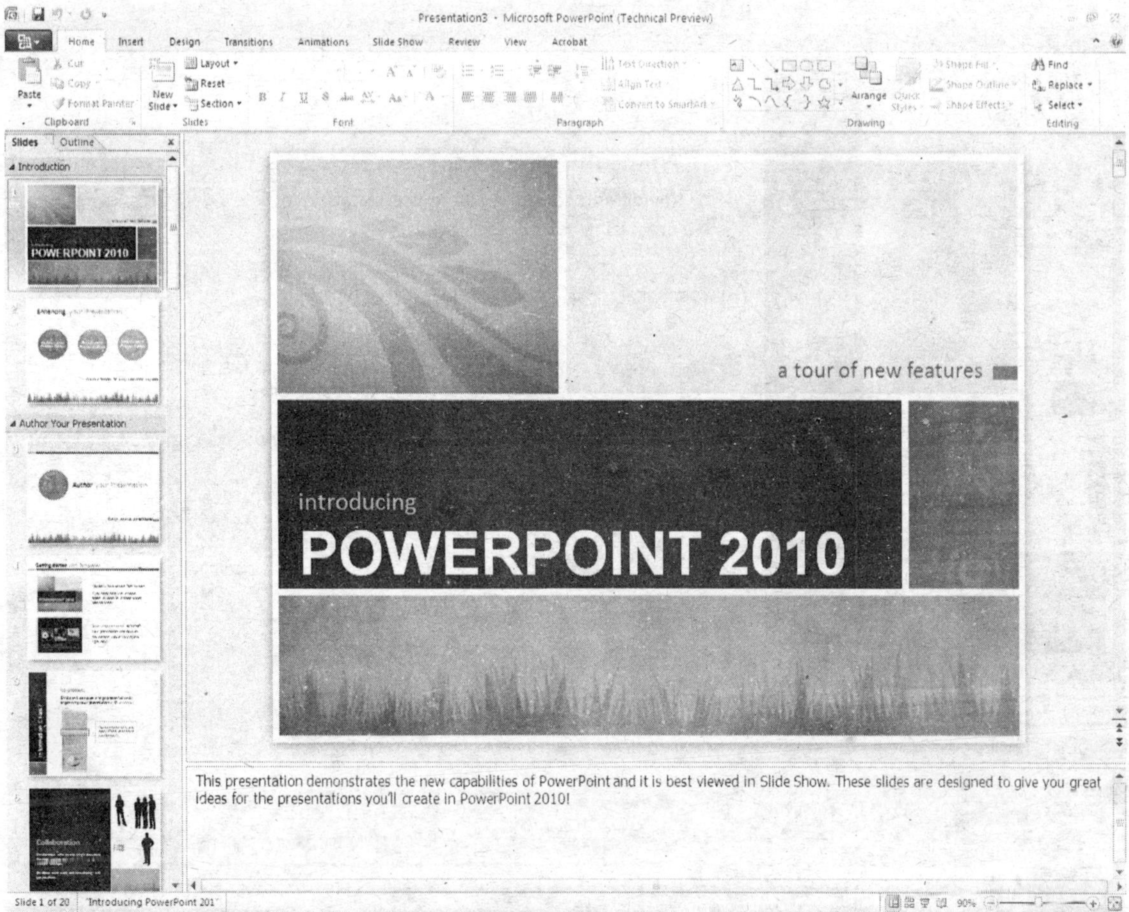

5. As you will that on the left panel 20 slides have been created and are thus numbered from 1 to 20.
6. You can see any one of them by just clicking at it. I am showing here the slide numbers 5, 9 and 18.

Creating a New Presentation

Another method of creating presentation is by using the option of New presentation using the Blank presentation option. You can select an option of text and graphics to make show on the screen.

1. Select New from the Office button.
2. Select Blank presentation and click Create.
3. A new slide is shown on the screen.

PowerPoint Views

There are different ways of looking at the presentations. These are called the views. There are as many as 5 different views in which you can see your presentation. They are:

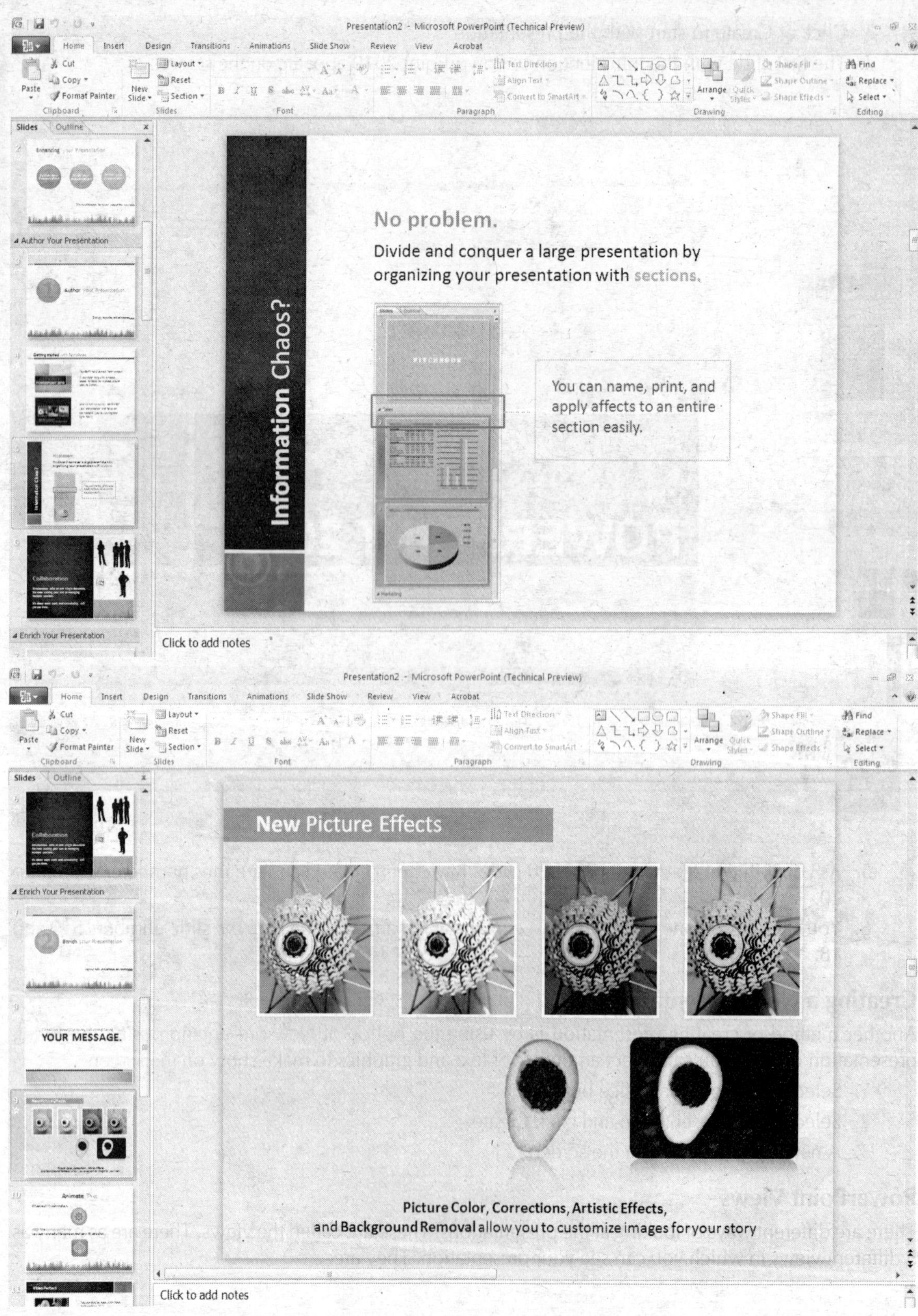
Presentation2 - Microsoft PowerPoint (Technical Preview)
Information Chaos?
No problem.
Divide and conquer a large presentation by organizing your presentation with sections.
You can name, print, and apply affects to an entire section easily.
Author Your Presentation
Enrich Your Presentation
Click to add notes
Presentation2 - Microsoft PowerPoint (Technical Preview)
New Picture Effects
Picture Color, Corrections, Artistic Effects,
and Background Removal allow you to customize images for your story
YOUR MESSAGE.
Click to add notes

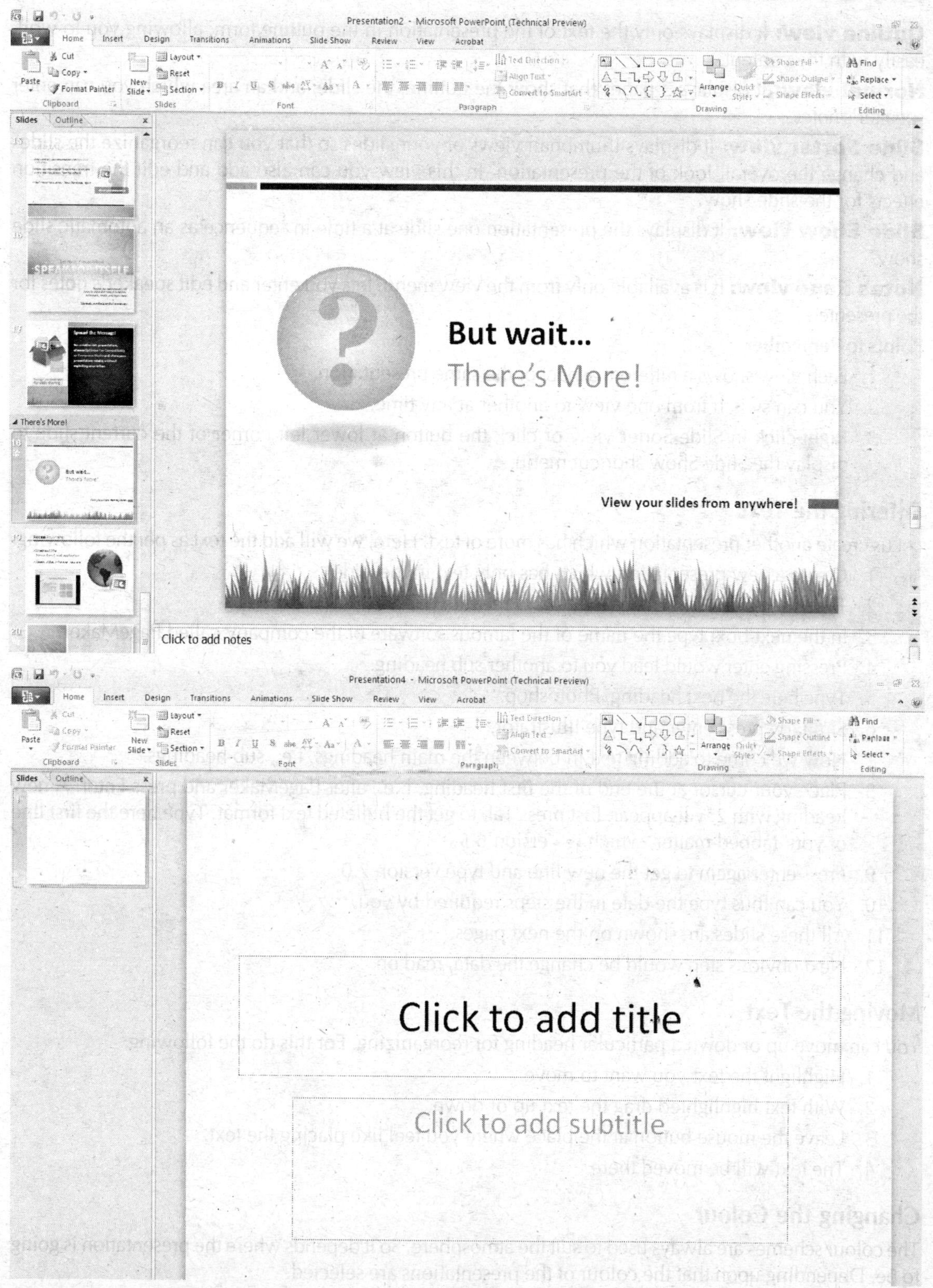
Presentation2 - Microsoft PowerPoint (Technical Preview)
But wait...
There's More!
View your slides from anywhere!
Click to add notes
Presentation4 - Microsoft PowerPoint (Technical Preview)
Click to add title
Click to add subtitle

Outline view: It displays only the text of the presentation in the outline form, allowing you to work easily with the content.

Normal view: It displays 3 panes that show the outline, the slide, and an area which you can enter speaker's notes.

Slide Sorter view: It displays thumbnail views of your slides so that you can reorganize the slides and change the overall look of the presentation. In this view you can also add and edit the transition effects for the slide show.

Slide Show view: It displays the presentation one slide at a time in sequence as an automatic slide show.

Notes Page view: It is available only from the view menu, lets you enter and edit speaker's notes for the presenter.

Points to Remember

1. Each view shows a different aspect of the same presentation.
2. You can switch from one view to another at any time.
3. Right-click in Slide Sorter view or click the button at lower left corner of the current slide to display the Slide Show shortcut menu.

Entering the Text

Let us create another presentation which has more of text. Here, we will add the text as per the following:

1. Create a new presentation which has only text in the slide.
2. Type the name Adobe Corporation in the title bar.
3. In the next box, type the name of the famous software of the company called PageMaker.
4. Pressing enter would lead you to another sub heading.
5. Type here the next heading, Photoshop.
6. Similarly press enter and type Illustrator.
7. Now we come to adding text in between the main headings, i.e., sub-headings.
8. Place your cursor at the end of the first heading, i..e., after PageMaker and press Enter. A new heading with 2 will appear. Just press Tab to get the bulleted text format. Type here the first line of your tabbed matter, which is Version 6.5.
9. Press enter again to get the new line and type version 7.0.
10. You can thus type the date in the steps required by you.
11. All these slides are shown on the next pages.
12. Next obvious step would be change the data, read on.

Moving the Text

You can move up or down a particular heading for reorganizing. For this do the following:

1. Highlight the text you want to move.
2. With text highlighted drag the text up or down.
3. Leave the mouse button at the place where you feel like placing the text.
4. The text will be moved there.

Changing the Colour

The colour schemes are always used to suit the atmosphere. So it depends where the presentation is going to be. Depending upon that the colour of the presentations are selected.

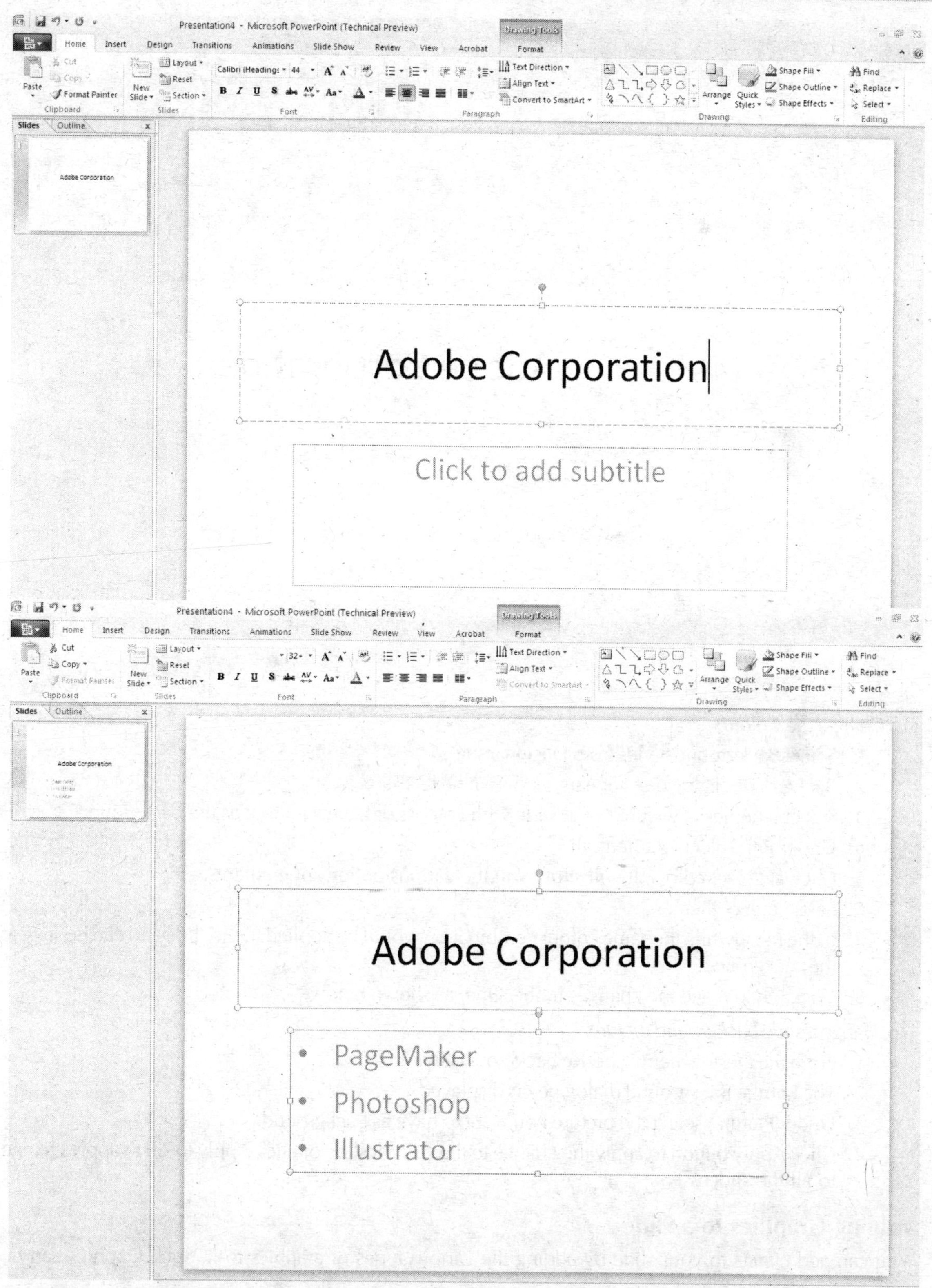
Presentation4 - Microsoft PowerPoint (Technical Preview)
Adobe Corporation
Click to add subtitle
Adobe Corporation
PageMaker
Photoshop
Illustrator

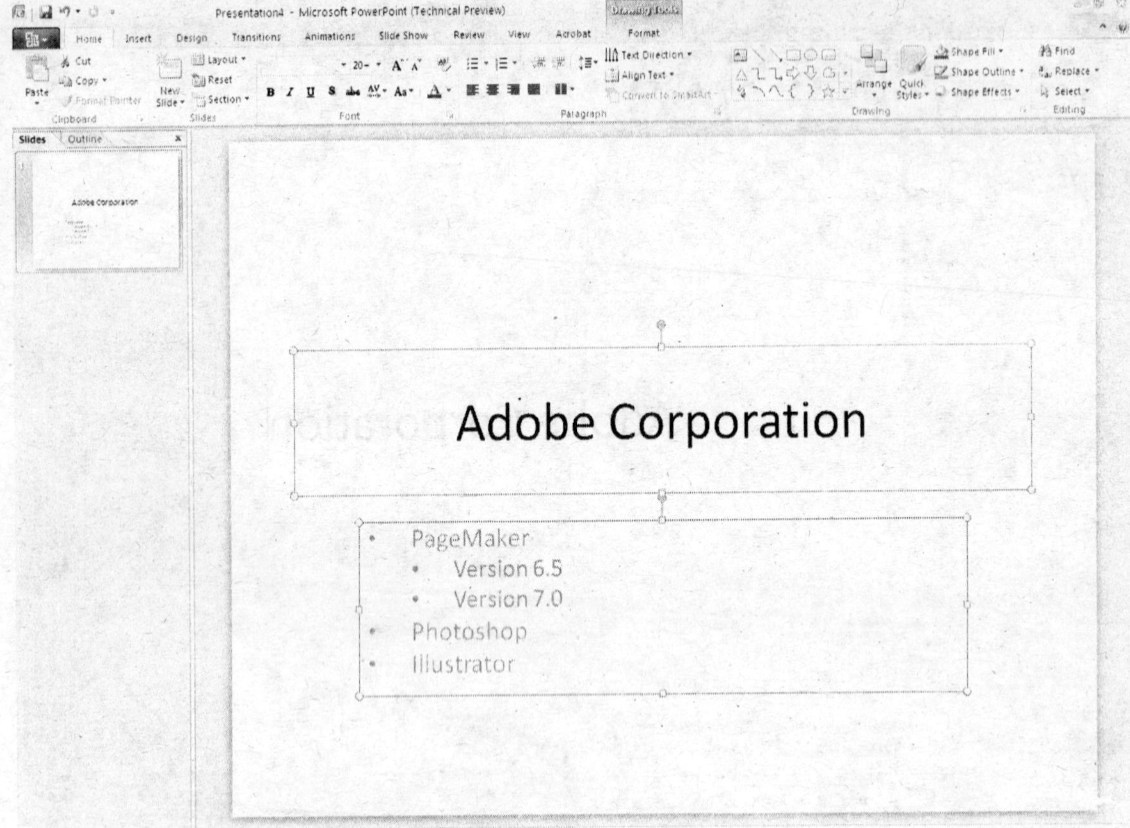

To Change the Colours

1. Select Background Styles from Design menu.
2. Background dialog box appears, as shown next.
3. Select whether you want to Fill slide with colours or have a picture as the background.
4. Under Fill, select Gradient fill.
5. Click at Preset colors, it will show you the various options of gradients.
6. Select one of them.
7. In the meanwhile the same colour combination would be applied to the slide and can be seen at the background.
8. Click Ok to make the changes in the slide, as shown below.

To change a slide background picture

1. From the Desing menu, choose background styles option.
2. The Format Background dialog box is displayed.
3. Under Picture, select the picture you want to have as background.
4. Click Apply button to apply the change to the current slide or click Apply to All to apply change to all the slides.

Adding Graphics to a Slide

You can add effects to your slide by adding the various types of graphics to it. Such graphics can be

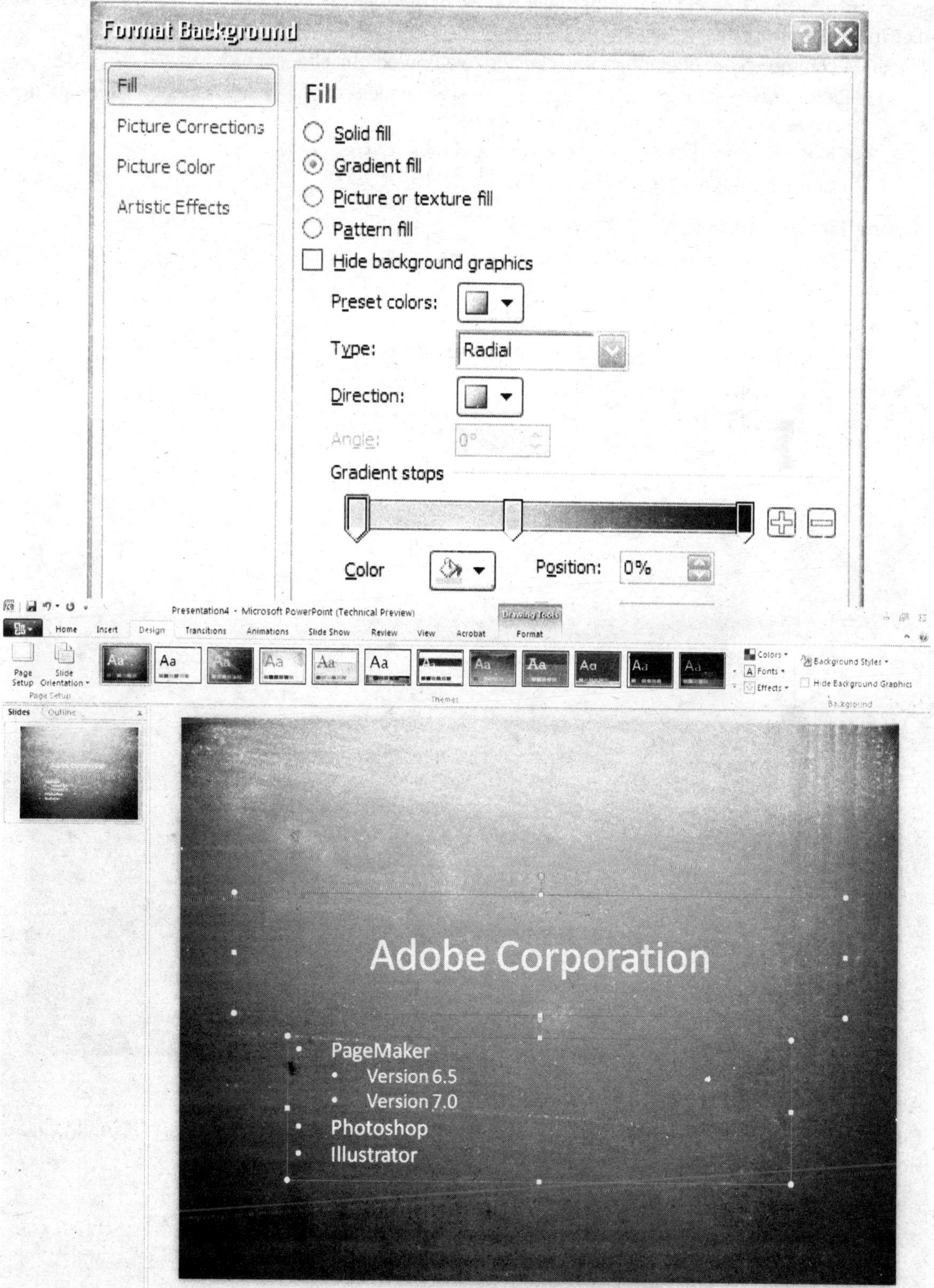

Format Background
Fill
Picture Corrections
Picture Color
Artistic Effects
Fill
Solid fill
Gradient fill
Picture or texture fill
Pattern fill
Hide background graphics
Preset colors:
Type:
Radial
Direction:
Angle:
0°
Gradient stops
Color
Position:
0%
Presentation4 - Microsoft PowerPoint (Technical Preview)
Home
Insert
Design
Transitions
Animations
Slide Show
Review
View
Acrobat
Format
Page Setup
Slide Orientation
Colors
Fonts
Effects
Background Styles
Hide Background Graphics
Slides
Outline
Adobe Corporation
PageMaker
Version 6.5
Version 7.0
Photoshop
Illustrator

informative, such as a chart that displays sales results; or they can be decorative, such as a cartoon smiley face that emphasizes the presentation's good news.

The three common types of graphics you can add to a PowerPoint slide include:

- **Picture files**: Includes clip art images as well as images you may have stored on your hard disk, such as photographs from your digital camera.
- **Charts**: Displays bar, column, line, pie, and other types of charts.
- **WordArt**: Displays text as colourful tex.

Adding Picture to the Presentation

1. Click a slide to which you want to add a picture.
2. Click the Insert tab.
3. Click the Picture icon in the Images group.
4. Click the picture file you want and then click Open.

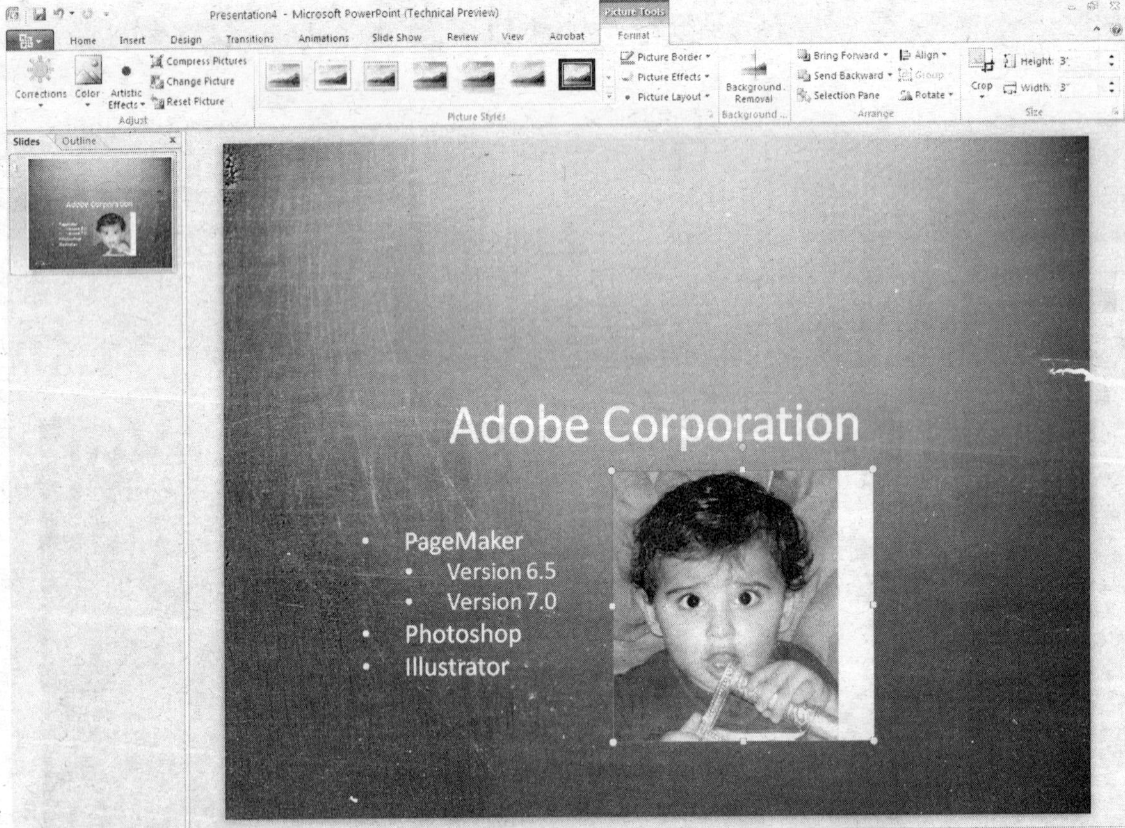

Adding Clip Art on a Slide

Clip Art consists of drawings that come with PowerPoint. To add a clip art image to a slide, follow these steps.:

1. Click a slide to which you want to add a click art.
2. Click the Insert tab.
3. Click the Clip ARt icon in the Illustrations group.

4. Click in the Search For text box and type a word that describes the type of image you want to find.
5. Click Ok.
6. Click the clip art image you want to use.

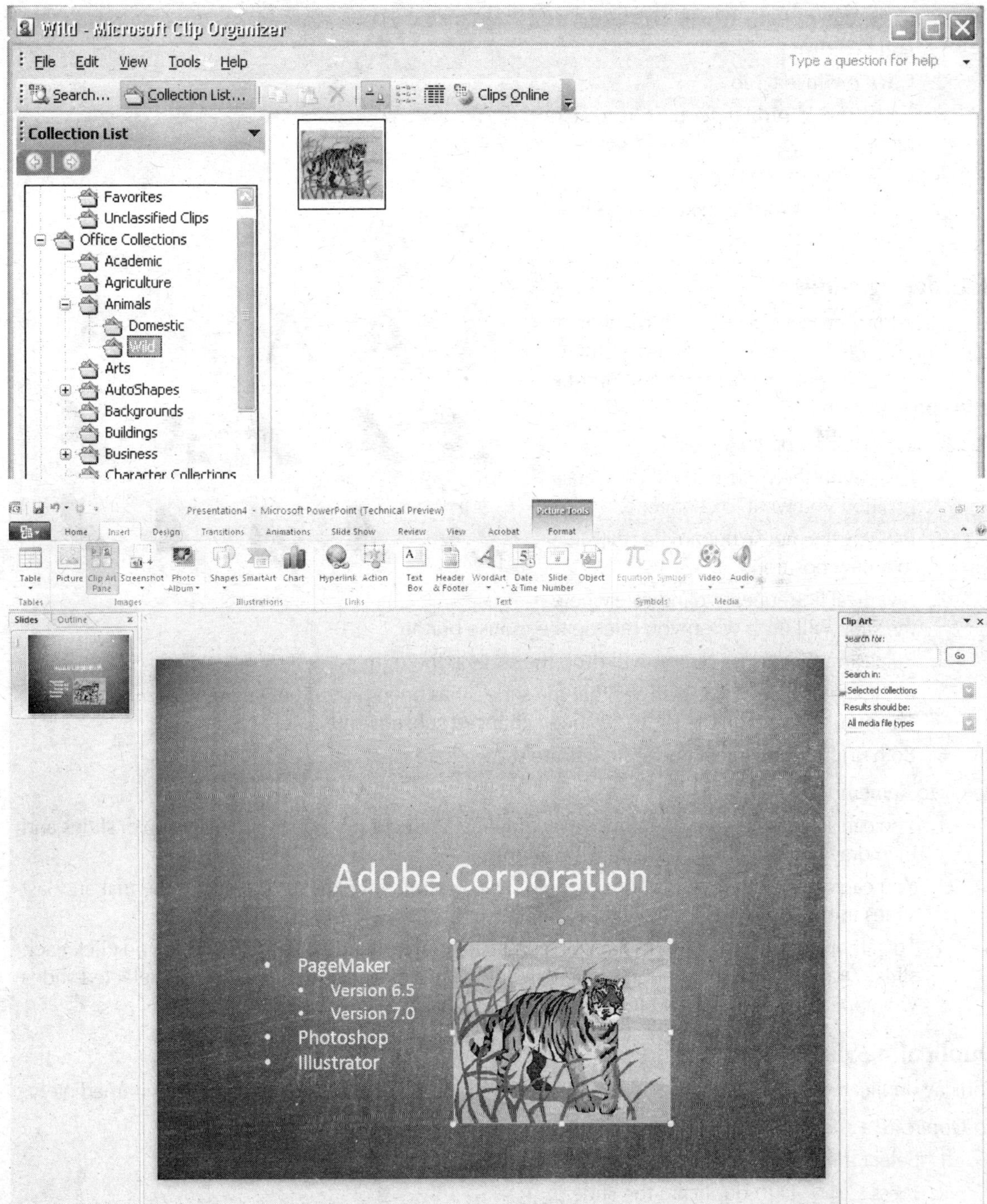

Adding from WordArt

WordArt is an independent program which allows you to create text in a presentable form and this text can be used in slides then. This is how it is done.

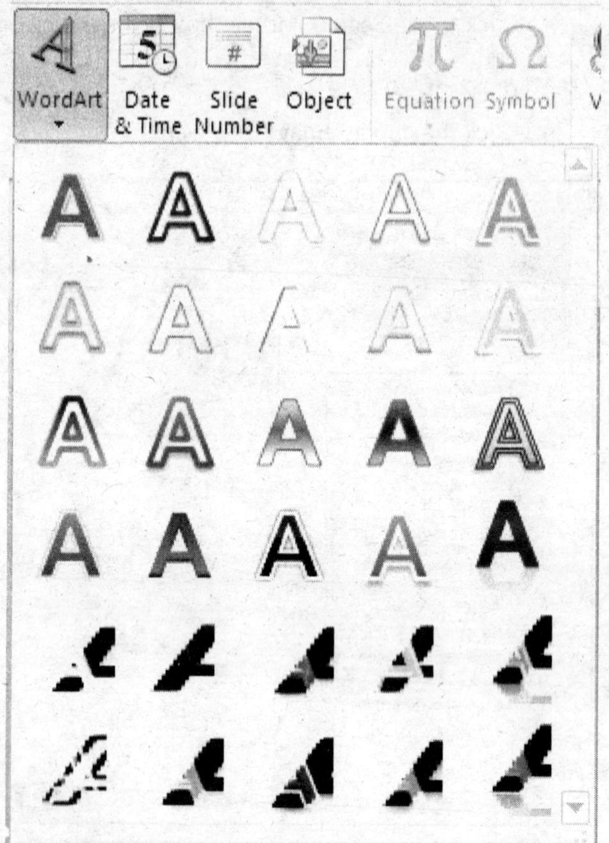

1. Click the slide to which you want to add WordArt.
2. Click the Insert Tab.
3. Click the WordArt icon in the Text group.
4. Click a WordArt style to use.
5. Click in the WordArt text box and type text.

Reordering Slides

As you see from the view, each slide is numbered. These number belong to their order of display. This order can be changed at any point of time in the presentation.

To Change the Order of the Slides:

1. Click with the mouse the slide whose position you want to change.
2. Pressing the mouse button drag the slide to a new position.
3. A vertical line appears to indicate where the slide will drop when you release the mouse button.
4. Releasing the mouse button will drop the slide at the right place.
5. In the figure below, you will see that the slide 3 has been placed between the number 1 and 2. The numbering of all the slides has been changed subsequently.
6. Both original and after change figures are shown here.

Points to Remember

1. You can select several slides to move by drawing a selection box around the group of slides and then dragging the group to the new position.
2. You can also select several slides by holding down the Shift key and selecting the first and last slides in the series.
3. To gather slides from different parts of a presentation, hold down the Ctrl key as you click each slide. Drag any one slide in the group to a new point in the presentation. All the selected slides will appear in sequence and in the same relative order at new position.

Duplicating Slides

You can duplicate selected slides in Slide Sorter view and see the effect on the flow of slides immediately.

To Duplicate a slide or slides:

1. Select the slide or slides you want to duplicate.
2. Press Ctrl + D to duplicate the slide.

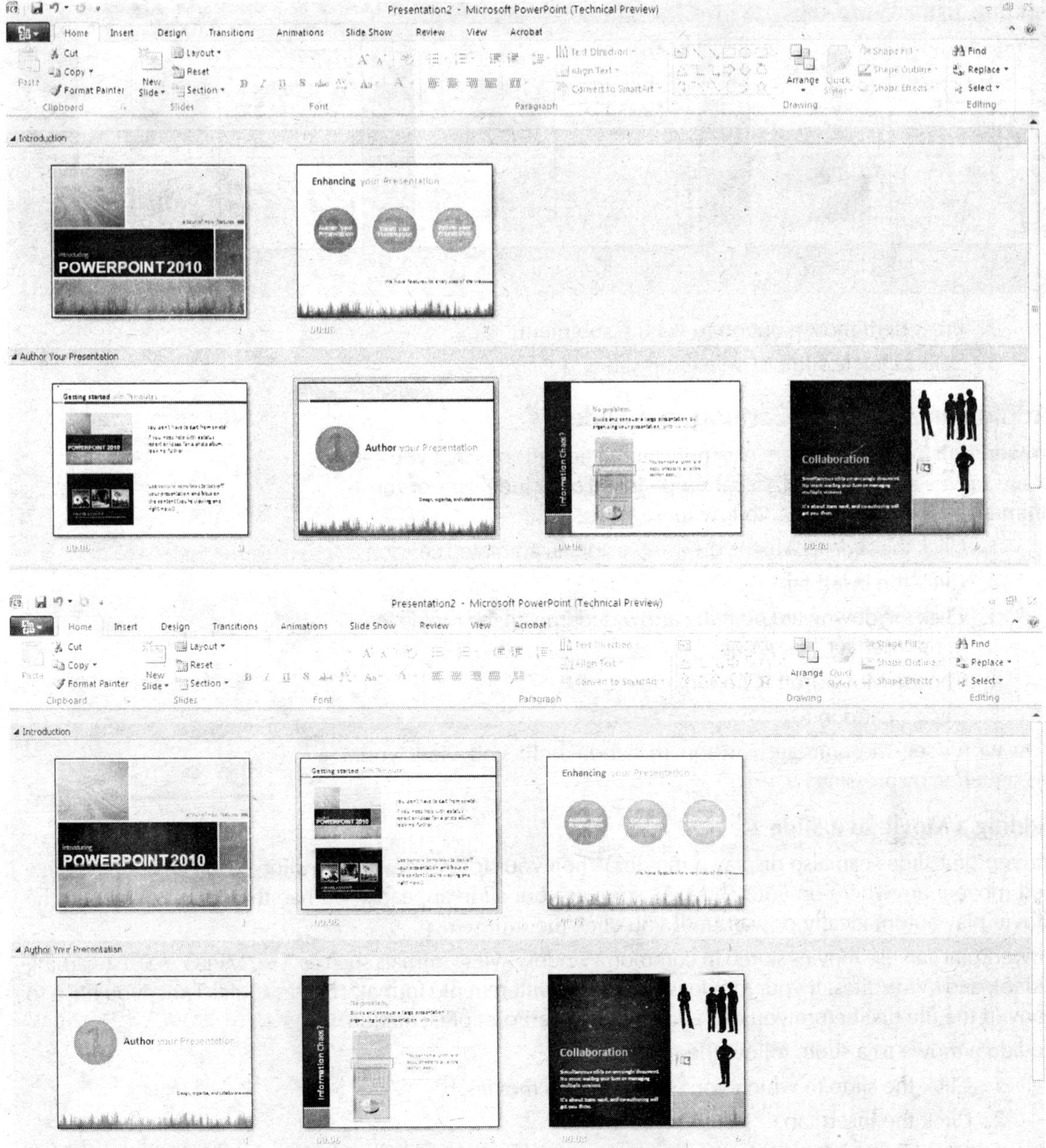

3. Slide would be duplicated.
4. In the following figure slide 18 has been duplicated as slide 19.

Deleting Slides

You can delete the selected slides in Slide Sorter view and see that the numbering of other slides change immediately.

To delete a slide or slides:

1. Select the slide or slides you want to delete.

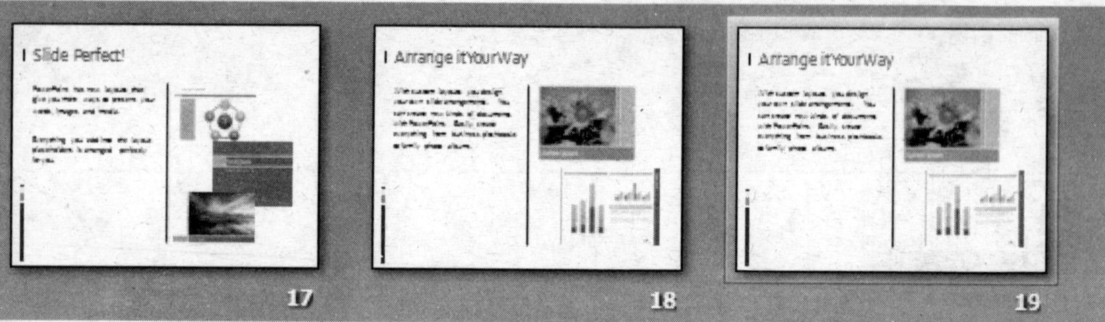

2. Press right mouse button to get the sub menu.
3. Select Delete slide to delete the slide.

Adding an Animated Cartoon to a Slide

PowerPoint includes a library of simple animated cartoons that you can place on a slide for added visual emphasis. To include one of these animate cartoons on a slide, follow these steps.

1. Click the slide to which you want to add an animated cartoons,
2. Click the Insert tab.
3. Click the downward pointing arrow underneath the Movie icon in the Media Clips group.
4. Choose Movie from Clip Organizer.
5. Click a cartoon.

You won't see the animate cartoon in action until you view your presentation by pressing F5.

Adding a Movie to a Slide

PowerPoint slides can also display a movie. When you store a movie on a slide, you can resize its size and move it anywhere on your slide. As soon as your slide appears, you hae the option of having the movie play automatically or wait until you click the mouse first.

PowerPoint can use movies stored in common Windows view formats such as AVI, MPEG, ASF (streaming video), and WMV files. If your movie is stored in a different file format, such as QuickTime, you have to convert the file first before you can add it to a PowerPoint presentation.

To add a movie to a slide, follow these steps:

1. Click the slide to which you want to add a movie.
2. Click the Insert tab.
3. Click the Movie icon in the Media Clips group.

   The Insert Movie dialog box appears.
4. Click the movie file you want to add and then click Ok.

   PowerPoint displays a box on your slide where your movie will appear along with a dialog box, asking whether you want the movie to play automatically or when you click the mouse.
5. Clikc Automatically or When clicked.
6. Move the mouse pointer over the movie.

   The mouse pointer turns into a long-way pointing arrow.

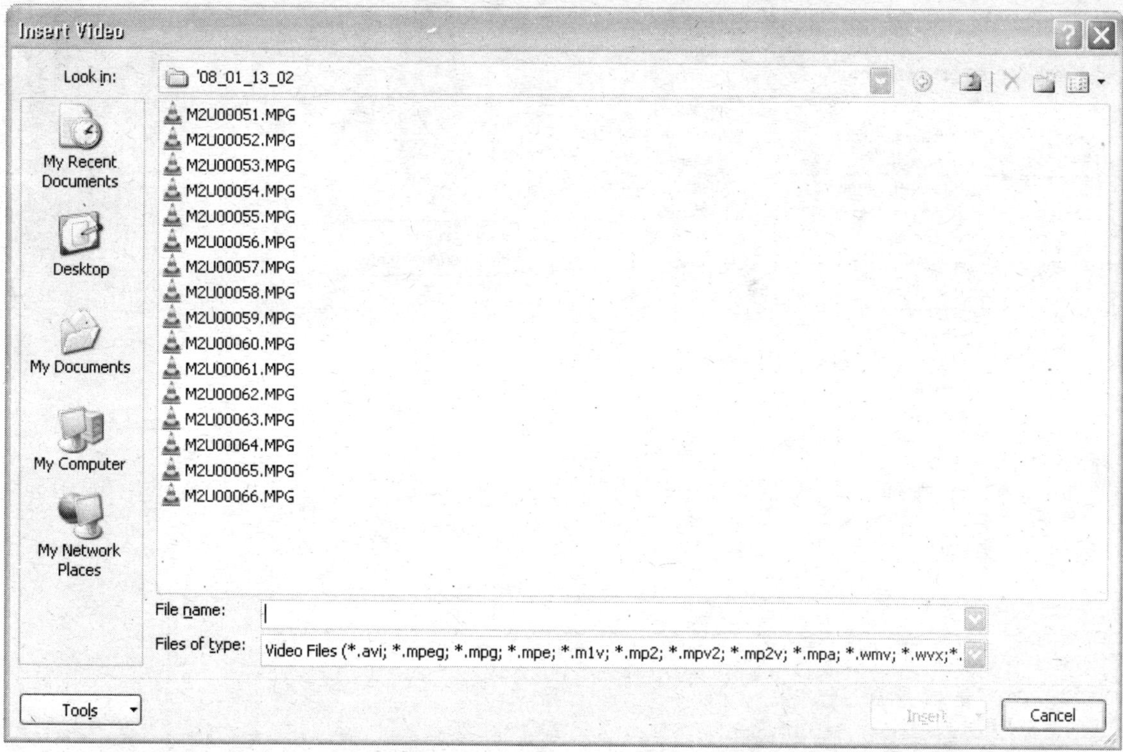

7. Hold down the left mouse button and drap (move) the mouse to place the movie where you want it to appear on the slide.
8. Move the mouse pointer over one corner of the movie until the mouse pointer turns into a two-way pointing arrow.
9. Hold down the left mouse button and drag (move) the mouse to resize the movie.

Adding Sound

You can add sounds to the transition effects and to the preset animation. You can also add audio to your presentation by inserting files from the Clip Art Gallery or from other folders available to you.

PowerPoint can use audio files stored in common formats such as AIFF, MIDI, MP3, and WAV file. If your audio file is stored in a different file format, such as Real Audio, you will have to convert the file first before you can add it to a PowerPoint presentation.

To Add an Audio File

1. Select the slide where you want to put this audio.
2. Click the Insert tab.
3. Click the downward-pointing arrow underneath the Sound icon to the Media Clips group.
4. Choose Sound from File

   The Insert Sound dialog box appears.
5. Click the audio file you want to add and thne click Ok.

   PowerPoint adds you audio file to the currently displayed slide (reprresent as a horn icon) and displays a dialog box, asking whether you want the sound to play automatically or when you click the mouse.

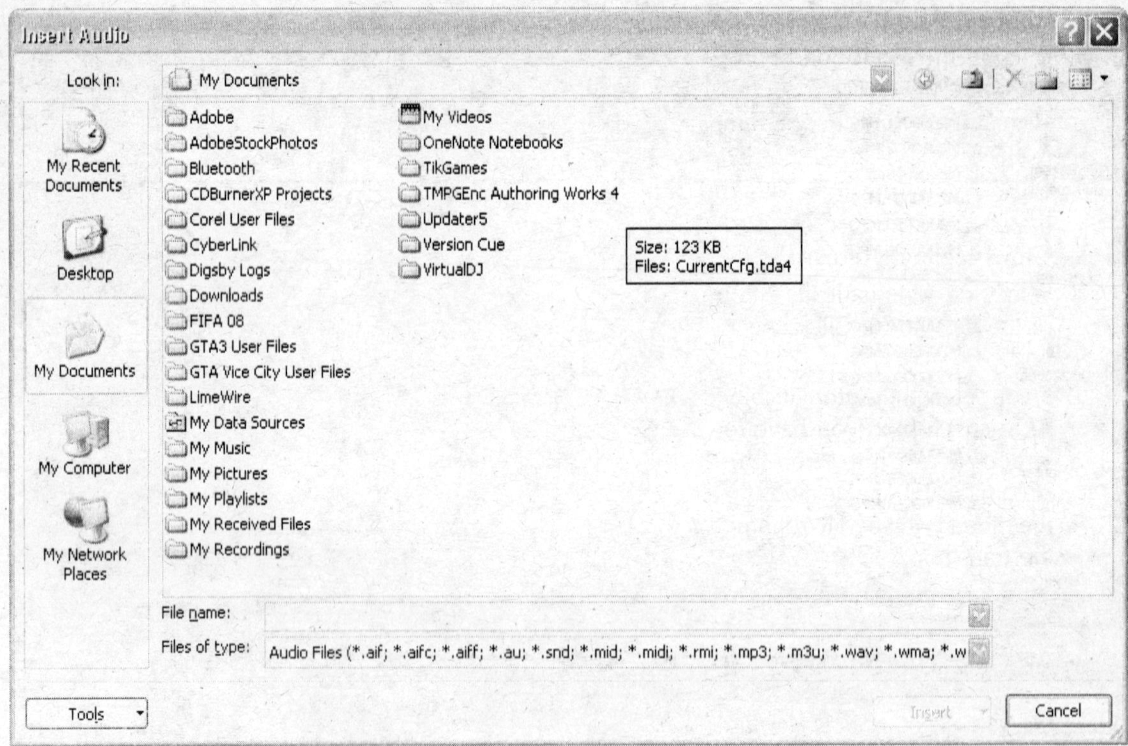

6. Click Automatically or When Clicked.

   PowerPoint displays your audio file as a sound icon on your slide. You may want to move the sound icon on your slide so it doesn't obscure part of your slide.

Adding Slide Transitions

These effects can be of the form of wipes, splits, dissolves, etc., which you usually see in the film show. For this you have to work in the Slide Sorter view.

When creating a transition, you need to define the following:

- The actual visual appearance of the transition.
- The speed of the transition (Slow, Medium, or Fast).
- Any sound effects you want to play during the transition (these can get really annoying, so use them sparingly)
- When to display the transition (after a certain time period or when you click the mouse).

To Add a Transition View

1. Click a slide (in the Slide or Outline view pane).

   Any transition you choose will end by displaying the slide you choose in this step.
2. Click the Animations tab.

   PowerPoint displays the different animation.
3. Click the More button of the Transition To This Slide group.

   A pull-down menu appears listing all the different transitions available. If you move the mouse over the a transition, PowerPoint shows you what that transition will look like on your chosen slide.

4. Click the transition you want.
5. Click in the Transition Sound list box and choose a sound, such as Cash Register or Drum Roll.
6. Click in the Transition Speed list box and choose a speed (Slow, Medium, or Fast).
7. Select the Automatically After or the On Mouse Click check box.

   If you select the Automatically After check box, you have to specify a time in the Automatically After text box for the slide to wait before running the transition.

   You can select both the On Mouse Click and Automatically After check boxes, so the slide transition waits until you click the mouse or until a certain amount of time passes.
8. Click Apply to All to apply your transition to every slide in your presentation.

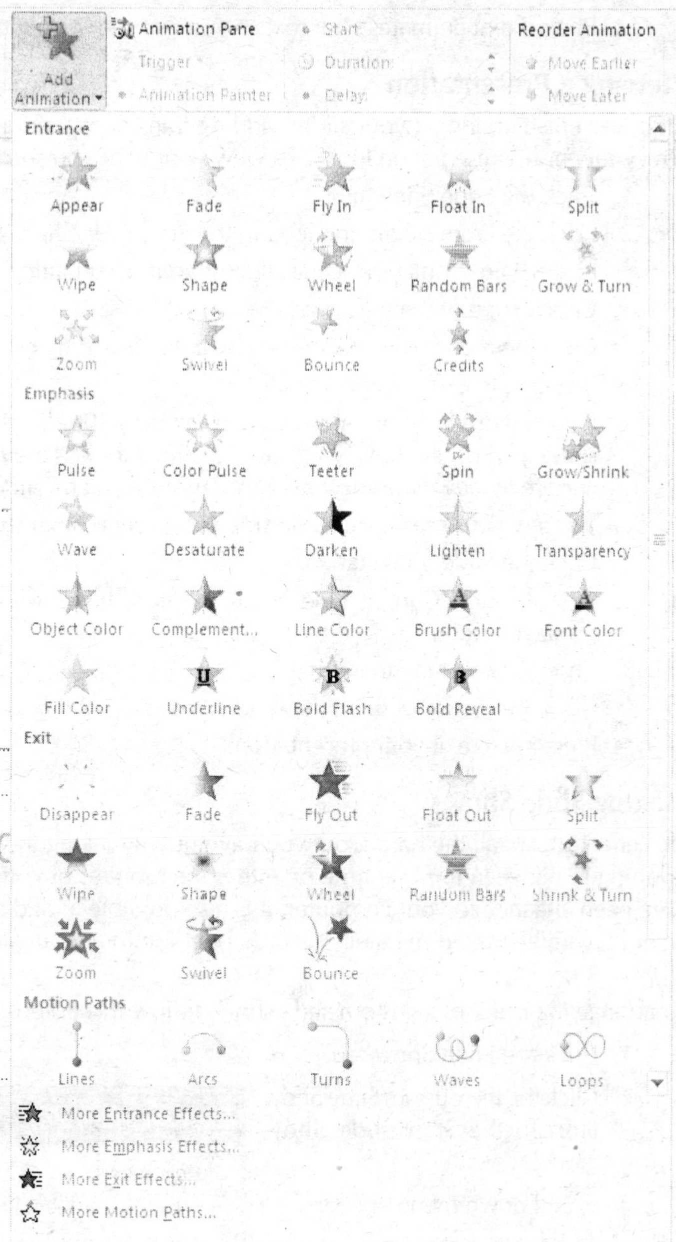

Adding Texl Transitions

Besides animating how your slides appear and disappear you can also add transitions to your text boxes or graphics so they fly or drop into place across a slide.

Use text transitions sparingly becaust eht transitions can get distracting when people just want to read your presentation without having to watch letters zoom around the screen.

To Create a simple text ransition, follow these steps:

1. Click a text box or picture on a slide.

   PowerPoint displays handles around your chosen item.
2. Click the Animations tab.
3. Click the Animate list box in the Animations group.

   A list of different animation schemes appear.
4. Click an animation, such as Fly In or Wipe.

PowerPoint animates your text so you can see how it looks.

Viewing a Presentation

After you finish arranging your slides, adding transitions, and adding hyper links, you are ready to test how your entire presentation looks. To view your entire presentation, follow these steps:

1. Click the Slide Show tab.
2. Click the From Beginning icon in the Start Slide Show group.

   PowerPoint displays the first slide of your presentation.
3. Choose one of the following:

- Click the mouse or press the spacebar to view the next slide.
- Press Esc to exit your presentation.

If you have a large presentation consisting of 300 slides, you may not want ot view the first 290 slides just to test how your last 10 slides look. To avoid this problem, PowerPoint lets you choose to view your presentation starting with any slide.

To view your presentation starting with a slide other than the first one, follow these steps:

1. Click the Slide Show tab.
2. Click the From Current Slide icon in the Start Slide Show group. PowerPoint displays the currently displayed slide.
3. Choose one of the following:

- Click the mouse or press the spacebar to view the next slide.
- Press Esc to exit your presentation.

Making Slide Shows

This effect shows all the hard work you have put in making the slides. It shows one slide after another, stopping in between for a set time on either the monitor of your screen or on the projector which may have been attached to your computer. It is also possible to add animated effects on the slides and show them in a sophisticated manner. It is also possible to add audio, video, narration, music, etc., to your slides.

To arrange the order of a custom slide show, follow these steps:

1. Click the Slide Show tab.
2. Click the the Custom Slide Show icon in the Start Slide Show group.

   A pull down menu appears.
3. Choose Custom Shows.

   The Custom Shows dialog box appears.
4. Click New.

   The Define Custom Show dialog box appears.
5. Click in the Slide Show Name text box and type a name for your custom slide show.

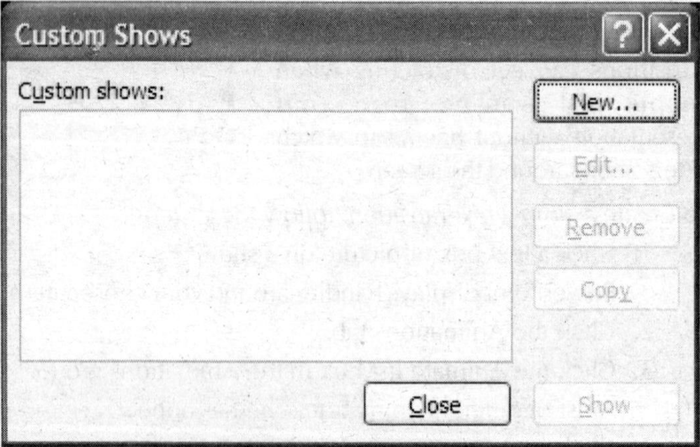

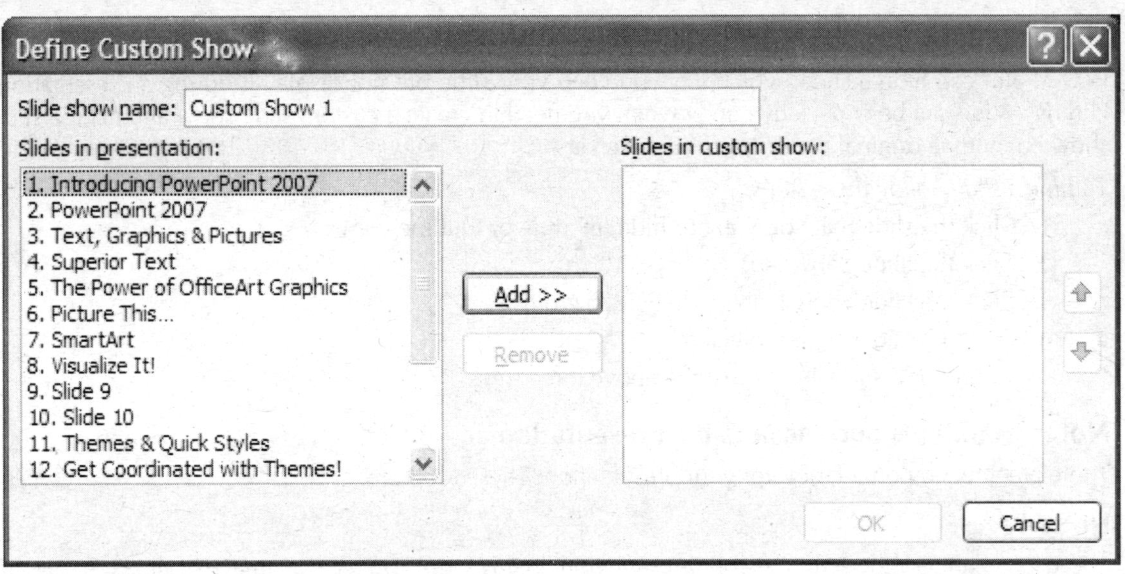

6. Clcik a slide in the Slides in Presentation list box and then click the Add button.

   This tells PowerPoint which existing slides you want to resuse in your custom slide show.

7. Repeat Step 6 for each slide you want to include in your custom slide show.
8. Click a slide in the Slides in Custom Show list box and click the Up or Down arrow button to rearrange their order.
9. Repeat Step 8 for each slide you want to rearrange in your custom slide show.
10. Click Ok.

    The Custom Shows dialog box appears again.

11. Click the name of your custom slide show and then click Show.

    PowerPoint shows your new, customized presentation.

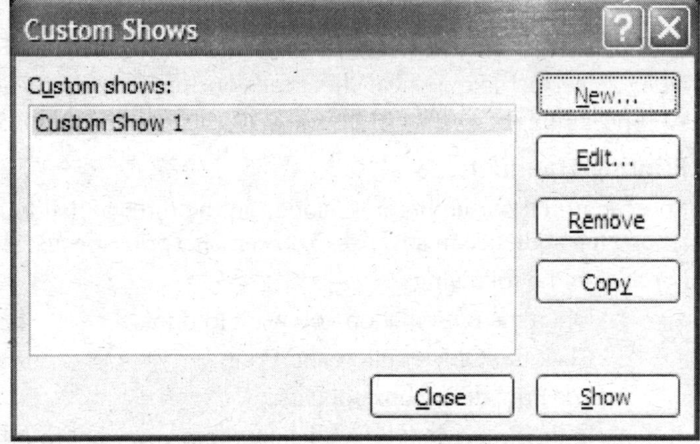

To present a custom slide show, follow these steps:

1. Click the Slide Show tab.
2. Click the Custom Slide Show icon in the Start Slide Show group.

   A pull-down menu appears that lists the names of all the custom slide shows you have created.

3. Click the name of the custom slide show you want to view.
4. Choose one of the following:

- Click the mouse or press the spacebar to view the next slide.
- Press Esc to exit your presentation.

Hiding a Slide

PowerPoint can hide a slide, which lets you keep your slide but not display it during a presentation. Hiding a slide can be expecially handy when you need to create a custom slide show and need a slide show but not the original presentation (or vice versa).

To hide a slide, followthese steps:

1. Click the slide that you want to hide (in Slide or Outline view).
2. Click the Slide Show tab.
3. Click the Hide Show icon in the Set Up group.

   PowerPoint dims your selected slide.

   To unhide a slide, just repeat the above three steps.

Notes, Handouts and Masters for Presentation

There are three important tools for your presentation. These tools are:

Notes Pages

These pages are like the script for your presentation. In this script you have an image of slides along with the words you want to deliver for the specific slide.

Handouts

These printed pages are the hard copies of the presentation slides which you can distribute to your audience.

Master

These are control elements of a slide like the title master which controls appearance of the title on all the slides.

Using Notes Pages

Notes Pages act like a cheat sheet for your presentation. You would write the text you want to read without letting the audience know that you are reading during the course of a presentation for each slide.

Printing Handouts

You can print your entire presentation in the form of handouts. These handouts are used to distribute among the audience in advance. You can also print specific slides, notes pages or outline pages.

For this do the following:

1. Open the presentation you want to print.
2. Click the Office button and Print.
3. The Print dialog box appears.
4. In the Print what: box, click the item you want to print.
5. If you select Handouts, you can then select a number of slides per page and whether the order should be horizontal or vertical,
6. Select any other options you want to apply.
7. After applying the option in the handouts section, click OK.

Handouts Master

The Handouts Master can be used to modify your Handout format.

For this do the following:

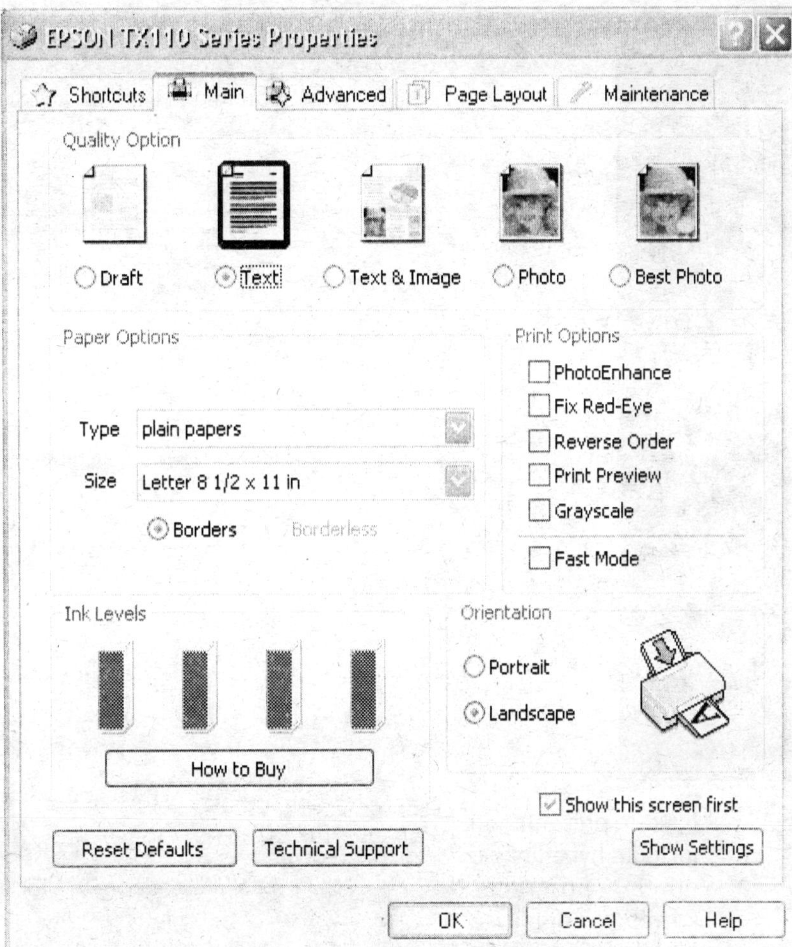

1. Click the View menu, highlight Master and choose Handout Master. The Handout Master appears.
2. In the Handout Master view, you can select the two slide per page, three slides per page or the six slides per page formats by clicking on the Handout Master toolbar as shown.
3. To apply any changes to the Handout Master, just follow the procedure as for the Notes master.
4. Save the presentation file to save any changes you make to the Handout Master.
5. You cannot change the position of the slide images on the Handout Master.
6. There is no notes text placeholder on the Handout Master.

Packing Presentations to Go

Many people use their laptops to display their PowerPoint presentations, but occasionally, you may need to use a different computer to run your presentaion. Because that other computer may not have a copy of PowerPoint, you can store your entire PowerPoint presentation on a CD that you can run on another computer.

To package up your presentation, follow these steps:

1. Click the Office button and choose Share <Publish for CD.

   The Package for CD dialog box appears.

   Rather than save a presentation to a CD, you can click the Copy to Folder button and specify a different drive and folder, such as a USB removeable drive.
2. Click in the Name the CD text box and type a descriptive name for your presentation.
3. Insert a blank CD in your rewritable CD drives.
4. Click Copy to CD.

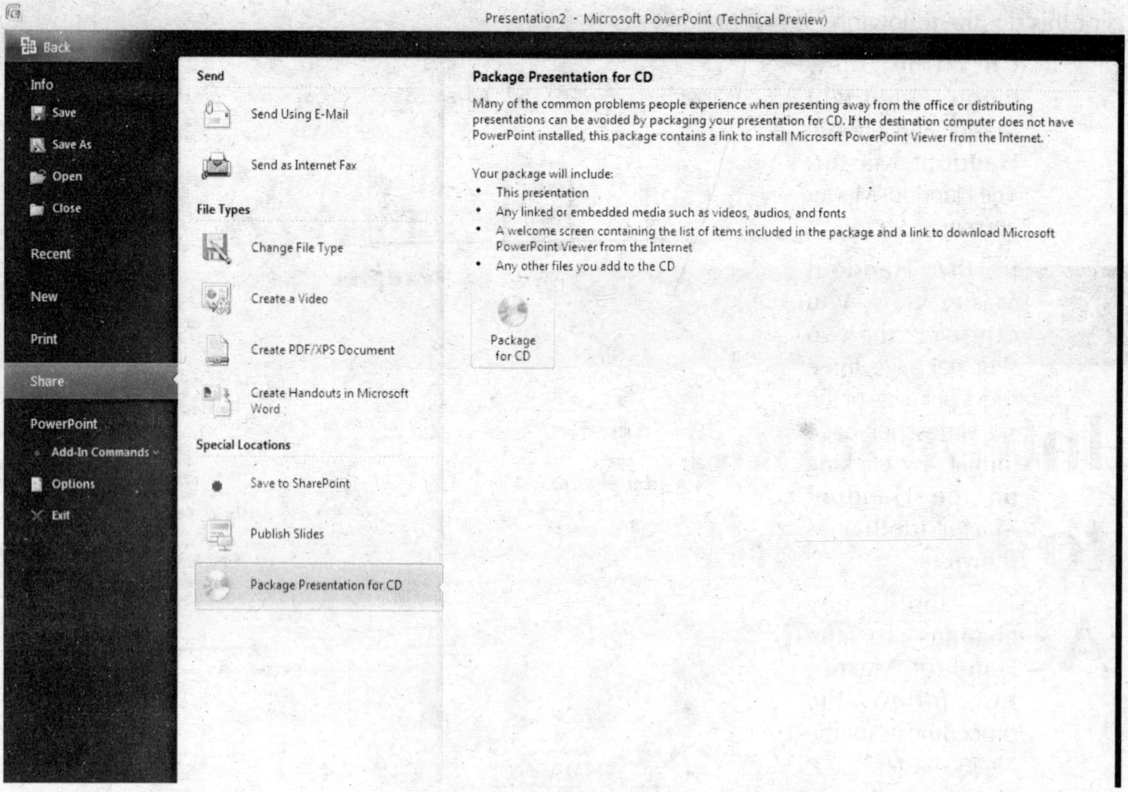

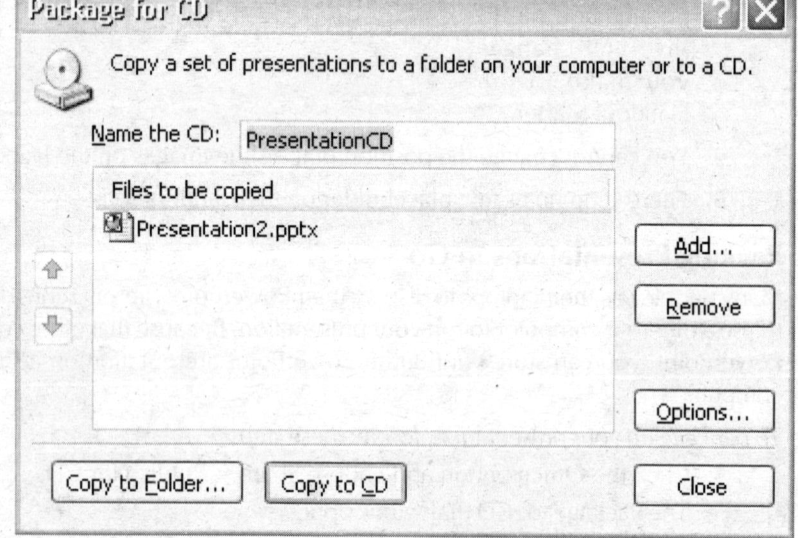

If your presentation includes hyperlinks to other programs, PowerPoint displays a dialog box to alert you. This dialog box is meant to keep you from accidentally creating a presentation that could spread viruses or Trojan Horses.

5. Click Close.

CHAPTER 5

Introduction to Microsoft Access 2010

Introduction

A software to take care of most of your database requirements. It allows you to store and organize information in sets of tables, which can be displayed in the form of columns and rows to look like a table or an index card. What's more it allows you to perform calculations and find for you simple statistics like totals and averages. It allows you to sort the data in any form and extract the required information based on the key given by you.

Creating a Database

Creating database with a Wizard is probably the easiest and fastest method of creating a database where you have to fill up some information and the database is ready for you. It not only creates Tables for you but all the Forms, Reports, etc., connected with it are done too.

Creating Database using the Wizard

Access can create a blank database or a database using one of many templates available from the Microsoft Web site. No matter how you create a database, you will likely need to modify it to customize it for the type of data you want.

To create a blank database, follow these steps:

1. Click the Office button and choose New.
   The Getting Started with Microsoft Access screen appears.
2. Click the Blank Database icon.
   The file name text box appears in the right corner of the screen.
3. Type a descriptive filename for your database.
   You may want to click the Browse icon to specify a different folder or drive to store your database.
4. Click Create.
   Access displays a blank table and an Add New Field text box. Displaying your database in rows and columns in Datasheet view.

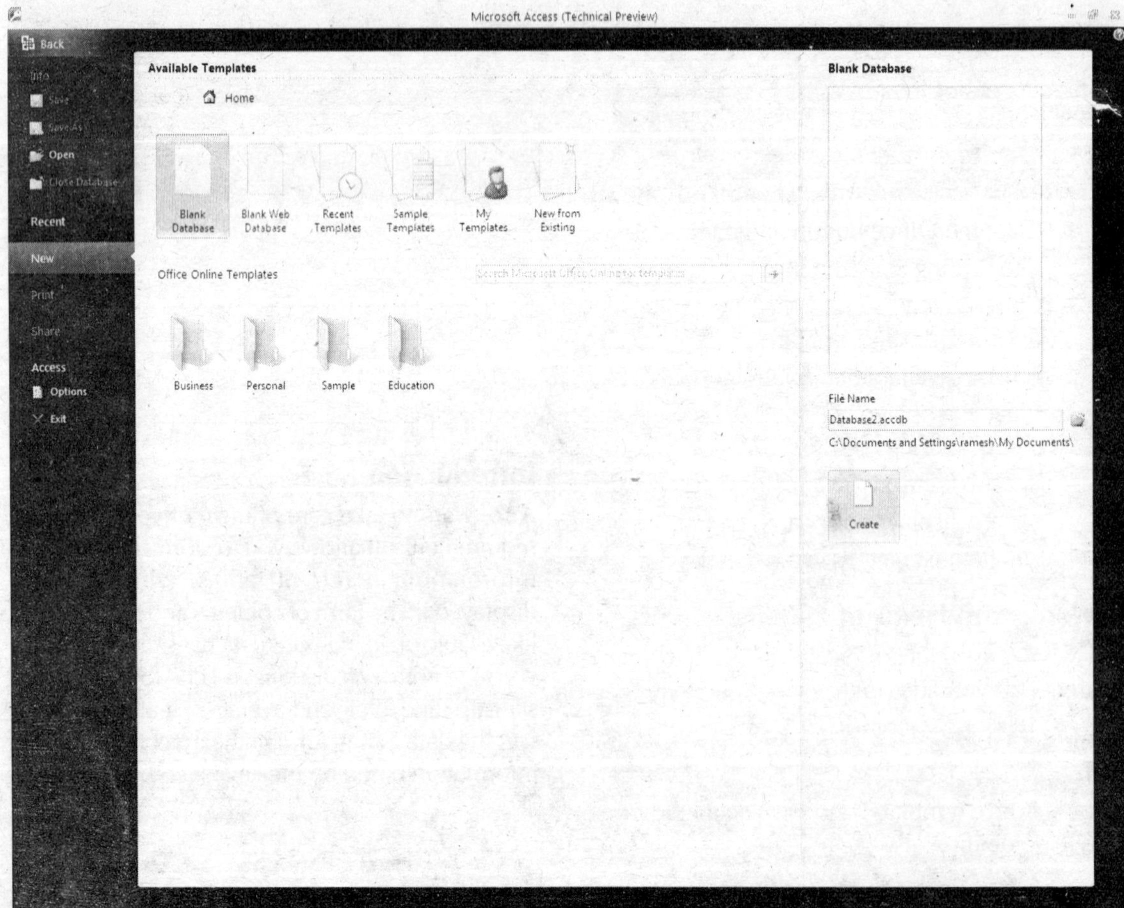

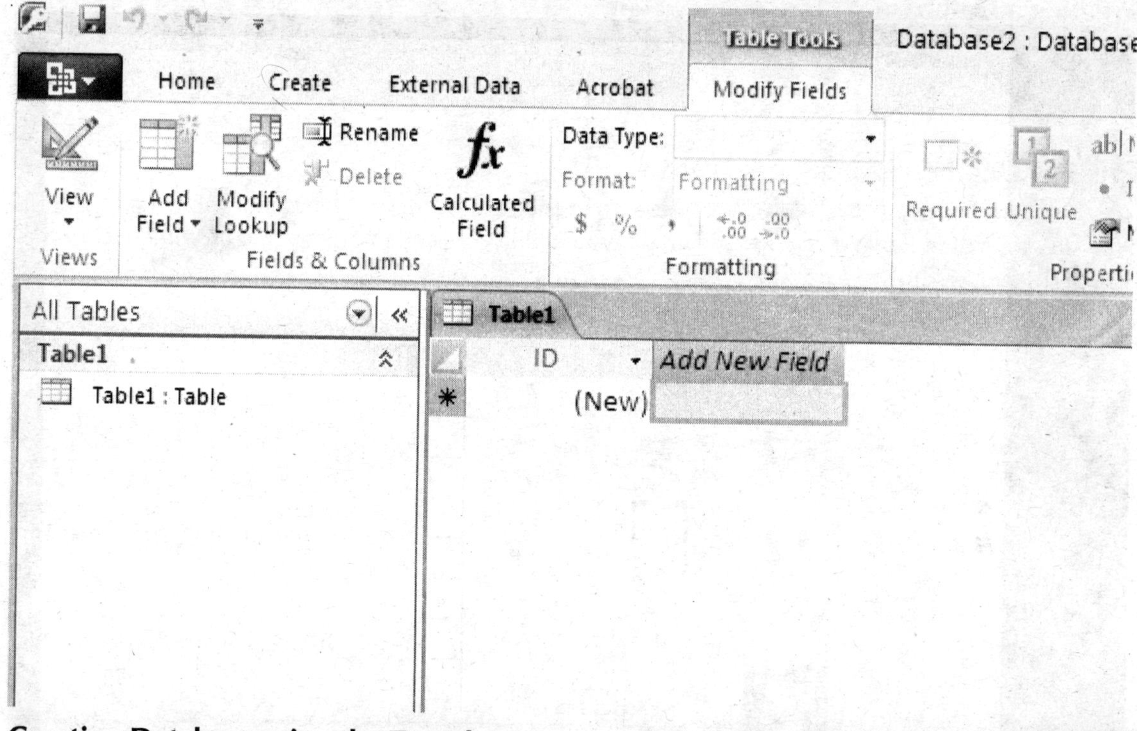

Creating Database using the Template

Just like it's easier to copy someone else's work, it's easier to use an existing database templates and modify it for your own needs. You need an Internet connection to retrieve any database templates from the Microsoft Web site.

To create a database file from a template, follow these steps:

1. Click the Office button and choose New.
   The Getting Started with Microsoft Access screen appears.
2. Click a category under the From Microsoft Office Online categroy such as Business or Education or choose Local Templates.
   A list of available templates appear.
3. Click a template. Access displays a default name in the File Name text box in the bottom right corner of the screen.
4. Type a descriptive name for your database in the File Name text box and then click Create.
   Access displays your database in rows and columns (Datasheet View).
   On the next page, see the database of Marketing Project.

Working with Fields of Database

After you have created a database and it has given you a database in the Datasheet View. It becomes apparent that you add fields, name them and then fill up the data in them (or import it).

Naming a Field

If you create a database from scratch, Access displays generic field names such as Field1. If you create a database from a template, you will see the descriptive field names, but you may still want to rename the fields to something else

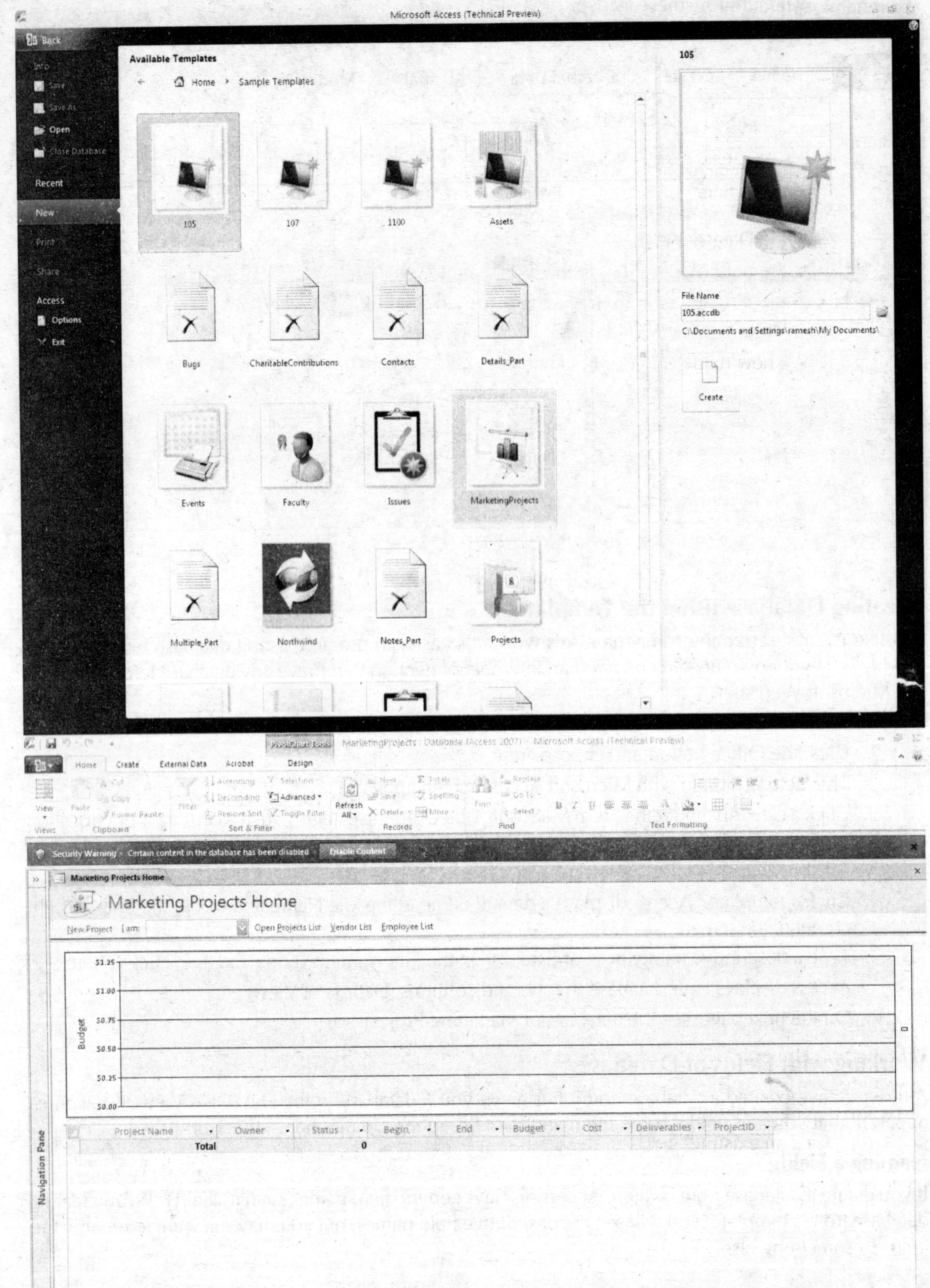
Microsoft Access (Technical Preview)
Available Templates
Home
Sample Templates
105
107
1100
Assets
Bugs
CharitableContributions
Contacts
Details_Part
Events
Faculty
Issues
MarketingProjects
Multiple_Part
Northwind
Notes_Part
Projects
File Name
105.accdb
C:\Documents and Settings\ramesh\My Documents\
Create
Security Warning
Certain content in the database has been disabled
Enable Content
Marketing Projects Home
New Project
Open Projects List
Vendor List
Employee List
Budget
Project Name
Owner
Status
Begin
End
Cost
Deliverables
ProjectID
Total
Navigation Pane

To rename a field, follow these steps:

1. Click the Office Button and then choose Open.
   The Open dialog box appears.
2. Click the Access database file you want to modify and then click Open.
   Access displays your chosen database.
3. In the All Tables pane on the left of the screen, double-click the table that contains the fields you want to rename.
   Access displays the Datasheet view of your database.
4. Click the Datasheet tab.
5. Click the field (column head) that you want to rename.
6. Click the Rename icon in the Fields & Columns group.
   Access highlights the field name.
7. Type a new name for your field and then click outside the field name when you are done.

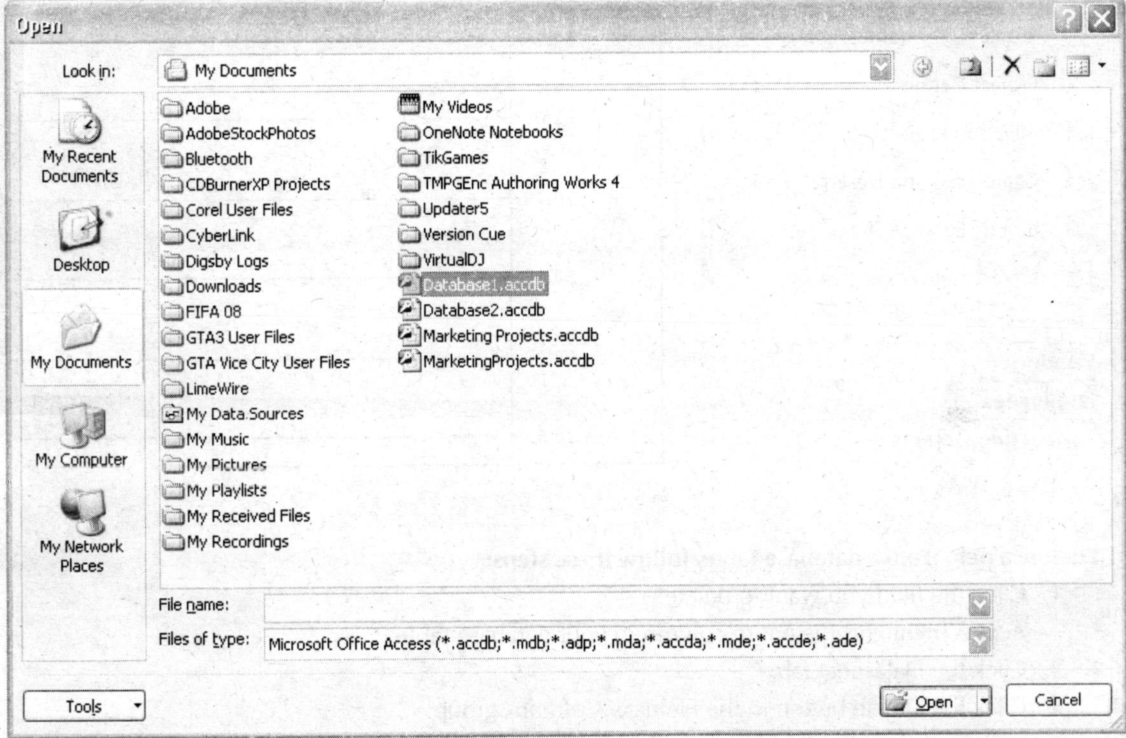

Adding/Deleting a Field

Sometimes you may need to add a field to make room to store new information. Other times, you may want to delete a field that you don't really want after all.

To add a field to a database table, follow these steps:

1. Click an existing field in your database table.
2. Click the Datasheet tab.
3. Click the Insert button in the Fields & Columns group.
   Access inserts a new field (column) in your database table.

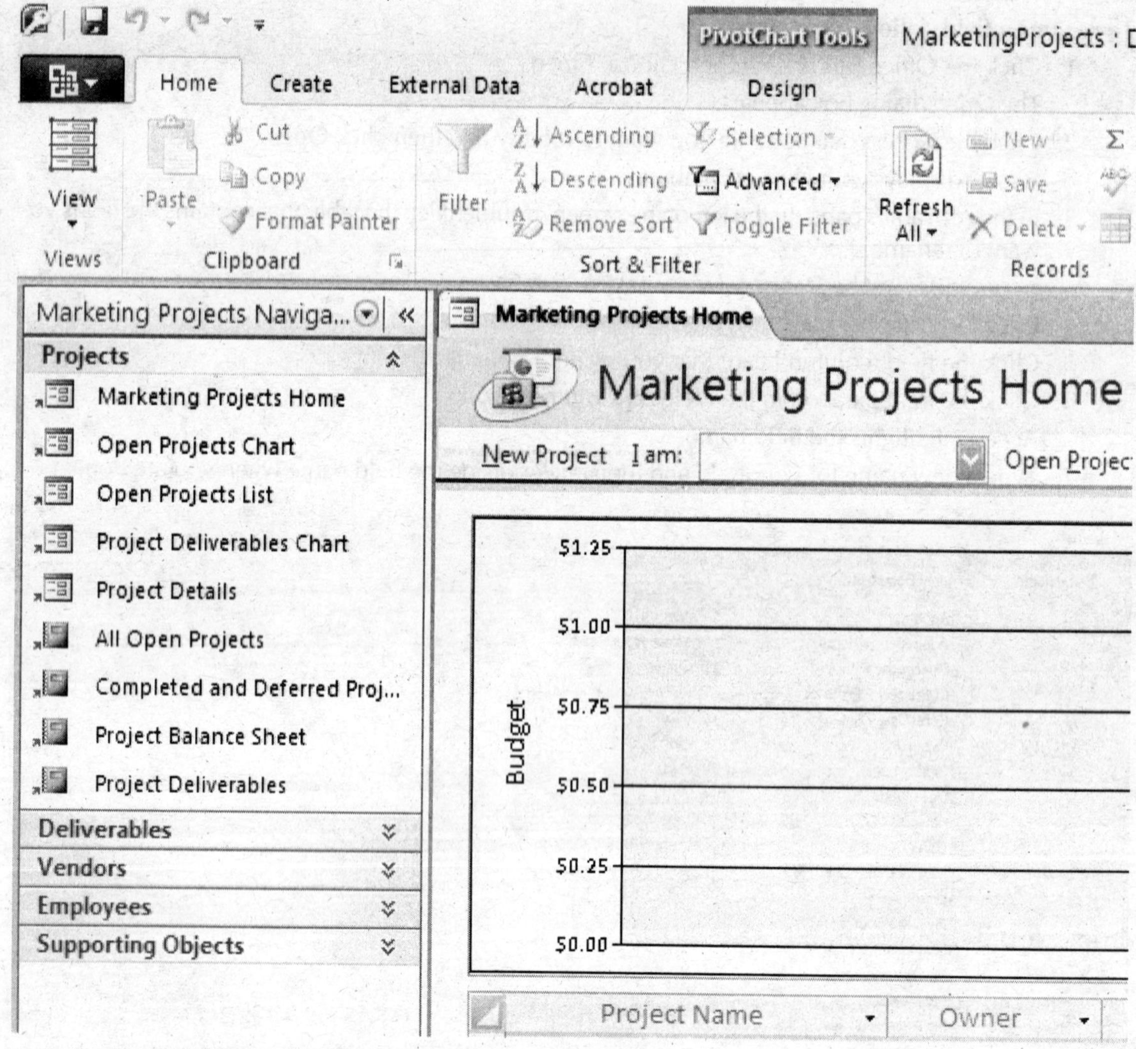

To delete a field from a database table, follow these steps:

1. Click the field you want to delete.

   Access highlights the entire column in your database table.
2. Click the Datasheet tab.
3. Click the Delete button in the Fields & Columns group.

   A dialog box appears, asking whether you want to permanently delete all the data in the field. If you delete a field, you also delete any data that may be stored in the field. Depending on how much data you have stored, you could wipe out a lot of information by deleting a signle field, so be careful.
4. Click Yest (or No).

   If you click Yes, Access deletes your chosen field.

Setting the Type and Size of a Field

The type of a field defines the type of data the field can hold (numbers, text, dataes, and so on), and the

Employee Details
Project1
Go to E-mail Create Outlook Contact Save and New Close
General Projects Tasks
First Name
Last Name Project1
Company
Job Title
E-mail
Web Page
Phone Numbers
Business Phone
Home Phone
Mobile Phone
Fax Number
Notes
Address
Street
City
State/Province
Zip/Postal Code
Country/Region
Record: 1 of 1 No Filter Search

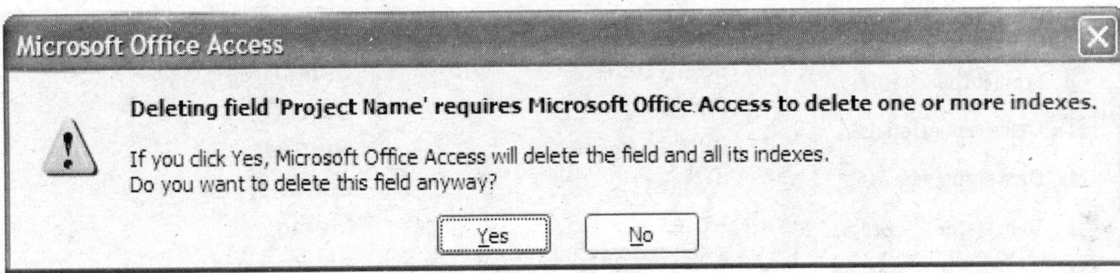

size of a field defines the amount of data the field can hold (no numbers larger than 250 digits, any text string fewer than 120 characters, and so on).

To define the type and amount of a data a field can store, follow these steps:

1. Click the Home or Datasheet tab.
2. In the All Tables pane on the left of the screen, double-click the table that contains the fields you want to define.

   Access displays the Datasheet view of your table.
3. Click the downward-pointing arrow underneath the View icon, which appears in the Views group.

A pull down menu appears.

4. Click Design View.

   Access displays the Design view of your database table.

5. Click in the Field Name column and edit an existing filed name.

   If you click in a blank row, you can add a field to a database table.

6. Click in the Data Type column.

   A downward-pointing arrow appears.

7. Click the downward-pointing arrow.

   A pull-down menu appears, listing all the different types of data you can define to store in a field.

8. Choose a data type, such as Number, Text or Data/Time. Access displays a General tab that contains different options for modifying your chosen data type.

9. Click one of the data type options, such as Format or Input Mask, listed under the General tab.

   Sometimes you have to type a value directly into a data type option. Other time a pull-down menu appears, from which you can choose an option.

10. Repeat Step 9 for each data type option you want to modify.

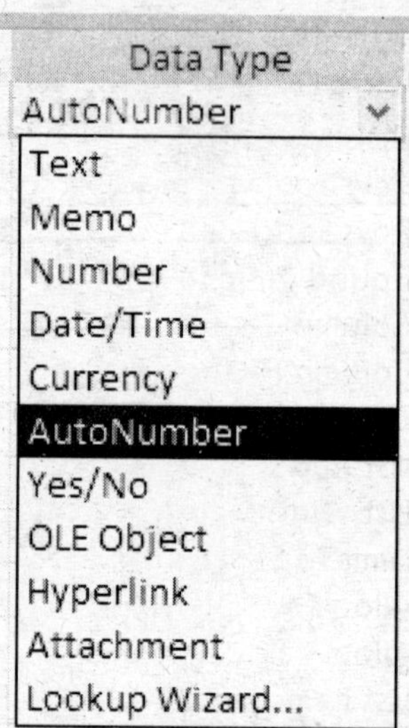

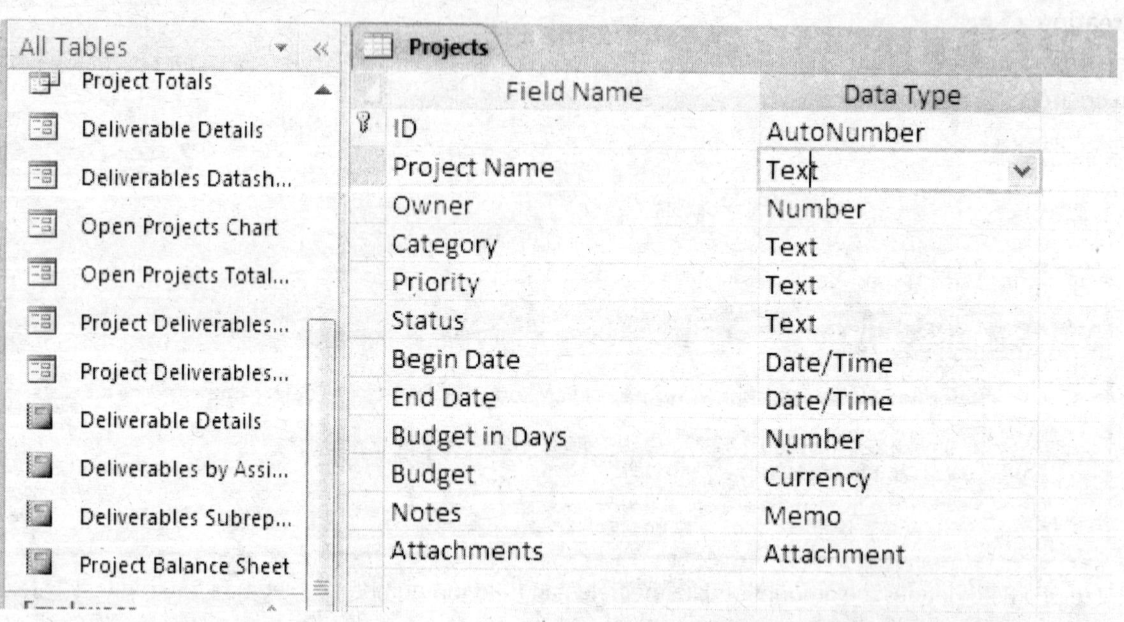

Creating a Form

The biggest problem with Datasheet view is that it can be confusing to find a field for a specific record. Because most people are familiar with paper forms or index cards that arrange related data (fields) on a page, Access offers you Form view. Form view simply displays the fields of a single record onscreen. To use Form

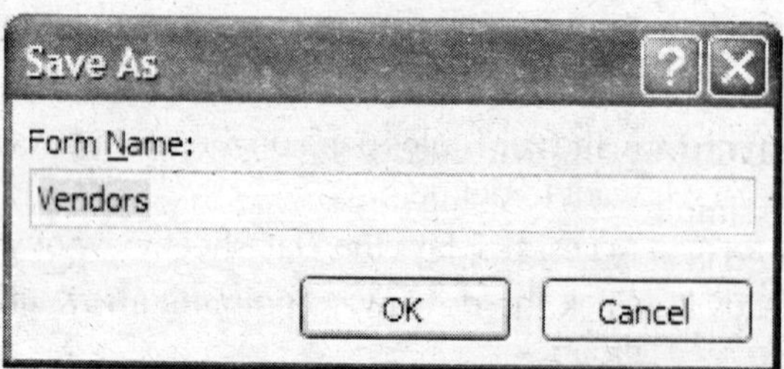

General | Lookup

Display Control	Combo Box
Row Source Type	Table/Query
Row Source	SELECT [Employees Extended].ID, [Employees Extended].[Employee Name]
Bound Column	1
Column Count	2
Column Heads	No
Column Widths	0";2"
List Rows	16
List Width	2"
Limit To List	Yes
Allow Multiple Values	No
Allow Value List Edits	Yes
List Items Edit Form	Employee Details
Show Only Row Source V	No

view, you must first create a form and arrange your fields on that form. After you create a form, you can add, edit and view data through that form.

Creating a Form

The simplest way to create a form to let Access desing one for you, which you can modify.

To create a form quickly, follow these steps:

1. Click the Office Button and then choose Open.
   The Open dialog box appears.
2. Click the Access database file you want to add or edit data. Then click Open.
   Access displays your chosen database.
3. In the All Tables pane on the left of the screen, double-click a table.
   Access displays the Datasheet view of your database.
4. Click the Create tab.
5. Click the Form icon in the Forms group.
   Access creates a form. Notice that the form name automatically uses the name of the database table you choose in Step 3.
6. Click the Office Button and then choose Save (or click the Save icon on the Quick Access toolbar).
   The Save As dialog box appears, asking you to type a name for your form.
7. Type a descriptive name for your form in the Form Name text box and then click Ok.
   Acess displays your form's name underneath the All Tables pabe. The next time you open this database and want to view the form, you can double-click the form's name in the left pane.

Searching a Database

The simplest type of search ooks for a specific record. To search for a record, you need to know the data stored in at least one of its fields, such as a phone number and e-mail address. The more information you already know, the more likely Access will find the one record you want. If you search for all records that

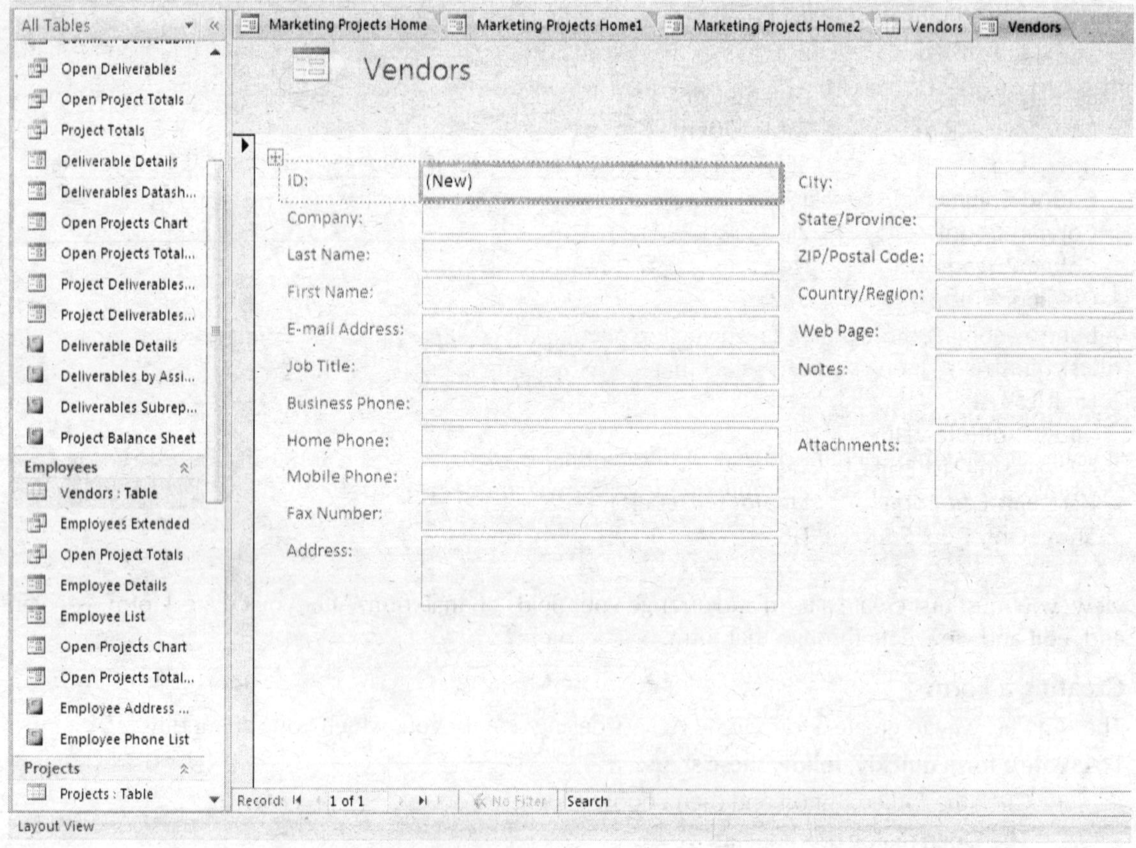

contain the first name, Access could find dozens of records. But, if you feed in the name and surname, your search would narrow down to just few records.

To search for a specific record in a database table, follow these steps:

1. In the All Tables pane on the left of the screen, double-click the name of the databse table you want to search.

   Access displays the Datasheet view of your database.
2. Click the Home tab.
3. Click the Find icon in the Find group.

   The Find and Replace dialog box appears.
4. Click in the Find What text box and type in the data you know is stored in the record in the record you want to find.

   For example, if you want to find the phone number of a person but you know only that person's last name in the Find What text box.
5. Click the Look In list box and choose the name of the entire databse table.
6. Click in the Match list box and choose one of the following:

- Any Part of Field: The Find What text can appear in any part of a field.
- Whole Field: The Find What text is the only text stored in a field.
- Start of Field: The Find What text can be only at the beginning of a field.

7. Click in the Search list box and choose one of the following:.
   - Up: Searches from the record where the cursor appears, up to the beginning of the database table.
   - Down: Searches from the record where the cursor appears, down to the end of the database table.
   - All: Searches the entire database table.
8. Click Find Next.
9. Repeat Step 8 to search for more records that might contain the text you typed in Step 4.
10. Click Cancel or the Close button.

Creating a Query

A query is nothing more than a saved version of your sort or filter criteria. By saving the particular sort or filter criteria as a query, you can select that query by name later.

Creating a Simple Query

If your databse table contains dozens of different fields, you may find it confusing to make sense of all your information. As an aid, a simple query strips away fields so you see only the fields containing data you want to see, such as a person's name and phone number but not her hire date or employee number.

To create a query, follow these steps:

1. Click the Create tab.
2. Click the Query Wizard icon in the Other group.
   The New Query dialog box appears.
3. Click Simple Query Wizard and then click Ok.
   The Simple Query Wizard dialog box appears.

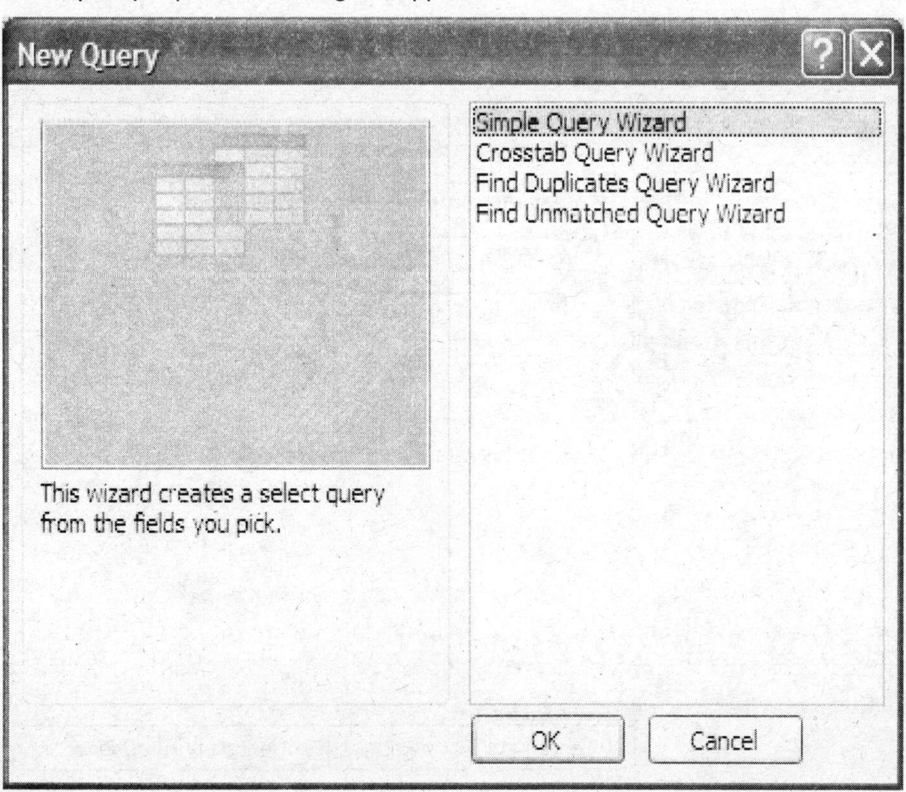

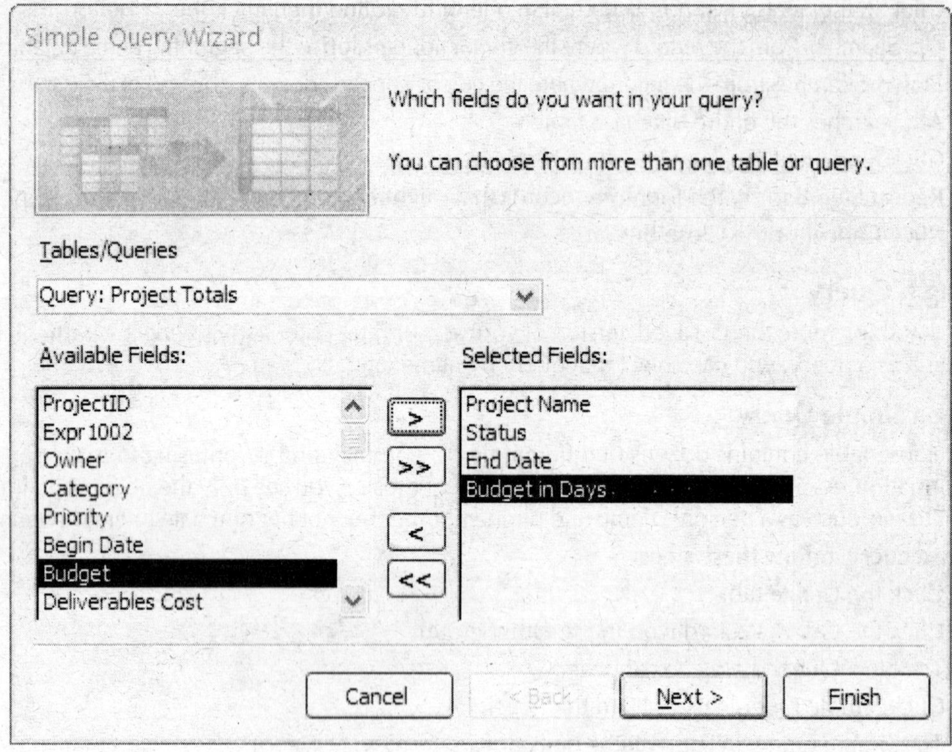
Simple Query Wizard
Which fields do you want in your query?
You can choose from more than one table or query.
Tables/Queries
Query: Project Totals
Available Fields:
ProjectID
Expr1002
Owner
Category
Priority
Begin Date
Budget
Deliverables Cost
Selected Fields:
Project Name
Status
End Date
Budget in Days
Cancel
< Back
Next >
Finish

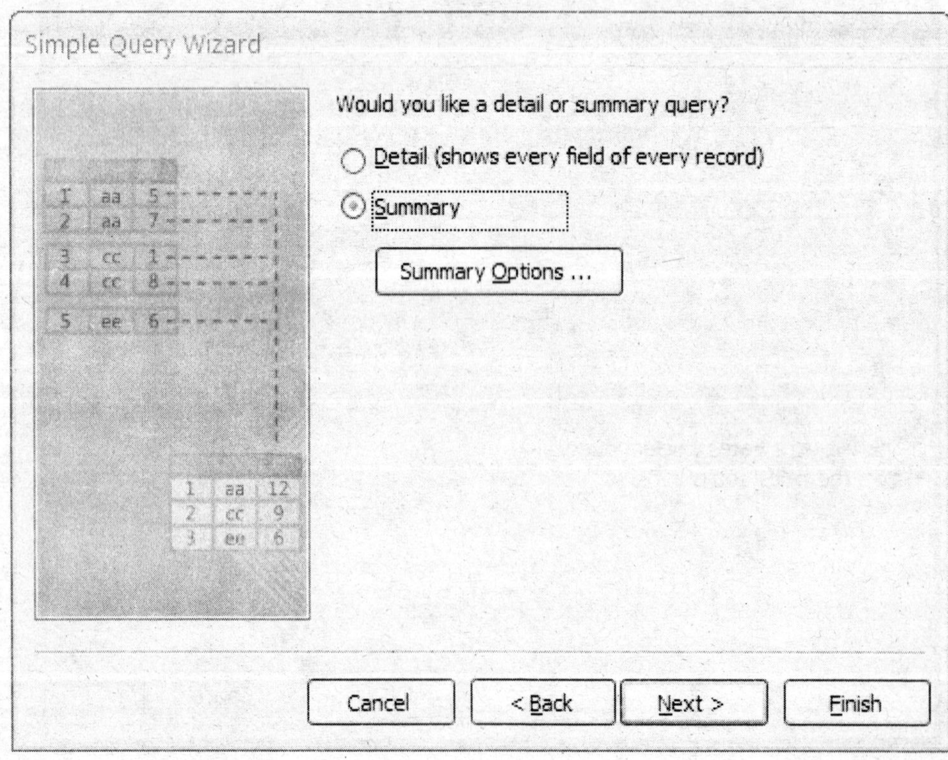
Simple Query Wizard
Would you like a detail or summary query?
Detail (shows every field of every record)
Summary
Summary Options ...
Cancel
< Back
Next >
Finish

4. Click a field name listed in the Available Fields box and then click the > button.
   Access displays your chosen filed in the Selected Fields box.
5. Repeat Step 4 for each field you want to use in your query.
6. Click Next.
   Another dialog box appears. This dialog box asks whether you want to display a Detail or Summary (shows numerical information such as the total number of records found, the average value, and the minimum/maximum value) view of your data.
7. Select the Detail or Summary radio button and then click Next.
   Another dialog box appears, asking you to type a descriptive name for your query.
8. Click to the text box, type a descriptive name for your query, and then click Finish.
9. Click the Office Button and then choose Save to save your query.

Creating a Crosstab Query

A crosstab query lets you combine tow or more fields to calculate and display a calculation based on a third field. For example, if your database contains the names of salespeople and the products they sold, you can use those two fields to create a crosstab that tells you how much each salesperson sold of each product.

To create a crosstab query, you need to identify three types of fields.

- One to three fields to identify each record (such as the First Name and Last Name fields)
- A single field to dsiplay specific data from each record (such as the Product field, which displays the actual product names like Nails, Barbed Wire, and Screws)
- A crosstab field that dsiplays a calculate result (such as Sales)

To create a crosstab query, follow these steps:

1. Click the Create tab.
2. Click the Query Wizard icon in the Other group.
   The New Query dialog box appears.
3. Click Crosstab Query Wizard and then click Ok.
   The Crosstab Query Wizard dialog box appears.
4. Click a database table and then click Next.
   Another Crosstab Query Wizard dialog box appears that asks for between one and three fields to identify each row (record).
5. Click a field in the Available Fields box and then click the > button to move your chosen field to the Selected Fields box.
6. Repeat Step 5 for each additional field you want to include.
7. Click Next.
   Another dialog box appears, asking for a single field to use to crosstabular data with the fields you choose in Steps 5 and 6.
8. Click a field name and then click Next.
9. Click a field that contains numerical data and then click a matematical function that you want Access to calculate, such as Sum, Avg., or Count.
10. Click Next.
    Another dialog box appears.
11. Type a descriptive name for your query in the text box at the top of the dialog box and then click Finish.

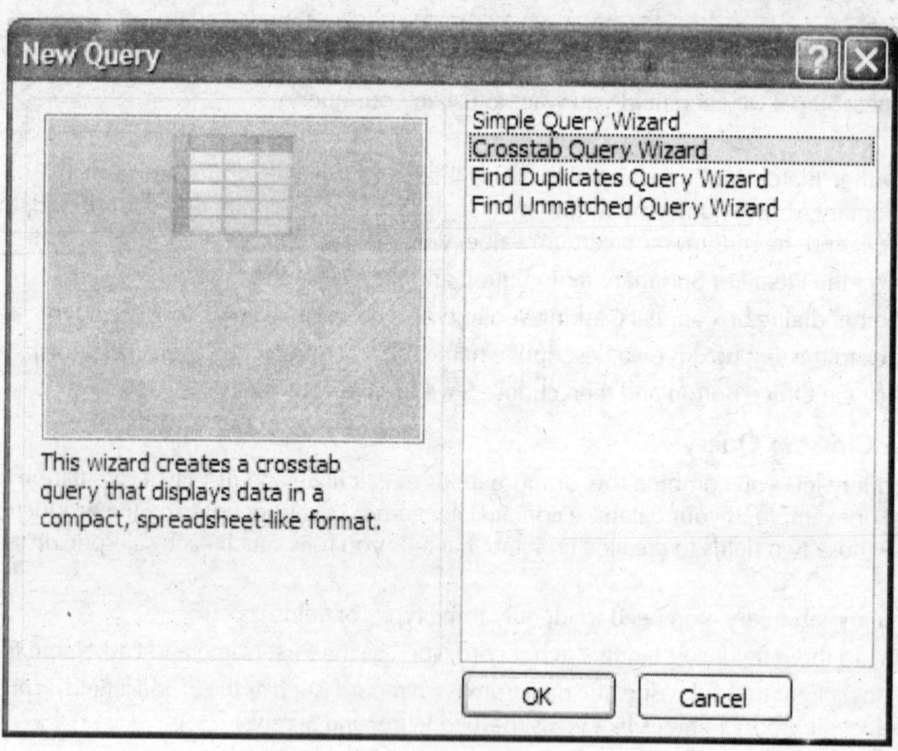
New Query
Simple Query Wizard
Crosstab Query Wizard
Find Duplicates Query Wizard
Find Unmatched Query Wizard
This wizard creates a crosstab query that displays data in a compact, spreadsheet-like format.
OK
Cancel

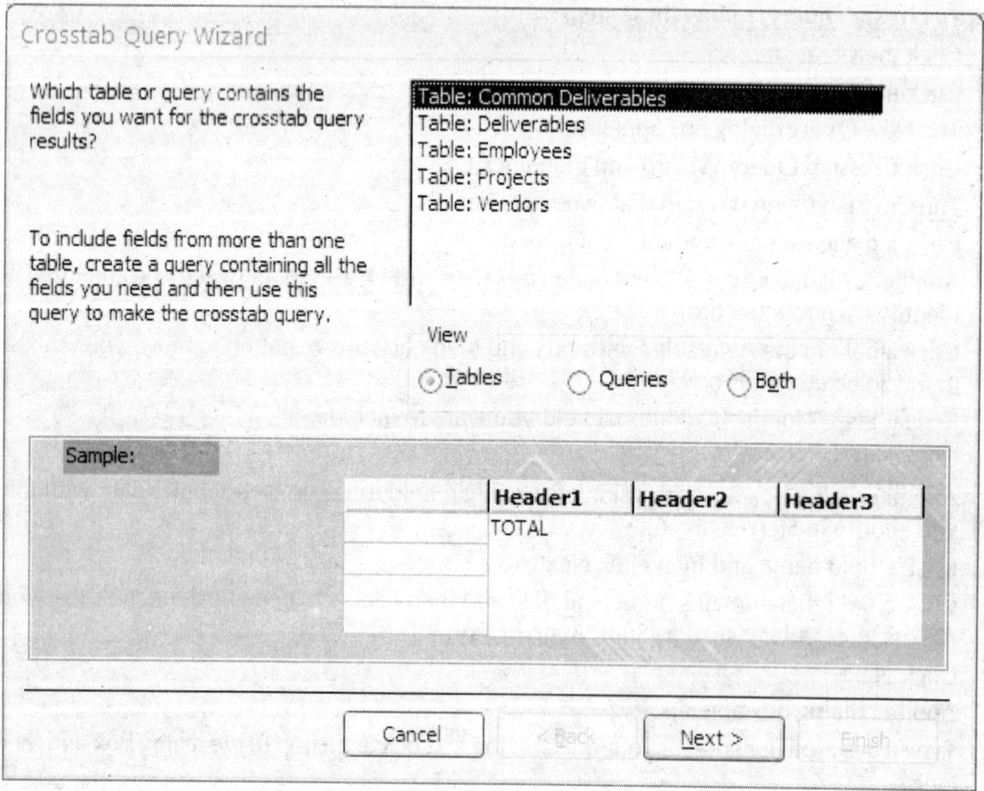
Crosstab Query Wizard
Which table or query contains the fields you want for the crosstab query results?
Table: Common Deliverables
Table: Deliverables
Table: Employees
Table: Projects
Table: Vendors
To include fields from more than one table, create a query containing all the fields you need and then use this query to make the crosstab query.
View
Tables
Queries
Both
Sample:
Header1
Header2
Header3
TOTAL
Cancel
< Back
Next >
Finish

Crosstab Query Wizard

Which fields' values do you want as row headings?

You can select up to three fields.

Select fields in the order you want information sorted. For example, you could sort and group values by Country and then Region.

Available Fields:

- Add
- Priority
- Cost
- % Complete
- Assigned To
- Start Date
- Due Date
- Attachments.FileData
- Attachments.FileFlags
- Attachments.FileName

> >> < <<

Selected Fields:

- Deliverable
- Vendor
- Cost In Days

Sample:

Deliverable	Vendor	Cost In Days	Header1	Header2	Header3
Deliverable1	Vendor1	Cost In Days1	TOTAL		
Deliverable2	Vendor2	Cost In Days2			
Deliverable3	Vendor3	Cost In Days3			
Deliverable4	Vendor4	Cost In Days4			

Crosstab Query Wizard

Which field's values do you want as column headings?

For example, you would select Employee Name to see each employee's name as a column heading.

- Add
- Priority
- Cost
- % Complete
- Assigned To
- Start Date
- Due Date
- Attachments.FileData
- Attachments.FileFlags
- Attachments.FileName

Sample:

Deliverable	Vendor	Cost In Days	Add1	Add2	Add3
Deliverable1	Vendor1	Cost In Days1	TOTAL		
Deliverable2	Vendor2	Cost In Days2			
Deliverable3	Vendor3	Cost In Days3			
Deliverable4	Vendor4	Cost In Days4			

Cancel | < Back | Next > | Finish

CHAPTER 5

Crosstab Query Wizard

What number do you want calculated for each column and row intersection?

For example, you could calculate the sum of the field Order Amount for each employee (column) by country and region (row).

Do you want to summarize each row?

☑ Yes, include row sums.

Fields:

Priority
Cost
% Complete
Assigned To
Start Date
Due Date
Attachments.FileData
Attachments.FileFlags
Attachments.FileName

Functions:

Count
First
Last
Max
Min

Sample:

Deliverable	Vendor	Cost In Days	Add1	Add2	Add3
Deliverable1	Vendor1	Cost In Days1	Count(Priority)		
Deliverable2	Vendor2	Cost In Days2			
Deliverable3	Vendor3	Cost In Days3			
Deliverable4	Vendor4	Cost In Days4			

Crosstab Query Wizard

What do you want to name your query?

Common Deliverables_Crosstab

That's all the information the wizard needs to create the query.

Do you want to view the query, or modify the query design?

◉ View the query.

○ Modify the design.

Cancel | < Back | Next > | Finish

12. Click the Office Button and choose Save to save your query.

Creating a Report

Each software has its own method of giving the output in the form of a print out, which can either be on printer or on screen. Access also has the same. But for this you have to first create a report design and then send it either to printer or monitor.

Creating Report using Wizard

The easiest way to create a report is to use the Report Wizard, which guides you step by step through arranging and selecting which data to print on a report along with sorting your data at the same time.

To use the Report Wizard, follow these steps:

1. Click the Create tab.
2. Click the Report Wizard icon in the Reports group.

   The Report Wizard dialog box appears.

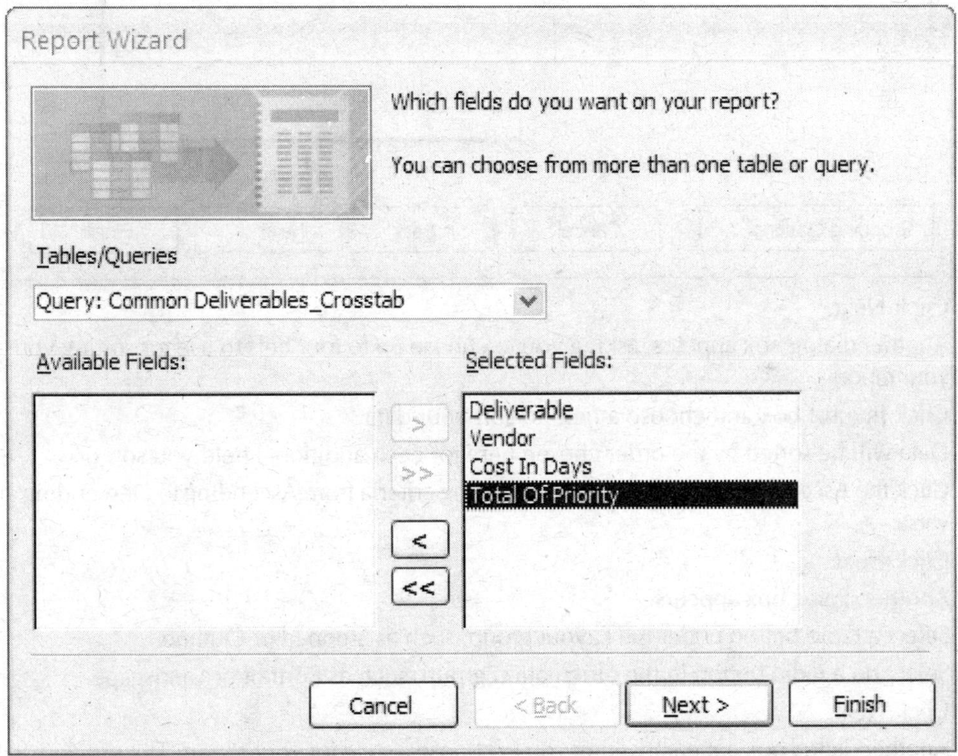

3. Click in the Tables/Queries list box and choose the table or query that contains the data you want to print in a report.
4. Click a field in the Available Fields box and then click this > button. Report this step for each additional field you want to display in your report.
5. Click Next.

   Another dialog box appears, asking whether you want to group your data by a speecific field such as Last Name or Employee Number.
6. Click a field name displayed in the box and then click the > button. Repeat this step for each additional field you want to use to group your data on the report.

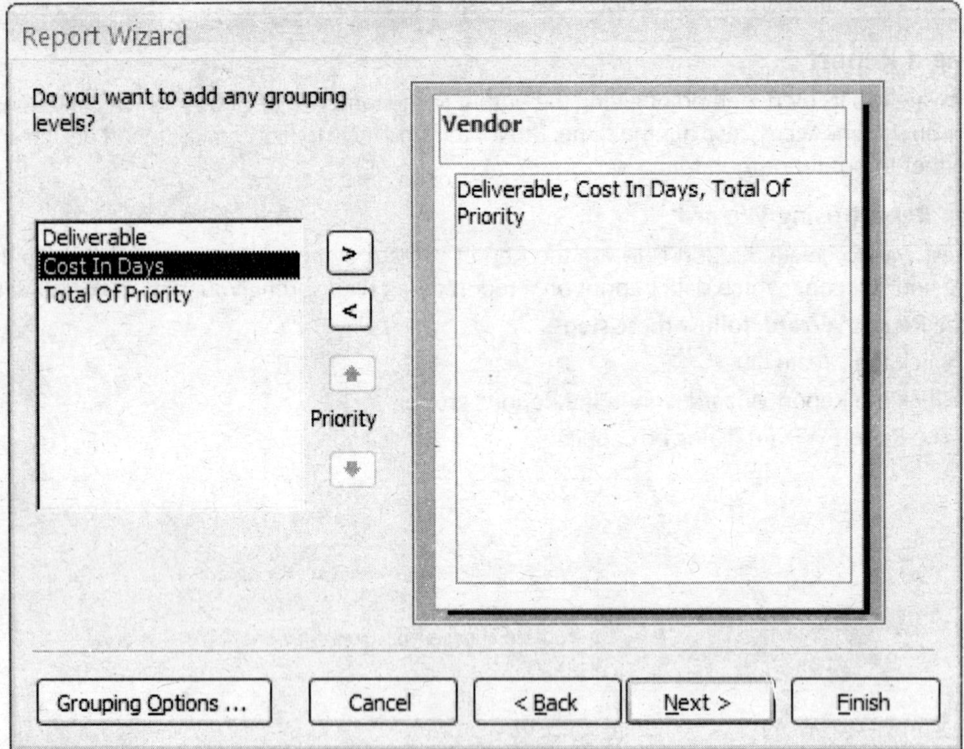

7. Click Next.

   Another dialog box appears, asking you to choose up to four fiels to use for sorting your data in your report.

8. Click in a list box and choose a field to sort your data.

   Data will be sorted by the order chosen here for each additional field you sort on.

9. Click the Ascending button to change the soring criteria from Ascending to Descending and vice versa.

10. Click Next.

    Another dialog box appears.

11. Select a radio button under the Layout group, such as Stepped or Outline.

12. Select on a radio button in the Orientation group, such as Portrait or Landscape.

13. Click Next.

    Another dialog box appears, asking you to choose a style for your report. The preview to the left will give you an indication of what the printed report will look like.

14. Click Next.

    Another dialog box appears, asking you for a descriptive name for your report.

15. Type a descriptive name for your report and then click Finish.

    Access displays your report.

16. Right-click the Report tab.

    A pop-up menu appears.

17. Click Close.

    A dialog box appears.

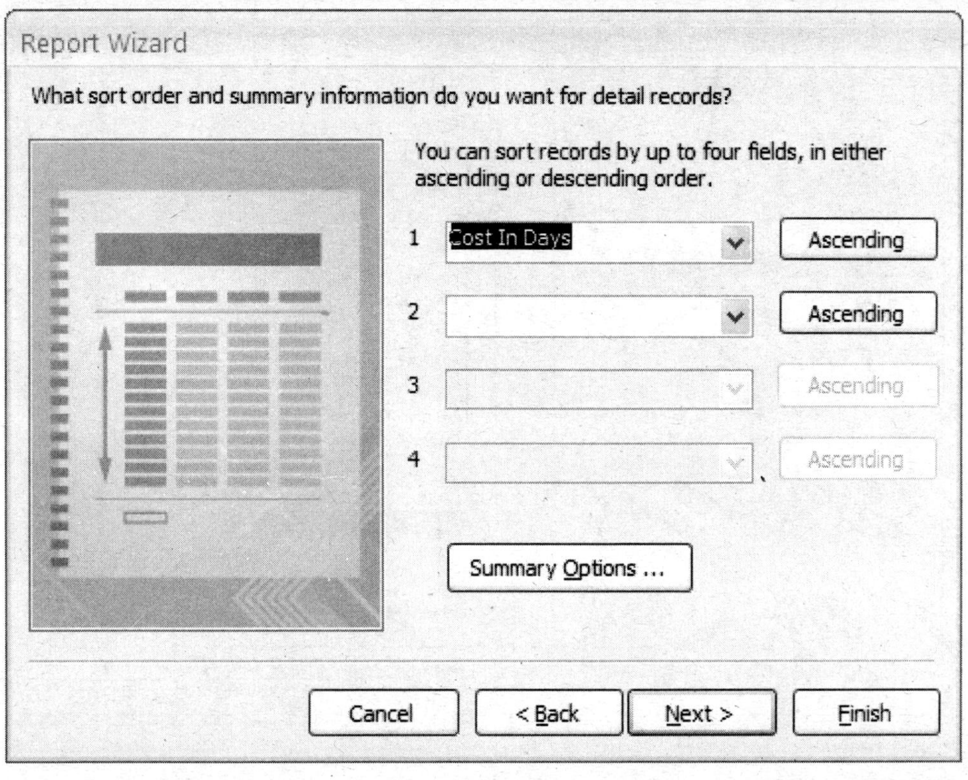
Report Wizard
What sort order and summary information do you want for detail records?
You can sort records by up to four fields, in either ascending or descending order.
1
Cost In Days
Ascending
2
Ascending
3
Ascending
4
Ascending
Summary Options ...
Cancel
< Back
Next >
Finish

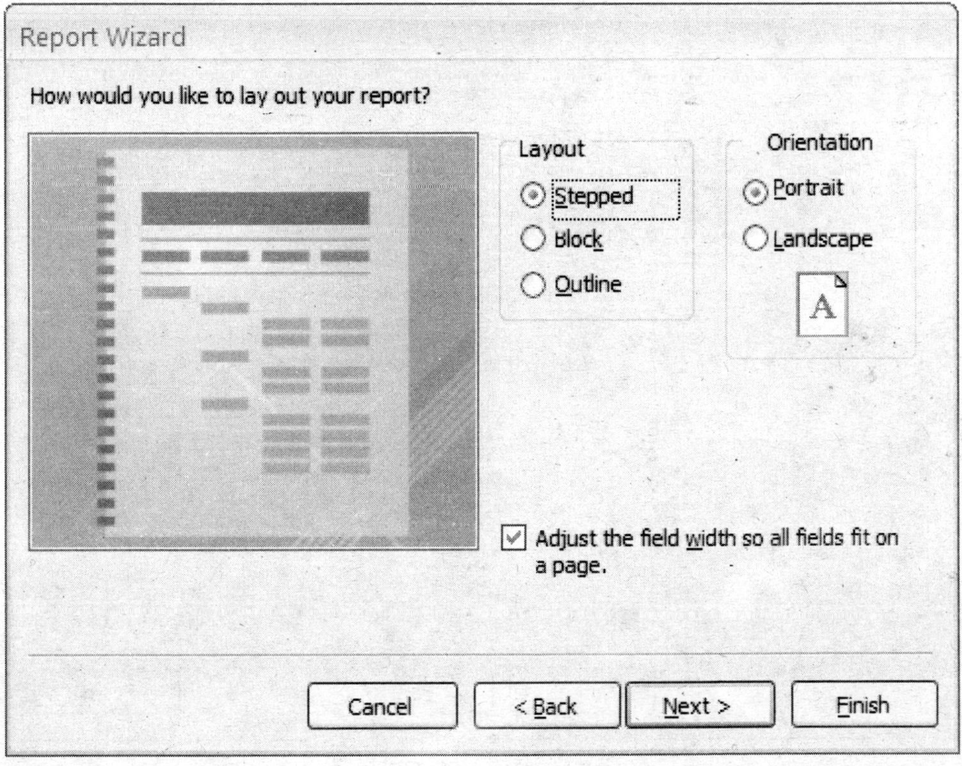
Report Wizard
How would you like to lay out your report?
Layout
Stepped
Block
Outline
Orientation
Portrait
Landscape
A
Adjust the field width so all fields fit on a page.
Cancel
< Back
Next >
Finish

CHAPTER 5

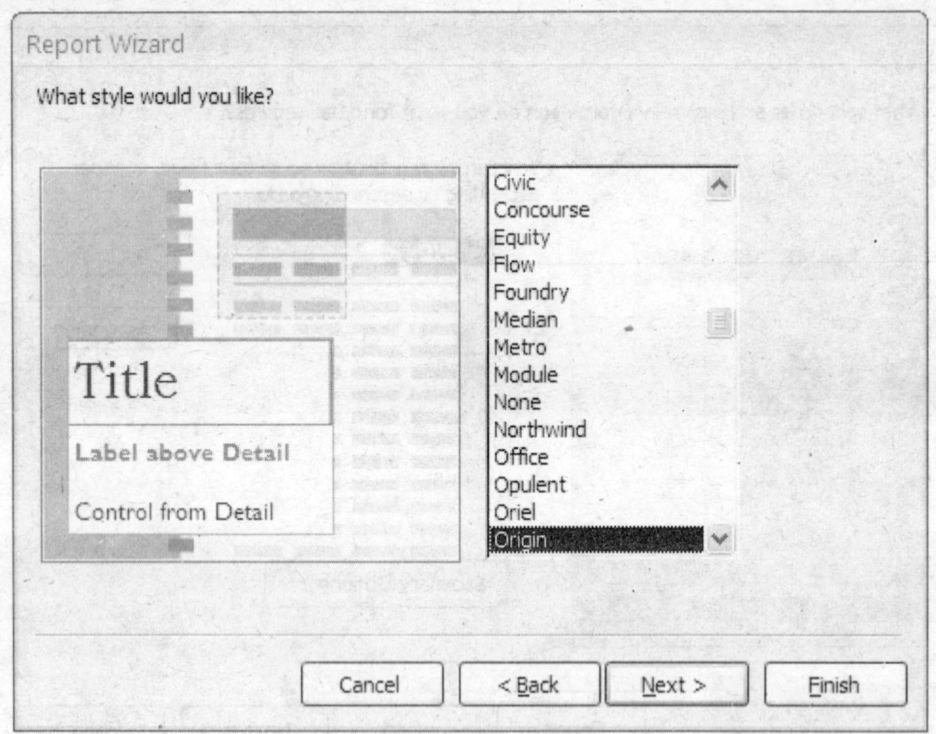

18. Click Yes.
    Access saves your report for future use and removes it from view.

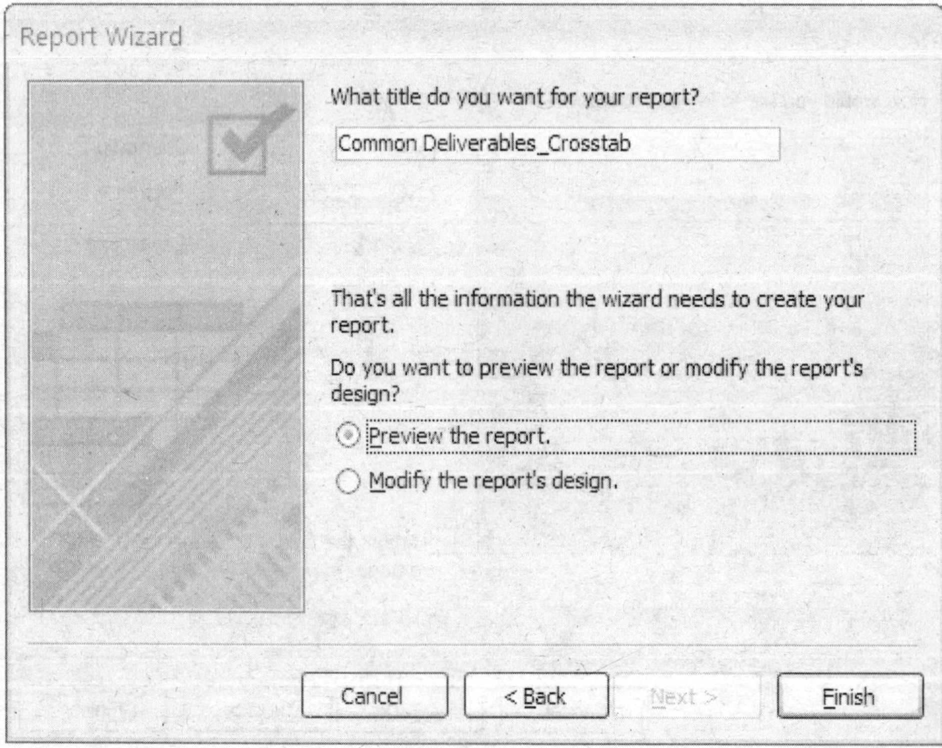

CHAPTER 6

Other Software of Microsoft Office 2010

Introduction

Publisher 2010 Microsoft's answer to the various other publishing software available in the market like PageMaker. It allows you to create invitations, design business-cards, and letter-heads, make your own calenders, produce newsletter, etc.

OneNote 2010 used to gather information during meetings, brainstorming sessions, interviews, and more. The notes you create can include text, drawings, images, and audio recordings. OneNote uses a freeform page layout, so you can place and move information wherever you want.

InfoPath 2010 helps you collect and work with data by using dynamic, online forms that have a familiar Office interface. Based on the Extensible Markup Language (XML), InfoPath makes it easy to create and use robust forms to more effectively gather and share information throughout your organization.

Microsoft Office Groove 2010 is Internet software for making direct connections with the people who are important to you. With Office Groove 2007, you can bring together team members from both inside and outside your company, with no IT assistance required and no need to waste time thinking about firewalls, servers, security, or network access. Additionally, you can enjoy the efficiency of always knowing each other's virtual location, or online presence, thus allowing for organic and quick conversation and collaboration.

CHAPTER 6

Microsoft Office OneNote 2010

With OneNote, you can jot down ideas generated in a meeting session, sketch your original vision, record your interviews and assemble material from your online reference sources.

You can enter original notes by typing on a keyboard. Your virtual notebook works much like a physical one – your notes are organized on pages and in sections. But you can also mark and highlight your notes as well as rearrange them, search them and create Microsoft Outlook tasks from them – try that with a physical notebook!

For your convenience, OneNote automatically saves your notes at regular intervals, so you don't have to stop working to save. Simply close OneNote at the end of a session and when you open it again, all your notes – in all the sections and all the pages – are there for you to continue your work.

Getting Started with OneNote

As usual I would show how you can start with OneNote and make your own notes for future use. Here I am making plans for the World Book Fair and what sort of activities to be taken up there.

Follow the following steps for this:

1. Click the Start button, point to All Programs, point to Microsoft Office and then click Microsoft OneNote 2010.

   OneNote 2010 opens with two sections: General, on the blue tab and Meetings on the green tab.
2. On the General section, click the Title box at the top of the page and type World Book Fair.
3. In the body of the page, directly below the title, click the shaded area and type **What we would like to do**.
4. Press enter and type Meet all the publishers.

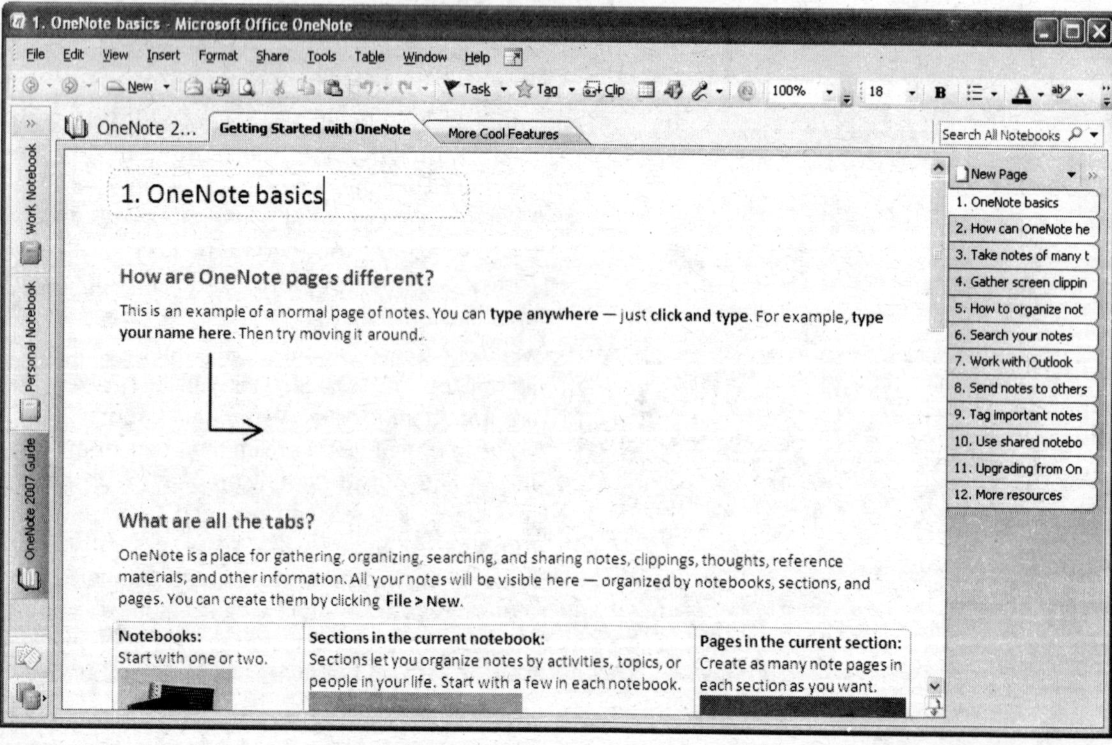

5. Press enter and type Select the books to be purchased.
6. Press enter and type Pick up catalog of competitors.
7. Select the first line, what we'd like to present and on the Formatting toolbar, click the Bold button.
8. Select the remaining three lines of text on the page and on the Formatting toolbar, click the Bullets button.
9. At this stage your screen would look like the one shown on the next page.
10. Near the top of the window, click the Meetings section tab.

    OneNote 2010 displays the Meetings section of the notebook. This is where you'll record your notes during a meeting with the various publishers.
11. Click the Title box and type Planning Session.
12. Click in the body of the page, type Stall Decoration.
13. Press the down key and type Arrange books category wise.
14. Press enter and type Arrange banners.
15. Press enter and type Arrange posters.
16. Select the three lines you just typed and on the Formatting toolbar, click the Bullet button.
17. On the File menu, click Exit.

OneNote closes. Your notes are saved as you crate them, so there's no need to save them when you close the program.

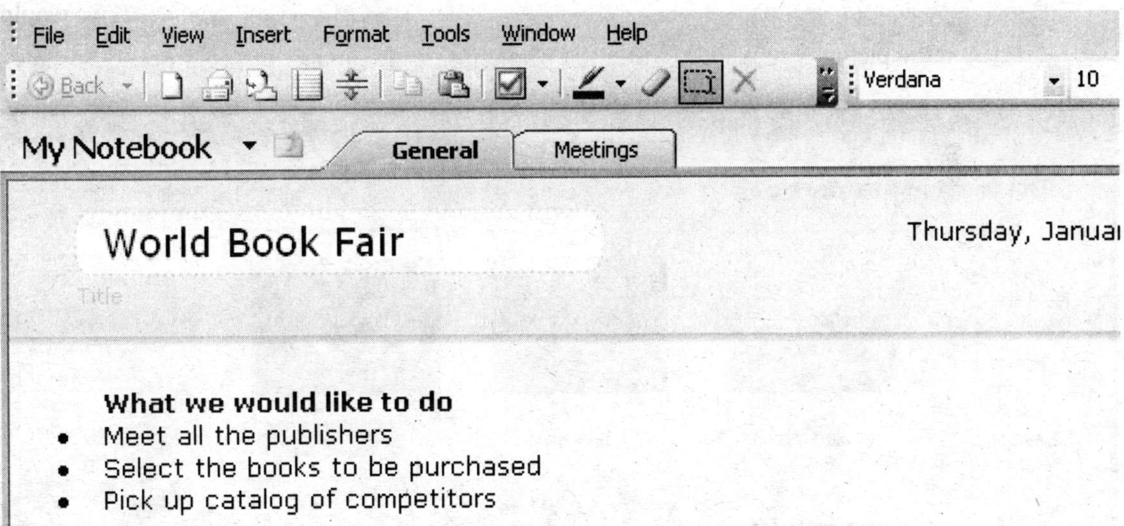

Adding Drawings and Images

To make your notes look more presentable, add the drawings, pictures or images. This can be done like this:

1. Click the Start button, point to All Programs, point to Microsoft Office and then click Microsoft OneNote 2010.

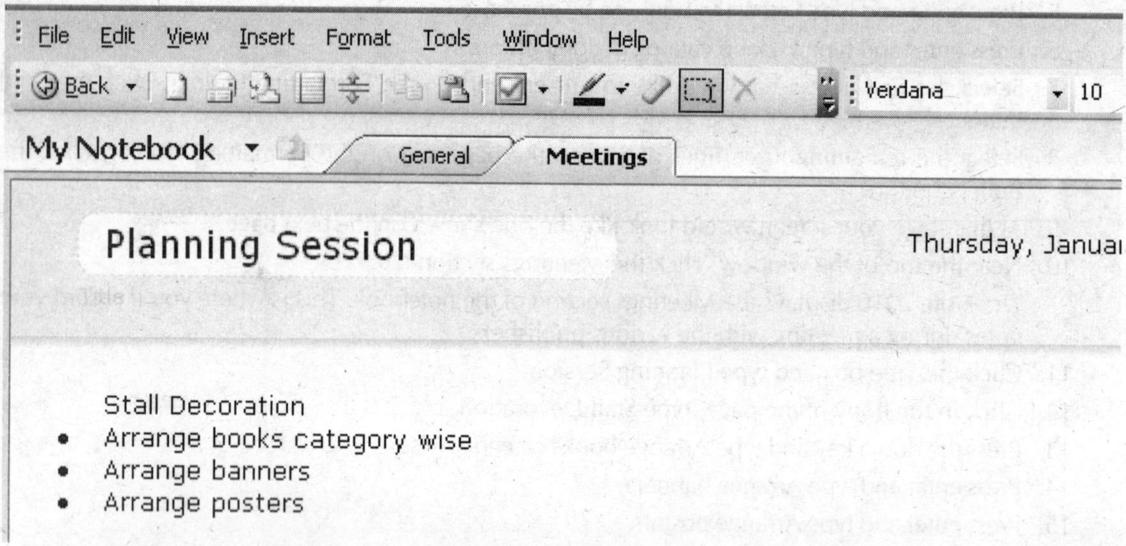

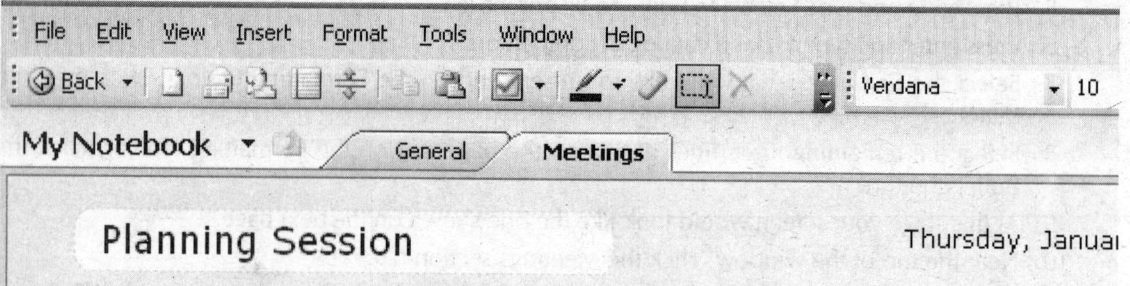

OneNote 2010 opens, showing the Meetings section because that section was active when you closed OneNote.

2. Click the General section tab and click the blank area below the text on the page.
3. On the Insert menu, click Picture.

   The Insert Picture dialog box appears.
4. Click at the picture you want to insert. OneNote inserts the image into your notes, as shown here.

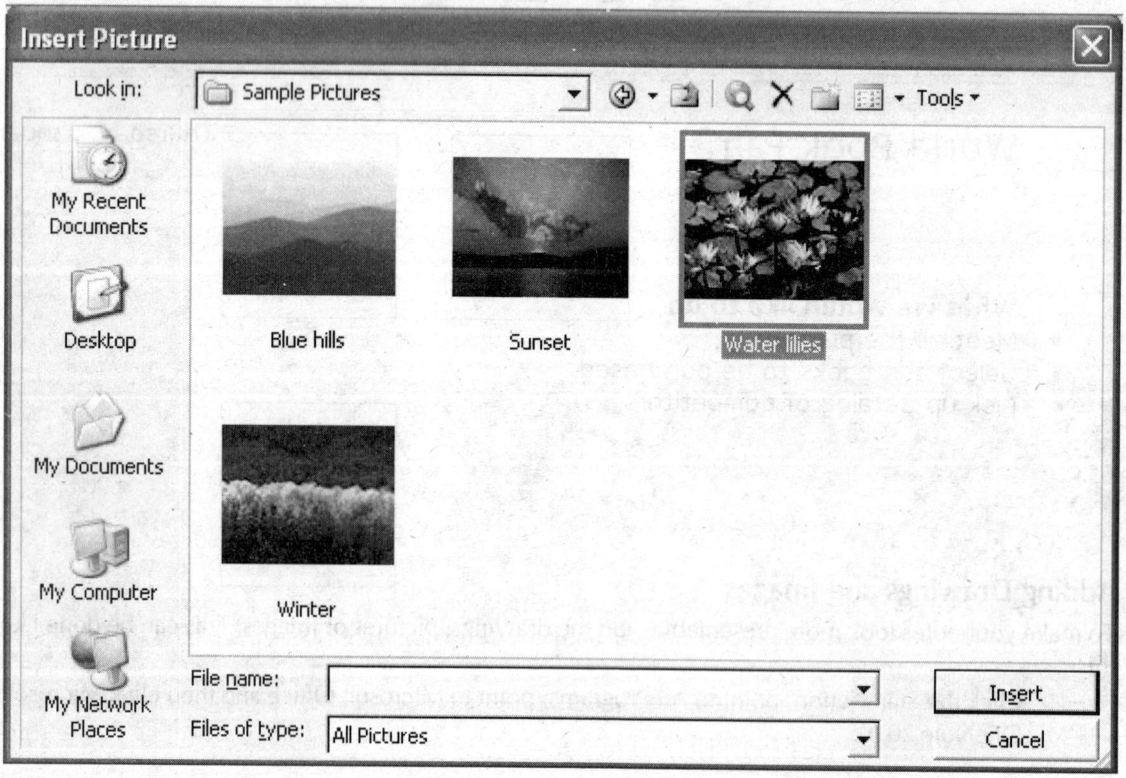

5. On the Standard toolbar, click the Pen button and move your mouse pointer over the note page. Your mouse pointer becomes a small colored dot.
6. In any blank area of the note page, drag the shape of a square with mouse pointer. Don't worry about making your lines straight – this is a rough sketch!
7. Click the down arrow to the right of the Pen button and click another color.
8. Position the mouse pointer over one edge of the square you just drew and drag the pointer to divide the square into two sections. This section can be any size or shape you 'd like – this will represent the layout for your exhibition booth.
9. On the Standard toolbar, click the Selection Tool button.
10. Click in the larger portion of your exhibition booth drawing and type main visitor area.
11. Click the smaller portion of the booth and type demo area.
12. See how we have drawn the various portions of the stall.

Organizing Notes into Sections and Folders

As you work with OneNote over time, you might collect notes about a wide variety of topics and your virtual notebook could get disorganized. To help you keep track of them, you can divide your notebook into sections and folders. Sections can contain one or more pages or groups of pages. Folders can contain pages, sections or other folders.

Be sure to start OneNote before beginning this exercise.

1. On the Insert menu, click New Section.

OneNote creates a new section as a tab at the top of the note page. Ready for you to name.

2. Type World Book Fair as the section name and press enter.
3. Right-click the new section tab, point to Section Color on the shortcut menu and click Magenta.
4. In the Title box, type Publisher Here.
5. On the Insert menu, click the New Folder.

   OneNote creates a new folder as a tab at the top of the note page, ready for you to name.
6. Type Books Displayed as the folder name and press enter.
7. Right-click the World Book Fair section tab and click Move on the shortcut menu.

   The Move Section to dialog box appears, as shown on the next page.
8. In the Move section to list, select the Meetings folder and click Move.
9. The World Book Fair section is no longer visible because it is contained within the Meetings folder.
10. Click the Meetings tab. The Meetings folder opens, displaying the World Book Fair tab.
11. Click the down arrow to the right of the folder name.

    The drop-down list shows all the sections and folders in your notebook.
12. In the list, click Meetings.
13. The Meetings section is displayed and the Event Planning folder again appears as a tab at the top of the page.

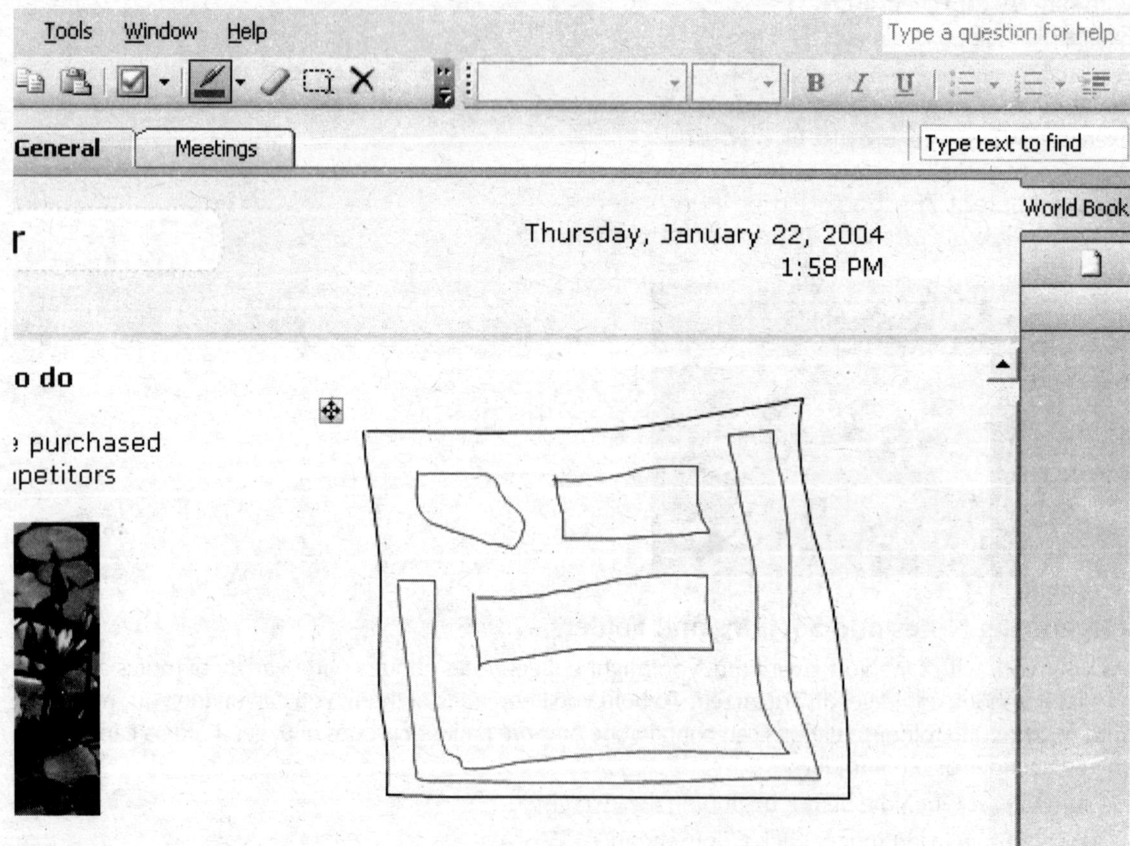

CHAPTER 6

14. Close One Note.

Remember

With OneNote you can do the following:

- You can easily take notes made up of typed text, handwritten text, images, Web clippings, drawings and sound recordings.
- You take notes on pages and can group pages with related content.
- You can organize pages into sections and sections into folders.
- You can rearrange your notebook by moving notes and pages.
- OneNote automatically saves your notebook at regular intervals and each time you close the program.

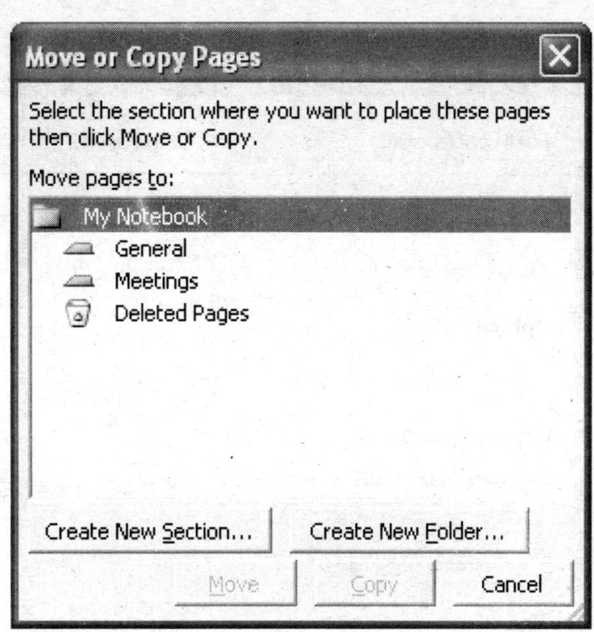

Microsoft Office InfoPath 2010

Microsoft InfoPath, a new application in the Microsoft Office System 2010, helps you gather and use information through dynamic forms. The information collected through InfoPath forms can be shared with others, published to the Web, and easily reused, because the data is stored in industry standard Extensible Markup Language.

As usual, I will take up a live example of completing a time card from and then familiarize yourself with the travel itinerary form. Be sure to start your computer, but don't start InfoPath before beginning this exercise.

1. Click Start, point to All Programs, point to Microsoft Office and then click Microsoft Office InfoPath 2010.

   InfoPath opens with the fill Out a Form task pane Displayed.
2. In the task pane, in the Fill out a form area, click More Forms.

   The Forms dialog box appears.
3. Click the Sample Forms tab.

   The collection of sample form is displayed on the tab.
4. Scroll down, click the Time Card (Simple) form and then click OK.

   The task pane closes and the Time Card form opens.
5. At the right end of the Week of button. A calendar appears, showing the current date.
6. Click the date required by you or leave it for TODAY.
7. In the Name box, type Bharat Nangia.
8. In the E-mail Address box, type bbn@hotmail.com and then press the tab key.
9. In the Work Telephone Number box, type 91-11-31001976 and press tab twice.
10. Enter the following regular hours into the Attendance Reporting table: 0 on Sunday, 12 for all other days except for saturday where you type 6.
11. On the File menu, click Close.
12. When prompted to save the form, click Yes.

CHAPTER 6

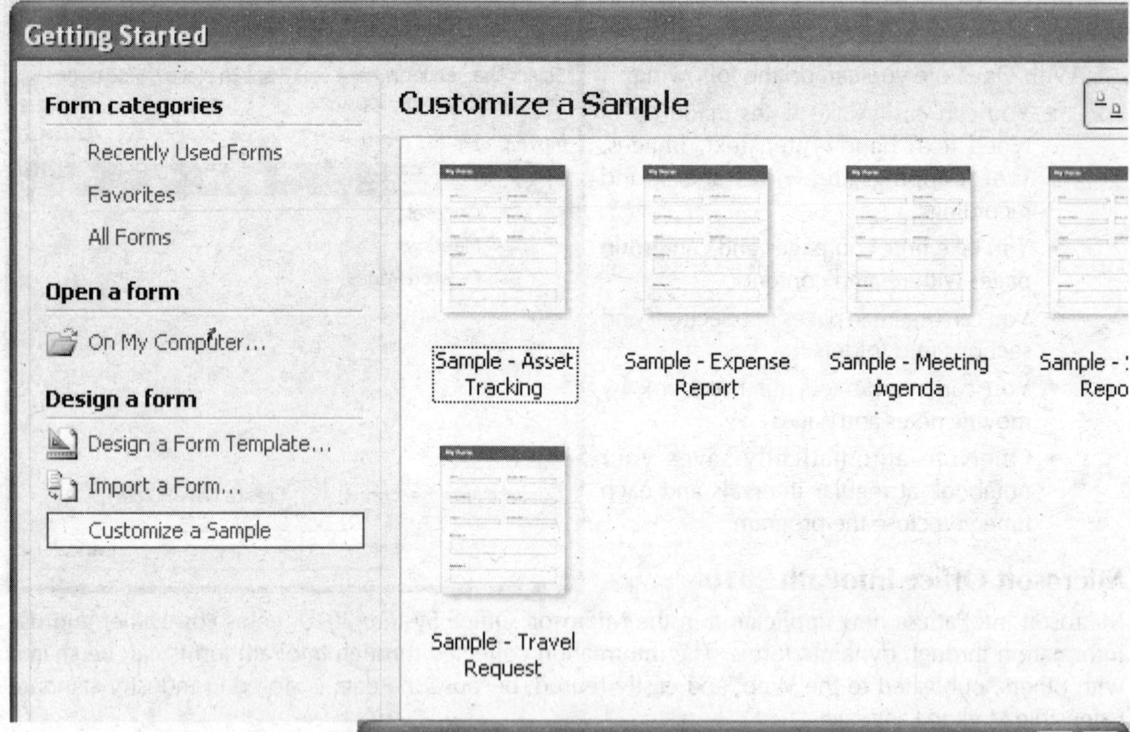

13. The Save As dialog box appears.
14. Type the name which you want to give and click Save. InfoPath saves your form data and closes the form.
15. In the Fill Out a Form task pane, click again at More Forms.
16. On the Sample Forms tab, click at Travel itinerary and then click OK.

    A travel itinerary form opens.
17. In the Purpose box, type Meeting with Client.
18. In the Traveler box, type Bharat Nangia.
19. In the Start date box, type the date and in the End date box, type the date following the start date you are entered.

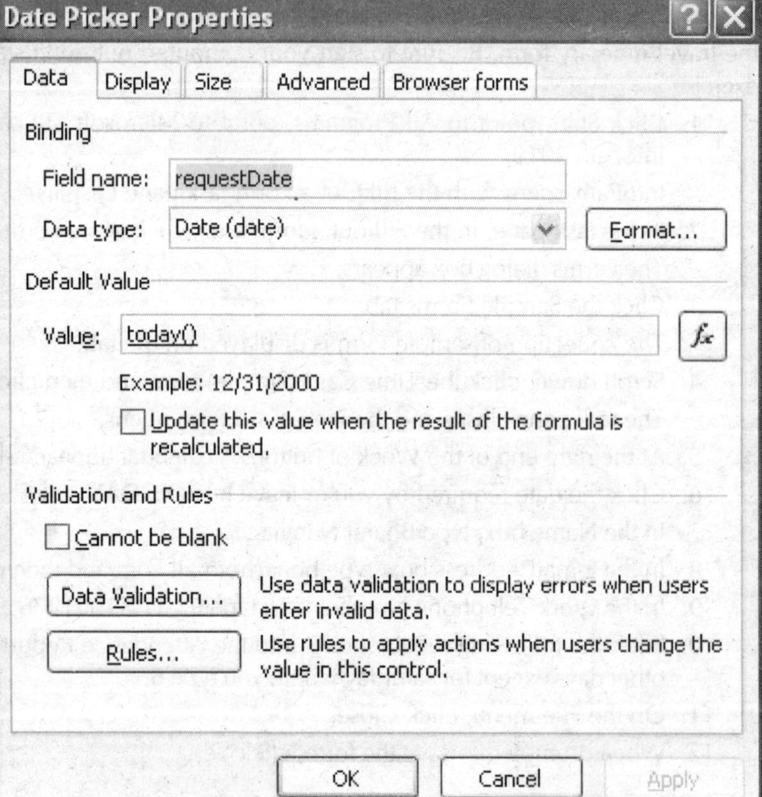

(Design) Template1 - Microsoft Office InfoPath

File Edit View Insert Format Tools Table Help

Preview Design Tasks

Verdana 10

Draw Table No border 1 pt Insert

TRAVEL REQUEST

Business Purpose:

Traveler Information

Name: E-mail

Trips

TRIP

From: To:

Departure Date: Departure Time: Anytime

Round trip

Return Date: Return Time: Anytime

Section

Repeating Section

Preferences

Trip Class: Select... Car Cl Sele

Seat Location:

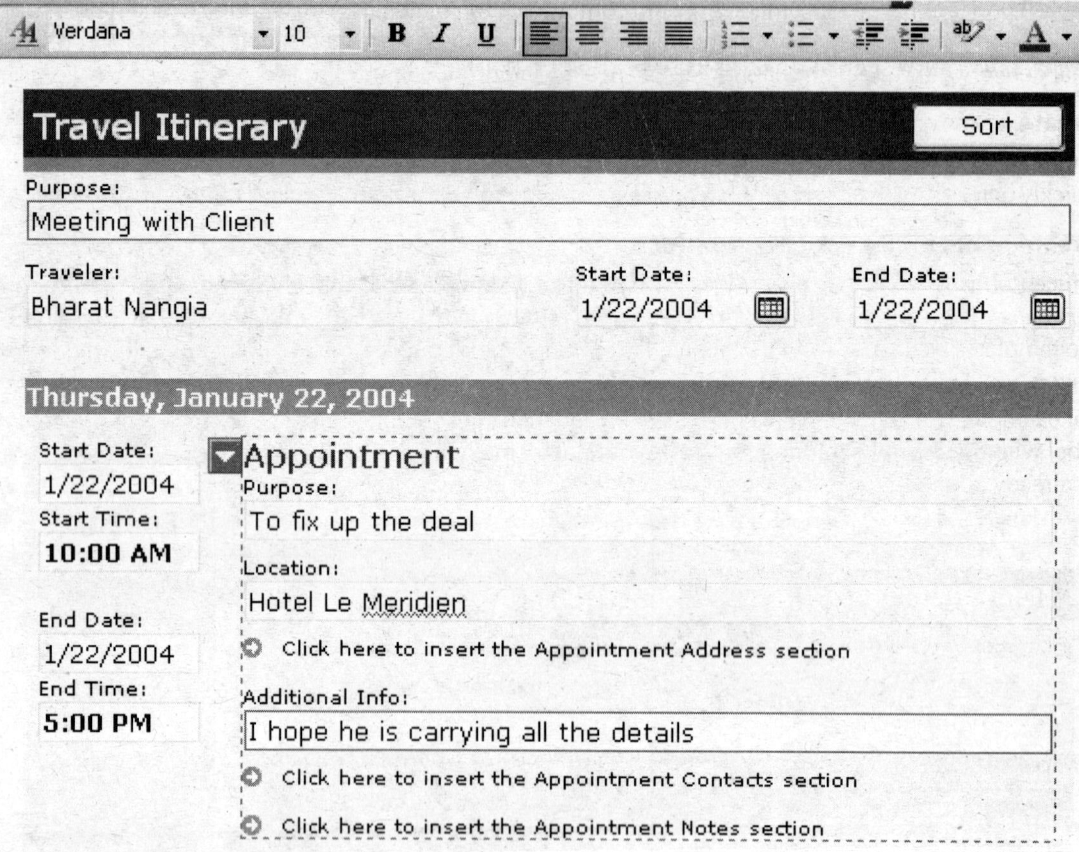

20. In the Appointment section, in the Start Date box, type the same start date you entered earlier and in the Start Time box, type 5:00pm.
21. In the Purpose box, type of To fix up the deal and in the Location box, type Hotel Le Meridien.
22. Click the right arrow below the Location box to insert the Appointment Address section.

    Address fields are inserted into the form.
23. Point to the blue bar at the top of the Appointment section, which contains the start date of the appointment.

    A dotted-line box appears around the section and a down arrow appears to the left of the bar.
24. Click the down arrow and in the drop-down list, click Insert Appointment Entry below.

    A second appointment section is inserted into the form.
25. In the first Appointment section, point to any of the address fields.

    A dotted-line box appears around the section and a down arrow appears to the left of the first address field (Address Line 1).
26. Click the down arrow and in the drop-down list, click Remove Appointment Address. The address fields are removed from the form.
27. On the File menu, click Close.

Microsoft Office Publisher 2010

Microsoft Office Publisher 2010 is the business publishing program that helps you create, design, and publish professional-looking marketing and communication materials. You can create materials for print, e-mail, and the Web with an intuitive, task-based environment that guides you from initial concept to final delivery in-house without professional design and production expertise.

Create branded, professional-looking publications

Office Publisher 2010 is designed to help businesses create professional-looking publications in-house quickly and easily. Even a beginner can create a publication for print, e-mail, or the Web.

Create publications easier and faster

Office Publisher 2010 has been redesigned to make it even easier to quickly start or open publications. You can create your own publications with the professionally designed Publisher templates, customize the templates as needed, and then change from one type of publication to another by clicking a single button.

For example, you can start with a business card and then click Change Template to create a return mailing label with the Business Information set — your name, mailing address, business logo, and design colors — already applied.

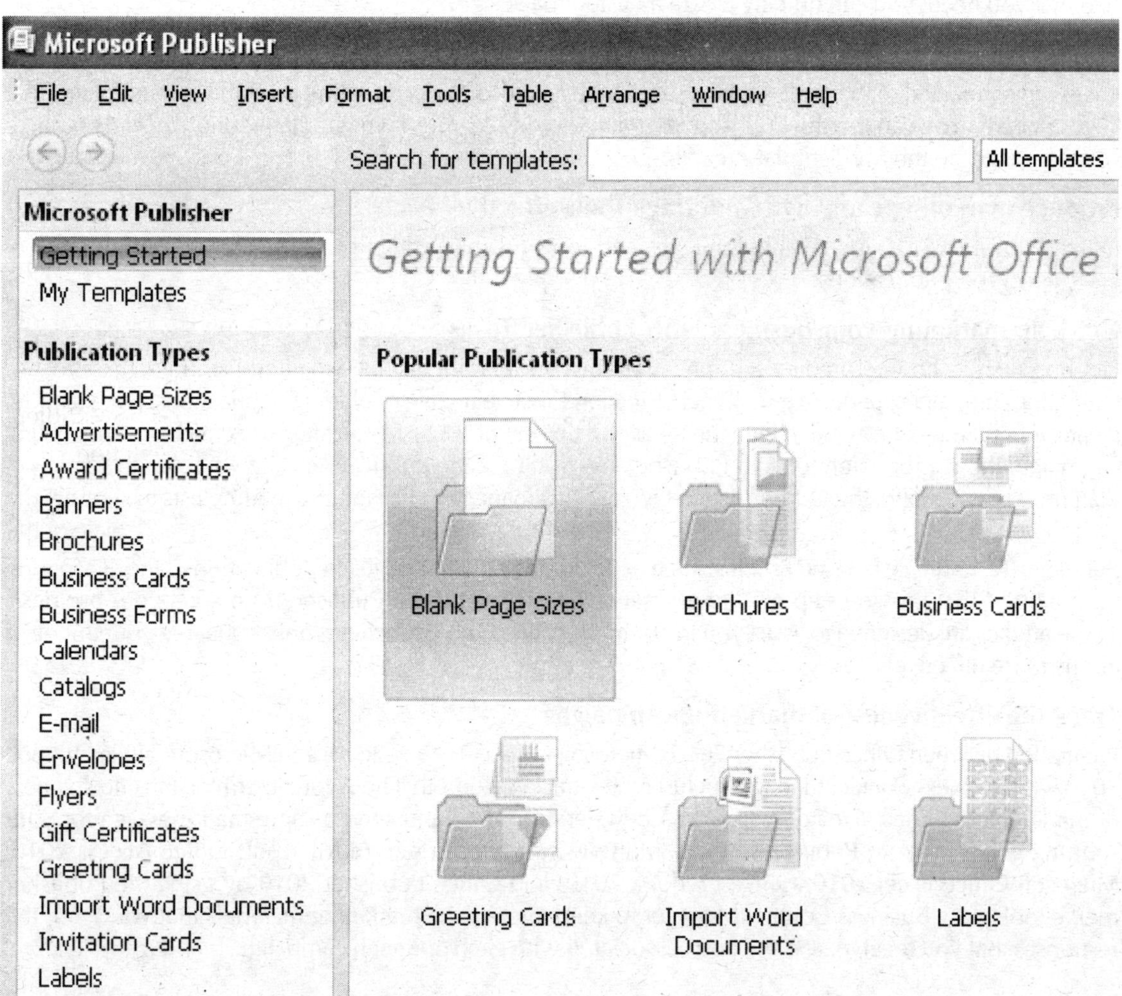

Open recent publications with a single click

If you worked on a publication recently, you can open it again by clicking its icon in the Recent Publications list.

Click to create a new publication

The most popular publication types, such as Newsletters, have large icons in the center of the workspace when you start Publisher. Just double-click the icon, and you can begin customizing your new publication.

Easily locate the page size that you need

Select your page size from the wide variety of page sizes (the paper dimensions are listed) in the Page Setup dialog box.

In Office Publisher 2010, you can see page, envelope, and label sizes. All of the sizes are listed with their common printing names, such as A4 and Size 10, and their dimensions.

If you can't find what you want, you can create the page size that you need. Unusual page sizes for admission tickets, big banners, business cards, or flyers are no problem.

You can also preview an example of how your publication type and template design will fit on the paper — so you can quickly see how your publication will look before it is printed. If you don't see the page size that you need, you can quickly create a custom page size.

Choose from more Publisher templates and manage your own templates

If you are connected to the Internet, you can search Microsoft Office Online for Publisher templates that fit your needs. You can use the Publisher templates to design your own templates, and you can organize your templates in the My Templates catalog.

Produce marketing campaigns and track their effectiveness

Office Publisher 2010 includes helpful tips and tools for marketing your business with print, mail, e-mail, and Web publications.

Get help marketing your business with Publisher Tasks

Get tips such as how to prepare a publication for your mailing list or e-mailing list, track the effect of marketing campaigns, perform e-mail marketing, and write effective marketing publications. For example, create your marketing campaign with the ideas and tips in Publisher Tasks. After you create your marketing campaign, the compression tools in Publisher can optimize the publications that you plan to send as e-mail messages. Finally, the Catalog Merge Wizard can manage your multiple mailing lists to simplify the e-mail process.

Publisher Tasks are task-based articles, such as "Adding text and images to publications" and "Preparing for mailing," that provide step-by-step assistance and help you use Publisher to market your business. These articles are designed to assist you in communicating with your clients and managing your outreach efforts more effectively.

Track the effectiveness of marketing campaigns

Integration between Office Publisher 2010, Microsoft Office Outlook 2010, and Microsoft Office Outlook 2010 with Business Contact Manager includes new tracking tools that help you determine the effectiveness of marketing mailings. Create flyers and a newsletter to mail and send as an e-mail message for your sporting goods store in Publisher. Merge multiple customer lists from Microsoft Office Access 2010, Microsoft Office Excel 2010, Office Outlook 2010, and Office Publisher 2010 by using the Publisher merge tools. Use Business Contact Manager to keep track of the marketing materials that you send, the responses that you receive, and the costs associated with each outreach campaign.

Customize and reuse design elements and information

Office Publisher 2010 makes it really easy to create content one time and then reuse it in many different publications. Start with one of the professionally designed templates, and then add your business's colors, logo, personnel names, and contact information.

You can also customize a template's font scheme and other options before you apply the template to your publication.

Store and organize reusable content in the Content Library

Create and store content such as logos, lists of services, success stories, maps to a business location, testimonials, and pictures that can be inserted into publications later and reused for faster, professional-looking publications.

Reuse business information and branding

Create Business Information sets that can be easily inserted into publications or transferred from one publication to another. When you finish creating a business card and then create a mailing label, the business information is automatically added in the appropriate places.

Get reminders before reusable content is deleted

As you convert one type of publication to another, Publisher moves any content from the previous publication type that doesn't easily fit into the new publication type to the Extra Content task pane. When you try to close a publication with content in the Extra Content task pane, Publisher notifies you, so that you won't lose your work.

Microsoft Office Groove 2010

Microsoft Office Groove 2010 is Internet software for making direct connections with the people who are important to you. With Office Groove 2010, you can bring together team members from both inside and outside your company, with no IT assistance required and no need to waste time thinking about firewalls, servers, security, or network access. Additionally, you can enjoy the efficiency of always knowing each other's virtual location, or online presence, thus allowing for organic and quick conversation and collaboration. Microsoft Office Groove 2010 can be used for the followings:

Contact Search

Office Groove 2010 provides a simplified process for searching for contacts. The search facility now allows you to simply type in the name or email address you are looking for and click Find. Groove will search all available directories to find a match for your entry. You can also optionally enable searching in the Public Groove Directory.

Groove/Messenger integration

If you have Integrate Messenger Contacts enabled in your preferences (the default setting), you can view Messenger online status for all Groove contacts who also run Messenger, and start Messenger activities with these contacts, such as text-chatting or voice-over-IP (VOIP). Additionally, the first time you start up Groove after installation or upgrade, you are prompted to add all Messenger contacts who also have Groove to your contact list.

Groove SharePoint Files Tool

The Groove SharePoint Files Tool is an enhanced version of the Groove Files Tool, with features intended for synchronizing file content between Groove and SharePoint document libraries.

Groove InfoPath Forms Tool

The Groove InfoPath Forms Tool enables application developers to create and lay out most design objects (forms and the fields that display on forms) in Microsoft InfoPath 2010, and then import the solution into the Groove InfoPath Forms Tool designer. Alternatively, developers can also use the Groove Forms Tool to create custom applications.

Groove Discussion Tool

The Groove Discussion Tool is now a custom Forms tool. It looks and behaves the same as the Discussion tool from earlier versions of Groove, with the addition of a Category field and views for sorting Discussion threads either by category or by date.

Groove Meetings Tool

In the Groove Meetings Tool, the "Participants" tab is renamed to the "Attendees" tab. The tool now supports assigning permissions to Groove user roles.

Features and tools no longer available in this release

The list below describes the features and tools no longer available in this release. The lengthy number of items mostly reflects adjustments to the feature set as the Groove application becomes part of Microsoft's Office offerings. Additionally, this release focuses on ensuring the highest quality of the key features that receive the most use.

- The following tools and toolsets are no longer available for adding to new or existing workspaces: Contact Manager, Discussion, Document Review, Outliner, Task Manager, Text, Tic-Tac-Toe, Web Links, Welcome Page, Advanced Project Toolset, and Mobile Workspace for SharePoint.
- Instances of these tools in existing workspaces will continue to function.
- A new version of the Groove Discussion Tool (as described above) is now available.
- The Groove SharePoint Files Tool replaces Mobile Workspace for SharePoint. Note that you can no longer synchronize data between an existing mobile workspace and its associated SharePoint site.
- Chat-only workspaces. Chat is now available only as part of standard or file sharing workspaces.
- Co-editing of Word documents.
- Presenting of PowerPoint slide shows.
- File viewers in the Groove Files Tool.
- Outlook Calendar integration with the Groove Calendar and Groove Meetings tools.
- Launching Netmeeting.
- Sending an Outlook email thread to a Groove workspace.
- Sending Lotus Notes documents to a Groove workspace.
- XMPP Proxy Server and Client features (i.e., interacting with Jabber users).
- Options in account preferences for presence settings for idle behavior.
- Docking the Groove Launchbar.
- The "Auto-create record" feature in the Groove Forms tool.
- Forms tools created in Groove versions prior to Groove 2.5 will not be accessible.
- Forms tools created in Groove 2.5 will be accessible only for the purpose of exporting data. Exported data can then be imported into a new Forms tool.
- Groove no longer supports installing new tools via component injection. That is, you can no longer install new tools in your Groove account by opening a .grv or .gcd file. Additionally, tools previously installed via component injection will no longer function in existing or new workspaces.
- Groove accounts can no longer be uploaded to groove.net for backup or for setting up use on multiple computers. Multiple computers usage now requires saving your account file manually.

CHAPTER 7

Keyboard Shortcuts of Microsoft Office 2010

Introduction

Shortcut keys are key combinations that start commands. For example, you can press CTRL + O to open a file and CTRL + S to save a file, which is the same result as choosing Open and Save from the File menu. .

Microsoft Office Basics

Switch to the next window.	ALT+TAB
Switch to the previous window.	ALT+SHIFT+TAB
Close the active window.	CTRL+W or CTRL+F4
Restore the size of the active window after you maximize it.	ALT+F5
Move to a task pane from another pane in the program window (clockwise direction). You may need to press F6 more than once.	F6
Move to a task pane from another pane in the program window (counterclockwise direction).	SHIFT+F6
When more than one window is open, switch to the next window.	CTRL+F6
Switch to the previous window.	CTRL+SHIFT+F6
Maximize or restore a selected window.	CTRL+F10
Copy a picture of the screen to the Clipboard.	PRINT SCREEN
Copy a picture of the selected window to the Clipboard.	ALT+PRINT SCREEN
Move from an open dialog box back to the document, for dialog boxes such as Find and Replace that support this behavior.	ALT+F6
Move to the next option or option group.	TAB
Move to the previous option or option group.	SHIFT+TAB
Switch to the next tab in a dialog box.	CTRL+TAB
Switch to the previous tab in a dialog box.	CTRL+SHIFT+TAB
Move between options in an open drop-down list, or between options in a group of options.	Arrow keys
Perform the action assigned to the selected button; select or clear the selected check box.	SPACEBAR
Select an option; select or clear a check box.	ALT+ the letter underlined in an option
Open a selected drop-down list.	ALT+DOWN ARROW
Select an option from a drop-down list.	First letter of an option in a drop-down list
Close a selected drop-down list; cancel a command and close a dialog box.	ESC
Run the selected command.	ENTER
Move to the beginning of the entry.	HOME
Move to the end of the entry.	END
Move one character to the left or right.	LEFT ARROW or RIGHT ARROW
Move one word to the left.	CTRL+LEFT ARROW
Move one word to the right.	CTRL+RIGHT ARROW
Select or unselect one character to the left.	SHIFT+LEFT ARROW
Select or unselect one character to the right.	SHIFT+RIGHT ARROW
Select or unselect one word to the left.	CTRL+SHIFT+LEFT ARROW
Select or unselect one word to the right.	CTRL+SHIFT+RIGHT ARROW
Select from the insertion point to the beginning of the entry.	SHIFT+HOME
Select from the insertion point to the end of the entry.	SHIFT+END

Use the Open and Save As dialog boxes

Display the Open dialog box.	CTRL+F12 or CTRL+O
Display the Save As dialog box.	F12
Go to the previous folder.	ALT+1
Up One Level button: Open the folder one level above the open folder.	ALT+2
Delete button: Delete the selected folder or file.	DELETE
Create New Folder button: Create a new folder.	ALT+4

Views button: Switch among available folder views.	ALT+5
Display a shortcut menu for a selected item such as a folder or file.	SHIFT+F10
Move between options or areas in the dialog box.	TAB
Open the Look in list.	F4 or ALT+I
Update the file list.	F5

Undo and redo actions

Cancel an action.	ESC
Undo an action.	CTRL+Z
Redo or repeat an action.	CTRL+Y

Access and use task panes and galleries

Move to a task pane from another pane in the program window. (You may need to press F6 more than once.)	F6
When a menu is active, move to a task pane. (You may need to press CTRL+TAB more than once.)	CTRL+TAB
When a task pane is active, select the next or previous option in the task pane.	TÁB or SHIFT+TAB
Display the full set of commands on the task pane menu.	CTRL+SPACEBAR
Perform the action assigned to the selected button.	SPACEBAR or ENTER
Open a drop-down menu for the selected gallery item.	SHIFT+F10
Select the first or last item in a gallery.	HOME or END
Scroll up or down in the selected gallery list.	PAGE UP or PAGE DOWN
Close a task pane	
Press F6 to move to the task pane, if necessary.	Press CTRL+SPACEBAR.
Use the arrow keys to select Close, and then press ENTER.	

Access and use smart tags

Display the shortcut menu for the selected item.	SHIFT+F10
Display the menu or message for a smart tag or for the AutoCorrect Options button or the Paste options button . If more than one smart tag is present, switch to the next smart tag and display its menu or message.	ALT+SHIFT+F10
Select the next item on a smart tag menu.	DOWN ARROW
Select the previous item on a smart tag menu.	UP ARROW
Perform the action for the selected item on a smart tag menu.	ENTER
Close the smart tag menu or message.	ESC

Change the keyboard focus without using the mouse

Another way to use the keyboard to work with Ribbon programs is to move the focus among the tabs and commands until you find the feature that you want to use. The following table lists some ways to move the keyboard focus without using the mouse.

Select the active tab of the Ribbon and activate the access keys.	ALT or F10. Press either of these keys again to move back to the document and cancel the access keys.
Move to another tab of the Ribbon.	F10 to select the active tab, and then LEFT ARROW or RIGHT ARROW
Hide or show the Ribbon.	CTRL+F1

Display the shortcut menu for the selected command. SHIFT+F10 Move the focus to select each of the following areas of the window:

Move the focus to each command on the Ribbon, forward or backward, respectively.	TAB or SHIFT+TAB
Move down, up, left, or right, respectively, among the items on the Ribbon.	DOWN ARROW, UP ARROW, LEFT ARROW, or RIGHT ARROW
Activate the selected command or control on the Ribbon.	SPACEBAR or ENTER
Open the selected menu or gallery on the Ribbon.	SPACEBAR or ENTER
Activate a command or control on the Ribbon so you can modify a value.	ENTER
Finish modifying a value in a control on the Ribbon, and move focus back to the document.	ENTER
Get help on the selected command or control on the Ribbon. (If no Help topic is associated with the selected command, a general Help topic about the program is shown instead.)	F1

Quick reference for Microsoft Office Word

Create a nonbreaking space.	CTRL+SHIFT+SPACEBAR
Create a nonbreaking hyphen.	CTRL+HYPHEN
Make letters bold.	CTRL+B
Make letters italic.	CTRL+I
Make letters underline.	CTRL+U
Decrease font size one value.	CTRL+SHIFT+<
Increase font size one value.	CTRL+SHIFT+>
Decrease font size 1 point.	CTRL+[
Increase font size 1 point.	CTRL+]
Remove paragraph or character formatting.	CTRL+SPACEBAR
Copy the selected text or object.	CTRL+C
Cut the selected text or object.	CTRL+X
Paste text or an object.	CTRL+V
Paste special	CTRL+ALT+V
Paste formatting only	CTRL+SHIFT+V
Undo the last action.	CTRL+Z
Redo the last action.	CTRL+Y
Open the Word Count dialog box.	CTRL+SHIFT+G

Working with documents and Web pages

Create, view, and save documents

Create a new document of the same type as the current or most recent document.	CTRL+N
Open a document.	CTRL+O
Close a document.	CTRL+W
Split the document window.	ALT+CTRL+S
Remove the document window split.	ALT+SHIFT+C
Save a document.	CTRL+S

Find, replace, and browse through text

Find text, formatting, and special items.	CTRL+F
Repeat find (after closing Find and Replace window).	ALT+CTRL+Y
Replace text, specific formatting, and special items.	CTRL+H

Go to a page, bookmark, footnote, table, comment, graphic, or other location.	CTRL+G
Switch between the last four places that you have edited.	ALT+CTRL+Z
Open a list of browse options. Press the arrow keys to select an option, and then press ENTER to browse through a document by using the selected option.	ALT+CTRL+HOME
Move to the previous edit location.	CTRL+PAGE UP
Move to the next edit location.	CTRL+PAGE DOWN

Switch to another view

Switch to Print Layout view.	ALT+CTRL+P
Switch to Outline view.	ALT+CTRL+O
Switch to Draft view.	ALT+CTRL+N

Outline view

Promote a paragraph.	ALT+SHIFT+LEFT ARROW
Demote a paragraph.	ALT+SHIFT+RIGHT ARROW
Demote to body text.	CTRL+SHIFT+N
Move selected paragraphs up.	ALT+SHIFT+UP ARROW
Move selected paragraphs down.	ALT+SHIFT+DOWN ARROW
Expand text under a heading.	ALT+SHIFT+PLUS SIGN
Collapse text under a heading.	ALT+SHIFT+MINUS SIGN
Expand or collapse all text or headings.	ALT+SHIFT+A
Hide or display character formatting.	The slash (/) key on the numeric keypad
Show the first line of body text or all body text.	ALT+SHIFT+L
Show all headings with the Heading 1 style.	ALT+SHIFT+1
Show all headings up to Heading n.	ALT+SHIFT+n
Insert a tab character.	CTRL+TAB

Print and preview documents

Print a document.	CTRL+P
Switch in or out of print preview.	ALT+CTRL+I
Move around the preview page when zoomed in.	Arrow keys
Move by one preview page when zoomed out.	PAGE UP or PAGE DOWN
Move to the first preview page when zoomed out.	CTRL+HOME
Move to the last preview page when zoomed out.	CTRL+END

Review documents

Insert a comment.	ALT+CTRL+M
Turn change tracking on or off.	CTRL+SHIFT+E
Close the Reviewing Pane if it is open.	ALT+SHIFT+C

Full Screen Reading view

Some screen readers may not be compatible with Full Screen Reading view.

Go to beginning of document.	HOME
Go to end of document.	END
Go to page n.	n, ENTER
Exit reading layout view.	ESC

References, footnotes, and endnotes

Mark a table of contents entry.	ALT+SHIFT+O
Mark a table of authorities entry (citation).	ALT+SHIFT+I

Mark an index entry.	ALT+SHIFT+X
Insert a footnote.	ALT+CTRL+F
Insert an endnote.	ALT+CTRL+D

Work with Web pages

Insert a hyperlink.	CTRL+K
Go back one page.	ALT+LEFT ARROW
Go forward one page.	ALT+RIGHT ARROW
Refresh.	F9

Edit and move text and graphics

Delete one character to the left.	BACKSPACE
Delete one word to the left.	CTRL+BACKSPACE
Delete one character to the right.	DELETE
Delete one word to the right.	CTRL+DELETE
Cut selected text to the Office Clipboard.	CTRL+X
Undo the last action.	CTRL+Z
Cut to the Spike.	CTRL+F3

Copy and move text and graphics

Open the Office Clipboard	Press ALT+H to move to the Home tab, and then press F,O.
Copy selected text or graphics to the Office Clipboard.	CTRL+C
Cut selected text or graphics to the Office Clipboard.	CTRL+X
Paste the most recent addition to the Office Clipboard.	CTRL+V
Move text or graphics once.	F2 (then move the cursor and press ENTER)
Copy text or graphics once.	SHIFT+F2 (then move the cursor and press ENTER)
When text or an object is selected, open the Create New Building Block dialog box.	ALT+F3
When the building block — for example, a SmartArt graphic — is selected, display the shortcut menu that is associated with it.	SHIFT+F10
Cut to the Spike.	CTRL+F3
Paste the Spike contents.	CTRL+SHIFT+F3
Copy the header or footer used in the previous section of the document.	ALT+SHIFT+R

Insert special characters

A field	CTRL+F9
A line break	SHIFT+ENTER
A page break	CTRL+ENTER
A column break	CTRL+SHIFT+ENTER
An em dash	ALT+CTRL+MINUS SIGN
An en dash	CTRL+MINUS SIGN
An optional hyphen	CTRL+HYPHEN
A nonbreaking hyphen	CTRL+SHIFT+HYPHEN
A nonbreaking space	CTRL+SHIFT+SPACEBAR
The copyright symbol	ALT+CTRL+C
The registered trademark symbol	ALT+CTRL+R
The trademark symbol	ALT+CTRL+T
An ellipsis	ALT+CTRL+PERIOD
A single opening quotation mark	CTRL+'(single quotation mark), '(single quotation mark)
A single closing quotation mark	CTRL+' (single quotation mark), ' (single quotation mark)

Double opening quotation marks	CTRL+' (single quotation mark), SHIFT+' (single quotation mark)
Double closing quotation marks	CTRL+' (single quotation mark), SHIFT+' (single quotation mark)
An AutoText entry	ENTER (after you type the first few characters of the AutoText entry name and when the ScreenTip appears)

Insert characters by using character codes

Insert the Unicode character for the specified Unicode (hexadecimal) character code. For example, to insert the euro currency symbol ( ), type 20AC, and then hold down ALT and press X.	The character code, ALT+X
Find out the Unicode character code for the selected character	ALT+X
Insert the ANSI character for the specified ANSI (decimal) character code. For example, to insert the euro currency symbol, hold down ALT and press 0128 on the numeric keypad.	ALT+the character code (on the numeric keypad)

Select text and graphics

Select text by holding down SHIFT and using the arrow keys to move the cursor.

Extend a selection

Turn extend mode on.	F8
Select the nearest character.	F8, and then press LEFT ARROW or RIGHT ARROW
Increase the size of a selection.	F8 (press once to select a word, twice to select a sentence, and so on)
Reduce the size of a selection.	SHIFT+F8
Turn extend mode off.	ESC
Extend a selection one character to the right.	SHIFT+RIGHT ARROW
Extend a selection one character to the left.	SHIFT+LEFT ARROW
Extend a selection to the end of a word.	CTRL+SHIFT+RIGHT ARROW
Extend a selection to the beginning of a word.	CTRL+SHIFT+LEFT ARROW
Extend a selection to the end of a line.	SHIFT+END
Extend a selection to the beginning of a line.	SHIFT+HOME
Extend a selection one line down.	SHIFT+DOWN ARROW
Extend a selection one line up.	SHIFT+UP ARROW
Extend a selection to the end of a paragraph.	CTRL+SHIFT+DOWN ARROW
Extend a selection to the beginning of a paragraph.	CTRL+SHIFT+UP ARROW
Extend a selection one screen down.	SHIFT+PAGE DOWN
Extend a selection one screen up.	SHIFT+PAGE UP
Extend a selection to the beginning of a document.	CTRL+SHIFT+HOME
Extend a selection to the end of a document.	CTRL+SHIFT+END
Extend a selection to the end of a window.	ALT+CTRL+SHIFT+PAGE DOWN
Extend a selection to include the entire document.	CTRL+A
Select a vertical block of text.	CTRL+SHIFT+F8, and then use the arrow keys; press ESC to cancel selection mode
Extend a selection to a specific location in a document.	F8+arrow keys; press ESC to cancel selection mode

Select text and graphics in a table

Select the next cell's contents.	TAB
Select the preceding cell's contents.	SHIFT+TAB
Select an entire table.	ALT+5 on the numeric keypad (with NUM LOCK off)

Move through your document

One character to the left	LEFT ARROW
One character to the right	RIGHT ARROW
One word to the left	CTRL + LEFT ARROW
One word to the right	CTRL + RIGHT ARROW
One paragraph up	CTRL + UP ARROW
One paragraph down	CTRL + DOWN ARROW
One cell to the left (in a table)	SHIFT + TAB
One cell to the right (in a table)	TAB
Up one line	UP ARROW
Down one line	DOWN ARROW
To the end of a line	END
To the beginning of a line	HOME
To the top of the window	ALT + CTRL + PAGE UP
To the end of the window	ALT + CTRL + PAGE DOWN
Up one screen (scrolling)	PAGE UP
Down one screen (scrolling)	PAGE DOWN
To the top of the next page	CTRL + PAGE DOWN
To the top of the previous page	CTRL + PAGE UP
To the end of a document	CTRL + END
To the beginning of a document	CTRL + HOME
To a previous revision	SHIFT + F5
After opening a document, to the location you were working in when the document was last closed	SHIFT + F5

Move around in a table

To the next cell in a row	TAB
To the previous cell in a row	SHIFT + TAB
To the first cell in a row	ALT + HOME
To the last cell in a row	ALT + END
To the first cell in a column	ALT + PAGE UP
To the last cell in a column	ALT + PAGE DOWN
To the previous row	UP ARROW
To the next row	DOWN ARROW
One row up	ALT + SHIFT + UP ARROW
One row down	ALT + SHIFT + DOWN ARROW

Insert paragraphs and tab characters in a table

New paragraphs in a cell	ENTER
Tab characters in a cell	CTRL + TAB

Character and paragraph formatting

Copy formatting

Copy formatting from text.	CTRL + SHIFT + C
Apply copied formatting to text.	CTRL + SHIFT + V

Change or resize the font

The following keyboard shortcuts do not work in Full Screen Reading mode.

Open the Font dialog box to change the font.	CTRL + SHIFT + F
Increase the font size.	CTRL + SHIFT + >
Decrease the font size.	CTRL + SHIFT + <
Increase the font size by 1 point.	CTRL +]

Decrease the font size by 1 point.	CTRL+[
Apply character formats	
Open the Font dialog box to change the formatting of characters.	CTRL+D
Change the case of letters.	SHIFT+F3
Format all letters as capitals.	CTRL+SHIFT+A
Apply bold formatting.	CTRL+B
Apply an underline.	CTRL+U
Underline words but not spaces.	CTRL+SHIFT+W
Double-underline text.	CTRL+SHIFT+D
Apply hidden text formatting.	CTRL+SHIFT+H
Apply italic formatting.	CTRL+I
Format letters as small capitals.	CTRL+SHIFT+K
Apply subscript formatting (automatic spacing).	CTRL+EQUAL SIGN
Apply superscript formatting (automatic spacing).	CTRL+SHIFT+PLUS SIGN
Remove manual character formatting.	CTRL+SPACEBAR
Change the selection to the Symbol font.	CTRL+SHIFT+Q
View and copy text formats	
Display nonprinting characters.	CTRL+SHIFT+* (asterisk on numeric keypad does not work)
Review text formatting.	SHIFT+F1 (then click the text with the formatting you want to review)
Copy formats.	CTRL+SHIFT+C
Paste formats.	CTRL+SHIFT+V
Set the line spacing	
Single-space lines.	CTRL+1
Double-space lines.	CTRL+2
Set 1.5-line spacing.	CTRL+5
Add or remove one line space preceding a paragraph.	CTRL+0 (zero)
Align paragraphs	
Switch a paragraph between centered and left-aligned.	CTRL+E
Switch a paragraph between justified and left-aligned.	CTRL+J
Switch a paragraph between right-aligned and left-aligned.	CTRL+R
Left align a paragraph.	CTRL+L
Indent a paragraph from the left	CTRL+M
Remove a paragraph indent from the left.	CTRL+SHIFT+M
Create a hanging indent.	CTRL+T
Reduce a hanging indent.	CTRL+SHIFT+T
Remove paragraph formatting.	CTRL+Q
Apply paragraph styles	
Open Apply Styles task pane.	CTRL+SHIFT+S
Open Styles task pane.	ALT+CTRL+SHIFT+S
Start AutoFormat.	ALT+CTRL+K
Apply the Normal style.	CTRL+SHIFT+N
Apply the Heading 1 style.	ALT+CTRL+1
Apply the Heading 2 style.	ALT+CTRL+2
Apply the Heading 3 style.	ALT+CTRL+3

Close the Styles task pane

If the Styles task pane is not selected, press F6 to select it. Use the arrow keys to select Close, and then press ENTER.	Press CTRL+SPACEBAR.

Insert and edit objects

Insert an object	Press ALT, N, J, and then J to open the Object dialog box.

Mail Merge and Fields

Perform a mail merge

You must be on the Mailings tab to use these keyboard shortcuts.

Preview a mail merge.	ALT+SHIFT+K
Merge a document.	ALT+SHIFT+N
Print the merged document.	ALT+SHIFT+M
Edit a mail-merge data document.	ALT+SHIFT+E
Insert a merge field.	ALT+SHIFT+F

Work with fields

Insert a DATE field.	ALT+SHIFT+D
Insert a LISTNUM field.	ALT+CTRL+L
Insert a PAGE field.	ALT+SHIFT+P
Insert a TIME field.	ALT+SHIFT+T
Insert an empty field.	CTRL+F9
Update linked information in a Microsoft Office Word source document.	CTRL+SHIFT+F7
Update selected fields.	F9
Unlink a field.	CTRL+SHIFT+F9
Switch between a selected field code and its result.	SHIFT+F9
Switch between all field codes and their results.	ALT+F9
Run GOTOBUTTON or MACROBUTTON from the field that displays the field results.	ALT+SHIFT+F9
Go to the next field.	F11
Go to the previous field.	SHIFT+F11
Lock a field.	CTRL+F11
Unlock a field.	CTRL+SHIFT+F11

Language bar

Handwriting recognition

Switch between languages or keyboard layouts.	Left ALT+SHIFT
Display a list of correction alternatives.	+C
Turn handwriting on or off.	+H
Turn Japanese Input Method Editor (IME) on 101 keyboard on or off.	ALT+ ~
Turn Korean IME on 101 keyboard on or off.	Right ALT
Turn Chinese IME on 101 keyboard on or off.	CTRL+SPACEBAR

Function key reference

Function keys

Get Help or visit Microsoft Office Online.	F1
Move text or graphics.	F2
Repeat the last action.	F4
Choose the Go To command (Home tab).	F5
Go to the next pane or frame.	F6
Choose the Spelling command (Review tab).	F7
Extend a selection.	F8
Update the selected fields.	F9
Show KeyTips.	F10

Go to the next field.	F11
Choose the Save As command (Microsoft Office Button).	F12

SHIFT + Function key

Start context-sensitive Help or reveal formatting.	SHIFT+F1
Copy text.	SHIFT+F2
Change the case of letters.	SHIFT+F3
Repeat a Find or Go To action.	SHIFT+F4
Move to the last change.	SHIFT+F5
Go to the previous pane or frame (after pressing F6).	SHIFT+F6
Choose the Thesaurus command (Review tab, Proofing group).	SHIFT+F7
Shrink a selection.	SHIFT+F8
Switch between a field code and its result.	SHIFT+F9
Display a shortcut menu.	SHIFT+F10
Go to the previous field.	SHIFT+F11
Choose the Save command (Microsoft Office Button).	SHIFT+F12

CTRL + Function key

Choose the Print Preview command (Microsoft Office Button).	CTRL+F2
Cut to the Spike.	CTRL+F3
Close the window.	CTRL+F4
Go to the next window.	CTRL+F6
Insert an empty field.	CTRL+F9
Maximize the document window.	CTRL+F10
Lock a field.	CTRL+F11
Choose the Open command (Microsoft Office Button).	CTRL+F12

CTRL + SHIFT + Function key

Insert the contents of the Spike.	CTRL+SHIFT+F3
Edit a bookmark.	CTRL+SHIFT+F5
Go to the previous window.	CTRL+SHIFT+F6
Update linked information in an Office Word 2010 source document.	CTRL+SHIFT+F7
Extend a selection or block.	CTRL+SHIFT+F8, and then press an arrow key
Unlink a field.	CTRL+SHIFT+F9
Unlock a field.	CTRL+SHIFT+F11
Choose the Print command (Microsoft Office Button).	CTRL+SHIFT+F12

ALT + Function key

To do this	Press
Go to the next field.	ALT+F1
Create a new Building Block.	ALT+F3
Exit Office Word 2010.	ALT+F4
Restore the program window size.	ALT+F5
Move from an open dialog box back to the document, for dialog boxes such as Find and Replace that support this behavior.	ALT+F6
Find the next misspelling or grammatical error.	ALT+F7
Run a macro.	ALT+F8
Switch between all field codes and their results.	ALT+F9
Maximize the program window.	ALT+F10
Display Microsoft Visual Basic code.	ALT+F11

ALT + SHIFT + Function key

Go to the previous field.	ALT+SHIFT+F1
Choose the Save command (Microsoft Office Button).	ALT+SHIFT+F2

Display the Research task pane. ALT+SHIFT+F7

Run GOTOBUTTON or MACROBUTTON from the field that displays the field results. ALT+SHIFT+F9

Display a menu or message for a smart tag. ALT+SHIFT+F10

CTRL+ALT+Function key

Display Microsoft System Information. CTRL+ALT+F1

Choose the Open command (Microsoft Office Button). CTRL+ALT+F2

Microsoft Excel

Ctrl combination shortcut keys

Key	*Description*
Ctrl+Shift+(	Unhides any hidden rows within the selection.
Ctrl+Shift+)	Unhides any hidden columns within the selection.
Ctrl+Shift+&	Applies the outline border to the selected cells.
Ctrl+SHIFT_	Removes the outline border from the selected cells.
Ctrl+Shift+~	Applies the General number format.
Ctrl+Shift+$	Applies the Currency format with two decimal places (negative numbers in parentheses).
Ctrl+Shift+%	Applies the Percentage format with no decimal places.
Ctrl+Shift+^	Applies the Exponential number format with two decimal places.
Ctrl+Shift+#	Applies the Date format with the day, month, and year.
Ctrl+Shift+@	Applies the Time format with the hour and minute, and AM or PM.
Ctrl+Shift+!	Applies the Number format with two decimal places, thousands separator, and minus sign (-) for negative values.
Ctrl+Shift+*	Selects the current region around the active cell (the data area enclosed by blank rows and blank columns). In a PivotTable, it selects the entire PivotTable report.
Ctrl+Shift+:	Enters the current time.
Ctrl+Shift+"	Copies the value from the cell above the active cell into the cell or the Formula Bar.
Ctrl+Shift+Plus (+)	Displays the Insert dialog box to insert blank cells.
Ctrl+Minus (-)	Displays the Delete dialog box to delete the selected cells.
Ctrl+;	Enters the current date.
Ctrl+‘	Alternates between displaying cell values and displaying formulas in the worksheet.
Ctrl+’	Copies a formula from the cell above the active cell into the cell or the Formula Bar.
Ctrl+1	Displays the Format Cells dialog box.
Ctrl+2	Applies or removes bold formatting.
Ctrl+3	Applies or removes italic formatting.
Ctrl+4	Applies or removes underlining.
Ctrl+5	Applies or removes strikethrough.
Ctrl+6	Alternates between hiding objects, displaying objects, and displaying placeholders for objects.
Ctrl+8	Displays or hides the outline symbols.
Ctrl+9	Hides the selected rows.
Ctrl+0	Hides the selected columns.
Ctrl+A	Selects the entire worksheet. If the worksheet contains data, Ctrl+A selects the current region. Pressing Ctrl+A a second time selects the current region and its summary rows. Pressing Ctrl+A a third time selects the entire worksheet.When the insertion point is to the right of a function name in a formula, displays the Function Arguments dialog box.Ctrl+Shift+A inserts the argument names and

	parentheses when the insertion point is to the right of a function name in a formula.
Ctrl + B	Applies or removes bold formatting.
Ctrl + C	Copies the selected cells. Ctrl + C followed by another Ctrl + C displays the Clipboard.
Ctrl + D	Uses the Fill Down command to copy the contents and format of the topmost cell of a selected range into the cells below.
Ctrl + F	Displays the Find and Replace dialog box, with the Find tab selected. Shift + F5 also displays this tab, while Shift + F4 repeats the last Find action.Ctrl + Shift + F opens the Format Cells dialog box with the Font tab selected.
Ctrl + G	Displays the Go To dialog box. F5 also displays this dialog box.
Ctrl + H	Displays the Find and Replace dialog box, with the Replace tab selected.
Ctrl + I	Applies or removes italic formatting.
Ctrl + K	Displays the Insert Hyperlink dialog box for new hyperlinks or the Edit Hyperlink dialog box for selected existing hyperlinks.
Ctrl + N	Creates a new, blank workbook.
Ctrl + O	Displays the Open dialog box to open or find a file. Ctrl + Shift + O selects all cells that contain comments.
Ctrl + P	Displays the Print dialog box. Ctrl + Shift + P opens the Format Cells dialog box with the Font tab selected.
Ctrl + R	Uses the Fill Right command to copy the contents and format of the leftmost cell of a selected range into the cells to the right.
Ctrl + S	Saves the active file with its current file name, location, and file format.
Ctrl + T	Displays the Create Table dialog box.
Ctrl + U	Applies or removes underlining. Ctrl + Shift + U switches between expanding and collapsing of the formula bar.
Ctrl + V	Inserts the contents of the Clipboard at the insertion point and replaces any selection. Available only after you have cut or copied an object, text, or cell contents.
Ctrl + W	Closes the selected workbook window.
Ctrl + X	Cuts the selected cells.
Ctrl + Y	Repeats the last command or action, if possible.
Ctrl + Z	Uses the Undo command to reverse the last command or to delete the last entry that you typed. Ctrl + Shift + Z uses the Undo or Redo command to reverse or restore the last automatic correction when AutoCorrect Smart Tags are displayed.

Function keys

Key	***Description***
F1	Displays the Microsoft Office Excel Help task pane. Ctrl + F1 displays or hides the ribbon.Alt + F1 creates a chart of the data in the current range.Alt + Shift + F1 inserts a new worksheet.
F2	Edits the active cell and positions the insertion point at the end of the cell contents. It also moves the insertion point into the Formula Bar when editing in a cell is turned off. Shift + F2 adds or edits a cell comment.Ctrl + F2 displays the Print Preview window.
F3	Displays the Paste Name dialog box. Shift + F3 displays the Insert Function dialog box.
F4	Repeats the last command or action, if possible. Ctrl + F4 closes the selected workbook window.
F5	Displays the Go To dialog box. Ctrl + F5 restores the window size of the selected workbook window.
F6	Switches between the worksheet, ribbon, task pane, and Zoom controls. In a worksheet that has been split (View menu, Manage This Window, Freeze Panes, Split Window command), F6 includes the split panes when switching between panes and the ribbon

	area. Shift+F6 switches between the worksheet, Zoom controls, task pane, and ribbon.Ctrl+F6 switches to the next workbook window when more than one workbook window is open.
F7	Displays the Spelling dialog box to check spelling in the active worksheet or selected range. Ctrl+F7 performs the Move command on the workbook window when it is not maximized. Use the arrow keys to move the window, and when finished press Enter, or Esc to cancel.
F8	Turns extend mode on or off. In extend mode, Extended Selection appears in the status line, and the arrow keys extend the selection. Shift+F8 enables you to add a nonadjacent cell or range to a selection of cells by using the arrow keys.Ctrl+F8 performs the Size command (on the Control menu for the workbook window) when a workbook is not maximized.Alt+F8 displays the Macro dialog box to create, run, edit, or delete a macro.
F9	Calculates all worksheets in all open workbooks. Shift+F9 calculates the active worksheet.Ctrl+Alt+F9 calculates all worksheets in all open workbooks, regardless of whether they have changed since the last calculation.Ctrl+Alt+Shift+F9 rechecks dependent formulas, and then calculates all cells in all open workbooks, including cells not marked as needing to be calculated.Ctrl+F9 minimizes a workbook window to an icon.
F10	Turns key tips on or off. Shift+F10 displays the shortcut menu for a selected item.Alt+Shift+F10 displays the menu or message for a smart tag. If more than one smart tag is present, it switches to the next smart tag and displays its menu or message.Ctrl+F10 maximizes or restores the selected workbook window.
F11	Creates a chart of the data in the current range. Shift+F11 inserts a new worksheet.Alt+F11 opens the Microsoft Visual Basic Editor, in which you can create a macro by using Visual Basic for Applications (VBA).
F12	Displays the Save As dialog box.

Other useful shortcut keys

Key	***Description***
Arrow Keys	Move one cell up, down, left, or right in a worksheet. Ctrl+ARROW KEY moves to the edge of the current data region (data region: A range of cells that contains data and that is bounded by empty cells or datasheet borders.) in a worksheet.Shift+ARROW KEY extends the selection of cells by one cell.Ctrl+Shift+ARROW KEY extends the selection of cells to the last nonblank cell in the same column or row as the active cell, or if the next cell is blank, extends the selection to the next nonblank cell.Left Arrow or Right Arrow selects the tab to the left or right when the ribbon is selected. When a submenu is open or selected, these arrow keys switch between the main menu and the submenu. When a ribbon tab is selected, these keys navigate the tab buttons.Down Arrow or Up Arrow selects the next or previous command when a menu or submenu is open. When a ribbon tab is selected, these keys navigate up or down the tab group.In a dialog box, arrow keys move between options in an open drop-down list, or between options in a group of options.Down Arrow or Alt+Down Arrow opens a selected drop-down list.
Backspace	Deletes one character to the left in the Formula Bar. Also clears the content of the active cell.In cell editing mode, it deletes the character to the left of the insertion point.
Delete	Removes the cell contents (data and formulas) from selected cells without affecting cell formats or comments. In cell editing mode, it deletes the character to the right of the insertion point.
End	Moves to the cell in the lower-right corner of the window when SCROLL LOCK is turned on. Also selects the last command on the menu when a menu or submenu is visible.Ctrl+End moves to the last cell on a worksheet, in the lowest used row of the rightmost used column. If the cursor is in the formula bar, Ctrl+End moves the cursor to the end of the text. Ctrl+Shift+End extends the selection of cells to the last used cell on the worksheet

	(lower-right corner). If the cursor is in the formula bar, Ctrl + Shift + End selects all text in the formula bar from the cursor position to the end—this does not affect the height of the formula bar.
Enter	Completes a cell entry from the cell or the Formula Bar, and selects the cell below (by default). In a data form, it moves to the first field in the next record.Opens a selected menu (press F10 to activate the menu bar) or performs the action for a selected command.In a dialog box, it performs the action for the default command button in the dialog box (the button with the bold outline, often the OK button).Alt + Enter starts a new line in the same cell.Ctrl + Enter fills the selected cell range with the current entry.Shift + Enter completes a cell entry and selects the cell above.
Esc	Cancels an entry in the cell or Formula Bar. Closes an open menu or submenu, dialog box, or message window.It also closes full screen mode when this mode has been applied, and returns to normal screen mode to display the Ribbon and status bar again.
Home	Moves to the beginning of a row in a worksheet. Moves to the cell in the upper-left corner of the window when SCROLL LOCK is turned on.Selects the first command on the menu when a menu or submenu is visible.Ctrl + Home moves to the beginning of a worksheet.Ctrl + Shift + Home extends the selection of cells to the beginning of the worksheet.
Page Down	Moves one screen down in a worksheet. Alt + Page Down moves one screen to the right in a worksheet.Ctrl + Page Down moves to the next sheet in a workbook.Ctrl + Shift + Page Down selects the current and next sheet in a workbook.

Keyboard shortcuts for using the Help window

The Help window provides access to all Office Help content. The Help window displays topics and other Help content.

Open the Help window.	F1
Close the Help window.	Alt + F4
Switch between the Help window and the active program.	Alt + Tab
Go back to Program Name Home.	Alt + Home
Select the next item in the Help window.	Tab
Select the previous item in the Help window.	Shift + Tab
Perform the action for the selected item.	Enter
In the Browse Program Name Help section of the Help window, select the next or previous item.	Tab or Shift + Tab
In the Browse Program Name Help section of the Help window, expand or collapse the selected item.	Enter
Select the next hidden text or hyperlink, including Show All or Hide All at the top of a Help topic.	Tab
Select the previous hidden text or hyperlink.	Shift + Tab
Perform the action for the selected Show All, Hide All, hidden text, or hyperlink.	Enter
Move to the previous Help topic (Back button).	Alt + Left Arrow or Backspace
Move to the next Help topic (Forward button).	Alt + Right Arrow
Scroll small amounts up or down within the current Help topic.	Up Arrow, Down Arrow
Scroll larger amounts up or down within the current Help topic.	Page Up, Page Down
Change whether the Help window appears connected to (tiled) or separate from (untiled) the active program.	Alt + U
Display a menu of commands for the Help window. This requires that the Help window is the active focus. (Click in the Help window.)	Shift + F10
Stop the last action (Stop button).	Esc
Refresh the window (Refresh button).	F5
Print the current Help topic. Note If the cursor is not in the current Help topic, press F6 and then press Ctrl + P.	Ctrl + P

Change the connection state.	F6, and then click Down Arrow
Type text in the Type words to search for box.	F6, and then click Down Arrow
Switch among areas in the Help window; for example, switch between the toolbar, Type words to search for box, and Search list.	F6
In a Table of Contents in tree view, select the next or previous item.	Up Arrow, Down Arrow
In a Table of Contents in tree view, expand or collapse the selected item.	Left Arrow, Right Arrow

Keyboard shortcuts for Microsoft Office basics

Display and use windows

Switch to the next window.	Alt + Tab
Switch to the previous window.	Alt + Shift + Tab
Close the active window.	Ctrl + W or Ctrl + F4
Restore the size of the active window after you maximize it.	Ctrl + F5
Move to a task pane from another pane in the program window (clockwise direction). You may need to press F6 more than once. Note If pressing F6 doesn't display the task pane that you want, try pressing Alt to place focus on the menu bar or the Ribbon, and then press Ctrl + Tab to move to the task pane.	F6
Move to a pane from another pane in the program window (counterclockwise direction).	Shift + F6
When more than one window is open, switch to the next window.	Ctrl + F6
Switch to the previous window.	Ctrl + Shift + F6
When a document window is not maximized, perform the Move command (on the Control menu for the window). Use the arrow keys to move the window, and, when finished, press Esc.	Ctrl + F7
When a document window is not maximized, perform the Size command (on the Control menu for the window). Press the arrow keys to resize the window, and, when finished, press Esc.	Ctrl + F8
Minimize a window to an icon (works for only some Microsoft Office programs).	Ctrl + F9
Maximize or restore a selected window.	Ctrl + F10
Copy a picture of the screen to the Clipboard.	Print Screen
Copy a picture of the selected window to the Clipboard.	Alt + Print Screen

Change or Resize the Font

Change the font.	Ctrl + Shift + F
Change the font size.	Ctrl + Shift + P
Increase the font size of the selected text.	Ctrl + Shift + >
Decrease the font size of the selected text.	Ctrl + Shift + <

Move around in text or cells

Move one character to the left.	Left Arrow
Move one character to the right.	Right Arrow
Move one line up.	Up Arrow
Move one line down.	Down Arrow
Move one word to the left.	Ctrl + Left Arrow
Move one word to the right.	Ctrl + Right Arrow
Move to the end of a line.	End
Move to the beginning of a line.	Home
Move up one paragraph.	Ctrl + Up Arrow
Move down one paragraph.	Ctrl + Down Arrow

Move to the end of a text box.	Ctrl + End
Move to the beginning of a text box.	Ctrl + Home
In Microsoft Office PowerPoint, move to the next title or body text placeholder. If it is the last placeholder on a slide, this will insert a new slide with the same slide layout as the original slide.	Ctrl + Enter
Repeat the last Find action.	Shift + F4

Move around in and work in tables

Move to the next cell.	Tab
Move to the preceding cell.	Shift + Tab
Move to the next row.	Down Arrow
Move to the preceding row.	Up Arrow
Insert a tab in a cell.	Ctrl + Tab
Start a new paragraph.	Enter
Add a new row at the bottom of the table.	Tab at the end of the last row

Access and use task panes

Move to a task pane from another pane in the program window. (You may need to press F6 more than once.) Note If pressing F6 doesn't display the task pane that you want, try pressing Alt to place focus on the menu bar, and then press Ctrl + Tab to move to the task pane.	F6
When a menu or toolbar is active, move to a task pane. (You may need to press Ctrl + Tab more than once.)	Ctrl + Tab
When a task pane is active, select the next or previous option in the task pane.	Tab or Shift + Tab
Display the full set of commands on the task pane menu.	Ctrl + Down Arrow
Move among choices on a selected submenu; move among certain options in a group of options in a dialog box.	Down Arrow or Up Arrow
Open the selected menu, or perform the action assigned to the selected button.	Spacebar or Enter
Open a shortcut menu; open a drop-down menu for the selected gallery item.	Shift + F10
When a menu or submenu is visible, select the first or last command on the menu or submenu.	Home or End
Scroll up or down in the selected gallery list.	Page Up or Page Down
Move to the top or bottom of the selected gallery list.	Ctrl + Home or Ctrl + End
Open the Research task pane. Note This keyboard shortcut does not work in Microsoft Office PowerPoint or Microsoft Office SharePoint Designer.	Alt + Click

Access and use smart tags

Display the menu or message for a smart tag. If more than one smart tag is present, switch to the next smart tag and display its menu or message.	Alt + Shift + F10
Select the next item on a smart tag menu.	Down Arrow
Select the previous item on a smart tag menu.	Up Arrow
Perform the action for the selected item on a smart tag menu.	Enter
Close the smart tag menu or message.	Esc

Press Ctrl + Tab repeatedly to select the toolbar or task pane that you want.

Use dialog boxes

Move to the next option or option group.	Tab
Move to the previous option or option group.	Shift + Tab
Switch to the next tab in a dialog box.	Ctrl + Tab
Switch to the previous tab in a dialog box.	Ctrl + Shift + Tab
Move between options in an open drop-down list, or between options in a group of options.	Arrow keys
Perform the action assigned to the selected button; select or clear the selected check box.	Spacebar
Open the list if it is closed and move to that option in the list.	First letter of an option in a drop-down list
Select an option; select or clear a check box.	Alt + the letter underlined in an option
Open a selected drop-down list.	Alt + Down Arrow
Close a selected drop-down list; cancel a command and close a dialog box.	Esc
Perform the action assigned to a default button in a dialog box.	Enter

Use edit boxes within dialog boxes

An edit box is a blank box in which you type or paste an entry, such as your user name or the path to a folder.

Move to the beginning of the entry.	Home
Move to the end of the entry.	End
Move one character to the left or right.	Left Arrow or Right Arrow
Move one word to the left.	Ctrl + Left Arrow
Move one word to the right.	Ctrl + Right Arrow
Select or cancel selection one character to the left.	Shift + Left Arrow
Select or cancel selection one character to the right.	Shift + Right Arrow
Select or cancel selection one word to the left.	Ctrl + Shift + Left Arrow
Select or cancel selection one word to the right.	Ctrl + Shift + Right Arrow
Select from the insertion point to the beginning of the entry.	Shift + Home
Select from the insertion point to the end of the entry.	Shift + End

Use the Open and Save As dialog boxes

Go to the previous folder.	Alt + 1
Up One Level button: open the folder up one level above the open folder.	Alt + 2
Search the Web button: close the dialog box and open your Web search page.	Alt + 3
Delete button: delete the selected folder or file.	Alt + 3
Create New Folder button: create a new folder.	Alt + 4
Views button: switch among available folder views.	Alt + 5
Tools button: show the Tools menu.	Alt + L
Display a shortcut menu for a selected item, such as a folder or file.	Shift + F10
Move between options or areas in the dialog box.	Tab
Open the Look in list.	F4 or Alt + I
Refresh the file list.	F5

Work with shapes in a SmartArt graphic

Select the next element in a SmartArt graphic.	Tab
Select the previous element in a SmartArt graphic.	Shift + Tab
Select all shapes.	Ctrl + A
Remove focus from the selected shape.	Esc
Nudge the selected shape up.	Up Arrow
Nudge the selected shape down.	Down Arrow
Nudge the selected shape left.	Left Arrow

Nudge the selected shape right.	Right Arrow
Edit text in the selected shape.	Enter or F2
Delete the selected shape.	Delete or Backspace
Cut the selected shape.	Ctrl + X or Shift + Delete
Copy the selected shape.	Ctrl + C
Paste the contents of the Clipboard.	Ctrl + V
Undo the last action.	Ctrl + Z

Move and resize shapes in a SmartArt graphic

Enlarge the selected shape horizontally.	Shift + Right Arrow
Reduce the selected shape horizontally.	Shift + Left Arrow
Enlarge the selected shape vertically.	Shift + Up Arrow
Reduce the selected shape vertically.	Shift + Down Arrow
Rotate the selected shape to the right.	Alt + Right Arrow
Rotate the selected shape to the left.	Alt + Left Arrow

Work with text in a SmartArt graphic

Move one character to the left.	Left Arrow
Move one character to the right.	Right Arrow
Move up one line.	Up Arrow
Move down one line.	Down Arrow
Move one word to the left.	Ctrl + Left Arrow
Move one word to the right.	Ctrl + Right Arrow
Move one paragraph up.	Ctrl + Up Arrow
Move one paragraph down.	Ctrl + Down Arrow
Move to the end of a line.	End
Move to the beginning of a line.	Home
Move to the end of a text box.	Ctrl + End
Move to the beginning of a text box.	Ctrl + Home
Cut selected text.	Ctrl + X
Copy selected text.	Ctrl + C
Paste selected text.	Ctrl + V
Undo the last action.	Ctrl + Z
Delete one character to the left.	Backspace
Delete one word to the left.	Ctrl + Backspace
Delete one character to the right.	Delete
Delete one word to the right.	Ctrl + Delete
Promote the selected text.	Alt + Shift + Right Arrow
Demote the selected text.	Alt + Shift + Left Arrow
Check the spelling (not available in Microsoft Office Word 2010).	F7

Apply character formatting

Open the Font dialog box.	Ctrl + Shift + F or Ctrl + Shift + P
Increase the font size of the selected text.	Ctrl + Shift + >
Decrease the font size of the selected text.	Ctrl + Shift + <
Switch the case of selected text (lower case, Title Case, Upper Case).	Shift + F3
Apply bold formatting to the selected text.	Ctrl + B
Apply an underline to the selected text (not available in Office Word 2010).	Ctrl + U
Apply italic formatting to the selected text.	Ctrl + I
Apply subscript formatting to the selected text.	Ctrl + Equal Sign
Apply superscript formatting to the selected text.	Ctrl + Shift + Plus Sign
Adjust the superscript/subscript offset up.	Ctrl + Alt + Shift + >

Adjust the superscript/subscript offset down.	Ctrl+Alt+Shift+<
Remove all character formatting from the selected text.	Ctrl+Spacebar

Copy text formatting

Copy formatting from the selected text.	Ctrl+Shift+C
Paste formatting to the selected text.	Ctrl+Shift+V

Apply paragraph formatting

Center a paragraph.	Ctrl+E
Justify a paragraph.	Ctrl+J
Left align a paragraph.	Ctrl+L
Right align a paragraph.	Ctrl+R
Demote a bullet point.	Tab or Alt+Shift+Right Arrow
Promote a bullet point.	Shift+Tab or Alt+Shift+Left Arrow

Use the Text pane

Merge two lines of text.	Delete at the end of the first line of text
Display the shortcut menu.	Shift+F10
Switch between the Text pane and the drawing canvas.	Ctrl+Shift+F2
Close the Text pane.	Alt+F4
Switch the focus from the Text pane to the border of the SmartArt graphic.	Esc
Open the SmartArt graphics Help topic.	Ctrl+Shift+F1

Microsoft PowerPoint

Display and use windows

Switch to the next window.	ALT+TAB
Switch to the previous window.	ALT+SHIFT+TAB
Close the active window.	CTRL+W or CTRL+F4
Restore the size of the active window after you maximize it.	CTRL+F5
Move to a task pane from another pane in the program window (clockwise direction). You may need to press F6 more than once. Note If pressing F6 doesn't display the task pane that you want, try pressing ALT to place focus on the menu bar or Ribbon and then pressing CTRL+TAB to move to the task pane.	F6
Move to a pane from another pane in the program window (counterclockwise direction).	SHIFT+F6
When more than one window is open, switch to the next window.	CTRL+F6
Switch to the previous window.	CTRL+SHIFT+F6
When a document window is not maximized, perform the Move command (on the Control menu for the window). Use the arrow keys to move the window and when finished, press ESC.	CTRL+F7
When a document window is not maximized, perform the Size command (on the Control menu for the window). Press the arrow keys to resize the window and when finished, press ESC.	CTRL+F8
Minimize a window to an icon (works for only some Microsoft Office programs).	CTRL+F9
Maximize or restore a selected window.	CTRL+F10

Copy a picture of the screen to the Clipboard.	PRINT SCREEN
Copy a picture of the selected window to the Clipboard.	ALT + PRINT SCREEN

Change or resize the font

Change the font.	CTRL + SHIFT + F
Change the font size.	CTRL + SHIFT + P
Increase the font size of the selected text.	CTRL + SHIFT + >
Decrease the font size of the selected text.	CTRL + SHIFT + <

Move around in text or cells

Move one character to the left.	LEFT ARROW
Move one character to the right.	RIGHT ARROW
Move one line up.	UP ARROW
Move one line down.	DOWN ARROW
Move one word to the left.	CTRL + LEFT ARROW
Move one word to the right.	CTRL + RIGHT ARROW
Move to the end of a line.	END
Move to the beginning of a line.	HOME
Move up one paragraph.	CTRL + UP ARROW
Move down one paragraph.	CTRL + DOWN ARROW
Move to the end of a text box.	CTRL + END
Move to the beginning of a text box.	CTRL + HOME
In Microsoft Office PowerPoint, move to the next title or body text placeholder. If it is the last placeholder on a slide, this will insert a new slide with the same slide layout as the original slide.	CTRL + ENTER
Repeat the last Find action.	SHIFT + F4

Find and replace

Open the Find dialog box.	CTRL + F
Open the Replace dialog box.	CTRL + H
Repeat the last Find action.	CTRL + F4

Move around in and work in tables

Move to the next cell.	TAB
Move to the preceding cell.	SHIFT + TAB
Move to the next row.	DOWN ARROW
Move to the preceding row.	UP ARROW
Insert a tab in a cell.	CTRL + TAB
Start a new paragraph.	ENTER
Add a new row at the bottom of the table.	TAB at the end of the last row

Access and use task panes

Move to a task pane from another pane in the program window. (You may need to press F6 more than once.) Note If pressing F6 doesn't display the task pane that you want, try pressing ALT to place focus on the menu bar and then pressing CTRL + TAB to move to the task pane.	F6
When a menu or toolbar is active, move to a task pane. (You may need to press CTRL + TAB more than once.)	CTRL + TAB
When a task pane is active, select the next or previous option in the task pane, respectively.	TAB, SHIFT + TAB

Display the full set of commands on the task pane menu.	CTRL+DOWN ARROW
Move among choices on a selected submenu; move among certain options in a group of options in a dialog box.	DOWN ARROW or UP ARROW
Open the selected menu, or perform the action assigned to the selected button.	SPACEBAR or ENTER
Open a shortcut menu; open a drop-down menu for the selected gallery item.	SHIFT+F10
When a menu or submenu is visible, select the first or last command, respectively, on the menu or submenu.	HOME, END
Scroll up or down in the selected gallery list, respectively.	PAGE UP, PAGE DOWN
Move to the top or bottom of the selected gallery list, respectively.	HOME, END
Close a task pane.	CTRL+SPACEBAR, C
Open the Clipboard.	ALT+H, F, O

Access and use smart tags

Display the menu or message for a smart tag. If more than one smart tag is present, switch to the next smart tag and display its menu or message.	ALT+SHIFT+F10
Select the next item on a smart tag menu.	DOWN ARROW
Select the previous item on a smart tag menu.	UP ARROW
Perform the action for the selected item on a smart tag menu.	ENTER
Close the smart tag menu or message.	ESC

Use dialog boxes

Move to the next option or option group.	TAB
Move to the previous option or option group.	SHIFT+TAB
Switch to the next tab in a dialog box.	CTRL+TAB
Switch to the previous tab in a dialog box.	CTRL+SHIFT+TAB
Open a selected drop-down list.	ALT+DOWN ARROW
Open the list if it is closed and move to an option in the list.	First letter of an option in a drop-down list
Move between options in an open drop-down list, or between options in a group of options.	Arrow keys
Close a selected drop-down list; cancel a command and close a dialog box.	ESC
Perform the action assigned to the selected button; select or clear the selected check box.	SPACEBAR
Select an option; select or clear a check box.	ALT+ the letter underlined in an option
Perform the action assigned to a default button in a dialog box.	ENTER

Use edit boxes within dialog boxes

An edit box is a blank in which you type or paste an entry, such as your user name or the path to a folder.

Move to the beginning of the entry.	HOME
Move to the end of the entry.	END
Move one character to the left or right, respectively.	LEFT ARROW, RIGHT ARROW
Move one word to the left.	CTRL+LEFT ARROW
Move one word to the right.	CTRL+RIGHT ARROW
Select or cancel selection one character to the left.	SHIFT+LEFT ARROW
Select or cancel selection one character to the right.	SHIFT+RIGHT ARROW
Select or cancel selection one word to the left.	CTRL+SHIFT+LEFT ARROW
Select or cancel selection one word to the right.	CTRL+SHIFT+RIGHT ARROW
Select from the cursor to the beginning of the entry.	SHIFT+HOME
Select from the cursor to the end of the entry.	SHIFT+END

Use the Open and Save As dialog boxes

Go to the previous folder.	ALT+1
Up One Level button: Open the folder up one level above the open folder.	ALT+2
Delete button: Delete the selected folder or file.	ALT+3 or DELETE
Create New Folder button: Create a new folder.	ALT+4
Views button: Switch among available folder views.	ALT+5
Tools button: Show the Tools menu.	ALT+L
Display a shortcut menu for a selected item, such as a folder or file.	SHIFT+F10
Move between options or areas in the dialog box.	TAB
Open the Look in list.	F4 or ALT+I
Refresh the file list.	F5

Microsoft Access 2010

General shortcut keys

Open a new database	CTRL+N
Open an existing database	CTRL+O
Exit Office Access 2010Access	ALT+F4
Printing and saving	
Print the current or selected object	CTRL+P
Open the Print dialog box from Print Preview	P or CTRL+P
Open the Page Setup dialog box from Print Preview	S
Cancel Print Preview or Layout Preview	C or ESC
Save a database object	CTRL+S or SHIFT+F12
Open the Save As dialog box	F12
Using a combo box or list box	
Open a combo box	F4 or ALT+DOWN ARROW
Refresh the contents of a Lookup field list box or combo box	F9
Move down one line	DOWN ARROW
Move down one page	PAGE DOWN
Move up one line	UP ARROW
Move up one page	PAGE UP
Exit the combo box or list box	TAB
Finding and replacing text or data	
Open the Find tab in the Find and Replace dialog box (Datasheet view and Form view only)	CTRL+F
Open the Replace tab in the Find and Replace dialog box (Datasheet view and Form view only)	CTRL+H
Find the next occurrence of the text specified in the Find and Replace dialog box when the dialog box is closed (Datasheet view and Form view only)	SHIFT+F4

Working in Design view

Switch between Edit mode (with insertion point displayed) and Navigation mode in a datasheet. When working in a form or report, press ESC to leave Navigation mode.	F2
Switch to the property sheet (Design view in forms and reports in both Access databases and Access projects)	F4
Switch to Form view from form Design view	F5
Switch between the upper and lower portions of a window (Design view of queries, and the Advanced Filter/Sort window)	F6

Cycle through the field grid, field properties, Navigation Pane, access keys in the Keyboard Access System, Zoom controls, and the security bar (Design view of tables)	F6
Open the Choose Builder dialog box (Design view window of forms and reports)	F7
Open the Visual Basic Editor from a selected property in the property sheet for a form or report	F7
Switch from the Visual Basic Editor back to form or report Design view	SHIFT + F7 or ALT + F11

Editing controls in form and report Design view

Copy the selected control to the Clipboard	CTRL + C
Cut the selected control and copy it to the Clipboard	CTRL + X
Paste the contents of the Clipboard in the upper-left corner of the selected section	CTRL + V
Move the selected control to the right (except controls that are part of a layout)	RIGHT ARROW or CTRL + RIGHT ARROW
Move the selected control to the left (except controls that are part of a layout)	LEFT ARROW or CTRL + LEFT ARROW
Move the selected control up	UP ARROW or CTRL + UP ARROW
Move the selected control down	DOWN ARROW or CTRL + DOWN ARROW
Increase the height of the selected control	SHIFT + DOWN ARROW
Increase the width of the selected control Note If used with controls that are in a layout, the entire layout is resized	SHIFT + RIGHT ARROW
Reduce the height of the selected control	SHIFT + UP ARROW
Reduce the width of the selected control Note If used with controls that are in a layout, the entire layout is resized	SHIFT + LEFT ARROW
Toggle the Navigation Pane	F11
Cycle between open windows	CTRL + F6
Restore the selected minimized window when all windows are minimized	ENTER
Turn on Resize mode for the active window when it is not maximized; press the arrow keys to resize the window	CTRL + F8
Display the Control menu	ALT + SPACEBAR
Display the shortcut menu	SHIFT + F10
Close the active window	CTRL + W or CTRL + F4
Switch between the Visual Basic Editor and the previous active window	ALT + F11

Working with Wizards

Toggle the focus forward between controls in the wizard	TAB
Move to the next page of the wizard	ALT + N
Move to the previous page of the wizard	ALT + B
Complete the wizard	ALT + F

Miscellaneous

Display the complete hyperlink address for a selected hyperlink	F2
Check spelling	F7
Open the Zoom box to conveniently enter expressions and other text in small input areas	SHIFT + F2
Display a property sheet in Design view	ALT + ENTER
Exit Access or close a dialog box	ALT + F4
Invoke a Builder	CTRL + F2
Toggle forward between views when in a table, query, form, report, page, PivotTable list, PivotChart report, stored procedure, or Access project (.adp) function. If there are	

additional views available, successive keystrokes will move to the next available view.	CTRL+RIGHT ARROW or CRTL+COMMA (,)
Toggle back between views when in a table, query, form, report, page, PivotTable list, PivotChart report, stored procedure, or .adp function. If there are additional views available, successive keystrokes will move to the previous view. Note CTRL+PERIOD (.) does not work under all conditions with all objects.	CTRL+LEFT ARROW or CRTL+PERIOD (.)

Navigation Pane shortcut keys

Editing and navigating the Object list	
Rename a selected object	F2
Move down one line	DOWN ARROW
Move down one window	PAGE DOWN
Move to the last object	END
Move up one line	UP ARROW
Move up one window	PAGE UP
Move to the first object	HOME
Navigating and opening objects	
Open the selected table or query in Datasheet view	ENTER
Open the selected form or report	ENTER
Run the selected macro	ENTER
Open the selected table, query, form, report, data access page, macro, or module in Design view	CTRL+ENTER
Display the Immediate window in the Visual Basic Editor	CTRL+G

Work with menus

Show the shortcut menu	SHIFT+F10
Show the access keys	ALT or F10
Show the program icon menu (on the program title bar)	ALT+SPACEBAR
With the menu or submenu visible, select the next or previous command	DOWN ARROW or UP ARROW
Select the menu to the left or right; or, when a submenu is visible, to switch between the main menu and the submenu	LEFT ARROW or RIGHT ARROW
Select the first or last command on the menu or submenu	HOME or END
Close the visible menu and submenu at the same time	ALT
Close the visible menu; or, with a submenu visible, to close the submenu only	ESC

Work in windows and dialog boxes

Using a program window	
Switch to the next program	ALT+TAB
Switch to the previous program	ALT+SHIFT+TAB
Show the Windows Start menu	CTRL+ESC
Close the active database window	CTRL+W
Switch to the next database window	CTRL+F6
Switch to the previous database window	CTRL+SHIFT+F6
Restore the selected minimized window when all windows are minimized	ENTER
Using a dialog box	
Switch to the next tab in a dialog box	CTRL+TAB

Switch to the previous tab in a dialog box	CTRL+SHIFT+TAB
Move to the next option or option group	TAB
Move to the previous option or option group	SHIFT+TAB
Move between options in the selected drop-down list box, or to move between some options in a group of options	Arrow keys
Perform the action assigned to the selected button; select or clear the check box	SPACEBAR
Move to the option by the first letter in the option name in a drop-down list box	Letter key for the first letter in the option name you want (when a drop-down list box is selected)
Select the option, or to select or clear the check box by the letter underlined in the option name	ALT+letter key
Open the selected drop-down list box	ALT+DOWN ARROW
Close the selected drop-down list box	ESC
Perform the action assigned to the default button in the dialog box	ENTER
Cancel the command and close the dialog box	ESC
Close a dialog box	ALT+F4
Editing in a text box	
Move to the beginning of the entry	HOME
Move to the end of the entry	END
Move one character to the left or right	LEFT ARROW or RIGHT ARROW
Move one word to the left or right	CTRL+LEFT ARROW or CTRL+RIGHT ARROW
Select from the insertion point to the beginning of the entry	SHIFT+HOME
Select from the insertion point to the end of the entry	SHIFT+END
Change the size of the selection by one character to the left	SHIFT+LEFT ARROW
Change the size of the selection by one character to the right	SHIFT+RIGHT ARROW
Change the size of the selection by one word to the left	CTRL+SHIFT+LEFT ARROW
Change the size of the selection by one word to the right	CTRL+SHIFT+RIGHT ARROW
Work with the Open, File New Database, and Save As dialog boxes	
Go to the previous folder ( )	ALT+1
Open the folder up one level from the open folder (Up One Level button)	ALT+2
Delete the selected folder or file (Delete button)	DEL
Create a new subfolder in the open folder (Create New Folder button)	ALT+4
Switch between Thumbnails, Tiles, Icons, List, Details, Properties, and Preview views	ALT+5
Show the Tools menu (Tools button)	ALT+L

Work with property sheets

Using a property sheet with a form or report	
Toggle the property sheet tab	F4
Move among choices in the control drop-down list one item at a time	DOWN ARROW or UP ARROW
Move among choices in the control drop-down list five items at a time	PAGE DOWN or PAGE UP
Move to the property sheet tabs from the control drop-down list	TAB
Move among the property sheet tabs with a tab selected, but no property selected	LEFT ARROW or RIGHT ARROW
With a property already selected, move down one property on a tab	TAB
With a property selected, move up one property on a tab; or if already at the top, move to the control drop-down list	SHIFT+TAB
Toggle forward between tabs when a property is selected	CTRL+TAB

Toggle backward between tabs when a property is selected CTRL+SHIFT+TAB

Using a property sheet with a table or query

Toggle the property sheet tab F4

With a tab selected, but no property selected, move among the property sheet tabs LEFT ARROW or RIGHT ARROW

Move to the property sheet tabs when a property is selected CTRL+TAB

Move to the first property of a tab when no property is selected TAB

Move down one property on a tab TAB

Move up one property on a tab; or if already at the top, select the tab itself SHIFT+TAB

Toggle forward between tabs when a property is selected CTRL+TAB

Toggle backward between tabs when a property is selected CTRL+SHIFT+TAB

Work with the Field List pane

Toggle the Field List pane ALT+F8

Add the selected field to the form or report detail section ENTER

Move up or down the Field List pane UP ARROW or DOWN ARROW

Move to the upper Field List pane from the lower pane SHIFT+TAB

Move to the lower Field List pane from the upper pane TAB

Keyboard shortcuts for using the Help window

Select the next hidden text or hyperlink, or Show All or Hide All at the top of a topic TAB

Select the previous hidden text or hyperlink, or the Browser View button at the top of a Microsoft Office Web site article SHIFT+TAB

Perform the action for the selected Show All, Hide All, hidden text, or hyperlink ENTER

Move back to the previous Help topic ALT+LEFT ARROW

Move forward to the next Help topic ALT+RIGHT ARROW

Open the Print dialog box CTRL+P

Scroll small amounts up and down, respectively, within the currently-displayed Help topic. UP ARROW AND DOWN ARROW

Scroll larger amounts up and down, respectively, within the currently-displayed Help topic. PAGE UP AND PAGE DOWN

Display a menu of commands for the Help window; requires that the Help window have active focus (click an item in the Help window). SHIFT+F10

Send e-mail messages

Send the active database object (the object selected in the Navigation Pane) as an e-mail message ALT+F+E

Open the Address Book from within Outlook CTRL+SHIFT+B

Check the names in the To, Cc, and Bcc boxes against the Address Book ALT+K or CTRL+K

Select the next box in the e-mail header or the body of the message when the last box in the e-mail header is active TAB

Select the previous field or button in the e-mail header SHIFT+TAB

Keys for working with text and data

Selecting text in a field

Change the size of the selection by one character to the right SHIFT+RIGHT ARROW

Change the size of the selection by one word to the right CTRL+SHIFT+RIGHT ARROW

Change the size of the selection by one character to the left SHIFT+LEFT ARROW

Change the size of the selection by one word to the left CTRL+SHIFT+LEFT ARROW

Selecting a field or record

Note To cancel a selection, use the opposite arrow key.

Select the next field TAB

Switch between Edit mode (with insertion point displayed) and Navigation mode in a datasheet. When using a form or report, press ESC to leave Navigation mode.	F2
Switch between selecting the current record and the first field of the current record, in Navigation mode	SHIFT + SPACEBAR
Extend selection to the previous record, if the current record is selected	SHIFT + UP ARROW
Extend selection to the next record, if the current record is selected	SHIFT + DOWN ARROW
Select all records	CTRL + A or CTRL + SHIFT + SPACEBAR

Extending a selection

Turn on Extend mode (in Datasheet view, Extended Selection appears in the lower-right corner of the window); pressing F8 repeatedly extends the selection to the word, the field, the record, and all records	F8
Extend a selection to adjacent fields in the same row in Datasheet view	LEFT ARROW or RIGHT ARROW
Extend a selection to adjacent rows in Datasheet view	UP ARROW or DOWN ARROW
Undo the previous extension	SHIFT + F8
Cancel Extend mode	ESC

Selecting and moving a column in Datasheet view

Select the current column or cancel the column selection, in Navigation mode only	CTRL + SPACEBAR
Select the column to the right, if the current column is selected	SHIFT + RIGHT ARROW
Select the column to the left, if the current column is selected	SHIFT + LEFT ARROW
Turn on Move mode; then press the RIGHT ARROW or LEFT ARROW key to move selected column(s) to the right or left	CTRL + SHIFT + F8

Edit text and data

Note If the insertion point is not visible, press F2 to display it.

Moving the insertion point in a field

Move the insertion point one character to the right	RIGHT ARROW
Move the insertion point one word to the right	CTRL + RIGHT ARROW
Move the insertion point one character to the left	LEFT ARROW
Move the insertion point one word to the left	CTRL + LEFT ARROW
Move the insertion point to the end of the field, in single-line fields; or to move it to the end of the line in multi-line fields	END
Move the insertion point to the end of the field, in multiple-line fields	CTRL + END
Move the insertion point to the beginning of the field, in single-line fields; or to move it to the beginning of the line in multi-line fields	HOME
Move the insertion point to the beginning of the field, in multiple-line fields	CTRL + HOME

Copying, moving, or deleting text

Copy the selection to the Clipboard	CTRL + C
Cut the selection and copy it to the Clipboard	CTRL + X
Paste the contents of the Clipboard at the insertion point	CTRL + V
Delete the selection or the character to the left of the insertion point	BACKSPACE
Delete the selection or the character to the right of the insertion point	DELETE
Delete all characters to the right of the insertion point	CTRL + DELETE

Undoing changes

Undo typing	CTRL + Z or ALT + BACKSPACE

Undo changes in the current field or current record; if both have been changed, press ESC twice to undo changes, first in the current field and then in the current record	ESC

Entering data in Datasheet or Form view

Insert the current date	CTRL+SEMICOLON (;)
Insert the current time	CTRL+SHIFT+COLON (:)
Insert the default value for a field	CTRL+ALT+SPACEBAR
Insert the value from the same field in the previous record	CTRL+APOSTROPHE (')
Add a new record	CTRL+PLUS SIGN (+)
In a datasheet, delete the current record	CTRL+MINUS SIGN (-)
Save changes to the current record	SHIFT+ENTER
Switch between the values in a check box or option button	SPACEBAR
Insert a new line	CTRL+ENTER

Refreshing fields with current data

Recalculate the fields in the window	F9
Requery the underlying tables; in a subform, this requeries the underlying table for the subform only	SHIFT+F9
Refresh the contents of a Lookup field list box or combo box	F9

Keys for navigating records

Navigate in Design view

Switch between Edit mode (with insertion point displayed) and Navigation mode	F2
Toggle the property sheet	F4
Switch to Form view from form Design view	F5
Switch between the upper and lower portions of a window (Design view of macros, queries, and the Advanced Filter/Sort window) Use F6 when the TAB key does not take you to the section of the screen you want.	F6
Toggle forward between the design pane, properties, Navigation Pane, access keys, and Zoom controls (Design view of tables, forms, and reports)	F6
Open the Visual Basic Editor from a selected property in the property sheet for a form or report	F7
Invokes the Field List pane in a form, report, or data access page. If the Field List pane is already open, focus moves to the Field List pane.	ALT+F8
When you have a code module open, switch from the Visual Basic Editor to form or report Design view	SHIFT+F7
Switch from a control's property sheet in form or report Design view to the design surface without changing the control focus	SHIFT+F7
Display a property sheet	ALT+ENTER
Copy the selected control to the Clipboard	CTRL+C
Cut the selected control and copy it to the Clipboard	CTRL+X
Paste the contents of the Clipboard in the upper-left corner of the selected section	CTRL+V
Move the selected control to the right by a pixel along the page's grid	RIGHT ARROW
Move the selected control to the left by a pixel along the page's grid	LEFT ARROW
Move the selected control up by a pixel along the page's grid Note For controls in a stacked layout, this switches the position of the selected control with the control directly above it, unless it is already the uppermost control in the layout.	UP ARROW

Move the selected control down by a pixel along the page's grid Note For controls in a stacked layout, this switches the position of the selected control with the control directly below it, unless it is already the lowermost control in the layout.	DOWN ARROW
Move the selected control to the right by a pixel (irrespective of the page's grid)	CTRL+RIGHT ARROW
Move the selected control to the left by a pixel (irrespective of the page's grid)	CTRL+LEFT ARROW
Move the selected control up by a pixel (irrespective of the page's grid) Note For controls in a stacked layout, this switches the position of the selected control with the control directly above it, unless it is already the uppermost control in the layout.	CTRL+UP ARROW
Move the selected control down by a pixel (irrespective of the page's grid) Note For controls in a stacked layout, this switches the position of the selected control with the control directly below it, unless it is already the lowermost control in the layout.	CTRL+DOWN ARROW
Increase the width of the selected control (to the right) by a pixel Note For controls in a stacked layout, this increases the width of the whole layout.	SHIFT+RIGHT ARROW
Decrease the width of the selected control (to the left) by a pixel Note For controls in a stacked layout, this decreases the width of the whole layout.	SHIFT+LEFT ARROW
Decrease the height of the selected control (from the bottom) by a pixel	SHIFT+UP ARROW
Increase the height of the selected control (from the bottom) by a pixel	SHIFT+DOWN ARROW

Navigate in Datasheet view

Going to a specific record

Move to the record number box; then type the record number and press ENTER	F5

Navigating between fields and records

Move to the next field	TAB or RIGHT ARROW
Move to the last field in the current record, in Navigation mode	END
Move to the previous field	SHIFT+TAB, or LEFT ARROW
Move to the first field in the current record, in Navigation mode	HOME
Move to the current field in the next record	DOWN ARROW
Move to the current field in the last record, in Navigation mode	CTRL+DOWN ARROW
Move to the last field in the last record, in Navigation mode	CTRL+END
Move to the current field in the previous record	UP ARROW
Move to the current field in the first record, in Navigation mode	CTRL+UP ARROW
Move to the first field in the first record, in Navigation mode	CTRL+HOME

Navigating to another screen of data

Move down one screen	PAGE DOWN
Move up one screen	PAGE UP
Move right one screen	CTRL+PAGE DOWN
Move left one screen	CTRL+PAGE UP

Navigate in subdatasheets

Going to a specific record

Move from the subdatasheet to move to the record number box; then type the record number and press ENTER	ALT+F5

Expanding and collapsing subdatasheet

Move from the datasheet to expand the record's subdatasheet	CTRL+SHIFT+DOWN ARROW
Collapse the subdatasheet	CTRL+SHIFT+UP ARROW

Navigating between the datasheet and subdatasheet

Enter the subdatasheet from the last field of the previous record in the datasheet	TAB
Enter the subdatasheet from the first field of the following record in the datasheet	SHIFT+TAB
Exit the subdatasheet and move to the first field of the next record in the datasheet	CTRL+TAB
Exit the subdatasheet and move to the last field of the previous record in the datasheet	CTRL+SHIFT+TAB
From the last field in the subdatasheet to enter the next field in the datasheet	TAB
From the datasheet to bypass the subdatasheet and move to the next record in the datasheet	DOWN ARROW
From the datasheet to bypass the subdatasheet and move to the previous record in the datasheet	UP ARROW

You can navigate between fields and records in a subdatasheet with the same shortcut keys used in Datasheet view.

Navigate in Form view

Going to a specific record

Move to the record number box; then type the record number and press ENTER	F5

Navigating between fields and records

Move to the next field	TAB
Move to the previous field	SHIFT+TAB
Move to the last control on the form and remain in the current record, in Navigation mode	END
Move to the last control on the form and set focus in the last record, in Navigation mode	CTRL+END
Move to the first control on the form and remain in the current record, in Navigation mode	HOME
Move to the first control on the form and set focus in the first record, in Navigation mode	CTRL+HOME
Move to the current field in the next record	CTRL+PAGE DOWN
Move to the current field in the previous record	CTRL+PAGE UP

Navigating in forms with more than one page

Move down one page; at the end of the record, moves to the equivalent page on the next record	PAGE DOWN
Move up one page; at the end of the record, moves to the equivalent page on the previous record	PAGE UP

Navigating between the main form and subform

Enter the subform from the preceding field in the main form	TAB
Enter the subform from the following field in the main form	SHIFT+TAB
Exit the subform and move to the next field in the master form or next record	CTRL+TAB
Exit the subform and move to the previous field in the main form or previous record	CTRL+SHIFT+TAB

Navigate in Print Preview and Layout Preview

Dialog box and window operations

Open the Print dialog box	P (for forms and reports) or CTRL+P (for datasheets, forms, and reports)

Open the Page Setup dialog box (forms and reports only)	S
Zoom in or out on a part of the page	Z
Cancel Print Preview or Layout Preview	C or ESC
Viewing different pages	
Move to the page number box; then type the page number and press ENTER	ALT+F5
View the next page (when Fit To Window is selected)	PAGE DOWN or DOWN ARROW
View the previous page (when Fit To Window is selected)	PAGE UP or UP ARROW
Navigating in Print and Layout Preview	
Scroll down in small increments	DOWN ARROW
Scroll down one full screen	PAGE DOWN
Move to the bottom of the page	CTRL+DOWN ARROW
Scroll up in small increments	UP ARROW
Scroll up one full screen	PAGE UP
Move to the top of the page	CTRL+UP ARROW
Scroll to the right in small increments	RIGHT ARROW
Move to the right edge of the page	END
Move to the lower-right corner of the page	CTRL+END
Scroll to the left in small increments	LEFT ARROW
Move to the left edge of the page	HOME
Move to the upper-left corner of the page	CTRL+HOME
Navigate in the Database Diagram window in an Access project	
Move from a table cell to the table's title bar	ESC
Move from a table's title bar to the last cell you edited	ENTER
Move from table title bar to table title bar, orfrom cell to cell inside a table	TAB
Expand a list inside a table	ALT + DOWN ARROW
Scroll through the items in a drop-down list from top to bottom	DOWN ARROW
Move to the previous item in a list	UP ARROW
Select an item in a list and move to the next cell	ENTER
Change the setting in a check box	SPACEBAR
Go to the first cell in the row, orto the beginning of the current cell	HOME
Go to the last cell in the row, orto the end of the current cell	END
Scroll to the next "page" inside a table, orto the next "page" of the diagram	PAGE DOWN
Scroll to the previous "page" inside a table, orto the previous "page" of the diagram	PAGE UP

Navigate in the Query Designer in an Access project

Any Pane	
Move among the Query Designer panes	F6, SHIFT+F6
Diagram Pane	
Move among tables, views, and functions, (and to join lines, if available)	TAB, or SHIFT+TAB
Move between columns in a table, view, or function	Arrow keys
Choose the selected data column for output	SPACEBAR or PLUS key
Remove the selected data column from the query output	SPACEBAR or MINUS key
Remove the selected table, view, or function, or join line from the query	DELETE

If multiple items are selected, pressing SPACEBAR affects all selected items. Select multiple items by holding down the SHIFT key while clicking them. Toggle the selected state of a single item by holding down CTRL while clicking it.

Grid Pane

Move among cells	Arrow keys or TAB or SHIFT+TAB
Move to the last row in the current column	CTRL+DOWN ARROW
Move to the first row in the current column	CTRL+UP ARROW
Move to the top left cell in the visible portion of grid	CTRL+HOME
Move to the bottom right cell	CTRL+END
Move in a drop-down list	UP ARROW or DOWN ARROW
Select an entire grid column	CTRL+SPACEBAR
Toggle between edit mode and cell selection mode	F2
Copy selected text in cell to the Clipboard (in edit mode)	CTRL+C
Cut selected text in cell and place it on the Clipboard (in edit mode)	CTRL+X
Paste text from the Clipboard (in edit mode)	CTRL+V
Toggle between insert and overstrike mode while editing in a cell	INS
Toggle the check box in the Output columnNote If multiple items are selected, pressing this key affects all selected items.	SPACEBAR
Clear the selected contents of a cell	DELETE
Remove row containing selected data column from the query Note If multiple items are selected, pressing this key affects all selected items.	DELETE
Clear all values for a selected grid column	DELETE
Insert row between existing rows	INS (after you select grid row)
Add an Or ... column	INS (after you select any Or ... column)

SQL Pane

You can use the standard Windows editing keys when working in the SQL pane, such as CTRL+ arrow keys to move between words, and the Cut, Copy, and Paste commands on the Edit menu.

Note You can only insert text; there is no overstrike mode.

Move the selection from left to right, and then down	The TAB key
Move the selection from top to bottom, and then to the right	ENTER
Select the cell to the left. If the current cell is the leftmost cell, SHIFT+TAB selects the last cell in the previous row.	SHIFT+TAB
Select the cell above the current cell. If the current cell is the topmost cell, SHIFT+ENTER selects the last cell in the previous column.	SHIFT+ENTER
Select the detail cells for the next item in the row area	CTRL+ENTER
Select the detail cells for the previous item in the row area	SHIFT+CTRL+ENTER
Move the selection in the direction of the arrow key. If a row or column field is selected, press DOWN ARROW to move to the first item of data in the field, and then press an arrow key to move to the next or previous item or back to the field. If a detail field is selected, press DOWN ARROW or RIGHT ARROW to move to the first cell in the detail area.	Arrow keys
Extend or reduce the selection in the direction of the arrow key	SHIFT+arrow keys
Move the selection to the last cell in the direction of the arrow key	CTRL+arrow keys
Move the selected item in the direction of the arrow key	SHIFT+ALT+arrow keys
Select the leftmost cell of the current row	HOME
Select the rightmost cell of the current row	END
Select the leftmost cell of the first row	CTRL+HOME
Select the last cell of the last row	CTRL+END
Extend selection to the leftmost cell of the first row	SHIFT+CTRL+HOME

Extend selection to the last cell of the last row	SHIFT+CTRL+END
Select the field for the currently selected item of data, total, or detail	CTRL+SPACEBAR
Select the entire row containing the currently selected cell	SHIFT+SPACEBAR
Select the entire PivotTable view	CTRL+A
Display the next screen	PAGE DOWN
Display the previous screen	PAGE UP
Extend the selection down one screen	SHIFT+PAGE DOWN
Reduce the selection by one screen	SHIFT+PAGE UP
Display the next screen to the right	ALT+PAGE DOWN
Display the previous screen to the left	ALT+PAGE UP
Extend the selection to the page on the right	SHIFT+ALT+PAGE DOWN
Extend the selection to the page on the left	SHIFT+ALT+PAGE UP

Keys for carrying out commands

Display Help topics	F1
Display the shortcut menu for the selected element of the PivotTable view. Use the shortcut menus to carry out commands in the PivotTable view.	SHIFT+F10
Carry out a command on the shortcut menu	Underlined letter
Close the shortcut menu without carrying out a command	ESC
Display the Properties dialog box	ALT+ENTER
Close the Properties dialog box	ALT+F4
Cancel a refresh operation in progress	ESC
Copy the selected data from the PivotTable view to the Clipboard	CTRL+C
Export the contents of the PivotTable view to Microsoft Office Excel 2010	CTRL+E

Keys for displaying, hiding, filtering, or sorting data

Show or hide the expand indicators (and boxes) beside items	CTRL+8
Expand the currently selected item	CTRL+PLUS SIGN (on the numeric keypad)
Hide the currently selected item	CTRL+MINUS SIGN (on the numeric keypad)
Open the list for the currently selected field	ALT+DOWN ARROW
Alternately move to the most recently selected item, the OK button, and the Cancel button in the drop-down list for a field	The TAB key
Move to the next item in the drop-down list for a field	Arrow keys
Select or clear the check box for the current item in the drop-down list for a field	SPACEBAR
Close the drop-down list for a field and apply any changes you made	ENTER
Close the drop-down list for a field without applying your changes	ESC
Turn AutoFilter on or off	CTRL+T
Sort data in the selected field or total in ascending order (A – Z 0 – 9)	CTRL+SHIFT+A
Sort data in the selected field or total in descending order (Z – A 9 – 0)	CTRL+SHIFT+Z
Move the selected member up or left	ALT+SHIFT+UP ARROW or ALT+SHIFT+LEFT ARROW
Move the selected member down or right	ALT+SHIFT+DOWN ARROW or ALT+SHIFT+RIGHT ARROW

Keys for adding fields and totals and changing the layout of a PivotTable view

Keys for working with the Field List pane

Display the Field List pane, or activate it if it is already displayed	CTRL+L
Move to the next item in the Field List pane	Arrow keys
Move to the previous item and include it in the selection	SHIFT+UP ARROW
Move to the next item and include it in the selection	SHIFT+DOWN ARROW
Move to the previous item, but don't include the item in the selection	CTRL+UP ARROW

Move to the next item, but don't include the item in the selection CTRL+DOWN ARROW
Remove the item from the selection, if the item that has focus is included in the selection, and vice versa CTRL+SPACEBAR
Expand the current item in the Field List pane to display its contents. Or expand Totals to display the available total fields. PLUS SIGN (numeric keypad)
Collapse the current item in the Field List pane to hide its contents. Or collapse Totals to hide the available total fields. MINUS SIGN (numeric keypad)
Alternately move to the most recently selected item, the Add to button, and the list next to the Add to button in the Field List pane The TAB key
Open the drop-down list next to the Add to button in the Field List pane. Use the arrow keys to move to the next item in the list, and then press ENTER to select an item. ALT+DOWN ARROW
Add the highlighted field in the Field List pane to the area in the PivotTable view that is displayed in the Add to list ENTER
Close the Field List pane ALT+F4

Keys for adding fields and totals

Add a new total field for the selected field in the PivotTable view by using the Sum summary function CTRL+SHIFT+S
Add a new total field for the selected field in the PivotTable view by using the Count summary function CTRL+SHIFT+C
Add a new total field for the selected field in the PivotTable view by using the Min summary function CTRL+SHIFT+M
Add a new total field for the selected field in the PivotTable view by using the Max summary function CTRL+SHIFT+X
Add a new total field for the selected field in the PivotTable view by using the Average summary function CTRL+SHIFT+E
Add a new total field for the selected field in the PivotTable view by using the Standard Deviation summary function CTRL+SHIFT+D
Add a new total field for the selected field in the PivotTable view by using the Standard Deviation Population summary function CTRL+SHIFT+T
Add a new total field for the selected field in the PivotTable view by using the Variance summary function CTRL+SHIFT+V
Add a new total field for the selected field in the PivotTable view by using the Variance Population summary function CTRL+SHIFT+R
Turn subtotals and grand totals on or off for the selected field in the PivotTable view CTRL+SHIFT+B
Add a calculated detail field CTRL+F

Keys for changing the layout

Note The following four shortcuts do not work if you press the keys 1, 2, 3, or 4 from the numeric pad of your keyboard.

Move the selected field in the PivotTable view to the row area CTRL+1
Move the selected field in the PivotTable view to the column area CTRL+2
Move the selected field in the PivotTable view to the filter area CTRL+3
Move the selected field in the PivotTable view to the detail area CTRL+4
Move the selected row or column field in the PivotTable view to a higher level CTRL+LEFT ARROW

Move the selected row or column field in the PivotTable view to a lower level	CTRL+RIGHT ARROW

Keys for formatting elements in PivotTable view

To use the following shortcuts, first select a detail field or a data cell for a total field. The first seven keyboard shortcuts change the number format of the selected field.

Apply the general number format to values in the selected total or detail field	CTRL+SHIFT+ ~ (tilde)
Apply the currency format, with two decimal places and negative numbers in parentheses, to values in the selected total or detail field	CTRL+SHIFT+$
Apply the percentage format, with no decimal places, to values in the selected total or detail field	CTRL+SHIFT+%
Apply the exponential number format, with two decimal places, to values in the selected total or detail field	CTRL+SHIFT+^
Apply the date format, with the day, month, and year, to values in the selected total or detail field	CTRL+SHIFT+#
Apply the time format, with the hour, minute, and AM or PM, to values in the selected total or detail field	CTRL+SHIFT+@
Apply the numeric format, with two decimal places, thousands separator, and a minus sign for negative values, to values in the selected total or detail field	CTRL+SHIFT+!
Make text bold in the selected field of the PivotTable view	CTRL+B
Make text underlined in the selected field of the PivotTable view	CTRL+U
Make text italic in the selected field of the PivotTable view	CTRL+I

PivotChart view

Keys for selecting items in a chart

Select the next item in the chart	RIGHT ARROW
Select the previous item in the chart	LEFT ARROW
Select the next group of items	DOWN ARROW
Select the previous group of items	UP ARROW

Keys for working with properties and options

Display the Properties dialog box	ALT+ENTER
Close the Properties dialog box	ALT+F4
When the Properties dialog box is active, select the next item on the active tab	The TAB key
When a tab in the Properties dialog box is active, select the next tab	RIGHT ARROW
When a tab in the Properties dialog box is active, select the previous tab	LEFT ARROW
Display a list or palette when a button that contains a list or palette is selected	DOWN ARROW
Display the shortcut menu	SHIFT+F10
Carry out a command on the shortcut menu	Underlined letter
Close the shortcut menu without carrying out a command	ESC

Keys for working with fields

Open the list for the currently selected field	ALT+DOWN ARROW
In the drop-down list for a field, alternately move to the most recently selected item, the OK button, and the Cancel button	The TAB key
In the drop-down list for a field, move to the next item	Arrow keys
In the drop-down list for a field, select or clear the check box for the current item	SPACEBAR
Close the drop-down list for a field and apply any changes you made	ENTER
Close the drop-down list for a field without applying your changes	ESC

Keys for working with the Field List pane

Display the Field List pane, or activate it if it is already displayed	CTRL+L

Move to the next item in the Field List pane	Arrow keys
Move to the previous item and include it in the selection	SHIFT + UP ARROW
Move to the next item and include it in the selection	SHIFT + DOWN ARROW
Move to the previous item, but don't include the item in the selection	CTRL + UP ARROW
Move to the next item, but don't include the item in the selection	CTRL + DOWN ARROW
Remove the item from the selection if the item that has focus is included in the selection, and vice versa	CTRL + SPACEBAR
Expand the current item in the Field List pane to display its contents, or expand Totals to display the available total fields	PLUS SIGN (numeric keypad)
Collapse the current item in the Field List pane to hide its contents, or collapse Totals to hide the available total fields.	MINUS SIGN (numeric keypad)
In the Field List pane, alternately move to the most recently selected item, the Add to button, and the list next to the Add to button	The TAB key
Open the drop-down list next to the Add to button in the Field List pane. Use the arrow keys to move to the next item in the list, and then press ENTER to select an item.	ALT + DOWN ARROW
Add the highlighted field in the Field List pane to the drop area that is displayed in the Add to list	ENTER
Close the Field List pane	ALT + F4

In the Help window

Open the Help window.	F1
Close the Help window	ALT + F4
Switch between the Help window and the active program.	ALT + TAB
Go back to *Program Name* Home.	ALT + HOME
Select the next item in the Help window.	TAB
Select the previous item in the Help window.	SHIFT + TAB
Perform the action for the selected item.	ENTER
In the Browse *Program Name* Help section of the Help window, select the next or previous item, respectively.	TAB or SHIFT + TAB
In the Browse *Program Name* Help section of the Help window, expand or collapse the selected item, respectively.	ENTER
Select the next hidden text or hyperlink, including Show All or Hide All at the top of a topic.	TAB
Select the previous hidden text or hyperlink.	SHIFT + TAB
Perform the action for the selected Show All, Hide All, hidden text, or hyperlink.	ENTER
Move back to the previous Help topic (Back button).	ALT + LEFT ARROW or BACKSPACE
Move forward to the next Help topic (Forward button).	ALT + RIGHT ARROW
Scroll small amounts up or down, respectively, within the currently displayed Help topic.	UP ARROW, DOWN ARROW
Scroll larger amounts up or down, respectively, within the currently displayed Help topic.	PAGE UP, PAGE DOWN
Display a menu of commands for the Help window. This requires that the Help window have the active focus (click in the Help window)	SHIFT + F10
Stop the last action (Stop button).	ESC
Refresh the window (Refresh button).	F5

Print the current Help topic. Note If the cursor is not in the current Help topic, press F6 and then press CTRL + P.	CTRL + P
Change the connection state.	F6, and then press ENTER to open the list of choices
Switch among areas in the Help window; for example, switch between the toolbar and the Search list.	F6
In a Table of Contents in tree view, select the next or previous item, respectively.	UP ARROW, DOWN ARROW
In a Table of Contents in tree view, expand or collapse the selected item, respectively.	LEFT ARROW, RIGHT ARROW

CHAPTER 8

Questions

Introduction

Questions help you in revising the matter read in the various chapters.

ANSWER THE FOLLOWING QUESTIONS

OBJECTIVE TYPE QUESTIONS

1. In word processing, you manipulate ______
   (a) numbers (b) text
2. You can set Left, Right and ______ alignment in word processing.
   (a) Center (b) Justify
   (c) Both
3. Can you spell check you text in word processing?
   (a) Yes (b) No
4. Can you locate a word in word processing?
   (a) No (b) Yes
5. Blinking point which shows your position in the text is called:
   (a) Cursor (b) Blinker
   (c) Position
6. Spacebar is used for :
   (a) giving space (b) deleting space
7. You can start Microsoft Word by using ______ button.
   (a) New (b) Start
   (c) Program
8. For creating a document, you use ____ command at File menu.
   (a) New (b) Open
   (c) Document
9. For saving a document, you need to have ______ for it.
   (a) Name (b) Surname
10. For opening an existing document, you need to give ____ command.
    (a) New (b) Open
    (c) Close
11. You can select the text by:
    (a) Keyboard (b) Mouse
    (c) Both
12. You click at B to make the text
    (a) Bold (b) Italics
    (c) Underline
13. Can you emboss you text?
    (a) Yes (b) No
14. You can change the size of the text from:
    (a) Formatting bar (b) Font dialog box
    (c) Both
15. You click at I to make the text
    (a) Bold (b) Italics
    (c) Underline

16. You can change the font of the text from
    (a) Formatting bar (b) Font dialog box
    (c) Box
17. Colour of the text can be changed:
    (a) Yes (b) No
18. You click at U to make the text
    (a) Bold (b) Italics
    (c) Underline
19. Word supports alignments like Left, Right, Center and ______
    (a) Justify (b) Up
    (c) Down
20. You can change the line and para spacing from ______ dialog box.
    (a) Font (b) Paragraph
    (c) Open
21. Header appears at the ______ of the page.
    (a) Top (b) Bottom
    (c) Center
22. Footer appears at the ________ of the page
    (a) Top (b) Bottom
    (c) Center
23. For printing a document you have to have _________ on.
    (a) Printer (b) Monitor
    (c) Scanner
24. Most of the editing tools are available under _____ menu.
    (a) File (b) Format
    (c) Edit
25. You can add picture in your document from the ______ menu.
    (a) File (b) Edit
    (c) Insert
26. Clip Art is
    (a) Text (b) Graphics
    (c) Both
27. Can Text be mingled with Graphics?
    (a) Yes (b) No
28. WordArt is a
    (a) Text (b) Graphic
    (c) Independent program
29. You can set margins by using the dialog box:
    (a) Font (b) Page Setup
    (c) Margins

30. Two main orientations are, Potrait and
    (a) Landscape (b) Photo
    (c) Lying
31. Can you shade your text?
    (a) Yes (b) No
32. Can you put border across your text in the document?
    (a) Yes (b) No
33. Decimal is tab?
    (a) Yes (b) No
34. In text you can find a word and replace it with another word using command ________.
    (a) Find (b) Replace
    (c) None
35. You can insert a table from ________ toolbar.
    (a) Formatting (b) Standard
    (c) Drawing
36. You can align data vertically in a table:
    (a) Yes (b) No
37. Can you insert more rows in a table?
    (a) Yes (b) No
38. Sending of same letter to different people is done by:
    (a) Send (b) Letter
    (c) Mailmerge
39. Headers are put:
    (a) at the top (b) at the bottom
    (c) in the middle
40. You can put page numbers :
    (a) at the top (b) at the bottom
    (c) both places
41. Footers are put:
    (a) at the top (b) at the bottom
    (c) in the middle
42. Table of contents has:
    (a) Page number (b) Marked entry
    (c) both
43. Borders can be shaded:
    (a) Yes (b) No
44. You can have line in between the columns:
    (a) Yes (b) No
45. Index has all marked enteries with page numbers:
    (a) Yes (b) No

46. Word count gives you :
   (a) Numuber of lines
   (b) Number of words
   (c) Both
47. For opening and closing of the file in Excel you can use which bar.
   (a) Formatting
   (b) Standard
   (c) Title
48. What are numbered from A to Z, etc?
   (a) Rows
   (b) Cells
   (c) Columns
49. You can move around the worksheet using which buttons?
   (a) Scroll
   (b) Logic
   (c) Start
50. For making the text bold in the cell, you use B in which bar.
   (a) Standard
   (b) Formatting
   (c) Title
51. For getting the short menu on the screen, you click which button of the mouse.
   (a) Right button
   (b) Left button
   (c) Centre button
52. Charts are created using which option.
   (a) Chart Wizard
   (b) Pivto Table
   (c) Pie Chart
53. For editing the chart, you ___________ the chart itself.
   (a) Click
   (b) Delete
   (c) Double click
54. In Excel formula starts with __________.
   (a) = sign
   (b) + sign
   (c) - sign
55. In Excel worksheets are given ____ extension.
   (a) .xls
   (b) .doc
   (c) .bmp
56. In Microsoft Excel, you use ______ for calcualtions.
   (a) Formula
   (b) Row
   (c) Cell
57. Formula which can be used directly from the Standard toolbar is
   (a) AutoSum
   (b) Auto
   (c) Sum
58. The result of AutoCalculate is shown at ___ bar.
   (a) Standard
   (b) Formatting
   (c) Status
59. Sum function needs to have _____ before it.
   (a) +
   (b) –
   (c) =

60. To access to any formula in Microsoft Excel, you need to go through _____
    (a) Function Wizard (b) File
    (c) Formula
61. Anything that is typed in a worksheet appears:
    (a) in both the active cell and the formula bar
    (b) in the active cell only
    (c) none of the above
62. The formatting toolbar
    (a) is placed just below the Standard toolbar (b) is used to apply common formats
    (c) both of above
63. The combination of the column letter and row number for a cell in an Excel worksheet is called a
    (a) cell identification number (b) cell reference
    (c) cell identity
64. In Excel the simplest way to move data from one location to another is
    (a) by menu commands (b) by mouse
    (c) by drag and drop method
65. Using borders you
    (a) can add lines above, below or to either side of a cell
    (b) can add a single line or multiple lines, along one side of a cell or around it.
    (c) both a and b above
66. Cell address B$6 in a formula means it is a
    (a) relative cell reference (b) absolute cell reference
    (c) mixed cell reference
67. A function in Excel
    (a) is a ready made formula (b) is a shortcut formula
    (c) both of above
68. PowerPoint is used for:
    (a) Word processing (b) Spreadsheets
    (c) Presentations
69. Overhead projections can be created using PoerPoint:
    (a) Yes (b) No
70. AutoContent Wizard creates a
    (a) Document (b) Presentation
    (c) Spreadsheet
71. There is no need to use templates in PowerPoint:
    (a) True (b) False
72. You can view your presentation through various views :
    (a) Yes (b) No
73. You can move your text in the slide, up and down:
    (a) Yes (b) No

74. A slide with background picture can be created in PowerPoint:
    (a) Yes (b) No
75. You can even have textured patterns in the background of a slide:
    (a) Yes (b) No
76. You can add organization format in the form of a :
    (a) Table (b) Chart
    (c) Graphic
77. You can use a picture as a background for a slide:
    (a) Yes (b) No
78. Various alignments available for text formatting in PowerPoint are Left, Right, Center and :
    (a) Justify (b) Natural
    (c) Reverse
79. Various tabs available in PowerPoint are, Left, Right, Center and :
    (a) Comma (b) Decimal
    (c) Full stop
80. Optional command which allows you to preset your errors is called:
    (a) Autoset (b) Autoplay
    (c) Autocorrect
81. Notes pages have on them:
    (a) text (b) graphic
    (c) pictures
82. You can view all slides continuously by using:
    (a) Show (b) Slide show
    (c) Slides
83. You can set tabs using
    (a) Ruler (b) Scale
    (c) Footer
84. For getting information from the database we use :
    (a) Table (b) Query
    (c) Report
85. It consists of various records having data:
    (a) Table (b) Query
    (c) Report
86. For printing the information from the Table we use:
    (a) Table (b) Query
    (c) Report
87. You can create a database using :
    (a) Home panel (b) Wizard
    (c) Programs
88. Main controlling point in Access is:
    (a) Switchboard (b) Home panel
    (c) Edit panel

89. Easy way of creating a Table is by using:
    (a) Wizard (b) Design View
    (c) New
90. A Table is a collection of :
    (a) Queries (b) Data
    (c) Reports
91. Forms are filled with :
    (a) Data (b) Database
    (c) Information
92. The number of forms which you can create from a Table:
    (a) One (b) Many
    (c) None
93. You can modify your report using :
    (a) Wizard (b) AutoFormat
    (c) Printer
94. Report can be created using :
    (a) Wizard (b) AutoFormat
    (c) Printer

ANSWERS TO OBJECTIVE TYPE QUESTIONS

1. b	2. c	3. a	4. b
5. a	6. a	7. b	8. a
9. a	10 b	11. c	12. a
13. a	14. c	15. a	16. c
17. a	18. a	19. a	20. b
21. a	22. b	23. a	24. c
25. c	26. b	27. a	28. c
29. b	30. a	31. a	32. a
33. a	34. b	35. a	36. a
37. a	38. c	39. a	40. c
41. b	42. a	43. a	44. a
45. a	46. c	47. b	48. c
49. a	50. b	51. a	52. a
53. c	54. a	55. a	56. a
57. a	58. c	59. c	60. a
61. a	62. c	63. b	64. c
65. c	66. b	67. c	68. c
69. a	70. b	71. b	72. a
73. a	74. a	75. a	76. b

77. a	78. a	79. b	80. c
81. a	82. b	83. a	84. b
85. a	86. c	87. b	88. a
89. a	90. b	91. a	92. b
93. b	94. a		

SUBJECTIVE TYPE QUESTIONS

Chapter 1 — Introduction to Windows 7

1. What is Windows 7?
2. Describe the various items available on the Desktop of Windows 7?
3. What is there on the Taskbar?
4. What is the use of Recycle Bin?
5. How would you create a shortcut?
6. Describe the various method of using mouse.
7. Describe the common keyboard commands.
8. How would you access Control Panel of Windows 7?
9. Write a short note on the following commands of Windows 7 Control Panel.

Add Hardware	Adminstrative Tools
AutoPlay	Backup and Restore Centre
BitLocker Drive Encryption	Color Management
Date and Time	Default Programs
Device Manager	Ease of Access
Folder Options	Fonts
Game Controllers	Indexing Options
Internet Options	iSCSI Initiator
Keyboard	Mail
Mouse	Network and Sharing Centre
Offline Files	Parental Controls
Pen and Input Devices	People Near Me
Performance Information	Personalize
Phone and Modem Options	Power Options
Printers	Problem Reports and Solutions
Programs and Features	Regional and Language Options
Scanners and Cameras	Security Center

Sound
Speech Recognition
System
Taskbar and Start Menu
User Accounts
Windows CardSpace
Windows Firewall
Windows SlideShow
SoundMAX
Sync Center
Table PC Settings
Text to Speech
Welcom Center
Windows Defender
Windows Sidebar Properties
Windows Update

Chapter 2 — Introduction to Microsoft Word 2010

1. Write a short note on the following commands of Microsoft Word.

   Applying Fonts
   Page Numbering
   Date and Time
   Sort
   Animate Text
   AutoFormat
   Columns
   Table of Contents
   Creating an Index
   File, Insert
   Footnotes and Endnotes
   Hyperlinks
   Protect Document
   Send To
   Tracking the Document Changes
   Versions
   Zoom
   Paragraph Setting
   Change Case
   Insert Picture
   Bullets and Numbering
   AutoCorrect
   Break, Insert
   Comments, Insert
   Creating a Table
   Drop Cap
   Find and Replace
   Header and Footer
   Macro
   Reveal Formatting
   Tabs
   Bookmarks
   Word Count

2. How would you save a document file?
3. Which alignments Word 2010 supports?
4. How would you apply various fonts?
5. Describe the process of Spell Checking in Word 2010.
6. What is Thesaurus?
7. What are Styles?
8. Describe the various Borders in Word 2010.
9. How would you close a document file?

10. Describe the various options of saving the document.
11. How would you print your document?
12. Describe the process of mailmerge in Word 2010.

Chapter 3 — Introduction to Microsoft Excel 2010

1. What conventions are used in Excel 2010?
2. How would you create a worksheet?
3. How would you copy a formula?
4. How are decision making formula used?
5. Write a short note on the following commands of Microsoft Excel.

   Styles
   Functions
   AutoCalculate
   Sum Function
   Average Function
   Creating Charts
   Auditing
   Comments
   Outlines
   Fitting on a page
   Function wizard
   Goal seeking
   Scenarios manager
   Pivot Table
   AutoFill
   Formatting Numbers and Labels
   Applying Themes
   Background Themes
   Protecting Worksheets
   Functions
   Adding/Deleting Rows
   Inserting Page Breaks
   Convert Text to Columns

Chapter 4 — Introduction to PowerPoint 2010

1. How would you create presentation from Template?
2. Describe the various PowerPoint views.
3. How would you change the background colour of the presentation?
4. How would you add graphics to the slide?
5. Describe the process of reordering the slides.
6. How would you add an animated cartoon to a slide?
7. What are slide transitions?
8. How would you create a Slide Show?
9. How would you pack the presentation?

Chapter 5 — Introduction to Access 2010

1. How would you create a database?
2. Describe the process of creating a database using the wizard.

3. How would you create a database using template?
4. What is a Form?
5. How would you create a Query?
6. How would you create a Report?

Chapter 5 — Other Software of Microsoft Office 2010

1. What is Publisher 2010 used for?
2. What all you can do using InfoPath Forms?
3. What is Groove 2010?
4. What in OneNote 2010 used for?